Praise for *Mending the Soul*

Mending the Soul sets the standard for integrating biblical foundations and research-based approaches to healing the trauma of abuse. This major upgrade incorporates the Tracys' lessons of fifteen years of worldwide utilization and is an essential resource for pastors, counselors, and teachers whose goal is to bring whole-person healing to traumatized and abused people.

> **Gerry Breshears,** PhD, professor of theology
> at Western Seminary, Portland, Oregon

Steven and Celestia Tracy have done a remarkable job updating, refining, and elaborating on their seminal work. This new edition is well-organized and clearly written, covering difficult material with grace, thoughtfulness, and careful exegesis without being either academically dry and heady or simplistic and naive, ensuring that *Mending the Soul* remains on the bookshelves of another generation of graduate students, pastors, and laypeople. This is essential reading for every abuse survivor, therapist, and ministry leader.

> **Justin Smith,** PsyD, LMFT, founder and
> director of The Family Room LLC

Mending the Soul is therapy with God.

> **Christina Tree-Lasiloo,** BBS, Indian Bible College

Regardless of how tidy everything may look on the outside, one thing is certain—sitting in the pews of every congregation are women and men who are living with the effects of unhealed trauma and abuse. As a pastor and someone whose own soul needed mending from the abuse I suffered as a young boy, I'm a firm believer in the Tracys' message and ministry. We must go beyond simply acknowledging that abuse exists to offering the healing power of Jesus embodied in people equipped to walk alongside those who travel their own mending journeys. While exposing the depths of abuse's darkness, Steven and Celestia always point to the power of God's healing strength with humility, grace, and the utmost care.

> **Rick McKinley,** founding pastor of Imago Dei Community,
> Portland, Oregon, and author of *This Beautiful Mess*

Steven and Celestia Tracy deliver a thorough examination of the devasting problem of abuse and suggest practical ways to listen to, understand, and support victims of abuse. They tap into their experience as scholars and clinical and pastoral counselors, as well as share the fruit of their work on the African continent. This is an excellent resource for professional counselors, pastors, church leaders, and lay counselors to help those who need to regain their wholeness.

Honoré Bunduki Kwany, PhD, professor and
rector at Université Chrétienne Bilingue du Congo
(Christian Bilingual University of the Congo)

Mending the Soul is powerful medicine for the ancient pandemic of abuse. This resource is unique because it is refreshingly holistic. Steven and Celestia Tracy are expert tour guides who do not shy away from revisioning the spiritual realities of victims, while also unpacking the complexity of trauma. This book should be in every pastor's library and be essential fodder for annual training.

Andrew J. Schmutzer, professor of Bible at Moody Bible Institute
and author of *Divine Suffering*

Mending the Soul is a penetrating, delicately documented, hands-on guide to wholeness. Its fresh approach, energizing language, tangible case studies, mastery of human experience, and simple yet effective model make it a manual for anyone who wants to understand what is wrong with humanity, grow in wholeness, and improve relationships. It helps survivors know where to begin. If you are a minister, social worker, nurse, educator, or caregiver, this book is for you.

Jean-Pasteur Kahindo Katavo, Christian education program officer
for the Baptist Community of Central Africa denomination

Mending the Soul is a game changer. I participated in a MTS small group years ago in which the *Mending the Soul* book and workbook guided us to work through our experiences in a truly transformative way and to forge deep bonds through the sharing of our stories of suffering. Together we encountered the healing power of Christ. Steven and Celestia Tracy are leading the way in helping us understand the nature of abuse and equipping us with practical ways to move forward in the healing power of Christ.

Joshua Ryan Butler, pastor of Redemption Tempe
and author of *Beautiful Union*

In this updated edition of *Mending the Soul*, you can expect to once again be even more deeply moved by God's healing love. Steven and Celestia Tracy guide the reader in tracing the emergence of beauty and dignity from the dark distortions of abuse and shame. They equip you to provide *real* help to survivors, look evil in the face, and see our Lord Jesus doing his most stunning work in those difficult places.

Michael Rehm, LPC, Stillwaters Counseling

Even with the explosion of technology, social media, and resources, hard truths remain about various forms of abuse that society and the church often want to ignore. Steven and Celestia Tracy boldly present the sobering truth about abuse and trauma with updated and relevant research and stories to educate the reader on today's more nuanced forms of abuse. However, the authors do not leave the reader in a place of despair. Rather, they courageously light the path forward with hope-infused stories of healing and redemption, along with the sharing of strong biblical evidence for God's hatred of abuse and for his redemptive plan to bring good from evil. This is a must-read for anyone searching for personal healing, as well as for caregivers who desire freedom and wholeness for those they love.

Kelsey Hawk, PhD, LMHC

After five years of teaching Mending the Soul courses in Spanish in eleven Latin American countries and the United States, we saw such powerful healing from abuse and trauma that we started a nonprofit—Resplandece Internacional—to empower us to reach more people. We're grateful for this new edition of *Mending the Soul* in which Steven and Celestia Tracy combine their expertise to amplify their compassionate, community-based healing We highly recommend *Mending the Soul* to all who want to better understand abuse and find healing for themselves and others.

Resplandece Internacional board members Magdalena Sánchez, interim president of the Centro Hispano de Estudios Teológicos; Carmen Quinche, Evangelical Covenant Church pastor; and Debbie Taylor, retired missionary, pastor, and therapist

Every Christian leader needs a theology of abuse in this broken world, and thus every Christian leader needs this book. For almost a decade, the *Mending the Soul* book and workbook have been used as an essential part of our transformational curriculum for upper-division students. I can testify to the power of this model to help heal and transform the lives of our Native American staff and students, many of whom are planning to take this approach back to their tribes. I'm thrilled at the additional information provided in this new edition.

Dr. Jason Koppen, DMin, president of Indian Bible College

In an era when we regularly learn of faith systems that not only condone but propagate and cover up abuse, *Mending the Soul* stands out as a trustworthy beacon of hope for survivors and those who care for them. With its integration of theology, social science, and practical application, this book serves as an essential resource for spiritual leaders to face head-on the dark and destructive nature of abuse and walk alongside victims in the painful journey of recovering from its staggering impact.

Cheryl M. C., survivor, Chandler, Arizona

For almost two decades, I have watched the MTS model mend the souls of our students and heal our broader community. The new edition of *Mending the Soul* is biblically sound, trauma-informed, tested, and proven. Steven and Celestia Tracy are authentic, faithful servants who travel the world offering help and hope to victims of abuse both outside and inside the church. This updated edition will surely bless the next generation.

John DelHousaye, PhD, professor of Bible and theology
at Arizona Christian University

There is no better resource for pastors and ministry leaders who desire to build healthy and thriving communities than *Mending the Soul*. During the past decade, we've introduced MTS models to churches in Ecuador, the United States, and Spain and have witnessed God's power at work in each of these church communities. Steve and Celestia Tracy not only help us understand abuse for what it is—the result of the sin that entered the world after the fall—but they also provide a road map for moving forward. The MTS model begins with individuals and in time transforms churches and broader communities and leads to wholeness and healing through Christ.

Titus Folden, WorldVenture, Spain

Mending the Soul

Understanding and Healing Abuse

Second Edition

Steven R. Tracy and
Celestia G. Tracy

ZONDERVAN
REFLECTIVE

ZONDERVAN REFLECTIVE

Mending the Soul
Copyright © 2005, 2022 by Steven R. Tracy and Celestia G. Tracy

Requests for information should be addressed to:
Zondervan, *3900 Sparks Dr. SE, Grand Rapids, Michigan 49546*

Zondervan titles may be purchased in bulk for educational, business, fundraising, or sales promotional use. For information, please email SpecialMarkets@Zondervan.com.

Library of Congress Cataloging-in-Publication Data

Names: Tracy, Steven R., author. | Tracy, Celestia G., 1958- author.
Title: Mending the soul : understanding and healing abuse / Steven R. Tracy and Celestia G. Tracy.
Description: Second edition. | Grand Rapids, Michigan : Zondervan Reflective, 2023. | Includes index.
Identifiers: LCCN 2022039055 (print) | LCCN 2022039056 (ebook) | ISBN 9780310121466 (hardcover) | ISBN 9780310121480 (audio) | ISBN 9780310121473 (ebook)
Subjects: LCSH: Christian teenagers—Religious life. | Abused Teenagers—Religious life.
Classification: LCC BV4531.3 .T73 2023 (print) | LCC BV4531.3 (ebook) | DDC 268/.433—dc23/eng/20221129
LC record available at https://lccn.loc.gov/2022039055
LC ebook record available at https://lccn.loc.gov/2022039056

Cover design: Thinkpen Design
Cover photo: © Pietro de Grandi / Unsplash
Interior design: Kait Lamphere

Printed in the United States of America

22 23 24 25 26 LBC 5 4 3 2 1

She said we are all part of a secret club.

Someday, she said, we will take over the earth.

It will be people like us that save the world, she said:

those who have walked the side of

sorrow and seen the dawn . . .

This is something I know:

no matter how far you have run,

no matter how long you have been lost,

it is never too late to be found.

Rene Denfeld, *The Child Finder*

Contents

Acknowledgments

We have been shaped by the stories we've heard and carried. Brave and honorable men, women, and children who have overcome indescribable forms of injustice and have not just survived but have transformed their suffering into redemptive purpose. This book is from you and for you.

Mending the Soul owes its existence to the many friends, partners, and colleagues who helped fund and support the research and writing of the first manuscript in 2003. There are too many of you to name, but you know who you are. You got us started. Thank you for believing in us and for your compassion for the oppressed. Your early investment has grown into a large not-for-profit organization that supports, trains, and resources trauma survivors around the world to not only heal their wounds but to help others do the same—all in Jesus' name. Many of you are still with us. Thank you for your trust and love.

We are also indebted to the hundreds of seminary students, international trainers, clients, faith leaders, and colleagues who have shared their experiences and knowledge with us. Your wisdom illuminates dark places. Thank you for your integrity and resolute compassion that think of all those who need help first. You humble us.

When we founded Mending the Soul, Inc., in 2003, we had no idea how much we would need our artists—extraordinarily gifted men and women who show the important truths that cannot be known any other way. Many of you are reflected on these pages and have chosen to remain anonymous. God knew we needed every contribution. Thank you for your compassionate gifts.

There is an artist who was the first one I asked to paint an image I would see every time I prayed for a survivor who couldn't pray for themselves—I desperately needed them to see it too. James Van Fossan, you were that artist! Since the inception of MTS, you have drawn or painted just what we needed, right when we needed it. How do we express adequate gratitude for such extraordinary offerings? You have given every piece of art to the survivors we serve, and you continue to be a significant part of every healing resource we create. May the thousands of lives that have seen their trauma transformed be your reward.

Additionally, we're deeply grateful for the generosity of our MTS board, staff, international resource teams, and partners who have given time and treasure to shape and translate this healing model for diverse groups of people worldwide. Thank you for giving to those whom you will never know. Your love encourages and inspires us and those we serve.

We're grateful for our gifted team at Zondervan. Thank you for believing in us in 2003 in what was then an idealistic vision that survivors would find trauma-informed care outside of a clinician's office. God picked you to be our starting place. And here we are again, working together on a revised and expanded book, the same team as before—lucky us! Thank you, Katya Covrett, for your encouragement and friendship over the years. Dirk Buursma, since editing Steve's first manuscript, you are now senior editor-at-large. We are honored to have your meticulous and skillful touch once again. Dr. Stan Gundry, you have over many years given us timely wisdom and direction just when we needed it. Thank you for believing in a healing model for communities like MTS. Today there are more than one hundred thousand people worldwide who have received free trauma-care in Jesus' name. Your support has helped us reach them.

Most of all, we're indebted to our family—our children Elizabeth, Luke, and Abigail—who each bring their own brand of psychological insight, compassion for the vulnerable, righteous indignation over abuse, and a commitment to do what they can, where they can. You've shaped us more than you know. Thank you for being in it with us. We love you dearly.

And finally, Mary—you're now an adult, married, and raising biological, foster, and adopted children of your own. Your passion for the "least of these" is infectious—you continue to shine a light that is uniquely your own. Your fire and compassionate voice continue to impact and inspire us. Thank you for being our starting place. We believe you know now: it's your spark that lights the world.

Preface to the
Second Edition

Abuse is as old as the human race. After all, the first child on earth grew up to murder his sibling! However, the specific manifestations and patterns of abuse are continually changing. In the seventeen years since *Mending the Soul* was published, we have witnessed significant abuse-related societal changes. The *Fourth National Incidence Study of Child Abuse and Neglect*, which was released in 2010, showed substantial drops in physical and sexual child abuse rates from the previous study released in 1996.[1] Today our society is much more knowledgeable about abuse and willing to discuss it in its various forms. The #MeToo movement has forced the evangelical church and the broader population to recognize and address abuse and sexual harassment. This has led to some significantly better responses to abuse in various cultural segments (note, for instance, changes in how professional sports teams are starting to respond to allegations of domestic violence or sexual assault by their athletes). There are now far more abuse education, prevention, and response resources, including many authored by Christians, than there were in 2005.

Unfortunately, our culture has shifted in other ways that aren't as positive. In spite of increased abuse awareness and the development of many new abuse-related policies and resources, we continue to struggle to respond properly. Abuse scandals and cover-ups, some institution-wide, continue with frightening frequency. Child neglect rates have dramatically increased due to the current opioid epidemic, and cyberbullying and sexual harassment (often

---

1. Andrea J. Sedlak et al., *Fourth National Incidence Study of Child Abuse and Neglect (NIS-4): Report to Congress* (Washington, DC: U. S. Department of Health and Human Services, Administration for Children and Families, 2010), https://cap.law.harvard.edu/wp-content/uploads/2015/07/sedlaknis .pdf. For an excellent assessment of the apparent dropping child abuse rates, see David Finkelhor, *Childhood Victimization: Violence, Crime, and Abuse in the Lives of Young People* (Oxford: Oxford University Press, 2008), 122–47.

done electronically) have dramatically increased. While these new technologically enabled forms of abuse leave no visible marks, their impact can be devastating and long-term. Furthermore, in just the past decade, isolation, anxiety, and depression rates have also dramatically increased. The United States now has higher suicide rates than it has seen in fifty years. Abuse is often the etiology of these and other mental health struggles. We now have universal access to the internet and widespread proliferation of smart phones that have dramatically expanded our ability to abuse each other, often anonymously. Clearly, there's a growing need for current, relevant, and accessible abuse resources to guide survivors, parents, and churches.

Not only has our culture mutated in the past seventeen years, but so have we! The faith leaders we've served from around the world have inalterably influenced our understanding of abuse and the essence of what is required for healing. We've seen the truths that transcend cultural differences and have been shaped by the leaders we've served. Since *Mending the Soul* was published in 2005, we've had the privilege of bringing trauma training and healing intensives to thousands of faith leaders around the world. Our faith has deepened and our healing model nuanced by the diverse cultures that have impacted it.

In 2007, we were invited to the Democratic Republic of the Congo to train faith leaders in a community-based model of care. We went, and four weeks later we returned as very different people. We witnessed the power of abuse to shatter God-given connections—within the self (mind, body, and emotions), between others (broken trust), and with God. Clinical care alone couldn't mend the pieces, but neither could a survivor do it alone. Abuse happens in relationship, and thus healing can only happen in relationship. We knew this theoretically, but in the Congo that year, we witnessed God's power unleashed among 139 faith leaders who faced their brokenness and the way misogyny and abuse had been encultured in their marriages, families, and churches. We had a front-row seat to miracles that month. We left East Africa, knowing they had few resources, such as the ones we take for granted—trauma books, mental health providers, counselors, and support groups. And yet when we went back one year later, we were astounded at what we witnessed—pastors boldly speaking out against gender violence and misogyny, domestic violence shelters established in churches, counseling offices established in schools, teachers caring for the psychological needs of their students, children's outreaches focused on abuse education and healing. They begged us for more—more biblical teaching on abuse and more resources—and Mending the Soul began to create them.

Most African churches can't outsource compassion, so the church stepped into the trauma-care gap and did it. The Congo taught us how healing was to be done—in safe community, one relationship at a time; how true healing must cross borders into homes, churches, schools, and villages. It was, and is, the most painful and beautiful thing we have ever seen.

The Congo taught us that healing rhythms are actually rhythms of biblical lament; that the Bible must be taken seriously, so when God says we are responsible for our neighbor, he means it; that Scripture is our only source of healing truth; that God's power to heal is bigger than the evil around and within us; that love is not a spoken word, but is action; that compassion isn't compassion unless it's costly; that trauma care is our responsibility to offer to one another; that there are no excuses; that no matter how broken a person is, Jesus is bigger yet; that night is dispelled with light; that one must courageously face the darkness inside in order to face it in others; that tears are healing and are to be wept along with comfort givers; that presence is just that—being right there with someone, and staying until they know they'll be okay; that real leaders of faith go first with their honest stories; that repentance is something one actually does and preaches from the pulpit; that Jesus is found in the face of an abused woman or man; that caregivers go to the suffering ones, and not the other way around; that real worship is best done on one's feet; that suffering turns into dancing in the end.

Some of the specific changes in this edition include substantially updated illustrations, abuse statistics, and endnotes. Based on our growing under-standing of abuse, as well as feedback from readers, we have incorporated additional data on domestic violence, abuse gender disparity, male victim-ization, spiritual abuse, sexual harassment, and abuse in the Majority World. We have thoroughly updated chapter 6 and retitled it "The Traumatized Brain." Additionally, while the healing model articulated in chapter 8 is essentially the same, we reworked the specific steps and incorporated recent trauma research. Most significantly, I have asked Celestia, my soul mate of forty-two years, to coauthor this revision. Celestia brings eighteen years of professional trauma therapy experience and another fourteen years of cross-cultural experience offering trauma healing intensives to faith leaders worldwide. We have written this revision together to incorporate a fuller integration of theology, social science, and practical application. Together, we've been privileged to resource and train faith leaders through our roles of pastor, counselor, seminary professor, trainer, and author. We believe that God's church is one without walls where people are equipped to provide for the emotional and spiritual needs of the community.

As we write today, we're different people. We've been softened, shaped, and molded by those we love. As you turn these pages, may you draw comfort and hope from the honest stories told here. They're not fairy tales, but real, living trophies of God's grace, proof that God is good and that he heals—anyone, anytime, anywhere. His hands are in our hands, his feet in our feet, his heart in our heart. If you haven't done so before, we invite you to take the first and most important journey into the unexplored recesses of your heart, to pick up any discarded pieces of your story, in order to integrate them with the present you. Then, once you're ready, come with us, because there's a suffering world waiting for trauma care in Jesus' name. We've never had more opened doors for those who are prepared and trained than we have today. They need us—and we need them.

It's our prayer that this revision will offer new insights and hope for a new generation of readers. May we together offer Jesus' redemptive love to a hurting world!

Introduction

Mary sobbed inconsolably on the bathroom floor. Her mother stroked her hair and held her until she could finally speak. Mary's first day of high school was a parent's worst nightmare. She had initiated a fight with a classmate, threatened the principal, and by three o'clock that afternoon was on the verge of being expelled. Mary's parents, missionaries with a Christian organization in the inner city of San Francisco, were beside themselves. Since the onset of puberty, Mary had grown increasingly rebellious and withdrawn. The precocious little girl who wore fairy dresses and drew pictures of puppies now wore black and drew pictures of corpses. In fits of rage, she would curse her parents for not aborting her before she was born. Her parents sought help from counselors, their youth pastor, and even the family doctor, but nothing seemed to help. It felt as though they were in a losing battle with a demon that was consuming their daughter's very soul.

Eventually, Mary began to speak to her mother in hushed whispers. She described a boy at school who had threatened her friend. As her mother began to question the depth of her rage at the boy, the long-invisible serpent began to take shape. Her cruel classmate had triggered dark memories she had spent years trying to escape. She was no longer able to hold back the horrifying images. She shamefully recounted that, five years earlier, an older and much-loved cousin had sexually molested her over a period of two years while he was babysitting her. The molestations stopped once her family moved to San Francisco, but her cousin continued to make sexually suggestive comments whenever he came to visit.

Mary's parents immediately contacted the authorities and the rest of the family. The authorities chose not to prosecute the case, since there was no physical evidence. Most of their relatives refused to believe Mary's disclosure, in spite of extensive mounting evidence. Even when three other children eventually came forward and reported that this same cousin had abused them, most of the family still refused to believe Mary. They argued that even *if* the cousin had "done something inappropriate" to Mary, it was in the past, and she was obligated to forgive and forget. To add insult to injury, teachers and grandparents told Mary that her anger showed how unchristian she was. Two years after disclosing the abuse, Mary still wasn't sure she could believe in a God who would allow something like this to happen to her and others.

We wish Mary's story were merely a hypothetical example. It is not. Our support of Mary and her family has permanently transformed our understanding of abuse. It also raises troubling questions for all Christians:

- How widespread is abuse?
- How can abuse that happened years earlier continue to have an impact?
- How can parents, youth workers, and single adults looking for life partners identify potential abusers?
- How can abuse victims heal?
- What does genuine healing look like?
- Where does forgiveness fit in?

These are some of the questions this book seeks to answer. For all too long, the church has ignored or, worse, perpetrated and covered up abuse. This must change!

Mending the Soul is divided into three parts. Part 1 addresses the nature of abuse. Here we'll give a biblical explanation for abuse, define exactly what constitutes abuse, and look at the characteristics of abusers and abusive families. We'll examine five different kinds of abuse, all of which distort the image of God and hence are extremely destructive.

Part 2 unpacks the confusing effects of abuse. Abuse survivors and those who seek to assist them must understand the way abuse impacts the body, mind, and soul before a plan for healing can be crafted. All too often, well-meaning Christians simplistically spout Bible verses to cure complex issues such as abuse. Scripture does give us a path to healing, but we cannot use Scripture properly until we have a keen grasp of the nature of abuse and the damage that needs to be healed.[1] More specifically, we'll look at shame,

---

1. The only offensive weapon listed in Scripture for spiritual warfare is "the sword of the Spirit, which is the word of God" (Ephesians 6:17). The language Paul uses in this passage is significant, for

hyperarousal, emotional constriction, and disconnection as four of the most persistent and pernicious effects of abuse, which can be best understood through the lens of our unique created design as bearers of God's image. This is the only way to validate the extent of soul damage caused by the perversion of abuse.

Part 3 illuminates an accessible healing path and explains the often complex nature of biblical forgiveness. This section concludes with an updated epilogue written by Mary, the sexual abuse survivor you were just introduced to.

At the end of the book there are three appendixes that include a listing of Bible passages that address abuse, a summary of warning signs of potential abusers, and guidelines for parents to reduce the risk of child sexual abuse and to know how to respond to abuse disclosures. We've written this book to be an accessible handbook for the wounded and for the shepherds (both lay and professional) who seek to care for them. Therefore, we've sought to keep technical discussions to a minimum. For those who desire more nuanced, detailed information about the issues discussed in this book, we've provided ample endnotes.

---

there are two words for "sword" used in the New Testament. The large *rhomphaia*, or broadsword, was typically used to slash from a distance (see Revelation 6:8), but it isn't the term used in this verse. Paul uses the other term for sword in Ephesians 6:17 (*machaira*), which indicates the short dagger used in close hand-to-hand combat to stab an open spot in the enemy's armor. This suggests that in spiritual warfare our goal is not to simply thrust large amounts of Scripture at a problem, but rather to gain a precise understanding of the issue (and Satan's lies) so that we can use the appropriate Scripture with precision to deal with the problem.

PART 1

The Nature of Abuse

Adolescents feel intense flashes of emotion, and our children were no exception. Our daughter burst into the car visibly agitated after church. Her youth pastor had taught that morning on family life and made some very strong admonitions with very few qualifications. He didn't nuance his topic or acknowledge the reality of abuse. Earlier that week, she had spent hours consoling a distraught classmate who had been sexually abused by a parent. To say the least, the youth pastor's teaching had hit a nerve.

We offered to support her by meeting with the pastor, but she wanted to talk to him herself. We helped her think through what she had heard that morning in light of Scripture. She crafted an articulate letter sharing her concerns, noting some of the damaging ways abuse survivors like her friend might have heard the lesson. We, and she, were stunned by his impulsive response. He stated that he was very sympathetic to our daughter's concerns, but as a pastor, he was compelled to teach only what he found in Scripture and that Scripture did not really address abuse. So neither could he.

In spite of the fact that this pastor was a seminary graduate, he clearly had no biblical framework for abuse. It is highly probable that in all his biblical and theological training, abuse was never mentioned. So too for Steve, whose twelve years of undergraduate, graduate, and doctoral training in theology and biblical studies did not include a single minute addressing abuse. Looking back, we are astonished by this void. Not only is abuse of power in all its forms a profoundly relevant and important topic, but it has created the greatest mission field of the twenty-first century.[1] Virtually every aspect of abuse is addressed in hundreds of biblical passages. We must understand abuse through the lens of God so that we are equipped to see it, hear the soul cries, and respond in trauma-informed ways to help heal it. Jesus beckons us to love others as he has loved us.

In the following four chapters, we'll draw from the rich and extensive biblical data to understand the nature of abuse, abusers, and abusive families.

---

1. See Diane Langberg, *Suffering and the Heart of God: How Trauma Destroys and Christ Restores* (Greensboro, NC: New Growth, 2015), 8.

CHAPTER 1

The Destructive Power and Astonishing Transformation of Abuse

Perhaps the most horrifying thing about nonconsensual sex is that, in an instant it erases you. Your own desires, your safety, and well-being, your ownership of the body that may very well have been the only thing you ever felt sure you owned—all of it becomes irrelevant, even nonexistent.

Nora Salem, "The Life Ruiner"

"There is no one righteous, not even one;
there is no one who understands;
there is no one who seeks God" . . .
"Their throats are open graves;
their tongues practice deceit."
"The poison of vipers is on their lips" . . .
"Their feet are swift to shed blood."

Romans 3:10–11, 13, 15

There are three truths that shape our model of abuse and healing. The first two are about the stunningly dark and destructive nature of abuse; the third premise has much greater power than the first two combined, shining a glimmer of hope's light into the blackest room.

Abuse Is Rampant

Thirty years ago, we naively struggled with the ugly reality and prevalence of abuse, particularly in Christian homes. During Steve's first pastorate, we served in a vibrant, large church. He had an unsettling conversation with the women's ministry director and was deeply offended when she invited an outside speaker to address the topic of domestic violence. Little did Steve (or anyone else) realize at the time that one of our well-respected elders had been beating his wife for years, having put her in the hospital several times. In addition, another one of our ministers was being criminally investigated for child sexual abuse. Thankfully, ministry to the marginalized and abused has opened our eyes and heart to the horrendous fact that abuse is not the occasional exception, but the grisly reality in both the church and secular society. The recent #MeToo movement has made this poignantly clear, yet still it remains difficult for most people to accept.[1]

Unfortunately, research among evangelicals shows a stubborn propensity for this population to grossly underestimate rates of physical and sexual abuse, particularly in their own congregations.[2] For instance, a 2014 survey of one thousand Protestant pastors conducted by Lifeway Research found that two out of three pastors preach on abuse less than once a year. The researchers concluded that this is because pastors dramatically underestimate the prevalence and seriousness of abuse in their congregations. The majority of ministers estimated that only 10 percent or less of their congregants have ever experienced physical or sexual abuse, and 37 percent of the pastors estimated that less than 5 percent of their congregation have been victims of sexual or domestic violence.[3] As we will see, these pastors' estimates are more than 300–400 percent low.

Sadly, we've discovered that Christians are typically much more likely to minimize the reality of abuse than non-Christians. While the church is blind to its own denial, it is well-known to abusers. To help Steve's seminary students wake up to the prevalence of abuse in religious settings, he shows them a filmed interview with an incarcerated child molester who has approximately one hundred victims. This perpetrator had worked as a youth pastor and preyed on young boys in the church and the nearby

---

1. For a survey of the #MeToo movement and lessons it gives the church, see Steven Tracy and Andy Maurer, "#MeToo and Evangelicalism: Shattering Myths about Sexual Abuse and Power," *Cultural Encounters* 14 (2019): 3–21.

2. See, for instance, Katie Brennan Homiak and Jon E. Singletary, "Family Violence in Congregations: An Exploratory Study of Clergy's Needs," *Social Work & Christianity* 34, no. 1 (March 2007): 18–46; Sharon G. Horne and Heidi M. Levitt, "Shelter from the Raging Wind: Religious Needs of Victims of Intimate Partner Violence and Faith Leaders' Responses," *Journal of Religion & Abuse* 5, no. 2 (2003): 83–98.

3. See Sojourners and IMA World Health, *Broken Silence: A Call for Churches to Speak Out: Protestant Pastors Survey on Sexual and Domestic Violence*, June 2014, 4, https://imaworldhealth.org /wp-content/uploads/2014/07/PastorsSurveyReport_final1.pdf.

community. When asked if he thought Christians were naive about abuse and hence easier to fool, he stated, "Oh yes, I believe Christians are very easy to fool. They are generally good people who want to believe the best about others." This child predator proudly recounted how church leaders quickly and vigorously defended him on two different occasions when he was accused of molesting boys. In their well-meaning but dangerously naive reasoning, these pastors discounted the possibility, let alone the prevalence, of abuse in their community. *Their flock and their town paid a tremendous price for this denial.*

It is thus essential that we have an accurate understanding of abuse rates. We will examine several categories of abuse and then compare prevalence statistics with Scripture. Thankfully, most people haven't experienced prosecutable Abuse (capital *A*), such as physical assault, rape, threatened use of a dangerous weapon, and so forth, but we have all experienced noncriminal (lowercase *a*) abuse. Most people have experienced painful verbal abuse; the vast majority of women have experienced sexual harassment; a majority of children and youth have been bullied, and we know that bullying, particularly cyberbullying, is an epidemic problem. For instance, almost one out of three (28 percent) of middle schoolers report being cyberbullied weekly.[4] Sadly, these abusive experiences are nearly universal and harmful. For a variety of reasons, abuse is challenging to quantify.[5] Thankfully, for several decades, extensive, careful abuse research has been conducted by social scientists. An indisputable picture has emerged: abuse, in all its forms, is rampant.

Sexual Assault

One of the most current and comprehensive sources for sexual violence rates in the United States is *The National Intimate Partner and Sexual Violence Survey* (NISVS), which is an ongoing survey developed by the Centers for Disease Control. The latest NISVS data reveals that:

- More than 43 percent of women experienced some form of contact sexual violence in their lifetime.

---

4. Cited in Melissa Diliberti et al., *Crime, Violence, Discipline, and Safety in U.S. Public Schools: Findings from the School Survey on Crime and Safety: 2017–18* (Washington, DC: U.S. Department of Education, 2019), 3, https://nces.ed.gov/pubs2019/2019061.pdf.

5. Thus it is essential for church leaders to listen carefully and proactively to those under their care to learn what they are experiencing. Leaders typically have very different experiences than their abused and disempowered parishioners have and thus will often lack an intuitive understanding of abuse prevalence.

- Nearly a quarter of men (24.8 percent) experienced some form of contact sexual violence in their lifetime.
- Approximately one in five women (21.3 percent) reported completed or attempted rape at some point in their lifetime.
- Nearly one in six women (16 percent) were victims of stalking in their lifetime, during which they felt fearful or believed someone close to them, would be harmed or killed.[6]

The highest rates of sexual abuse are found among young adult females.[7] A general population study of women found that 38 percent of all respondents reported at least one experience of sexual abuse in their lifetime, but for women thirty-one years old and younger, almost 42 percent reported sexual abuse.[8] For several decades, research has shown that 15 to 25 percent of college women experience some form of sexual violence while they are students. And sadly, these rates have risen in the past decade. For instance, the largest study of its kind to date (2019) found that 26 percent of female undergraduates and 2.5 percent of male undergraduates experienced non-consensual sexual contact by physical force or inability to consent while enrolled at school.[9] These sexual assault rates were up about 3 percent from the 2015 survey. Tragically these high abuse rates are also now seen among teens. In one major study of dating violence, 20 percent of American high school girls report being physically or sexually assaulted by a male partner.[10]

We'll illustrate abuse prevalence rates among college women with a personal example. After our son graduated from high school, he went to college

---

6. Cited in Sharon G. Smith et al., *The National Intimate Partner and Sexual Violence Survey: 2015 Data Brief—Updated Release* (Atlanta, GA: National Center for Injury Prevention and Control, Centers for Disease Control and Prevention, 2018), www.cdc.gov/violenceprevention/pdf/2015data-brief508.pdf.

7. See Erin A. Casey and Paula S. Nurius, "Trends in the Prevalence and Characteristics of Sexual Violence: A Cohort Analysis," *Violence and Victims* 21, no. 5 (October 2006): 629–44, www.academia.edu/13026120/Trends_in_the_Prevalence_and_Characteristics_of_Sexual_Violence_A_Cohort_Analysis.

8. Casey and Nurius, "Trends in the Prevalence," 635–37.

9. Cited in David Cantor et al., "Report on the AAU Campus Climate Survey on Sexual Assault and Misconduct," The Association of American Universities, revised January 17, 2020, www.aau.edu/sites/default/files/AAU-Files/Key-Issues/Campus-Safety/Revised%20Aggregate%20report%20%20and%20appendices%201-7_(01-16-2020_FINAL).pdf. This survey was the largest of its kind, with more than 181,000 students responding to the survey. One of the best overviews of research on sexual abuse among college women over the past fifty years is Leah E. Adams-Curtis and Gordon B. Forbes, "College Women's Experiences of Sexual Coercion: A Review of Cultural, Perpetrator, Victim, and Situational Variables," *Trauma, Violence, & Abuse* 5, no. 2 (April 2004): 91–122.

10. Cited in Jay G. Silverman et al., "Dating Violence against Adolescent Girls and Associated Substance Abuse, Unhealthy Weight Control, Sexual Risk Behavior, Pregnancy, and Suicidality," *Journal of the American Medical Association* 286, no. 5 (2001): 572–79.

at a state university. The week before classes began, we attended a weekend orientation for students and their parents. One of the presentations was on campus safety. The presenter shared campus crime statistics for the previous year. In light of our work, we were particularly interested in seeing the data on sexual assaults. The handout revealed that on the university campus, with an enrollment of almost forty thousand students, only a handful of sexual assaults were reported to have occurred over the previous year.

We were stunned, because we knew the research study outcomes of Dr. Mary Koss, one of the leading authorities on sexual assault on US college campuses and a faculty member of this university. Based on her research, corroborated by many other studies, we knew there must have been several thousand students sexually assaulted at this university over the previous year.[11] Yet this ugly truth was denied for the sake of everyone's comfort level. While distorting the hard realities of abuse may increase our levels of comfort in the beginning, it is a dangerous fool's paradise.

Sexual Harassment

As tragic as the high sexual abuse rates are in the United States, sexual harassment rates are even higher. A national study released in 2018 found that:

- more than four out of five women (81 percent) reported experiencing some form of sexual harassment and/or assault in their lifetime;
- more than three in four women (77 percent) experienced verbal sexual harassment;
- more than one in two women (51 percent) were sexually touched in an unwelcome way;
- around four in ten women experienced cybersexual harassment; and
- close to one in three women (30 percent) experienced unwanted genital flashing.[12]

---

11. See Sarah L. Cook and Mary P. Koss, "More Data Have Accumulated Supporting Date and Acquaintance Rape as Significant Problems for Women," in *Current Controversies on Family Violence* (Thousand Oaks, CA: Sage, 2005), 97–116; see also Sofi Sinozich and Lynn Langton, *Rape and Sexual Assault Victimization Among College-Age Females, 1995–2013* (Washington D.C., U.S. Department of Justice, 2014), https://permanent.fdlp.gov/gpo84729/rsavcaf9513.pdf. I am not accusing the university officials of consciously lying. They may well have been accurately reporting from some crime data report, but it certainly didn't accord with what we know about sexual assault rates.

12. Cited in Holly Kearl, "The Facts Behind the #MeToo Movement: A National Study on Sexual Harassment and Assault," Stop Street Harassment, Reston, VA, 2018. A national survey of more than two thousand college students from various colleges across the country had similar findings. Approximately two-thirds of the students reported experiencing sexual harassment defined narrowly as "unwanted and unwelcome sexual behavior which interferes with your life," Catherine Hill and Elena Silva, *Drawing the Line: Sexual Harassment on Campus* (Washington, DC: American Association of University Women Educational Foundation, 2005).

Again, let's personalize sexual assault and sexual violence with a real-world example. Mending the Soul conducted an abuse training seminar for local Christian leaders. One of the parachurch campus ministries at Arizona State sent twenty of their student leaders to our training. They were all college seniors; most had been working together and meeting in weekly small discipleship groups since their freshman year. What they learned that weekend about abuse, particularly sexual abuse, was so transformative that it provoked honest, vulnerable sharing for the first time. Every one of the female leaders shared their own sexual abuse story, some as children and some in college. Two of the male students confessed to having perpetrated some form of sexually abusive or coercive behavior while serving in leadership in this organization.

The campus minister who oversaw this ministry told us they were stunned at these disclosures. These were twenty of their most mature veteran student leaders, and they had told no one about their abuse experiences—not the campus minister or any of their friends. These students mobilized themselves into MTS small groups and began to, for the first time, heal invisible wounds. Upon the conclusion of their small groups, the students organized a series of public campus presentations on sexual abuse. The talks were extremely well attended. These young leaders shared their own personal stories. The campus minister reported that these presentations opened more doors for effectively sharing the gospel than anything else they had ever done.

Intimate Partner Violence (IPV) / Domestic Violence (DV)

Physical abuse comes in many forms and contexts but occurs most frequently in the context of marriage or intimate partnerships. Intimate partner violence is one of the leading causes of death and injury to women worldwide. In North America, numerous studies reveal that 22–33 percent of North American women and 20–30 percent of men will be assaulted by an intimate partner in their lifetime.[13] An estimated 50 percent of females

---

13. See Smith, *National Intimate Partner*. This study showed that men and women experienced almost identical intimate partner physical violence rates—31 percent. One of the largest older US surveys of DV—the Violence against Women Survey—found a female lifetime intimate partner assault rate of 22 percent (Patricia Tjaden and Nancy Thoennes, *Prevalence, Incidence, and Consequences of Violence against Women: Findings from the National Violence against Women Survey* [Washington, DC: National Institute of Justice and Centers for Disease Control, 1998], www.ojp.gov/pdffiles/172837.pdf). Using a screening tool recommended by the American Medical Association, other researchers found a 31 percent lifetime prevalence for DV among adult American women (see R. M. Siegel et al., "Screening for Domestic Violence in the Community Pediatric Setting," *Pediatrics* 104, no. 4 (1999): 874–77.

victimized by an intimate partner and 44 percent of males victimized by an intimate partner suffer a physical injury.[14] Just in terms of one category of DV impact—namely, economic—the lifetime costs of DV are estimated to be $3.6 trillion.[15] This equates to almost 90 percent of the entire federal budget for the year this study was published (2018).

Child Maltreatment

In my last pastorate, I chaired our child protection committee. This explains why Pastor John visited my office after visiting a new family in our church that had requested financial assistance. While John was in the home, an argument broke out among the children, at which time the father and eldest son left for several minutes. Upon their return, the father was highly agitated, while the son was listless and silent as a stone. From across the room, John could see a large, red welt the size and shape of a hand on the son's face. It was obvious the father had just struck his son. Pastor John discreetly pulled the father away and questioned him about what he had just witnessed. The father didn't deny hitting his son, but he was enraged that an outsider would "butt into their family business!" We reported the assault to the authorities, but the family left the church before any intervention could take place. They were never seen again. This is one of those rare cases of child abuse in which the evidence is immediate, tangible, and irrefutable. Most child maltreatment, however, is less obvious and thus more difficult to validate and address. As with other forms of abuse, while child maltreatment is often unseen, it is nevertheless quite common.

Large-scale research on child abuse reveals that child maltreatment—neglect, physical abuse, emotional abuse, and sexual abuse—occurs in every community. It is impossible to know for certain how prevalent child abuse is because the vast majority of abuse is not reported to the authorities. One of the most respected and thorough studies of reported child maltreatment is the *National Incidence Study of Child Abuse and Neglect*. The fourth, and most recent, study was released early in 2010. It collects data from child protective service agencies in all fifty states, as well as from community

---

14. Cited in Shannon Catalano, "Intimate Partner Violence: Attributes of Victimization, 1993–2011," U.S. Department of Justice, Bureau of Justice Statistics, November 2013, https://bjs.ojp.gov/content/pub/pdf/ipvav9311.pdf.

15. Cited in Cora Peterson et al., "Lifetime Economic Burden of Intimate Partner Violence Among U.S. Adults," *American Journal of Preventive Medicine*, 55, no. 4 (2018): 433–44. The costs factored in include those related to the treatment of injuries, lost productivity from work, and the criminal justice system. Lifetime cost of IPV for a female victim was calculated to be $103,767 and $23,414 for a male victim.

professionals.[16] This study found that roughly three million children were maltreated based on the "endangerment" definition of abuse. Of the children who were abused, more than twice as many were physically abused than sexually abused (58 percent versus 24 percent). By far the most common form of child maltreatment is neglect (77 percent of maltreated children, using the "endangerment" standard). It is not surprising that younger children are maltreated much more often than older children. For instance, children ages birth to three are three times more likely to be maltreated than sixteen- to seventeen-year-olds, and the vast majority (81 percent) of maltreated children are treated cruelly by their own parents. Finally, we note that poor children are five times more likely to be maltreated and seven times more likely to be neglected.

Even though child maltreatment rates, particularly physical and sexual abuse, declined markedly between the third and fourth incidence studies, this probably reflects the positive impact of abuse prevention and response strategies, changes in child protective services (CPS) data, and increased conservativism within CPS.[17] In the past decade, child maltreatment rates have dropped further, less so for neglect.[18] COVID-19 stress-related child maltreatment, particularly emotional abuse, neglect, and physical abuse, is dramatically rising, while calls to CPS have dramatically dropped—62–94 percent in various locations.[19] This is due to the fact that most maltreatment concerns are reported by school officials, and during a quarantine, children aren't in school. Numerous hospitals have seen alarming rises in severe child abuse injuries.[20]

Abuse Rates in Christian Families

Until recently, little research had been conducted to assess abuse specifically among evangelicals. The data we now have reveals that evangelicals

---

16. See Andrea J. Sedlak et al., *Fourth National Incidence Study of Child Abuse and Neglect (NIS–4): Report to Congress* (Washington, DC: U. S. Department of Health and Human Services, Administration for Children and Families, 2010), https://cap.law.harvard.edu/wp-content/uploads/2015/07/sedlaknis.pdf.

17. For an analysis of this decline, see Lisa Jones, David Finkelhor, and Kathy Kopiec, "Why Is Child Sexual Abuse Declining? A Survey of State Child Protection Administrators," *Child Abuse & Neglect* 25, no. 9 (2001): 1139–58.

18. For more recent trends, see David Finkelhor, Kei Saito, and Lisa Jones, "Updated Trends in Child Treatment, 2019," University of New Hampshire, Crimes against Children Research Center, February 2021, http://unh.edu/ccrc/pdf/CV203%20-%20Updated%20trends%202019_ks_df.pdf.

19. See Samantha Schmidt and Hannah Natanson, "With Kids Stuck at Home, ER Doctors See More Severe Cases of Child Abuse," *Washington Post*, April 30, 2020, www.washingtonpost.com/education/2020/04/30/child-abuse-reports-coronavirus.

20. See Schmidt and Natanson, "With Kids Stuck at Home."

experience high lifetime abuse rates that are comparable to the general population. For instance, in a survey of 1,476 women who self-identified as "fairly or deeply religious Christians," the majority (50.7 percent) reported that they had experienced one or more types of abuse (physical, emotional, sexual, stalking, or threats) from an intimate partner.[21] In terms of sexual abuse, a frequently cited sexuality survey of two thousand Christian women conducted by three well-respected evangelical social scientists revealed that 50 percent of the women surveyed reported they had experienced unwanted sexual touch.[22]

In terms of domestic violence, prevalence rates among Christians are rather complex. Conservative Protestant men (by and large evangelicals) who attend church regularly are the least likely group to perpetrate domestic violence, though conservative Protestant men who are irregular church attendees are the most likely to batter their wives.[23] While many theories have been put forward to explain these startling differences in DV rates among evangelicals, the bottom line is that overall DV rates among Christians, like sexual abuse rates, mirror rates in the general population.

Global Abuse Rates

Globally, we know that a person is most likely to experience abuse at the hands of family members or intimate partners.[24] This is particularly true for females. In one of the most frequently cited global abuse studies, based on interviews with twenty-four thousand women from fifteen sites in ten countries, more than 75 percent of the women who had been physically or sexually abused since age fifteen reported being abused by an intimate partner—someone they knew and trusted.[25] The World Health Organization

21. Cited in Mei-Chuan Wang et al., "Christian Women in IPV Relationships: An Exploratory Study of Religious Factors," *Journal of Psychology and Christianity* 28, no. 3 (2009): 224–35.

22. Cited in Archibald D. Hart, Catherine Hart Weber, and Debra L. Taylor, *Secrets of Eve: Understanding the Mystery of Female Sexuality* (Nashville: Word, 1998), 181.

23. See Christopher G. Ellison and Kristin L. Anderson, "Religious Involvement and Domestic Violence among U.S. Couples," *Journal for the Scientific Study of Religion* 40, no. 2 (2001): 269–86; Merlin B. Brinkerhoff, Elaine Grandin, and Eugen Lupri, "Religious Involvement and Spousal Violence: The Canadian Case," *Journal for the Scientific Study of Religion* 31, no. 1 (1991): 15–31; Christopher G. Ellison, John P. Bartkowski, and Kristin L. Anderson, "Are There Religious Variations in Domestic Violence?" *Journal of Family Issues* 20, no. 1 (1999): 87–113; W. Bradford Wilcox, *Soft Patriarchs, New Men: How Christianity Shapes Fathers and Husbands* (Chicago: University of Chicago Press, 2004), 181–83.

24. For an excellent overview of global violence against women, see Elaine Storkey, *Scars across Humanity: Understanding and Overcoming Violence against Women* (Downers Grove, IL: InterVarsity, 2018).

25. Claudia Garcia-Moreno et al., Summary Report: *WHO Multi-country Study on Women's Health and Domestic Violence against Women: Initial Results on Prevalence, Health Outcomes, and Women's Responses* (Geneva: WHO Press, 2005), xiv, https://onvg.fcsh.unl.pt/wp-content/uploads/sites/31/2019/11/924159358X_eng.pdf.

conducts some of the most extensive and careful global abuse assessments and has found that worldwide almost one-third (30 percent) of women who have been in a relationship have experienced physical or sexual violence by their partner.[26] In some regions, abuse is so pervasive that it is the accepted norm. For instance, 28 percent of South African men surveyed admitted having raped a woman and 54 percent of those who had raped had done so more than once. These sexual abuse rates mean that currently a woman born in South Africa has a greater chance of being raped than she has of learning to read.[27] The largest compilation of global statistics on violence against children, drawing from data on 190 countries, reveals that homicide is the leading cause of preventable injury and death for minors worldwide.[28]

These statistics are profoundly sobering, revealing that abuse is prevalent in the United States and around the world. We cannot ignore it. A study of world history strongly suggests that abuse has always been rampant. In fact, the writer of Ecclesiastes looked around and "saw all the oppressions that are done under the sun. And behold the tears of the oppressed, and they had no one to comfort them!" (Ecclesiastes 4:1 ESV). He concluded that the prevalence of abuse and the suffering it created were so great that it would be better to be dead in a peaceful grave than alive in this broken world. Or better yet is "he who has not yet been and has not seen the evil deeds that are done under the sun" (Ecclesiastes 4:3 ESV). Thankfully, this is not the final word on abuse. We will see shortly that God delights in healing and redeeming evil.

Abuse Is Predictable

The Role of Sin

> God hates sin not just because it violates his law but, more substantively, because it violates shalom, because it breaks the peace, because it interferes with the way things are supposed to be . . . God is for shalom and *therefore* against sin.[29]

---

26. Cited in World Health Organization, *Global and Regional Estimates of Violence against Women: Prevalence and Health Effects of Intimate Partner Violence and Non-Partner Sexual Violence* (Geneva: WHO Press, 2013), 2. This study was based on three large international data sets and seventy-seven studies covering fifty-six countries.

27. See Clare Kapp, "Rape on Trial in South Africa," *The Lancet* 367 (2006): 718–19; Rachel Jewkes et al., "Gender Inequitable Masculinity and Sexual Entitlement in Rape Perpetration South Africa: Findings of a Cross-Sectional Study," *PLoS One* 6, no. 12 (2011): 1–10.

28. Cited in Claudia Cappa, *Hidden in Plain Sight: Statistical Analysis of Violence against Children* (New York: United Nations Children's Fund [UNICEF], Division of Data, Research and Policy, 2014), www.unicef.org/media/66916/file/Hidden-in-plain-sight.pdf.

29. Cornelius Plantinga, *Not the Way It's Supposed to Be: A Breviary of Sin* (Grand Rapids: Eerdmans, 1995), 14, italics in original.

How do we make sense of worldwide rampant abuse rates? As Christians, we may be shocked but we should not be surprised by the prevalence of abuse. Orthodox Christianity has consistently declared that we live in a fallen world. Humans are not born morally neutral but are pervasively infected by sin. While evangelical theologians debate the effects of human depravity (especially the nature of free will), none question its universal presence. The biblical record makes this indictment inescapable, for no sooner had the forbidden fruit cleared Adam's and Eve's lips than a host of destructive and abusive behaviors ensued. On the heels of the first human sin (Genesis 3:1–6) came hiding from God (Genesis 3:8–10), blame shifting (Genesis 3:12–13), murder (Genesis 4:8), and universal evil so great that God almost destroyed the entire human race (Genesis 6:5–8).

The Bible is patently clear that all humans from the moment of conception are corrupted by sin (Psalm 51:5) and thus have the potential for evil cruelty. The Bible repeatedly warns of evil people whose greatest delight is violating and overpowering the weak and vulnerable, shedding their blood, and consuming them (Psalm 17:8–12; Proverbs 1:16–19; Micah 2:1–2; 3:1–3). Even if we do not murder with our hands, we are all quite capable of abusively murdering with our tongues (Proverbs 18:21; James 3:2–12). In the apostle Paul's overwhelming exposé of universal human depravity and resultant guilt, he notes that in their natural condition all humans are depraved and inclined to abuse others (Romans 3:9–18). He cites various Old Testament passages to show that the entire human race and every aspect of every human is depraved and has the potential of being abusively destructive.

Specifically, humans possess throats that are an open grave (they want to destructively consume); they have the poison of vipers under their lips, curse with their mouths, have feet swift to shed blood, and leave nothing but ruin and misery in their wake (Romans 3:13–16). This graphic language (drawn from Psalms 5:9; 10:7; 140:3; and Isaiah 59:7–8) describes the way universal human depravity is displayed in widespread abusive behavior.

Paul's assertions that depravity results in unrestricted abuse are validated from Genesis to Revelation by hundreds of accounts of verbal, physical, and sexual abuse. We read of abusive behavior that penetrates all sociodemographic sectors of biblical society. Various forms of abuse are committed by Jews as well as Gentiles, worshipers of Yahweh as well as worshipers of Baal, kings as well as peasants, men as well as women. Joseph's brothers abusively sought to kill him and eventually sold him into slavery in Egypt (Genesis 37:20–28), but Joseph also experienced abuse at the hands of the Egyptians (Genesis 39:11–20). The pagan prince Shechem raped Dinah (Genesis 34:1–2), but the Jewish prince Amnon raped his own sister, Tamar (2 Samuel 13:1–19). Pharaoh, king of Egypt, ordered the slaughter of baby Israelite boys (Exodus 1:15–22), but so did Herod, the king of Judea (Matthew 2:16–18). Idol-worshiping King Ahab used his power to murder the innocent (1 Kings 21), but so did King David, the writer of many psalms (2 Samuel 11:6–27).

The pagan inhabitants of Sodom sought to rape a man visiting their town (Genesis 19:1–6), but in similar circumstances Israelite men fatally gang-raped a traveling woman (Judges 19:16–28). The Egyptians physically abused their Israelite slaves (Exodus 1:11–14; 2:11), but the Israelites physically abused their inspired prophets (Jeremiah 20:1–2). The agents of the antichrist will behead saints for refusing to worship the beast (Revelation 20:4), while Herodias had John the Baptist beheaded for refusing to overlook her adulterous affair (Matthew 14:1–12). Jesus was tortured and executed by the barbaric Romans, but the sophisticated Jewish religious leaders had already tried to stone him to death (John 8:59) and peasants from Nazareth tried to throw him off a cliff (Luke 4:29). Arameans ripped open the wombs of pregnant women and killed their unborn children (2 Kings 8:12), but Israelite parents burned their own infants alive as an act of worship (2 Kings 17:17; Jeremiah 32:35).

Lest we attempt to limit abuse to the ranks of evil degenerates and religious hypocrites, we should tease out the biblical data a bit more. In the biblical record, orthodox religious leaders and even mature believers are repeatedly indicted for abuse and collaborating with abuse:

- Abraham, the greatest Israelite patriarch and hero of faith (Genesis 22; Hebrews 11:8–9, 17–19), twice deceitfully tried to protect himself by exposing his wife to sexual exploitation by a foreign monarch (Genesis 12:10; 20:2, 11).
- Sarah, the heroine of faith, almost fatally abused her own handmaid and child (Genesis 21:9–21; Hebrews 11:11).
- David, the man whose heart was wholly devoted to God and the greatest human monarch in Jewish history (1 Kings 11:4, 36–38), was guilty of murder and adultery (2 Samuel 11). He also failed to protect his own daughter from incestuous rape and engaged in a conspiracy of silence with her rapist (2 Samuel 13:7, 20–39).
- Lot, who in some respects was "righteous" (2 Peter 2:7–8), offered his own daughters to be gang-raped by the men of Sodom (Genesis 19:8).

- Judah, the father of one of the greatest tribes of Israel, tried to have his own daughter-in-law burned to death after he impregnated her (Genesis 38).
- Monotheistic Israelite priests used their religious power to sexually prey on women serving in the tabernacle (1 Samuel 2:22).
- Priests and other religious leaders used their power to physically exploit the vulnerable, especially widows and orphans (Micah 2:8–9; Malachi 3:5).
- Christians in the Corinthian church engaged in a form of incest that was more perverted than that practiced by their pagan neighbors (1 Corinthians 5:1).

We must not sanitize the biblical record to avoid the implications for our own families, churches, and communities. Humans are no less sinfully depraved now than they were in the past. Abuse is rampant today, as it has been throughout human history—a point we must emphasize because few Christians believe abuse is rampant through all segments of society and is committed by Christian leaders. Over and over, parents, congregations, and religious leaders deny abuse reports, in spite of the weight of the evidence. We must *never* assume a child who reports that beloved Uncle Bob has been sexually touching them must be lying. Unspeakable damage occurs when we deny the possibility that a pastor who powerfully communicates God's word on Sunday mornings could beat his wife, scream at his children, or molest his daughter on Monday.

Several years ago, Steve invited a team of child abuse professionals to give a guest lecture in one of his seminary classes. One of the presenters was a judge and former government prosecutor with years of experience in the criminal court system, particularly with child abusers. She soberly warned the students that twenty years in the courtroom had taught her that Christians were the most gullible group when it came to child abusers and were persistently unwilling to accept the potential for abuse in their own religious communities. She said she shuddered when church members testified in her courtroom as "character witnesses" on behalf of those accused of child abuse. Repeatedly she has listened to Christians defend the moral integrity of individuals who end up being convicted of hideous acts of abuse. These Christians simply can't believe a person they've experienced as "nice" could commit abuse.

After her presentation, John, one of the students who was a pastoral intern, shared—with a sheepish look on his face—that he had been a character witness defending a youth leader who had been accused of sexually molesting a junior high girl in his youth group. John recounted how he gave eloquent testimony about how wonderful this man was and how he was sure there was no way he could have abused a child; he just wasn't capable of that kind of behavior. John then told us that, after his glowing testimony of this man's character, the prosecuting attorney cross-examined him and asked if he knew that this "wonderful man" had previously been convicted in another state of raping a teen at knifepoint. John was flabbergasted. He hadn't known and yet he still couldn't believe that a kind church leader could molest a teen. Thankfully, the jury disregarded John's naive judgment, and the youth leader was convicted of child molestation and sentenced to several years in prison. In class that day, John shared his deep regret for his denial. Christians, of all people, must take the implications of universal depravity seriously and accept the fact that *all* humans are capable of abuse.

The Role of Satan and the Demonic

> Goodness is, so to speak, itself: badness is only spoiled goodness. And there must be something good first before it can be spoiled.[30]

Satan cannot create anything, and thus he perverts the best of what God has created. Cornelius Plantinga puts it this way: "Good is original, independent, and constructive; evil is derivative, dependent, and destructive. To be successful, evil needs what it hijacks from goodness."[31] Plantinga goes on: "Evil wants good; in fact, evil needs good to be evil. Satan himself, as C. S. Lewis explains, is *God's* Satan—a creature of God who can be really wicked only because he comes from the shop of a master and is made from his best stuff. 'The better stuff a creature is made of—the cleverer and stronger and freer it is—then the better it will be if it goes right, but also the worse it will be if it goes wrong.'"[32]

Let's further explore the role of Satan and his demonic legions.[33]

---

30. C. S. Lewis, *Mere Christianity* (New York: Macmillan, 1952), 49.

31. Plantinga, *Not the Way It's Supposed to Be*, 89.

32. Plantinga, *Not the Way It's Supposed to Be*, 90, italics in original; quoting C. S. Lewis, *Mere Christianity* (New York: Macmillan, 1949), 53.

33. For a basic overview of the nature and activity of angels, see C. Fred Dickason, *Angels Elect and Evil*, rev. ed. (Chicago: Moody, 1995). For a scholarly treatment of the biblical doctrine of angels, see Stephen F. Noll, *Angels of Light, Powers of Darkness* (Downers Grove, IL: InterVarsity, 1998). For a comprehensive biblical treatment of Satan and demons, see Sydney H. T. Page, *Powers of Evil: A Biblical Study of Satan and Demons* (Grand Rapids: Baker, 1995). More recent works on angels and demons, drawing heavily on ancient Near Eastern and Jewish sources, are Michael Heiser, *Angels: What The Bible Really Says about God's Heavenly Host* (Bellingham, WA: Lexham, 2018) and *Demons: What the*

Contemporary culture often makes Satan the butt of jokes, as evidenced in Adam Sandler's portrayal of Satan in the movie *Little Nicky* and in Gary Larson's comic images in the *Far Side* cartoons. Liberal theologians often assert that Satan and demons reflect the prescientific mythology of the biblical writers, and that evil is best understood as the result not of dark angelic forces but of unjust sociopolitical structures.[34] The writers of Scripture, however, treat Satan as real and unimaginably destructive.

- Nineteen of the twenty-seven books of the New Testament refer to Satan, and seven Old Testament books refer to him.
- Of the eight New Testament books that do not refer to Satan, four refer to demons.
- Of the twenty-nine references to Satan in the Gospels, twenty-five are made by Jesus himself.
- Satan's power and influence is vast. He is declared the ruler and god of this world (John 12:31; 2 Corinthians 4:4).
- Unbelievers are held captive to do his will (2 Timothy 2:26).
- He is the one who deceives nations and the whole world (Revelation 12:9; 20:3). Thus—temporarily—Satan is carrying out his will throughout world history.

One of the biblical titles given to Satan helps make the link clear between Satan's character and human abuse. Satan is repeatedly described as the "evil one" (Matthew 6:13; John 17:15; 1 John 2:13–14; 5:18–19). This phrase in Greek indicates that Satan is "the one intrinsically wicked who is not content to be corrupt in himself but must seek to corrupt others."[35] As we'll see in the following chapters, abuse is one of Satan's most powerful tools for corrupting and destroying individuals in every aspect of their being (physically, emotionally, relationally, and spiritually). Repeatedly, the Bible describes Satan's work and influence in the world as one of abusive evil. Cain, the man who committed the first act of physical violence recorded in Scripture, drew his inspiration from Satan, the "evil one" who was a butcher (physically abusing murderer) from the very beginning (John 8:44;

Bible Says about the Powers of Darkness (Bellingham, WA: Lexham, 2020). We are not convinced by Heiser's proposal of three angelic falls, but he is an excellent writer with many helpful insights.

34. For an excellent overview of historical and contemporary theological models of evil, see Hans Schwarz, *Evil: A Historical and Theological Perspective* (Minneapolis: Fortress, 1995).

35. Dickason, *Angels Elect and Evil*, 130, regarding the articular use of the adjective *poneros* to refer to Satan. On other uses of this phrase to refer to Satan, particularly in Matthew, see Page, *Powers of Evil*, 112–14.

1 John 3:12).[36] Satan is said to promote the persecution, abuse, and even murder of God's people (Revelation 2:10; 12:13). In this context, the most significant satanic title is found in Revelation 9:11, where Satan is called *Apollyon* (that is, the Destroyer), the king of all demons. In this passage Satan the Destroyer sends out demons with scorpion-like tails to abuse and physically torment humans all over the earth.

However, God's Word is abundantly clear that God's power to heal and redeem suffering is greater than Satan's power to destroy. The apostle Paul powerfully articulates this truth:

> No, in all these things we are more than conquerors through him who loved us. For I am convinced that neither death nor life, neither angels nor demons, neither the present nor the future, nor any powers, neither height nor depth, nor anything else in all creation, will be able to separate us from the love of God that is in Christ Jesus our Lord. (Romans 8:37–39)

Fleming Rutledge helpfully connects the presence of destructive evil with God's good plan and the believers' response, paving the way for redemption:

> Evil is *in no way* part of God's good purpose, and cannot be, since it does not have existence as a created good. Evil is neither rationally nor morally intelligible and must simply be loathed and resisted. The beginning of resistance is not to *explain*, but *to see*. Seeing is itself a form of action—seeing evil for what it is, not a part of God's plan, but a colossal *x* factor in creation, a monstrous contradiction, a prodigious negation that must be identified, denounced, and opposed wherever it occurs.[37]

Satan is the architect of abuse. He is the one who promotes evil, death, and destruction—from the Garden of Eden to the end of the age. But the cosmic destruction unleashed in Eden is merely the first chapter of human history. God will triumph over evil. And he calls us, his children, to engage in this battle.

---

36. The use of the verb *sphazo* highlights the brutal nature of Cain's act, for it means to kill by violence, to slaughter (Jeremiah 52:10 [Septuagint]; Revelation 6:4, 9). Satan's being "a murderer from the beginning" may refer to his influence on Cain but more likely refers to his influence in the temptation of Adam, which would then make Satan the murderer of the entire human race (Romans 5:12–21; Wisdom of Solomon 2:23–24).

37. Fleming Rutledge, *The Crucifixion: Understanding the Death of Jesus Christ* (Grand Rapids: Eerdmans, 2015), 434, italics in original.

Abuse Is Redeemable

If abuse is widely distributed throughout all sectors of society—and it has been so throughout human history—due to human depravity and satanic influence, what hope is there? It is precisely at the juncture of intractable evil, abuse, and human misery that the Christian gospel offers the only possible hope. The God declared in the Bible is not like the Greek gods on Mount Olympus that drank ambrosia and consorted with nymphs while humans squirmed and screamed on earth. Rather, God is deeply moved by human suffering (Hosea 11:8; Matthew 9:36; John 11:35) and is committed to healing and redeeming the vulnerable and oppressed at the greatest possible cost (Exodus 2:23–25; 12:1–42; Romans 5:8). Jesus Christ did not come for the healthy, but to redeem the sick and broken (Matthew 9:12–13). The writer of Hebrews beautifully declares that Christ took on human flesh so that he could die and, in so doing, render Satan and death impotent—to break the chains of human bondage (Hebrews 2:14–15).

The inconceivable irony of the gospel is that Jesus suffered the most extreme form of physical abuse so that the abused and their repentant abusers could be restored—"by his wounds we are healed" (Isaiah 53:5). In fact, this irony is so great that the dominant symbol of Christianity is an instrument of sadistic abuse—a cross. When one understands the grotesque nature of crucifixion, by which the founder of Christianity and many early Christian leaders were tortured to death, it's shocking that Christians image their faith with a cross (1 Corinthians 2:2). It would be comparable to Jews making the symbol of Judaism a miniature crematorium that they wear around their necks and place on their synagogues. The cross is the most poignant symbol imaginable of God's goodness and power to heal and redeem abuse.

This side of heaven, no one can offer a fully satisfactory answer for why God continues to allow evil and suffering.[38] We do know, however, that God delights in taking suffering and evil and creating great good out of them (Romans 8:28; 2 Corinthians 4:8–18; Philippians 1:12–14). One of the most beautiful statements of divine redemption of grotesque evil is found in Genesis 50:20, when Joseph declared to his abusive brothers, "You intended to harm me, but God intended it for good." This statement highlights the fact that God is sovereign—even over evil. What the brothers intended for

---

38. For a brief overview of this subject, see Steven Tracy, "Where Is God in the Midst of the Suffering of Abuse?" *Africanus Journal* 2, no. 2 (2010): 45–52, https://mlhlsi.infiniteuploads.cloud /2018/09/WhereIsGodInMidstofSufferingandAbuse.pdf.

Joseph's destruction God providentially redeemed in the most dramatic fashion. He brought individual healing and restoration to Joseph by using the very circumstances created by their devious abuse to bring about the deliverance of their entire family—and ultimately the Israelite nation.

The apostle Paul, a collaborator in the fatal abuse of Stephen and a former physical abuser of Christians (Acts 8:1–3),[39] became the Christian church's greatest missionary and teacher. He, in turn, experienced layers of abuse—slander, beatings, whippings, stoning, imprisonments, and even murderous attempts (2 Corinthians 11:23–33). After enduring a lifetime of suffering, Paul declared that through all of the abuse, Christ was sweeter and stronger in his life than he had ever been (2 Corinthians 4:8–18; 12:10). God desires to heal our brokenness and to use it to draw us deeper into a joy-filled intimacy with him and to use the very scars created by abuse to comfort others who are also suffering (Romans 8:17; 2 Corinthians 1:4–6).

The biblical data is clear—God delights in redeeming every form of evil, including abuse. He supremely did this on the cross, using the worst imaginable abuse to ultimately destroy death, suffering, and Satan. For some readers, this truth may seem too abstract and hypothetical to be real. So we would like to close this chapter with another personal story. Recently we led an MTS training team to East Africa to provide trauma intensives for refugees, as well as for Congolese pastors and caregivers. As is always the case with such work, it was physically, emotionally, and spiritually exhausting and demanding. But it was a small price to pay for what we saw, heard, and experienced—life purpose, healing, and redemption. Each member of our MTS training team shared their story of abuse, healing, and redemption. Together we got to experience seeing God use our pain for the comfort of others. This is exactly the principle the apostle Paul gave to the Corinthians: "Praise be to the God and Father of our Lord Jesus Christ, the Father of compassion and the God of all comfort, who comforts us in all our troubles, so that we can comfort those in any trouble with the comfort we ourselves receive from God (2 Corinthians 1:3–4).

We reflect now on that trip and see Mama Nora, a quiet, humble American grandmother who survived years of childhood sexual abuse, chronic intimate partner abuse, her daughters' sexual abuse, the deaths of her daughter and brother, and life-threatening cancer. Mama Nora has

---

39. The use of the Greek verb *suneudokeo* in Acts 8:1 makes it clear that Paul did not passively consent to Stephen's murder, for this term indicates active consent and hearty approval (Acts 22:20; Romans 1:32; 1 Corinthians 7:12). Furthermore, Acts 8:3 shows that Paul was actively ravaging the church (*elumaineto*—the imperfect tense indicates ongoing action).

become a celebrity in Africa. Why? Because she stands as a trophy of God's grace and power to heal. Most Africans have never met an American who has suffered so much and yet has such robust faith, contagious joy, and deep compassion. Her gentle yet bold, vulnerable sharing of her trauma story has provided hope and healing to thousands.[40] We can see her embracing Pastor J, a gentle brother who, as a young child, stood by helplessly as he watched his family drown after fleeing a militia attack. Mama Nora's story of family loss gave him hope that his suffering could be redeemed. Today Pastor J is a leader in his denomination, guiding hundreds of pastors in offering trauma-informed care to hurting families.

We remember Mama Leah. Our team sat with tears streaming down our faces as we heard the harrowing story of her abduction, torture, and abuse at the hands of those in a local militia. She was abused in every unspeakable way for seven days before being thrown into a pit. She lay there until a ransom was paid and she was finally released. The year before her abduction, in God's providence, Mama Leah's pastor had participated in an MTS trauma training and healing intensive. After Mama Leah's release, Pastor Richard gathered a trained team to care for her physically and psychologically. She slowly began to heal. Upon the anniversary of her release, Mama Leah decided to go back into the bush to find the rebels who had kidnapped her. When they saw her, they began to shout and threaten her, interrogating her about her reasons for coming. She boldly declared, "God sent me to you because you need Jesus. What you did was evil, but God loves you and Jesus died for you. I forgive you for what you did to me, and I'm here to tell you about God's love and forgiveness." She ended up staying for three days, teaching them about Jesus through the lens of trauma care. Since that day, Mama Leah has gone on to share her story with thousands of Congolese trauma survivors. She has become a tremendous source of inspiration for other Congolese Christians. Her story has spread like wildfire throughout the North Kivu region of the DRC. God heals and redeems.

We remember Jumah, our MTS Africa director, and can hear his contagious laughter and see his magnetic smile. His childhood home was violent and laced with physical abuse, abandonment, and poverty because of his polygamous family. He was bounced from home to home, never finding the security and safety his heart longed for. He bears the scars from the physical abuse; he was cut with knives and burned by his stepmother and

---

40. Nora's "five-heart" story is found in Steven and Celestia Tracy, *By His Wounds: Trauma Healing for Africa* (Phoenix, AZ: Mending the Soul Ministries, 2014), 177–88.

violent father. He grew up in abject poverty and soul-grinding injustice. Humanly, Jumah didn't stand a chance in life. But over the course of many years, God was miraculously healing and redeeming his trauma. God has used those very wounds to mold Jumah into a godly husband, faithful father, and unstoppable advocate for the marginalized. Year after year, we've seen Jumah boldly, powerfully, and lovingly share his story with abusive government officials, massacre survivors, Muslim leaders, soldiers, incarcerated youth, and traumatized children. Jumah is known to say, "I will spend the rest of my life, until God takes me home, serving the abused! This is my life mission. This is what gives me hope, joy, and life purpose. God has given me healing, and I must share it with others!" We get it. We feel exactly the same way.

In this life, we bear scars—physical and emotional—yet there is no evil that the crucified, resurrected Jesus can't redeem. Your pain need not be wasted. There is purpose in suffering. Satan does not have the final word!

CHAPTER 2

Abuse as a Perversion of the Image of God

What makes sin so heinous is that
man is prostituting such splendid gifts.
Corruptio optimi pessima: the corruption
of the best is the worst.

Anthony A. Hoekema,
Created in God's Image

What is mankind that you are mindful of them,
human beings that you care for them?
You have made them a little lower than the angels
and crowned them with glory and honor.

Psalm 8:4–5

Until God brought Mary into our lives, we simply couldn't comprehend the staggering impact of abuse. We were particularly stunned at the way in which this beautiful little girl was haunted by traumatic memories that followed her like a toxic cloud of self-annihilating shame. Her body held the horror of what she had experienced. How could sexual fondling that had occurred years before cause a bright and gifted girl who had grown up in a loving Christian family to have such self-loathing and shame that she had to cut herself for a destructive sense of release?

After Mary disclosed her abuse, her parents sought counsel from a Christian psychologist who specialized in working with high-risk adolescents in the California juvenile justice system. Dr. Jones (not her real name) explained to Mary's bewildered parents that in her ten-year practice, a high percentage of her young patients who self-mutilated had been sexually abused. In some strange way, the uninvited internal anguish was mitigated by creating physical pain in their bodies.[1]

Abuse opens a Pandora's box of horrifying destruction that raises a host of troubling questions: Why are women who have been abused during childhood significantly more likely to be revictimized in adulthood? Why are women who have experienced sexual assault 250 to 400 percent more likely to develop PTSD than soldiers returning from combat?[2] Why are adult female prostitutes three to four times more likely than nonprostitutes to have been physically or sexually abused in childhood?[3] Why is it that 70–80 percent of sex addicts are survivors of physical or sexual abuse?[4] Why is it that the majority of men who beat their wives and/or children experienced childhood physical abuse?[5] One might logically expect that men who experienced the horror of abuse in childhood would be the *least* likely to be abusers themselves, not wanting to inflict the kind of pain on their loved ones that was inflicted on their mother, siblings, or on them.[6]

---

1. Steven Levenkron, a psychologist who specializes in treating self-mutilators, estimates that there are two million Americans who self-mutilate, and the majority do so because of unresolved childhood trauma, especially sexual abuse (*Cutting: Understanding and Overcoming Self-Mutilation* [New York: Norton, 1999]).

2. Cited in Steven Tracy and Andy Maurer, "#MeToo and Evangelicalism: Shattering Myths about Sexual Abuse and Power," *Cultural Encounters* 14, no. 2 (2019): 15.

3. Kathleen Potter, Judy Martin, and Sarah Romans conducted a study of prostitutes in New Zealand and found that 80 percent of them had experienced physical abuse and 36 percent experienced genital sexual abuse before the age of sixteen ("Early Developmental Experiences of Female Sex Workers: A Comparative Study," *Australian and New Zealand Journal of Psychiatry* 33, no. 6 [1999]: 935–40). A larger study of 237 prostitutes and 407 comparison women at an STD clinic found that 32 percent of the prostitutes had experienced severe childhood sexual abuse (nonconsensual prepubertal intercourse). This rate was two and a half times higher than that experienced by the control group from an STD clinic—and a control group from an STD clinic will most likely reflect considerably higher childhood abuse rates than the general populace (see John J. Potterat et al., "Pathways to Prostitution: The Chronology of Sexual and Drug Abuse Milestones," *Journal of Sex Research* 35, no. 4 [1998]: 333–40). These abuse rates are three to four times the national average.

4. Studies conducted by Patrick Carnes reveal that 72 percent of the sex addicts surveyed reported physical abuse in their history, and 81 percent reported a history of sexual abuse (*Don't Call It Love: Recovery from Sexual Addiction* [New York: Bantam, 1991], 146). Interestingly, the partners of sex addicts have histories of physical and sexual abuse mirroring that of the addicts.

5. See Lex L. Merrill, Linda K. Hervig, and Joel S. Milner, "Childhood Parenting Experiences, Intimate Partner Conflict Resolution, and Adult Risk for Child Physical Abuse," *Child Abuse & Neglect* 20, no. 11 (1996): 1049–65. A shockingly high percentage of parents who experienced abuse as children will become abusers. Joan Kaufman and Edward Zigler report that approximately 30 percent of abused children become physically abusing parents ("Do Abused Children Become Abusive Parents?" *American Journal of Orthopsychiatry* 57, no. 2 [1987]: 186–92).

6. The transmission of violence from parents to children is a complex but very real phenomenon. For instance, in a nationally representative victims survey of over 11,000 adults, researchers found that the most important risk marker for perpetrating parental violence is having experienced parental violence (78 percent of the abusive parents in the study had experienced parental violence themselves), Deborah Hellmann et al., "(Why) Do Victims Become Perpetrators? Intergenerational Transmission of Parental Violence in a Representative German Sample," *Journal of Family Psychology* 32 (2018): 286.

The unsettling truth is that abuse has profound, wildly irrational consequences. It shatters the soul. The only way to fully understand the effects of abuse is to clarify what it means to be a human being created in God's image. Once you can see through this lens, you will more fully understand and validate abuse—in all its forms—as the evil it is.

Made in the Image of God—Genesis 1 and 2

Christian theology asserts that humans are not just the most highly evolved mammals at the top of a food chain, nor are we complex machines that spontaneously arose out of a "primordial soup" millions of years ago. Rather, humans are dazzlingly unique among God's entire created realm, for only humans are made in the very image of God. As one theologian wisely notes, being made in God's image "confers on the human subject the highest possible distinction, leaving the world of the animals far behind. Here is language used of no other creature, language that teaches us to understand ourselves in terms of God rather than in terms of the animals."[7] The Bible is patently clear: all humans bear God's image in a unique way (Genesis 1:26–28; 9:6; James 3:9); at the core of what it means to be human is to be made "in his own image" (Genesis 1:27).

Our challenge is to understand more precisely what "image of God" means, since the Bible nowhere defines this monumentally important phrase. The best way to make sense of the image of God is to look at the creation account in Genesis 1:26–28, where this phrase first appears. We should note first that the biblical account of human creation is distinctly different from other ancient Mesopotamian creation accounts in which humans are created as an afterthought to provide the gods with food and relieve them of work. Moses, on the other hand, tells us that humans are the apex of all creation, for only after Adam and Eve are created does God pronounce his finished work as "very good" (Genesis 1:31). The first chapter of the Bible describes God's magnificent, unique creation of the first human beings as mirroring the sovereign Lord of the universe.

Being made in God's image refers to *all that we are* as humans.[8] Genesis 1:26 helps us understand the *relational* implications of our created selves:

---

7. Paul K. Jewett, *Who We Are: Our Dignity as Humans* (Grand Rapids: Eerdmans, 1996), 54.

8. I'm indebted to Anthony A. Hoekema for this perspective of the image of God. He argues that the image of God in humans is multifaceted and involves a structural aspect (innate qualities such as rationality) as well as relational and functional aspects (*Created in God's Image* [Grand Rapids: Eerdmans, 1986], 66–101); see also Wayne Grudem, *Systematic Theology* 2nd ed. (Grand Rapids: Zondervan, 2020), 567–69.

humans have the capacity, longing, and desperate drive for intimate relation-ship based on a relational God who is in intimate relationship within his own divine being. Jesus himself spoke of the loving intimacy he had with the Father and prays that his followers would reflect God through intimate human relationships (John 17:21–23). Apparently when God chose to create creatures who would mirror who he is, the best (and maybe the only) way to do so was to create not just an individual but a pair whose very sexuality as male and female complements and attracts each to the other.[9]

This helps to explain why the New Testament teaches that intimate relationships in the Christian community are essential for spiritual growth (Acts 4:32–34; Hebrews 10:24–25; James 5:16). Furthermore, social scientists have discovered that healthy relationships are essential for social, intellectual, and emotional growth. Children who are cut off from human contact develop permanent social and intellectual impairment. Research on attachment has shown the tremendous long-term social and emotional significance for chil-dren to have a safe, secure attachment with their parents.[10] The human need for relationship is so profound that infants who are fed, clothed, and given medical care but are deprived of affectionate touch will often fail to thrive and, left untouched, may eventually die.[11] Our need and capacity for intimate relationships creates great vulnerability in a sinful, abusive world.

There is also a visible aspect of image of God seen in the language of Genesis 1:26 when God says, "Let us make mankind in our image, in our likeness." This is the aspect of the image of God in which humans visi-bly demonstrate God's attributes. We see this in the very terminology of this verse ("image" and "likeness").[12] The point here is that humans are to

9. Anthony Hoekema notes, "Men and women cannot attain to true humanity in isolation; they need the fellowship and stimulation of others. We are social beings" (*Created in God's Image*, 77); see also Ranald Macaulay and Jerram Barrs, *Being Human: The Nature of Spiritual Experience* (Downers Grove, IL: InterVarsity, 1978), 171.

10. The literature on attachment is voluminous. Robert Karen gives an excellent overview of the research (*Becoming Attached: First Relationships and How They Shape Our Capacity to Love* [New York: Oxford University Press, 1998]). A more recent nontechnical overview of attachment is Peter Lovenheim, *The Attachment Effect: Exploring the Powerful Ways Our Earliest Bond Shapes Our Relationships and Lives* (New York: TarcherPerigee, 2018). As a theologian, I'm amazed at the way secular attachment research harmonizes with the biblical teaching on the relational aspect of the image of God, especially the profound significance of intimate relationships.

11. *Marasmus* (wasting away) is the medical term for this condition, which was identified after World War II when large numbers of infant orphans, cared for in Allied orphanages, began dying for no apparent medical reason. Once these infants who were being changed, fed, and given warm cribs but receiving little or no physical contact by the busy nurses began to be held by caregivers, the exploding infant mortality rates dramatically reversed.

12. The Hebrew word for "image" (*tselem*) indicates concrete similarity, such as that found in a coin or a statue (Daniel 3:1). The word for "likeness" (*demut*) indicates abstract similarity (Daniel 10:16). The terms are probably mutually defining.

visibly manifest who God is—to make visible the invisible God (compare Colossians 1:15). Sadly, as with the relational aspect of the image of God, abuse can grotesquely distort how God is imaged because of an abusive spouse or parent. This explains why we find such harsh statements in Scripture against religious leaders who abuse their power to exploit the vulnerable ones in their care (Ezekiel 34:1–10; Matthew 23; etc.), especially when they were tasked to use their power to serve, nurture, and protect so those who don't know God will see his character in those who do.

A third aspect of God's image is the *functional* aspect in which humans serve as God's representatives on earth.[13] In terms of creation, we are his vice-regents, or representatives, in caring for his creation. This is clearly stated in Genesis 1:26 where "so that they may rule" immediately follows "Let us make mankind in our image." We also see this in Genesis 2, when God waited to create some of the plants until Adam and Eve had been created to care for them (Genesis 2:5). God put man and woman in the garden to "work it and take care of it" (Genesis 2:15). While the Bible assigns the ultimate providential care over the created world to God himself (Psalm 104:14–30; 135:7; Acts 14:17), he made humans in his image as his functional representatives to care for all he had created. This involves both control (Genesis 1:26; Psalm 8:5–6) and cultivation (Genesis 2:15). Again, we can easily see how this aspect of the image of God can be distorted. Instead of functioning properly as God's representatives to care for creation, we can rule harshly over creation and grossly misrepresent who God is. When humans do not function as God's representatives but use their power to dominate rather than nurture, long-term damage is done.

The Effects of Sin—Genesis 3

While Genesis 2 ends on an incredibly beautiful note of relational intimacy—"Adam and his wife were both naked, and they felt no shame"— this intimacy is immediately shattered by sin in Genesis 3. As soon as Adam and Eve eat the forbidden fruit, all three aspects of the image of God are disrupted and distorted. Instead of mirroring and enjoying relational intimacy, immediately after eating the fruit they try to hide from each other and from God (Genesis 3:7–8); soul-satisfying intimacy is perverted into something shameful. Instead of visibly manifesting the character of God, they manifest ungodliness and unholiness. Instead of functioning as God's

---

13. See Erich Sauer, *The King of the Earth* (Exeter, England: Paternoster, 1959), 72–91.

representatives in caring for creation, their sin harmed and cursed creation (Genesis 3:14–16). At every level, sin corrupted the image of God, though it did not eliminate it.

At this juncture, we should note the relevance of the curse recorded in Genesis 3:16 to the issue of abuse:

- Instead of joyfully living out the image of God through physical reproduction (a very godlike activity), the woman would now experience pain in childbirth.
- Instead of acting as a spiritual equal who complements the man, the woman would have an unhealthy, slavish dependence on the man ("your desire will be for your husband").[14]
- Instead of the man treating the woman as a divine gift who could complement him as an intimate equal, the fallen man would seek to harshly rule over the woman as an inferior ("he will rule over you").[15]

Scripture and human history repeatedly bear out the accuracy of this horrifying forecast. Throughout history, men have repeatedly abused their power over women, and women have often been destructively codependent on men. Several years ago, we developed curriculum and trainings for organizations serving sex-trafficked girls. In preparation, we conducted extensive academic and field research on prostitution. In coordination with local law enforcement officials, Celestia and a team of counselors worked with two dozen girls and young women who had been trafficked. In the process, we repeatedly witnessed graphic, truly outrageous manifestations of the "rule over/desire" prediction. Prostituted girls endured extreme levels

---

14. The prediction that Eve's desire would be for her husband is difficult to interpret. Susan Foh forcefully argues that, based on the use of the same word in Genesis 4:7, this refers to the woman's desire to master or usurp her husband's authority (*Women and the Word of God: A Response to Biblical Feminism* [Grand Rapids: Baker, 1979], 67–69). While this view is exegetically viable, we believe it places too much emphasis on the meaning of "desire" in Genesis 4:7 while ignoring the fact that the only other time the term is used in the Old Testament, it refers to emotional, romantic desire (Song of Songs 7:10). It also seriously fails to account for human experience. Women very commonly seek from a man what can only be obtained from God. We might call this "codependence."

15. The majority of commentators recognize that "he will rule over you" is no divine prescription but a tragic prediction of sin's effects on the human race. The Hebrew term for "rule" found in Genesis 3:16 is the same term found in Genesis 4:7 of Cain's need to harshly dominate or master that which would harm him—namely, sin. This lexical observation, along with the fact that Genesis 3:16 gives several unfortunate negative consequences of the fall, lead me to conclude that "he will rule over you" reflects not God's desire but a realistic prediction of the results of sinful depravity on males who will routinely seek to abuse their power. Thus, Victor Hamilton argues that this phrase means "the sinful husband will try to be a tyrant over his wife" (*The Book of Genesis Chapters 1–17* [Grand Rapids: Eerdmans, 1990], 202).

of violence from their male pimps and "customers." One study of prostituted women in nine different countries found that 70–95 percent of the women had been physically assaulted while in prostitution, and 95 percent of the US women in this study had experienced head injuries.[16] This is similar to findings from studies done exclusively in the US.[17]

Ironically, it is extremely difficult for prostituted women to leave "the life" in spite of the fact that they are subject to humiliation, degradation, and violence on a daily basis. As if that abuse isn't costly and demeaning enough, they usually are required to give 100 percent of their earnings to the very pimp who abuses and exploits them. They have a tragic, self-destructive "desire" for their pimps.

One of the first girls Celestia worked with in a juvenile detention facility drew pictures of her "boyfriend" and described in detail his love for her (see figure 1). When Celestia asked her how she knew her "boyfriend" loved her, she thought for a moment and then, in all seriousness, declared, "Because he buys me Cheetos." We knew the background to this seventeen-year-old's story—her history of childhood abuse, years on the run, and subsequent drug abuse. The detective who asked Mending the Soul to help kids like her warned us to be careful because her pimp was a violent and dangerous man who had been labeled by the federal authorities as a "gorilla pimp."

Celestia had the privilege of counseling this beautiful girl for four more months before she aged out of the system on her eighteenth

Figure 1

16. Melissa Farley et al., "Prostitution and Trafficking in Nine Countries: An Update on Violence and Posttraumatic Stress Disorder," in Melissa Farley, ed., *Prostitution, Trafficking, and Traumatic Stress* (Birmingham, NY: Haworth Maltreatment & Trauma Press, 2003), 54, 56.

17. A study of almost three hundred prostituted women in Miami found that in just the previous three months, almost three-fourths of the women had experienced a "violent encounter" (Hilary Surratt et al., "The Connections of Mental Health Problems, Violent Life Experiences, and the Social Milieu of the 'Stroll' with the HIV Risk Behaviors of Female Street Sex Workers," *Journal of Psychology & Human Sexuality* 17, no. 1–2 [2005]: 23–44, https://nsuworks.nova.edu/cgi/viewcontent .cgi?article=1274&context=shss_facarticles).

birthday. Even though she was transferred to a "safe house," she escaped out of a bathroom window to return to her "boyfriend." Sadly, she was killed a month before her nineteenth birthday.

Pimps astutely understand and shamelessly exploit women's codependent "desire." Mickey Royal, a self-professed "pimp king," wrote an instructional manual on prostitution. It is a pathological expression of the desire/rule prophesy. His advice to other men for securing and exploiting women for prostitution includes the following:

> How to knock a b**** and transform her into a ho? It is an intricate process of psychological destruction and emotional construction . . .
>
> A ho's desire can't be fed because she has a need that isn't material—love, security, acceptance, confirmation of one's self worth, etc. Just as young men join gangs for the same reason, a ho exchanges something she can see for something she can't. This leaves the door open for exploitation, abuse and misuse . . .
>
> A ho to a pimp is worth nothing. She is actually worth everything, but he must make her believe that she is worthless. A pimp buys her soul . . .
>
> The strength of a pimp comes from the ho's belief that the pimp loves her. You have to know everything about your ho. Some hos need physical abuse. Some hos need emotional mistreatment. Some hos need lies and fantasies . . .
>
> A ho is driven by her insecurities. You find out what her insecurities are and use them against her.[18]

While prostitution represents an extreme expression of Genesis 3:16, the general principle can be seen in many other abuse contexts. For instance, it helps explain the common question outsiders often ask regarding women who are being battered by their partners: "Why doesn't she just leave him since he keeps beating her up?" Obviously, men often stay in unhealthy, even abusive relationships. But it is much less common for outsiders to ask, "Why doesn't he just leave her since she keeps beating him up?" It rarely works that way.

Let's extend this discussion of abuse, gender, and power a bit further.

---

18. Mickey Royal, *The Pimp Game: Instructional Guide* (Los Angeles: Sharif, 1998), 3, 40, 52, 70, 76. On the sophisticated way pimps emotionally manipulate and dominate ("rule") women, using their "desire" against them, see Harvey Schwartz, Jody Williams, and Melissa Farley, "Pimp Subjugation of Women by Mind Control," in *Prostitution & Trafficking in Nevada: Making the Connection*, ed. Melissa Farley (San Francisco: Prostitution Research & Education, 2007), 49–84.

The Bible describes numerous instances (Isaiah 10:1–2; Ezekiel 22:6–12; Micah 2:9; 3:1–3, for example) where those with power, particularly civil and religious authorities, used their power to exploit and abuse those with less power, particularly orphans, widows, and the poor.[19] Scripture also suggests that those who are marginalized and suddenly gain power can become the very oppressors they had previously feared. This dynamic appears to lie behind the statement in Proverbs 30:21–22 that one of three times the earth trembles is when a slave becomes king. Obviously, the sin nature is evenly distributed by gender, so the issue is not being male or female per se. Men and women are equally fallen and can become abusers as well as victims. Some of the most wounded abuse survivors we have worked with were men who had been abused (physically, sexually, or verbally) by their mothers.

Scripture certainly gives examples of females misusing their power by abusing others. Murderous Jezebel, Athaliah, and Herodias are notable examples (1 Kings 21:7–14; 2 Kings 11:1–3; Matthew 14:1–11). We particularly witness female abuse of power in the context of parenting, since children are dependent on others for their care. The most recent National Incidence Study shows that 68 percent of all maltreated children are maltreated by a female. Furthermore, when children are maltreated by a birth parent, 75 percent of the time they are maltreated by their mother. The Fourth National Incidence Study also found that children are more than twice as likely to be neglected by a female as a male.[20] We should not misconstrue these statistics to suggest that mothers are more inherently abusive than fathers. Mothers are statistically more likely than fathers to maltreat their children, primarily because mothers are much more likely to be the primary caregivers than are fathers.

Are Males More Likely to Abuse Than Women?

Various scholars argue that the perpetration of intimate partner violence is essentially gender-symmetrical, that is, women are just as likely as men to perpetrate abuse, particularly intimate partner violence.[21] Some studies, particularly self-report surveys of adolescents and young adults, have found that

19. For a superb treatment of abuse and the misuse of spiritual and social power, see Diane Langberg, *Redeeming Power: Understanding Authority and Abuse in the Church* (Grand Rapids: Brazos, 2020).

20. Andrea J. Sedlak et al., *Fourth National Incidence Study of Child Abuse and Neglect (NIS–4): Report to Congress* (Washington, DC: U. S. Department of Health and Human Services, Administration for Children and Families, 2010), https://cap.law.harvard.edu/wp-content/uploads/2015/07/sedlaknis.pdf.

21. See Donald G. Dutton, "My Back Pages: Reflections on Thirty Years of Domestic Violence Research," *Trauma, Violence, and Abuse* 9, no. 3 (2008): 131–43.

females are more likely than males to physically assault their male partner.[22] These findings have led to strident controversy and have created a significant backlash, prompting some to reject previous IPV models and responses. For several decades, since the "second wave" of feminism in the 1960s and 1970s, feminists have proclaimed that male-perpetrated physical and sexual abuse is a long-standing, overwhelming social problem that must be decisively addressed. Some of the abuse literature in the '70s was extreme in its indictment of males as *the* cause of abuse. For instance, Susan Brownmiller in her classic early feminist work on rape, stated that rape "is nothing more or less than a conscious process by which *all men* keep *all women* in a state of fear."[23]

But in the past two decades, the pendulum has swung to the other extreme. Some are now asserting that, in fact, men are most often the victims of abuse, particularly IPV, and are the ones most in need of protection, and that women are the primary perpetrators of abuse. Various political and religious conservatives have joined this chorus.[24] For instance, evangelical author Beth Impson asserts that current male-perpetrated IPV and sexual violence statistics are greatly inflated, inaccurate "scare numbers." In other words, male-perpetrated abuse is not a significant problem. She then goes on to suggest that women are the bigger problem. She asks, "Where are the resources to help battered men? Where are the resources to help violent women learn to control their anger?"[25] She answers her questions by suggesting that feminists, in love with their own power, are responsible for distorting the truth about abuse.

What are we to make of this controversy? As we noted previously, women

---

22. Murray A. Straus, "Dominance and Symmetry in Partner Violence by Male and Female University Students in 32 Nations," *Children and Youth Services Review* 30, no. 3 (2008): 252–275; Carrie Mulford and Peggy Giordano, "Teen Dating Violence: A Closer Look at Adolescent Romantic Relationships," *National Institute of Justice Journal* 261 (2008): 34–40. While Mulford and Giordano noted gender parity regarding perpetration of violence, they emphasized that the motivation for the violence was different, with males more frequently reporting the need to control as a motivating factor and girls often reporting self-defense as a motivating factor.

23. Susan Brownmiller, *Against Our Will* (New York: Simon & Schuster, 1975), 5, italics original.

24. See, for instance, Janice Shaw Crouse (currently a senior fellow for Concerned Women for America), "The Violence Against Women Act Should Outrage Decent People," *U.S. News and World Report*, March 19, 2012, www.usnews.com/debate-club/should-the-violence-against-women -act-be-reauthorized/the-violence-against-women-act-should-outrage-decent-people; Tobin Grant, "Evangelical Leaders Split Over Violence Against Women Act," *Christianity Today* May 18, 2012, www .christianitytoday.com/ct/2012/mayweb-only/evangelical-leaders-split-over-violence-against-women -act.html; Kate O'Beirne [former president of the National Review Institute], *Women Who Made the World Worse* (New York: Sentinel, 2006), 17–18, 62–64; Suzanne Venker and Phyllis Schlafly [founder of Eagle Forum], *The Flipside of Feminism: What Conservative Women Know—and Men Can't Say* (Washington, DC: WND Books, 2011), 162–64.

25. Beth Impson, *Called to Womanhood: The Biblical View for Today's World* (Wheaton, IL: Crossway, 2006), 63–64.

are just as sinful and capable of abuse as men. At the same time, it is essential to recognize the overwhelming evidence of abuse asymmetry. All abuse is terribly wrong and can be exceedingly harmful. But it is very important to recognize that male-perpetrated physical and sexual abuse is a serious problem. Men are much more likely to abuse women (and other men) physically and sexually than women are likely to abuse men (or other women) physically or sexually. And when men do abuse women physically or sexually, it is generally more physically and psychologically harmful. Looking at this theologically, we believe it ultimately reflects innate biological differences designed by God (Genesis 2:18). In particular, men have ten to twenty times more testosterone than women, resulting in much greater physical aggression and strength. For instance, men have, on average, 40 percent greater upper-body and 33 percent greater lower-body strength than women do. Numerous secular scientists argue for a biological basis (particularly the impact of estrogen on females and testosterone on males) for dramatic gender asymmetry regarding the perpetration and impact of physical and sexual abuse.[26] Here is a summary of some of the data supporting this assertion.

- **Men perpetrate the overwhelming bulk of sexual abuse.** This is simply indisputable. In more than two decades of professional life dedicated to abuse research and service, we have heard of only one instance of an adult female raping an adult male. Female-perpetrated child sexual abuse does happen, but it is comparatively rare. In the vast majority of cases, 80–90 percent of the time when minors are sexually abused by an adult, it is by a man.

  And there is data to suggest that in the church, men are even more likely than women to be the sexual abusers of children. For instance, in an analysis of 326 cases of child sexual abuse in Protestant churches over a twenty-two-year period, 98.8 percent of the abusers were men.[27]

  And when it comes to adults, few men ever have to consider the possibility that they might be sexually assaulted. And the few who do have this fear, such as prison inmates, are threatened by men who

---

26. See, for instance, Simon Baron-Cohen, *The Essential Difference: Men, Women and the Extreme Male Brain* (New York: Penguin, 2012), 34–38, 99; Louann Brizendine, *The Male Brain: A Breakthrough Understanding of How Men and Boys Think* (New York: Harmony, 2010), 102–8, 168–70; David Geary, *Male, Female: The Evolution of Human Sex Differences*, 3rd ed. (Washington D.C: American Psychological Association, 2020).

27. Andrew S. Denney, Kent R. Kerley, and Nickolas G. Gross, "Child Sexual Abuse in Protestant Christian Congregations: A Descriptive Analysis of Offense and Offender Characteristics," *Religions* 9, no. 1 (2018), 6.

might assault them, never women. On the contrary, most women on some level factor the possibility of being assaulted into their daily lives. This fear influences where they park at night, where they walk, and the like. This is not a new phenomenon.

Sexual assault was apparently so common in Israel that Naomi advised Ruth to stay near Boaz's men, "lest in another field you be assaulted" (Ruth 2:22 ESV). In other words, women in ancient Israel had to factor into their daily lives the possibility of sexual assault by men, as do modern American women. Men overwhelmingly perpetrate the bulk of sexual abuse.

- **Men perpetrate the overwhelming bulk of criminal violence in general.** The most recent Justice Department analysis of criminal victimization, released in 2019, found that males were the perpetrators of 77 percent of all violent incidents, while females were the perpetrators of just 18.3 percent of all violent incidents, making men more than four times more likely than females to be the perpetrators of violence.[28] Similarly, in a study of US homicide trends over a twenty-eight-year period, almost 90 percent of the perpetrators were males.[29]

- **In terms of intimate partner violence, there is simply no gender parity when it comes to death, serious injury, or psychological harm.** A nineteen-year study of intimate partner violence found that females were almost two and a half times more likely to be seriously injured by an intimate partner than was a male.[30] In the US, almost one-third of female murder victims are killed by an intimate partner, while only 5 percent of male murder victims are killed by an intimate partner.[31]

Studies in developing world countries also reveal stark gender disparity regarding IPV homicides. The World Health Organization

28. We should note that 4.7 percent of the time, both a male and a female perpetrated the violence. See Rachel E. Morgan and Barbara A. Oudekerk, "Criminal Victimization 2018," U.S. Department of Justice, Bureau of Justice Statistics, September 2019, 12, www.bjs.gov/content/pub/pdf/cv18.pdf.

29. Alexia Cooper and Erica L. Smith, "Homicide Trends in the United States 1980–2008," U.S. Department of Justice, Bureau of Justice Statistics, November 2011, 3, www.bjs.gov/content/pub/pdf/htus8008.pdf. The lopsided preponderance of male-perpetrated violence, including homicide, appears to be a historical and transcultural reality. Martin Daly and Margo Wilson (*Homicide* [1988; repr., New York: Routledge, 2017], 146) conducted extensive studies of homicide records over many centuries from dozens of cultures. They conclude that there "is no known human society in which the level of lethal violence among women even approaches that among men" (146). They found that male-male homicide was 30 to 40 times more likely than female-female homicide.

30. Shannon Catalano, "Intimate Partner Violence: Attributes of Victimization, 1993–2011," U.S. Department of Justice, Bureau of Justice Statistics, November 2013, 6, www.bjs.gov/content/pub/pdf/ipvav9311.pdf.

31. Richard M. Hough and Kimberly D. McCorkle, *American Homicide*, 2nd ed. (Los Angeles: Sage, 2020) 86.

notes that research from Australia, Canada, Israel, South Africa, and the United States shows that 40–70 percent of female murder victims are murdered by their husbands, ex-husbands, or boyfriends, whereas in the United States, from 1976 to 1996, only 4 percent of the men murdered were killed by their wives, girlfriends, or ex-wives.[32]

Other studies in the US have found even greater IPV harm disparities, with women almost four times more likely than men to be injured (13.4 percent versus 3.5 percent), more than four times more likely to need medical care, and almost four times more likely to report having experienced one or more PTSD symptoms as a result of the IPV they experienced.[33] Female survivors of IPV are also three times more likely than male survivors to suffer depression and also three times more likely to suffer negative physical health outcomes.[34]

- **In terms of intimate partner violence, there is simply no gender parity when it comes to the context and motivation for violence.**[35] Women are much more likely than men to resort to violence as a means of self-defense. Studies show that the vast majority of women arrested for IPV had been previously victimized by that male partner.[36] Of particular importance is the role and impact that control plays in IPV. While all violence directed toward an intimate partner is obviously wrong and harmful, research has shown that some of the most harmful forms of IPV involve the use of "coercive control" in which the perpetrators,

32. Etienne G. Krug et al., eds., *World Report on Violence and Health* (Geneva: World Health Organization, 2002), 93, http://apps.who.int/iris/bitstream/handle/10665/42495/9241545615_eng.pdf.

33. Matthew Breiding et al., "Prevalence and Characteristics of Sexual Violence, Stalking, and Intimate Partner Violence Victimization—National Intimate Partner and Sexual Violence Survey, United States, 2011," Centers for Disease Control and Prevention, Morbidity and Mortality Weekly Report, September 5, 2014, www.cdc.gov/mmwr/preview/mmwrhtml/ss6308a1.htm.

34. Hyunkag Cho et al., "Gender Differences in the Relationship between the Nature of Intimate Partner Violence and the Survivor's Help-Seeking," *Violence Against Women* 26, no. 6–7 (2020): 714–15.

35. Gender IPV symmetry assertions are primarily the result of research using the Conflict Tactics Scale (CTS) developed by Murray Straus. Various abuse experts have shown that the CTS does not adequately disaggregate types of violence, thus overrepresenting minor female violence, and fails to account for the context of its use. When this is done, IPV gender parity largely disappears. See Sherry Hamby, "The Gender Debate about Intimate Partner Violence: Solutions and Dead Ends," *Psychological Trauma: Theory, Research, Practice, and Policy* 1, no. 1 (2009): 24–34; Lisa Young et al., "Understanding and Addressing Women's Use of Force in Intimate Relationships: A Retrospective," *Violence Against Women* 25, no. 1 (2019): 56–80.

36. Suzanne C. Swan et al., "Women's Use of Violence with Male Intimate Partners," in *Criminal Justice and the Law*, vol. 3 in *Violence against Women in Families and Relationships*, ed. Evan Stark and Eve S. Buzawa (New York: Praeger, 2009), 48–67; Evan Stark, "Do Violent Acts Equal Abuse? Resolving the Gender Parity/Asymmetry Dilemma," *Sex Roles* 62, no. 3 (2010): 201–11.

overwhelmingly males, engage in "patterns of emotionally abusive intimidation, coercion, and control coupled with physical violence against their partners."[37] Coercive control evidenced by behaviors such as threats of harm, extreme jealousy, and choking is highly correlated with fatal homicide.[38]

In summary, the motivation for IPV is different between the genders, with women being much more likely to perpetrate IPV as an act of self-defense. And the context for IPV is also gender-differentiated, with men much more likely to engage in intimidation and coercive control against their female partners. Coercive control is a most harmful form of abuse.

Challenge for Church Leaders

It is very important that we recognize a significant challenge faced by most church leaders. By definition, leaders have an enhanced level of power. In the evangelical world, church leaders are most often men. Those of us who are used to having physical, social, and religious power, particularly those of us who seek to use these blessings responsibly, can easily be blind to the experiences of others. After all, our experiences are what we intuitively understand. Others' weaknesses and vulnerabilities will not be intuitive to us if they are dramatically different from our own. The need to listen carefully to the needs and experiences of others might seem like common sense but it can be easily, harmfully overlooked.

This point was driven home to us several years ago when we were asked to help a large West Coast church that had been rocked by some high-profile abuse disclosures. In the course of our meetings and interviews, a woman we'll call Donna asked if she could meet with us privately. Donna shared that she was separated from her abusive husband. It was immediately apparent that she was absolutely terrified of this man. Others in the church who knew Donna and her husband were concerned for her well-being and asked if we could advocate with the church on her behalf. Donna had made a straightforward and, in our opinion, reasonable request that the church leaders ask her husband to attend the second Sunday morning service so she could attend the earlier service. Though it was a large church, every week her

---

37. Joan B. Kelly and Michael P. Johnson, "Differentiation among Types of Intimate Partner Violence: Research Update and Implications for Intervention," *Family Court Review* 46, no. 3 (2008): 478.

38. Jacquelyn Campbell et al., "Assessing Risk Factors for Intimate Partner Homicide," *National Institute of Justice Journal* 250 (2003): 14–19; Jacqueline Harden et al., "Examining Attempted and Completed Intimate Partner Homicide: A Qualitative Synthesis," *Violence and Victims* 34, no. 6 (2019): 869–88.

husband just "happened" to end up exactly where she was on the church campus. The previous week on her way to Sunday school, he had gone into the same elevator right after she entered. This incident was extremely traumatic for her. Unfortunately, the church leaders had not followed through on her request that he be asked to attend the second service.

So we met with the church leaders and discussed Donna's situation, seeking to explain the nature of abuse trauma and the needs of survivors. One of the pastors responded by explaining that he was personally discipling Donna's husband and was encouraged at his progress. He said the husband did acknowledge perpetrating some abusive behavior. But now, based on his own experiences with the husband, the pastor felt that Donna was exaggerating the extent and impact of the abuse. When we explained our observations about Donna's fears and the legitimacy of her traumatic responses, this leader simply couldn't accept the fact that Donna had any real reason to be fearful. His evidence? Earlier that week, he had met with the husband in his church office and "had not sensed anything whatsoever that should make anyone afraid."

We were left almost speechless. The pastor, seemingly very sincere, just didn't get it. He was making a value judgment, discounting this woman's fears and need for safety based on his own intuition, physical size, and personal potency when in the company of Donna's husband. The irony was that Donna was a 120-pound woman and this pastor was a large, former college athlete who possessed physical, social, and religious power far superior to that of Donna's husband. No wonder this pastor didn't sense any personal potential threat. No threat existed for him, so he assumed that no threat existed for her. It was tragic that this well-meaning pastor wasn't able to see the world outside his own privileged frame of experience.

Abuse as a Perversion of the Image of God

At its core, abuse involves the misuse of God-given power—verbal, physical, social, psychological, economic, cognitive, religious—to take advantage of another. Most often, abusers leverage some form of power against someone with less power, someone who is in some manner vulnerable. Hence, the prophet Micah excoriated powerful abusers in ancient Israel who "plot evil on their beds! At morning's light they carry it out *because it is in their power to do it*. They covet fields and seize them, and houses, and take them. They defraud people of their homes, they rob them of their inheritance" (Micah 2:1–2, emphasis added).

Sadly, the abuse of power against the vulnerable wasn't extinguished in ancient Israel. It is currently alive and well. The most vulnerable are still the most likely to be taken advantage of. For instance, research shows that children with disabilities are almost four times more likely than nondisabled children to be victims of violence, and three to four times more likely to experience physical or sexual abuse.[39] We have already noted that women are four times more likely than men to be physically injured by intimate partner violence. We are convinced that historical and present power disparities play a significant role in the fact that Native Americans have the highest physical and sexual abuse rates of any ethnic group in America, with more than four out of five Native men and women experiencing violence in their lifetime, and a third experiencing it within the previous year. And the 80 percent who do experience abuse in their lifetime are approximately two and a half times more likely to experience violence from a non-Native than a fellow Native (interracial versus intraracial perpetrators).[40]

The powerless are simply more vulnerable to abuse. The writer of Ecclesiastes put it this way: "Again I looked and saw all the oppression that was taking place under the sun: I saw the tears of the oppressed—and they have no comforter; *power was on the side of their oppressors*" (Ecclesiastes 4:1, emphasis added). Thankfully, our God-given power can just as surely be used to heal and to protect as to harm and destroy.

In the next few pages, we'll define five different kinds of abuse and explore how they pervert the image of God.[41]

Five Kinds of Abuse

Sexual abuse	A perversion of "one flesh"	Genesis 2:24
Physical abuse	A perversion of "let them rule"	Genesis 1:26
Neglect abuse	A perversion of "cultivate the ground"	Genesis 2:5
Spiritual abuse	A perversion of "image"	Genesis 1:26
Verbal/psychological abuse	A perversion of "be fruitful"	Genesis 1:28

39. Lisa Jones et al., "Prevalence and Risk of Violence against Children with Disabilities: A Systemic Review and Meta-Analysis of Observational Studies," *Lancet* 380, no. 9845 (2012): 899–907.

40. André Rosay, "Violence against American Indian and Alaska Native Women and Men," *NIJ Journal* 277 (2016): 1, 4, https://nij.ojp.gov/topics/articles/violence-against-american-indian-and-alaska-native-women-and-men.

41. While I'm focusing on five types of abuse, these are the major categories and by no means exhaust the spectrum of abuse. Paul Hegstrom, a man who physically abused his wife for years while serving as a Protestant pastor, charts sixteen different varieties of wife abuse, including stalking, economic abuse, intimidation, property violence, emotional abuse, and the use of children (*Angry Men and the Women Who Love Them* [Kansas City, MO: Beacon Hill, 1999], 30–42).

Sexual Abuse—A Perversion of "One Flesh"[42]

A woman once told us about a disturbing call she had received from a woman in her Sunday school class seeking advice on a moral dilemma. The woman and her husband frequently traveled with their three adolescent children. As do most families on a limited budget, they shared a hotel room when they traveled. Her dilemma? Her husband, an active member of a vibrant evangelical church known for solid Bible exposition, was pressuring her to have sex with him in the motel room with their three children in another bed a few feet away from theirs. He reasoned that the Bible nowhere prohibited this, thus she was obligated to comply with his demand. Apparently, this man did not realize (or care) that by deliberately exposing his children to his sex acts with his wife, he could be prosecuted by the state for child sexual abuse, and he could cause damage to his children. Sexual abuse is a broad category that encompasses a variety of behaviors (contact and noncontact) and victims (males and females, minors and adults).

Adult sexual abuse (often termed "sexual assault") is any nonconsensual sexual activity between adults. Several factors can make sexual activity nonconsensual: physical force, threat or coercion, or the inability of an individual to consent due to being unconscious or under the influence of mood-altering chemicals. Most sexual abuse survivors erroneously blame themselves for being assaulted, as do perpetrators and outsiders. Self-blame and other negative self-attributions are even more common when a victim's sexual abuse did not involve physical force. This dynamic helps explain research which shows that when a woman's first intercourse experience is coerced (or "persuaded"), she will have poorer physical and psychological health outcomes than if it had been "willing."[43]

Sexual abuse with a minor is the exploitation of a minor for the sexual gratification of another person through sexual contact or sexual interaction.[44] Abusive sexual contact can be described on a descending continuum

---

42. One of the best comprehensive treatments of sexual abuse by evangelicals is Andrew Schmutzer, ed., *The Long Journey Home: Understanding and Ministering to the Sexually Abused* (Eugene, OR: Wipf & Stock, 2011). One of the best practical healing resources for survivors by a leading evangelical sexual abuse expert is Diane Langberg, *On the Threshold of Hope: Opening the Door to Healing for Survivors of Sexual Abuse* (Wheaton, IL: Tyndale, 1999). One of the few books specifically for Christian men who are survivors of sexual abuse is Andrew Schmutzer, Daniel Gorski, and David Carlson, *Naming Our Abuse* (Grand Rapids: Kregel, 2016).

43. Simon McCarthy-Jones et al., "Associations between Forced and 'Persuaded' First Intercourse and Later Health Outcomes in Women," *Violence Against Women* 25, no. 5 (2019): 528–48. The most robust finding was that the physical and psychological well-being of "persuaded" women was poorer than that of the "willing" women (540).

44. Dan Allender's definition of sexual abuse is helpful: "Sexual abuse is any contact or interaction (visual, verbal, or psychological) between a child/adolescent and an adult when the child/adolescent

and includes intercourse, attempted intercourse, oral sex, genital contact, breast contact, intentional sexual touching of buttocks or thighs, simulated intercourse, touching of clothed breasts, and sexual kissing.[45] Abusive sexual interaction includes deliberate exposure of a minor to pornography or sexual activity and exhibitionism. This graphic description is necessary because many people mistakenly believe sexual abuse must involve sexual intercourse, or at least genital contact, with a minor. Furthermore, even when people accept that sexual abuse encompasses a broad range of behaviors, they often assume that only abuse involving intercourse creates severe damage. On the contrary, all sexual abuse is extremely damaging.

Diana Russell, one of America's foremost authorities on sexual abuse, found that in the cases of the "least severe" forms of sexual abuse (sexual kissing, sexual touching of buttocks or thighs, and the like), almost 20 percent of the abuse victims experienced extreme trauma, and in the next to least severe forms of sexual abuse (touching of clothed breasts and the like) 35 percent of victims experienced extreme trauma.[46] We have repeatedly witnessed the devastating effects of sexual abuse that did not involve sexual intercourse.

Sexual abuse is especially damaging because sex is the most powerful bonding activity in which we as creatures made in God's image can engage. God's intention is that in marriage a man shall leave his father and mother and cleave to his wife and become one flesh (Genesis 2:24). Loving marital sex can powerfully bond, but through abuse, it can just as powerfully wound.

We often hear faith leaders express agitated impatience with sexual abuse survivors who continue to struggle with the damaging effects of their abuse. They make remarks such as, "For crying out loud, that happened years ago." "Lots of girls get touched like that. Get over it!" "How long is she going to nurse this abuse?" These kinds of ignorant and destructive comments completely ignore the biblical data. In 1 Corinthians 6:15–18, drawing on the bonding imagery of Genesis 1 and 2, Paul declared that the sex act is unlike any other. When we sin sexually (or, by implication, are sinned against sexually), it forms a unique bonding, which creates damage that goes beyond anything else we can do with our body.[47] As Paul concluded

---

is being used for the sexual stimulation of the perpetrator or any other person" (*The Wounded Heart*, rev. ed. [Colorado Springs: NavPress, 1995], 48).

45. I'm utilizing Diana Russell's six categories of sexual abuse (*The Secret Trauma: Incest in the Lives of Girls and Women* [New York: Basic Books, 1986], 144).

46. Russell, *Secret Trauma*, 142–44. By way of contrast, 54 percent of severe sexual abuse resulted in extreme trauma.

47. For a technical exegesis that supports these conclusions, see Bruce Fisk, "*Porneuein* as Body Violation: The Unique Nature of Sexual Sin in 1 Corinthians 6:18," *New Testament Studies* 42, no. 4 (1996): 540–58.

in 1 Corinthians 6:18, "Flee from sexual immorality. All other sins a person commits are outside the body, but whoever sins sexually, sins against their own body."

Sexual relations are to be a beautiful divine gift that expresses unconditional love and should be a source of emotional and even physical life. Sexual abuse perverts the relational aspect of the image of God and his divine plan for sexuality. With sexual abuse, sex no longer gives life but destroys life. With sexual abuse, sex does not express selfless love but destructive selfishness. As a result, sexual abuse survivors struggle to accept their sexuality and their body, which makes it difficult to enjoy healthy, sanctified sex. Women who have been abused often can't admit to being enjoyed and desired by godly men. Sexual abuse is a sad perversion of the "one flesh" relationship.

Sexual abuse is addressed much more robustly in Scripture than most Christians realize.[48] The following are key biblical texts on sexual abuse:

- Genesis 19:4–5—attempted male rape by the inhabitants of Sodom
- Genesis 34—the rape of Dinah
- Deuteronomy 22:25–29—Mosaic legislation regarding rape
- 2 Samuel 11—the "power rape" of Bathsheba[49]
- 2 Samuel 13—the incestuous rape of Tamar
- Judges 19—the gang rape of the Levite's concubine

Physical Abuse—A Perversion of "Let Them Rule"

With respect to child abuse, physical abuse is legally defined as any non-accidental injury to a minor by an adult or caregiver. This could include blows, shakings, burnings, or other physical assaults that cause injury to the child. Physical abuse toward other adults is the use or threat of physical force against another person. The tendency of physical abusers also to verbally abuse, particularly to threaten, is well attested in Scripture.[50] When the other adult person is abused is an adult family member or intimate partner, this is

---

48. One of the best concise surveys of sexual abuse in the Old Testament is Richard M. Davidson, "Sexual Abuse in the Old Testament: An Overview of Laws, Narratives, and Oracles," in *The Long Journey Home*, Schmutzer, ed., 136–54. For a detailed nonevangelical treatment of sexual abuse in the Old Testament, see Susanne Scholz, *Sacred Witness: Rape in the Hebrew Bible* (Minneapolis: Fortress, 2010).

49. Richard Davidson makes an excellent case for this being an example of "power rape" by David, the sovereign Hebrew monarch. He gives eighteen different arguments to support this thesis (*Flame of Yahweh: Sexuality in the Old Testament* [Peabody, MA: Hendrickson, 2007], 523–32; cf. Larry W. Spielman, "David's Abuse of Power," *Word & World* 19, no. 3 [1999]: 251–59).

50. See, for instance, Psalm 73:6, 8: "Therefore pride is their necklace; they clothe themselves with violence . . . They scoff, and speak with malice; with arrogance they threaten oppression." See also 1 Kings 19:2–3; 22:27; 2 Kings 18:27–35; Jeremiah 26:8–9; Acts 4:21, 40; 9:1–2.

referred to as domestic violence (DV). Intimate partner violence (IPV) is virtually synonymous with DV except that it refers only to the abuse of intimate partners and not of other family members. IPV can be broadly described as the use or threat of force to control an adult family member, particularly a spouse or intimate partner.[51] This can include threats, shoving, slaps, hair pulling, punches, kicks, the injuring or killing of pets, destruction of personal possessions, assaults with inanimate objects, and assaults with lethal weapons. Abuse experts also include forced or coercive sexual activity in IPV.

It's important to recognize that the presence and damage of DV and IPV involve much more than physical attack or blatant threat, and thus its consequences cannot be measured merely by physical injury. Several years ago, a local church asked us to assist with a particularly difficult counseling situation they were facing. A young woman had come to the pastoral team asking for help, but her needs were far beyond their expertise. We agreed to meet with her and quickly realized her abuse history was one of the most extensive and abhorrent we had heard. She had suffered chronic abuse from childhood. Her mother, father, brother, and several others had repeatedly molested, beaten, and threatened her, and she had survived two murder attempts by her brother. As a result, she suffered extensive physical and psychological damage. Ironically, it became clear that out of all this abuse, the single most traumatic event was not the direct physical contact or verbal abuse she endured; it was the day her father came home in a rage, grabbed her pet dog, and shot him in the backyard. In this one act of noncontact DV, he had profoundly abused her. Similarly, when children are not physically assaulted or threatened but witness IPV between their parents, this is as traumatizing as direct contact abuse and leaves long-term physiological and psychological harm.[52] In some jurisdictions, committing adult-on-adult IPV in the presence of children is factored into sentencing guidelines, and in some states, it is considered in itself a form of child abuse.[53]

---

51. See Carol J. Adams, *Woman-Battering* (Minneapolis: Fortress, 1994), 12.

52. Bruce Perry has done groundbreaking work on the physiological impact on children's brains from witnessing DV (*Maltreated Children: Experience, Brain Development, and the Next Generation* [New York: Norton, 1996]). A recent survey of the destructive cognitive, emotional, and behavioral impact on children of witnessing IPV is Terra Pingley, "The Impact of Witnessing Domestic Violence on Children: A Systematic Review," *Master of Social Work Clinical Research Papers* (May 2017), http://sophia.stkate.edu/msw_papers/776. Excellent summaries of the impact of DV exposure on children can be found on the Child Welfare Information Gateway, www.childwelfare.gov/topics/systemwide/domviolence/assessment/child-exposure.

53. Child Welfare Information Gateway, "Child Witnesses to Domestic Violence" (Washington, DC: U.S. Department of Health and Human Services, Children's Bureau, 2016), www.childwelfare.gov/pubPDFs/witnessdv.pdf.

Physical abuse of children and spouses is a direct perversion of the functional aspect of the image of God. We are to care for creation as God's representatives by cultivating and exercising responsible dominion. Through physical abuse, we injure and demolish what we should nurture, sustain, and enhance. Instead of functioning as God's gracious representatives to care for creation, physical abuse distorts the image and character of God. Since God has put it in the human heart for children and spouses to crave love and affection from family members, physical abuse at the hands of parents and spouses—the very ones whose hands should caress us—is most destructive.

Mariam's story poignantly illustrates the perversion of IPV. Mariam Ibraheem was born in Sudan to a Christian mother and a Muslim father. Mariam's parents divorced when she was young, and she has had little contact with her father since then. Mariam professed Christ as a child, grew up as a Christian, married a Christian man when she was in her twenties, and soon became a mother determined to nurture her children to love Christ.

Based on these straightforward facts, the Western world was shocked to learn that in 2013, Mariam was arrested, convicted of apostasy and adultery, and given a capital sentence. Unless she denounced Christianity, she would be executed by hanging after being flogged with one hundred lashes. Her crimes were based on Sharia law, which declared her to be legally Muslim, and thus her profession of Christianity was considered apostasy. Additionally, her marriage to a Christian man was declared legally invalid, making her an adulterer. Mariam spent Christmas in a fetid prison cell, pregnant with her second child. She gave birth while in chains, causing her to fear serious harm to her child. During this time, the imam visited her regularly, admonishing her to renounce Christianity and thus reverse her death sentence. She refused and remained resolute in her faith, regardless of the cost.

Thankfully, after the relentless advocacy of foreign leaders, including US politicians, Mariam was eventually released from prison. She currently resides in the United States, where she cofounded a nonprofit that serves refugees who have escaped religious persecution.[54]

Recently, Mariam broke her silence about a different kind of suffering she had endured for years. Her husband had abused her (DV) throughout the duration of her marriage. She reported that the abuse escalated until she had to flee for her life. Mariam then said something truly staggering:

---

54. Mariam's story, as well as a link to a YouTube video in which Miriam shares her abuse story, can be found at www.tahriralnisa.org/about/mariam-ibraheem.

> The suffering I experienced in a Sudanese prison cell awaiting execu-
> tion was not nearly as traumatic as the trauma I have experienced from
> domestic violence by my husband. In prison I knew who my enemies
> were—unbelievers who wanted to kill me—enemies from outside. *But
> with domestic violence, the enemy destroying me was inside my own home.*
> This isn't supposed to be the place of destruction or the person who would
> attack and harm you.

Domestic violence perverts the heart of God's created design. This is what makes it so destructive.

Physical abuse is addressed in hundreds of Scripture passages. It appears immediately after sin enters the human race and spreads expeditiously. The first recorded post-Edenic sin is the fatal domestic violence Cain perpetrated against his brother Abel (Genesis 4:9). Later in that same chapter, we have the first example of spousal abuse, when Lamech threatens his two wives (4:23–24). Physical abuse rapidly became so rampant that in Genesis 6:13, God told Noah he would destroy the human race because "the earth is filled with violence." The threat or experience of physical abuse occasioned the writing of numerous psalms.[55] Physical violence and oppression is a domi-nant theme in most of the Major and Minor Prophets and precipitated the Babylonian captivity.[56] Paul gives physical abuse as evidence of universal human depravity in Romans 3:15 ("their feet are swift to shed blood"). Paul is so realistic about the potential for physical abuse in the church that he makes it a disqualifier for church eldership ("not violent," 1 Timothy 3:3). Scripture declares God's hatred of physical abuse and unrepentant abusers: "The bloodthirsty and deceitful you, LORD, detest (Psalm 5:6).[57]

Neglect Abuse—A Perversion of "Cultivate the Ground"[58]

Neglect abuse is essentially the opposite of physical abuse, but instead of destructive actions, it involves a destructive *lack of action*. Neglect is defined

---

55. For instance, Psalms 5; 10; 18; 22; 31; 35; 37; 40; 44; 52; 55; 59–60; 64; 70–74; 79; 83; 86; 94; 109; 137; 140; 142.

56. Isaiah 59:1–5; Jeremiah 7:6–11; Ezekiel 11:5–12; Hosea 4:1–2; Joel 3:19; Amos 2:6–7; 3:9; Obadiah 10; Jonah 3:8–9; Micah 3:10; 6:8; 7:2; Nahum 3:1–3; Habakkuk 1:2–3, 9; Zephaniah 3:1–4; Zechariah 7:9–10; Malachi 2:16. The Babylonian captivity was God's judgment for Israel's idolatry and for their abuse (Jeremiah 7:5–15; Ezekiel 22:27–31).

57. Similar statements of God's hatred of physical abuse and abusers are found in Psalms 7:11–16; 11:5; Proverbs 6:16–17.

58. A helpful overview of child neglect is Child Welfare Information Gateway, "Acts of Omission: An Overview of Child Neglect," Washington, DC: U.S. Department of Health and Human Services, Children's Bureau, 2018, www.childwelfare.gov/pubs/focus/acts.

as "parental failure to meet a child's basic needs."[59] These basic needs can be put into various categories and include adequate food and clothing, medical care, protection, supervision, and emotional support. Neglect is one of the least understood and researched forms of child maltreatment, in spite of the fact that more children die and are physically harmed by neglect than any other form of abuse. We do know that of all forms of child abuse, neglect is one of the most likely to be perpetrated by the child's biological parents, particularly their mother.

Many conditions or factors contribute to parental neglect, particularly the parents' own childhood maltreatment, as well as parental mental illness or drug addiction. We also know that poverty is tightly correlated with neglect, with poor children being seven times more likely than other children to suffer from it.[60] Emotional neglect is one of the most overlooked forms of child maltreatment largely because it is difficult to precisely define or identify. Other than the most extreme emotional neglect, which can result in an infant's failing to thrive and ultimately dying, emotional neglect leaves no physical wounds. Some have described emotional neglect as "a parent overlooking a child versus mistreating a child."[61] Emotional neglect involves a parent's being psychologically unavailable to the child, not responding to the child's direct and indirect calls for attention and emotional care. One of the most important things to understand about emotional neglect is that *it is every bit as harmful, and in some respects more harmful, than physical or sexual abuse.* For instance, one major longitudinal study (more than forty years) found that "73 percent of emotionally neglected children met criteria for two or more psychiatric disorders. Although the maltreatment experienced by emotionally neglected children was the most subtle of all forms, the consequences were very serious."[62]

Neglect, like physical abuse, is a perversion of the functional aspect of the image of God in which humans are to cultivate the ground (Genesis 2:5). We are to function as God's representatives by tenderly caring for his

59. Martha Farrell Erickson, Madelyn H. Labella, and Byron Egeland, "Child Neglect," in *The APSAC Handbook on Child Maltreatment*, 4th ed., J. Bart Klika and Jon R. Conte, eds. (Los Angeles: Sage, 2018), 128.

60. A. J. Sedlak et al., *Fourth National Incidence Study of Child Abuse and Neglect (NIS–4): Report to Congress Executive Summary* (Washington, DC: U.S. Department of Health and Human Services, Administration for Children and Families, 2010), 14.

61. Catherine Robertson Souter, "Psychologist Examines 'Childhood Emotional Neglect,'" *New England Psychologist*, March 1, 2015, www.nepsy.com/articles/leading-stories/psychologist-examines -childhood-emotional-neglect.

62. Erickson, Labella, and Egeland, "Child Neglect," 133. The study is the Minnesota Longitudinal Study of Risk and Adaptation.

creation. If we are called to responsibly care for the plants and animals God created, how much more should parents tenderly care for their own children, who are utterly dependent on them. Parental child neglect also distorts the character of God, our heavenly Father. God continually sees, listens to, and responds to his children.[63] He is so attentive that he knows everything about us, down to the number of hairs on our head (Matthew 10:30). He is continually thinking about his children (Psalms 40:5; 139:17). He sees our tears, always remembers them, and responds (Psalm 56:8–9). His attentiveness and care are so great that when we aren't taking our needs to him, the Holy Spirit and God's Son intercede to the Father on our behalf (Romans 8:26–27, 34). Neglectful parenting of any type egregiously distorts the character of God our heavenly Father. Thus, it is very harmful spiritually, relationally, and psychologically.[64]

The harm and perversion of parental neglect help us understand the exceedingly harsh indictment Paul gives to neglectful parents. He states that a Christian parent (in this case, a father) who is guilty of neglect by refusing "to provide for their relatives, and especially for their own household" has "denied the faith and is worse than an unbeliever" (1 Timothy 5:8). In other words, caring for your family is a fundamental responsibility that even unbelievers, who don't have the Scriptures or the power of the Holy Spirit, recognize and carry out. Thus, when a professing believer neglects their family, they are evidencing a moral condition worse than that of someone who rejects Christ.

Jasmin Lee Cori's poem titled "Mommy, Where Were You?" encapsulates well the experience and pain of childhood neglect. She ends her poem with these heartbreaking words: "Your warmth never reached my little girl's heart. Why did we miss each other, Mommy? Where were you? Was it because of me?"[65]

Spiritual Abuse—A Perversion of "Image"

Christy had grown up at First Presbyterian Church, where many of her relatives attended. When Christy was in junior high, Mark, her twenty-one-year-old youth pastor, formed a special relationship with her over an extended period of time. Mark took advantage of his spiritual authority

---

63. Numerous passages affirm this, including Exodus 6:5; 1 Kings 9:3; 2 Kings 20:5; Psalm 91:15; Isaiah 58:9; Jeremiah 33:3; Zechariah 10:6; 13:9.

64. Jasmin Lee Cori describes twenty-nine different relational and psychological effects of emotional neglect (*The Emotionally Absent Mother: A Guide to Self-Healing and Getting the Love You Missed*, 2nd ed. [New York: The Experiment, 2017], 111–25).

65. Cori, *Emotionally Absent Mother*, xi.

and her trust to develop a sexualized relationship with her. He told Christy that their relationship was pure and that it was ordained by God. He also threatened physical harm if she reported their relationship. Christy loved his attention but was in emotional turmoil over their "special" relationship. His caresses and sexual touch caused her shame, and in time she developed a severe eating disorder. She eventually gathered the courage to go to her senior pastor and disclose Mark's behavior. She documented her story and shared it with the pastor in his office. After reading her letter, he tore it up into tiny pieces and threw it in the trash can. He then informed her that the Bible tells us we must forgive others. He furthermore declared that she had a sinful heart in harboring anger toward Mark and that she needed to confess her sin of anger. The pastor prayed with Christy and cautioned her to never repeat the accusation.

Shortly after this, Christy's bulimia spun out of control. Sadly, Mark's abuse was enabled and continued for several more years. Eventually, through the help of a counselor, Christy gained the strength to oppose her church authorities and report Mark to the police. He was eventually convicted of felony sexual abuse for acts he perpetrated on other girls in the youth group. He was given a ten-year prison sentence. Initially after his conviction, Mark's church continued to run a weekly notice in the bulletin, publicizing the opportunity to donate toward Pastor Mark's legal defense fund. Thankfully, after a few years, a new leadership team arose and took thorough corrective action, owned and apologized for their failure to protect victims, and instituted extensive steps to educate the church on abuse and to prevent such harm from happening in the future. At the same time, tremendous long-term harm had been done to girls, their families, the entire congregation, and countless others who heard about this abuse. When spiritual authorities fail to protect the vulnerable in their care, it creates deep damage.

While Mark's sexual abuse of Christy was in the least severe category (it didn't involve sexual intercourse or fondling of the genitals or breasts), it was still extremely damaging, especially in combination with spiritual abuse.[66] When Christy began counseling in junior high, her Christian therapist asked her to draw a self-portrait—a helpful way for counselors to assess the impact of abuse on the child's sense of self. To the counselor's astonishment, Christy drew a picture of herself sitting in a chair with her back to the viewer

---

66. The combination of spiritual and sexual abuse is particularly harmful (see Danielle McGraw et al., "Consequences of Abuse by Religious Authorities: A Review," *Traumatology* 25, no. 4 [2019]: 242–55).

(see figure 2).[67] Her picture revealed overwhelming shame and powerlessness. The combination of sexual and spiritual abuse had a toxic synergistic effect.

Figure 2

Christy's experience illustrates the invisible damage of graphic sexual/spiritual abuse by two different pastors who should have been her protectors. Spiritual abuse is the *inappropriate* use of spiritual authority (the Bible, ecclesiastical tradition, or church authority) to force a person to do what the leader wants them to do.[68] Spiritual authority can be inappropriate in the way it is exercised—namely, through demeaning and domineering behavior—or in the demands being made—namely, ones that are not truly biblical. The former form of abuse is condemned in 1 Peter 5:3, where elders are admonished not to *lord it over* the church members God has entrusted to their care.[69] The Greek word used here means "to dominate" and is used in Matthew 20:25 of the Gentile rulers who used their power to dominate instead of humbly and sacrificially serving. Thus, one expert defines spiritual abuse as a "form of emotional and psychological abuse," which is "characterized by a systematic pattern of coercive and controlling

67. Art therapy pictures are included in several of the following chapters. The vast majority of these come from Celestia's counseling practice. They give the reader a graphic window into the world of abuse survivors and into the dynamics of abuse.

68. For more on spiritual abuse, see David Johnson and Jeff VanVonderen, *The Subtle Power of Spiritual Abuse* (Minneapolis: Bethany House, 1991), 20; Ken Blue, *Healing Spiritual Abuse: How to Break Free from Bad Church Experiences* (Downers Grove, IL: InterVarsity, 1992), 12. An excellent new resource focused on spiritual abuse perpetrated by narcissists is Chuck DeGroat, *When Narcissism Comes to Church: Healing Your Community from Emotional and Spiritual Abuse* (Downers Grove, IL: InverVarsity, 2020). The best treatment of spiritual power, healthy and destructive, is by Diane Langberg, one of the country's leading Christian abuse experts: *Redeeming Power: Understanding Authority and Power in the Church* (Grand Rapids: Brazos, 2020).

69. This is the Greek word *katakurieuo*, a compound word whose root means "to be Lord and Master of" (Walter Bauer et al., *A Greek-English Lexicon of the New Testament and Other Early Christian Literature*, 3d ed. [Chicago: University of Chicago Press, 2000], 519). This succinctly describes the goal of spiritual abusers.

behaviour in a religious context."[70] Often it involves a forceful or manipulative denial of the victim's feelings and convictions.

Ultimately, spiritual abuse is based on denial of one of the most precious pillar doctrines of Protestant Christianity—namely, the priesthood of all believers. This doctrine teaches that, while church leaders and spiritual teachers are necessary and helpful (Ephesians 4:11–12), every individual believer has the Holy Spirit and has direct access to God through Christ our great high priest (Hebrews 4:14–16). Thus, every believer has a right to discern the will of God for themselves through the Scriptures and the leading of the Spirit (Romans 14:4–5). It is in this context that John the apostle tells his readers, "The anointing you received from him remains in you, and you do not need anyone to teach you" (1 John 2:27).

The clearest biblical example of a spiritual abuser is seen in the Pharisees, who honed spiritual manipulation into an art form. They manifest both aspects of spiritual abuse—demeaning, dominating use of their authority and demands that were not harmonious with Scripture. They habitually twisted the Scriptures selfishly to manipulate others under the guise of spirituality (Matthew 15:1–9; 23:16–36; Mark 7:11–13). It's worth noting that the harshest words attributed to Jesus in all four Gospels are found in Matthew 23, and they are directed at the Pharisees for their spiritual abuse.[71] Jesus excoriated them for using Scripture and their own legalistic rules of spirituality to place unbearable, crushing spiritual demands on those under their authority, all for their own self-advancement and not the well-being of those under their spiritual care (Matthew 23:1–8). Jesus notes that if the Pharisees had used their spiritual authority properly, they would have de-emphasized their authority, rejected authoritative titles, and humbly served those under them (Matthew 23:8–12). Jesus places their sin of spiritual abuse in the same category as the most severe physical abuse, for he says these hypocritical Pharisees are "the descendants of those who murdered the prophets" (23:31).

David Johnson and Jeff VanVonderen give four characteristics of a spiritually abusive system:[72]

---

70. Lisa Oakley and Justin Humphreys, *Escaping the Maze of Spiritual Abuse: Creating Healthy Christian Cultures* (London: SPCK, 2019), 31.

71. Ken Blue organizes much of his book around Matthew 23 and the spiritual abuse of the Pharisees. He concludes by identifying seven symptoms of abusive religion seen in Matthew 23 (*Healing Spiritual Abuse*, 134–35).

72. See Johnson and VanVonderen, *Subtle Power of Spiritual Abuse*, 63–71. Sam Storms also gives an excellent, practical list of the characteristics of spiritually abusive pastors ("Pastoral Bullies," April 17, 2013), www.samstorms.org/enjoying-god-blog/post/pastoral-bullies.

- **Power posturing.** The leaders are preoccupied with their authority and continually remind people of it. This approach runs contrary to the Bible's teaching that church leaders are not to excessively leverage their authority but are to lead by example, not decree (Luke 22:25–26; 1 Peter 5:3).
- **Performance preoccupation.** Spirituality becomes a matter of external performance, not internal character (Matthew 15:1–12).
- **Unspoken rules.** Spiritually abusive churches have unspoken rules, such as, "Don't ever disagree with the pastor or you are disloyal and unspiritual"; these rules are not discussed openly but are enforced rigidly.
- **Lack of balance.** Spiritually abusive churches have little or no spiritual balance, and the leaders exhibit either extreme objectivity ("you must have graduate degrees to have any spiritual knowledge") or extreme subjectivity ("the Lord gave me this message, and you must accept it").

Pastoral Sexual Misconduct (PSM)[73]

Churches have historically labeled a pastor who has sexual relations with a parishioner as having had an "affair." But this misconstrues the power imbalance between pastors and parishioners and the gravity of PSM. (1) Pastors are entrusted with sacred authority from God (1 Timothy 5:17; Hebrews 13:17), an authority that parishioners do not possess. Making matters even worse, PSM often involves specific leveraging of "spiritual power resources" against the parishioner to manipulate—misusing Scripture, asserting one's potency as a spiritual leader to know what is right and best, and so forth. (2) Pastors are, by definition, shepherds. This means they are to serve, feed, and protect the flock (Acts 20:28–31; 1 Peter 5:2–3). Scripture pronounces severe judgment on "shepherds" who abuse those under their care.[74] Some of the harshest judgment is meted out to shepherds who, instead of feeding their sheep, feed *on* the sheep (Ezekiel 34:1–10; Zechariah 11:4–5; Jude 12). (3) Parishioners typically come to their pastor in moments of great need and are often emotionally vulnerable.[75] It is an outlandish abuse of power when

---

73. Portions of this section are taken from Steven Tracy and Andy Maurer, "#MeToo and Evangelicalism: Shattering Myths about Sexual Abuse and Power," *Cultural Encounters* 14, no. 2 (2019): 3–21. A concise overview of PSM is given by David Pooler and Amanda Frey, "Responding to Survivors of Clergy Sexual Abuse," in *Treating Trauma in Christian Counseling*, ed. Heather Davediuk Gingrich and Fred Gingrich (Downers Grove, IL: InterVarsity 2017), 188–207. Helpful case studies are found in Ruth Everhart, *The #MeToo Reckoning: Facing the Church's Complicity in Sexual Abuse and Misconduct* (Downers Grove, IL: InterVarsity 2020).

74. Jeremiah 12:10–13; 23:1–2; 25:34–38; Zechariah 10:3; see also Mathew 23:4, 13.

75. See Marie M. Fortune, *Is Nothing Sacred? The Story of a Pastor, the Women He Sexually Abused, and the Congregation He Nearly Destroyed* (Eugene, OR: Wipf & Stock, 1999), 18–42.

a pastor takes advantage of a parishioner's vulnerability to meet his own sexual and emotional needs.

Thus, in light of a pastor's greater power and the parishioner's frequent vulnerability, the parishioner's ability to fully consent to a sexual relationship is most often significantly compromised.[76] Thus, pastors who have sexual relations with those under their care are committing a grave form of spiritual abuse.

While spiritual abuse can be perpetrated by virtually anyone who claims spiritual authority, pastors, by virtue of their position and power, can wreak particularly broad swaths of destruction. While we would like to believe that spiritual abuse is rare among spiritual shepherds, evidence suggests otherwise. For instance, two researchers (both church leaders, one a pastor) conducted a survey of more than four hundred North American pastors. They found that 31 percent of the pastors surveyed met the full diagnostic criteria for narcissistic personality disorder.[77] This personality disorder particularly lends itself to spiritual abuse, for it is characterized by a sense of grandiosity and self-importance, the perception that one is "special," a deep lack of empathy, and arrogance. Thus, these researchers describe this group as "predatory pastors" who feed on their sheep. This is disturbingly similar to how the prophet Ezekiel described spiritually abusive shepherds in his day:

> Woe to you shepherds of Israel who only take care of yourselves! Should not shepherds take care of the flock? You eat the curds, clothe yourselves with the wool and slaughter the choice animals, but you do not take care of the flock. You have not strengthened the weak or healed the sick or bound up the injured. You have not brought back the strays or searched for the lost. You have ruled them harshly and brutally.
>
> Ezekiel 34:2–4

Spiritual abuse appears to be every bit as common today as it was in ancient Israel. This is strongly suggested or alleged in numerous recent scandals and subsequent removals or resignations of high-profile church leaders, including Mark Driscoll, founder of Mars Hill Church; James McDonald, founder of Harvest Bible Chapel; and Steve Timmis, CEO of

---

76. Fortune, *Is Nothing Sacred?*, 41; Diana Garland, "Clergy Sexual Misconduct: Don't Call It an Affair," *Journal of Family and Community Ministries* 26 (2013): 66–96.

77. R. Glenn Ball and Darrell Puls, *Let Us Prey: The Plague of Narcissist Pastors and What We Can Do about It* (Eugene, OR: Cascade, 2017), 114.

Acts 29, all reportedly due to their spiritual abuse manifested in chronic failure to accept accountability, bullying, misuse of church discipline, personal financial aggrandizement, and the like.[78]

The Bible is very clear that spiritual abuse by religious leaders is toxic. Religious leaders can, in the name of God and with the torch of Scripture, manipulate and destroy others for their own selfish purposes (Ezekiel 22:25–28; cf. Galatians 6:12–13). Spiritual abuse creates tremendous damage, for it generates extensive confusion and perverts the character of God, the people of God, and the Word of God. Often victims of spiritual abuse find church attendance, Bible teaching, and even the Scriptures themselves to be emotionally disturbing because these were the very things employed to manipulate and harm them. Spiritual abuse is also damaging because it grooms people to distrust their emotions and convictions and to give in to the demands of someone who claims to be more spiritual. Because spiritual abuse leaves no physical marks, it is often minimized by Christians.

Some of the most destructive spiritual abuse is that which is subtle; it does not involve physical or sexual abuse and has a veneer of biblical support. Several years ago, Celestia had a counseling session with a client we'll call Cathy, who demonstrated the destructive power of subtle spiritual abuse. Cathy, immaculately dressed, sat on the edge of the sofa. Her beautiful auburn hair and brown eyes were a stark contrast to her stiff demeanor. In her hour-long session, she never relaxed or leaned back on the sofa. From the outset she cried and kept apologizing for being sad.

Cathy had limited vocabulary for her sorrow. She had sought counseling because of debilitating anxiety that was making it difficult for her to leave her home. Cathy was married to a well-known elder in a large evangelical church and homeschooled their four children. She had

---

78. Some of the most extensive analysis and documentation of Mark Driscoll's alleged pattern of behavior is reported by blogger and psychology professor Warren Throckmorton, www.wthrock morton.com/category/mars-hill-church. See also Kate Shellnutt, "Former Mars Hill Elders: Mark Driscoll Is Still 'Unrepentant,' Unfit to Pastor," *Christianity Today*, July 26, 2021, www.christianity today.com/news/2021/july/mars-hill-elders-letter-mark-driscoll-pastor-resign-trinity.html. Some of the most extensive analysis and documentation of James McDonald's alleged pattern of abusive behavior is reported by blogger and journalist Julie Roys, https://julieroys.com/tag/james-macdonald. On Steve Timmis, see Kate Shellnutt, "Acts 29 CEO Removed Amid 'Accusations of Abusive Leadership,'" *Christianity Today*, February 7, 2020, www.christianitytoday.com/news/2020/february/acts-29-ceo -steve-timmis-removed-spiritual-abuse-tch.html. The article goes on to report, ironically, that in 2015 five staff members serving under Timmis documented in a nineteen-page letter to the Acts 29 board their concerns about his bullying, overcontrolling, and development of a culture of fear. Reportedly, all five were fired after the meeting and asked to sign nondisclosure agreements as a condition of their severance packages. Matt Chandler, who was the Acts 29 president at the time, contests this account.

few friends and had "no time" for personal friendships or for discretionary reading and activities. When Celestia asked her about this, she dispassionately explained that five years earlier, she had made a $50 purchase without her husband's permission. When he found out, he became enraged and in front of the children lectured her on how God, in his love, punished the children of Israel when they disobeyed. He declared that he was to "love" her in the same way. She was to be punished from that point on. He would no longer give her money for groceries or other household expenses. She would need to babysit to "earn" that money in her spare hours. That evening, he confiscated her checkbook and credit cards. In the days that followed, he continued to refer to "God's loving punishment" and threatened her with even greater consequences if she didn't exhibit total obedience.

As Celestia heard her story and began to describe the true nature of God's love reflected in the way Jesus respectfully and gently responded to Mary Magdalene and to other women, Cathy began to cry. Her heart resonated with this truth. She knew she was created for that kind of love. In fact, she was starving for it, having been manipulated and bullied by a self-righteous husband who twisted Scripture to humiliate her and make her feel inferior. Cathy left the session in tears, continuing to apologize for her well-earned sorrow. Sadly, she never came back. It's unlikely that anyone in Cathy's church would ever realize how profoundly and destructively her husband was spiritually abusing her. Spiritual abuse is a pernicious evil.

Verbal/Psychological Abuse—A Perversion of "Be Fruitful"

Verbal abuse is a form of emotional maltreatment in which words are systematically used to belittle, undermine, scapegoat, or maliciously manipulate another person. Psychological abuse is essentially the same as verbal abuse (the communication of demeaning, belittling, harmful messages), but the communication is achieved nonverbally. Thus, we call this form of abusive communication "psychological." Nonverbal communication includes body movement, facial expressions, tone of voice, and eye gaze, with the latter being one of the most powerful forms. Abuse survivors can be utterly frozen by the fixed stare of their abuser, a reality that malevolent abusers delight in.

Psychological abuse is well attested in Scripture. For instance, Jeremiah describes abusive enemies who "scoff and gnash their teeth" (Lamentations 2:16). Both of these are nonverbal forms of communication.

(The ESV translates the first verb "hiss," which highlights its nonverbal expression). Elsewhere Scripture describes abusers sneering and making sounds of disgust (Psalm 35:21), scornfully shaking their heads (Psalm 109:25), and menacingly staring and gloating (Psalm 22:17).

Verbal/psychological abuse is every bit as damaging as physical or sexual abuse and in some cases even more damaging. The somewhat subjective nature of verbal/psychological abuse can make it more insidious and difficult to confront (which also makes it more damaging). Verbal/psychological abuse perverts the beautiful truth of divine creation. Nine times in Genesis 1, Moses tells us, "And God said" (or "Then God said"), and six times he follows it up with, "And it was so." Thus, God's very words are efficacious; they have the power to create the universe and all life that exists in it.

Humans as "image of God" creatures are also called to create life ("be fruitful and multiply" [Genesis 1:28 ESV]). While humans obviously do this through sexual relations, we also metaphorically give life through our words. The Bible tells us that "the tongue has the power of life and death" (Proverbs 18:21). Pleasant words are "sweet to the soul and healing to the bones" (Proverbs 16:24). Kind words have the power to enliven and refresh a downcast heart (Proverbs 12:25). Given the power of words to encourage and to give life, Satan will surely prompt people to use their God-given verbal power not to bless but to curse, not to give life but to take life. The perversion of life-giving words helps explain why almost half of the seven sins identified as the ones God particularly hates are expressly verbal (a lying tongue; a false witness; one who stirs up conflict in the community [Proverbs 6:16–19]).

While the psychological community readily accepts the axiom that verbal abuse can cause tremendous long-term psychological damage, any Christian familiar with the Bible should easily agree with this premise as well. Rash words ravage the soul the way a sword ravages the body (Proverbs 12:18). A godly tongue gives life, but a perverse tongue crushes the spirit (Proverbs 15:4). The tongue's power for emotional and spiritual destruction is so great that James describes it as a fire that consumes life and is itself set on fire by hell (James 3:6).

Betty, an extremely pleasant woman with a soft Northern accent, has a gentle demeanor that belies her troubled spirit. In the course of discussing her difficult marriage and family life, Betty disclosed one of the most tragic stories of abuse we've ever heard. Betty's father was a musician who frequently moved his family from town to town as he sought work. Sadly, he was also an alcoholic who became abusive when he drank. Betty would lie awake at night listening to him curse and batter her mother. On several occasions, he would beat Betty and her brothers.

When Betty was six, her father came home drunk in the middle of the night. She awakened to his footsteps pounding up the stairs, but instead of hearing him stumble into his bedroom to curse at her mother, his shadow appeared in the doorway of her room. He moved to Betty's bed and raped her. From that point on, the rapes continued for ten years until she was sixteen. For the duration of her childhood, Betty went to bed every night hypervigilant and afraid. As Betty finished her story, what shocked us the most was the comparison she made of her mother's verbal abuse with the twenty years of physical abuse and ten years of rape at the hands of her father. Her mother's verbal abuse had damaged her more deeply.

One of her most vivid and life-imprinting incidents occurred, again, at the tender age of six. She was practicing her spelling words with her mother. When Betty misspelled the word *butter,* her mother scowled and with piercing eyes declared, "You are such a stupid little bastard." Now, almost fifty years later, Betty chokes back tears as she recounts her mother's venomous words. Though she had been a Christian for many years, Betty still struggled with the deep-seated conviction that she really is nothing more than a stupid little bastard. In fact, acting on this message had all but destroyed her marriage, as well as her relationship with her son, who at the time of our session had just been sentenced to life in prison.

Undoubtedly, what deleteriously reinforced her mother's toxic words was sexual abuse throughout her childhood. When Betty was twelve, she had finally gathered the courage to tell her mother that her father had been molesting her. When she did so, her mother flew into a rage and accused Betty of trying to destroy their family by slandering her father. Betty never brought up the topic again.[79] Unfortunately, the sexual abuse continued, and a broken, sexualized adolescent girl concluded that she could not trust her feelings and deserved to be abused.[80]

---

79. Caregivers' responses to children's abuse disclosures often have profound long-term effects. Inappropriate responses to an abuse disclosure (shaming, blaming, denial, passivity, and the like) can be just as damaging as the abuse itself. See Leonard T. Gries et al., "Positive Reaction to Disclosure and Recovery from Child Sexual Abuse," *Journal of Child Sexual Abuse* 9, no. 1 (2000): 29–51; Thomas A. Roesler, "Reactions to Disclosure of Childhood Sexual Abuse: The Effect on Adult Symptoms," *Journal of Nervous and Mental Disease* 182, no. 11 (1994): 618–24.

80. Tragically, parents often do not respond properly to disclosures of abuse. In a study of 755 adult women who had disclosed incest to a nonoffending parent in childhood (before age eighteen), 52 percent of the time the incest continued for more than one year after the disclosure. In a high

Born to Shimmer

All forms of abuse—sexual, physical, neglect, spiritual, and verbal—are highly damaging because of the manner in which they pervert the image of God in us. Apart from the redeeming grace of God, abuse leaves lifelong soul scars.

Shawn Mullins has captured the battle humans face in living out their divinely ordained destiny in a fallen world. He declares that we are born to shimmer, born to shine, born to radiate. This is God's beautiful plan, which abuse perverts.

Shimmer

Sharing with us what he knows
Shining eyes are big and blue
And all around him water flows
This world to him is new . . .
The essence of a child . . .
He's born to shimmer, he's born to shine
He's born to radiate
He's born to live, he's born to love
But we will teach him how to hate . . .
I heard a brilliant woman say
She said you know it's crazy
How I want to try to capture mine . . .
I think I love this woman's way she shimmers, the way she shines
The way she radiates
The way she lives, the way she loves
The way she never hates . . .
You know I drink a whole bottle of my pride
And I toast to change to keep these demons off my back . . .
'Cause I want to shimmer, I want to shine
I want to radiate
I want to live, I want to love . . .
We're born to shimmer, we're born to shine
We're born to radiate

percentage of instances, mothers disbelieved or blamed their daughters for the incest (see Thomas A. Roesler and Tiffany Weissmann Wind, "Telling the Secret: Adult Women Describe Their Disclosure of Incest," *Journal of Interpersonal Violence* 9 [1994]: 327–38).

We're born to live, we're born to love
We're born to never hate.[81]

Now that we understand the perversion of abuse through an "image of God" lens, we'll take a look at some general and specific characteristics of abusers in the next chapter.

---

81. "Shimmer," words and music by Shawn Mullins. Copyright © 1998 EMI BLACKWOOD MUSIC, INC., and ROADIEODIE MUSIC, Inc. All rights reserved. International rights secured. Used by permission.

CHAPTER 3

Profiles of Abusers

Murderers are not monsters, they're men. And
that's the most frightening thing about them.

Alice Sebold, *The Lovely Bones*

"Their mouths are full of cursing and bitterness."
"Their feet are swift to shed blood;
ruin and misery mark their ways."

Romans 3:14–16

John was well-known in his community. As a successful businessman, his baritone voice was widely recognized from his radio commercials. He was heavily involved in civic events and charitable organizations and had even dabbled in local politics. Thus, his arrest for the sexual exploitation of a minor made headlines in the midsize city where he lived. The community quickly polarized, with dozens of friends, neighbors, and employees coming to his defense.

After a lengthy trial, John was convicted of sex crimes against two adolescent girls. Reporters immediately sought interviews with John's friends and neighbors, most of whom declared that John was innocent and had been falsely accused by the district attorney. What we found most surprising was the logic used by his defenders. Several told reporters he couldn't possibly be guilty of sex crimes because he was such a nice guy who had helped many people in the community. One elderly neighbor recounted how he had shoveled her sidewalks one winter—something she was quite sure a child molester would never do. After prolonged questioning by a reporter regarding John's guilt or innocence, one exasperated defender declared, "Just look at this man. Look at his face. Anybody with half a brain can see he's not a child molester."

This instinctual response is one of the most common myths regarding abusers—namely, that *you'll know one when you see one*. It's most disturbing to discover that this comforting bromide has no factual basis. In 1960, the Israelis captured Nazi war criminal Adolf Eichmann and put him on trial in Jerusalem for war crimes and crimes against humanity because of his extensive role in orchestrating the murders of up to six million Jews in Nazi death camps. When Eichmann's trial began in 1961, *The New Yorker* magazine sent philosopher and writer Hannah Arendt to Jerusalem to cover the trial. Her reaction upon seeing Eichmann for the first time was one of shock, because as she looked into the face of this indescribably evil man, she did not recognize evil. She mused that his deeds were monstrous, but the doer appeared quite ordinary and commonplace. As she continued to reflect on Eichmann, she coined a phrase to describe him: "the banality of evil."[1] Hence, what is exceptional about abusers is their commonness.

Abusers come from all strata of society. For instance, several years ago the US Customs Office undertook a large child pornography sting operation. They arrested dozens of men and in the process documented approximately sixty different professions represented among the defendants. The list read like a vocational cross section of American society: attorney, actuary, butcher, college music teacher, janitor, owner of a funeral home, salesman, police officer, farmer, graphic artist, defense contractor, school bus driver, house painter, and structural engineer.[2]

Abusers cannot be predicted by race, occupation, demeanor, education, or facial features. Thus, one of the most chilling aspects of physical and sexual abusers is their invisibility, which leads to a disturbing situation for those who want to protect the vulnerable from abuse. If the family dentist, our child's Sunday school teacher, the retired engineer next door, or our auto mechanic could be a malignant perpetrator, then what do we look for? If abusers cannot be visually identified, then what common characteristics do they possess? In the next section, we'll identify four general characteristics of abusers.

---

1. Hannah Arendt, *Eichmann in Jerusalem: A Report on the Banality of Evil*, rev. ed. (New York: Penguin, 1965).
2. Anna C. Salter, *Transforming Trauma: A Guide to Understanding and Treating Adult Survivors of Child Sexual Abuse* (Thousand Oaks, CA: Sage, 1995), 27–28.

General Characteristics of Abusers

Pervasive Denial of Responsibility

We've worked with abusers and their victims for more than twenty-five years, and the single most consistent characteristic we've observed in abusers is their utter unwillingness to accept full responsibility for their behavior. They typically do not confess to abuse unless there is crystal-clear, overwhelming evidence of their misbehavior—and even when there is this evidence, they'll minimize what they've done and shift the blame. Adolf Eichmann repeatedly declared his innocence by insisting that his only crime was being virtuous, that is, that he was an obedient, law-abiding German citizen, and thus, his obedient nature had been exploited by the Nazi leaders since all he did was "follow orders."[3]

Rapists are another example, as they typically blame victims for dressing seductively and the like and relabel the rape as consensual sex. Physical abusers blame family members for making them mad, so what else could they do but lash out? We've listened to child molesters explain how a child seduced them into having sex.[4] We've witnessed a molester in court, who was later convicted for raping two children, tell the jury that the children held him down and forced him to have sex with them. What made this denial even more outrageous was the fact that the children he molested were five and seven years old, and he, the perpetrator was a three-hundred-pound man. Needless to say, the jury dismissed his repulsive attempt to shift blame onto his innocent victims. Similarly, spiritual abusers ironically use Scripture to justify their misuse of Scripture and their authority, all to harm instead of help.

In summary, abusers, when caught, will (if pressed to the wall) admit to *some* inappropriate behavior but will fixate on the sins (real or imagined) of their victims. Unrepentant abusers demonstrate a predictable inability to fully own their sin.

Two studies illustrate how consistently abusers deny their responsibility for harming others. The first involved two researchers who interviewed eighty-six convicted child molesters about their sexual offenses against children. This group of offenders gave 250 different reasons for their acts

---

3. See Arendt, *Eichmann in Jerusalem*, 21–25. The extreme extent to which Eichmann denied responsibility is seen in his last statement to the court (247).

4. Eric Leberg gives helpful insights into the various ways child molesters maintain secrecy and deny responsibility (*Understanding Child Molesters: Taking Charge* [Thousand Oaks, CA: Sage, 1997], 57–80).

of abuse. The most frequent justification was that the child consented to having sex (29 percent); 24 percent said they did it because they had been denied conventional sex by their partners; 23 percent blamed it on being intoxicated; 22 percent blamed the child because they had initiated sex.[5]

The second study highlights patterns of denial and blame shifting in men convicted of IPV. James Ptacek conducted interviews with men who had been in a Boston-area counseling service for physically abusive men and discovered shocking patterns of denial of responsibility. Most frequently they reported beating their wives because they had lost control due to alcohol or built-up frustration. They made such statements as these:

> I think I reach a point where I can't tolerate anything anymore, and it's at that time whatever it is that shouldn't be tolerated in the first place now is a major issue in my life. . . . I couldn't hold it back anymore.

> It was all the booze. I didn't think. . . . It was temporary insanity. I really, all's I really wanted to do was crush her.[6]

The second primary way these men victimized themselves by denying responsibility was to blame their wives for their beating.[7] Here are some examples:

> Women can verbally abuse you. They can rip your clothes off, without even touching you, the way women know how to talk, converse. But men don't . . . so it was a resort to violence if I couldn't get through to her by words.

> On some occasions she was the provoker . . . You know, you're married for that long, if somebody gets antagonistic, you want to defend yourself.

---

5. Nathan L. Pollock and Judith M. Hashmall, "The Excuses of Child Molesters," *Behavioral Sciences & the Law* 9, no. 1 (1991): 53–59. Howard E. Barbaree and William L. Marshall argue regarding child molesters that "denial of the offense and minimization of the offender's responsibility and the harm he has done is so common . . . as to be regarded as a defining characteristic of this population" ("Treatment of the Sexual Offender," in *Treatment of Offenders with Mental Disorders*, ed. Robert M. Wettstein [New York: Guilford, 1998], 294).

6. Cited in James Ptacek, "How Men Who Batter Rationalize Their Behavior," in *Abuse and Religion: When Praying Isn't Enough*, ed. Anne L. Horton and Judith A. Williamson (Lexington, MA: Lexington, 1988), 249–50.

7. For an excellent discussion of the way child molesters blame victims and victims' mothers, see Leberg, *Understanding Child Molesters*, 81–87.

It [the beating] was over sex, and it happened I guess because I was
trying to motivate her [to want sex more often] and she didn't seem too
motivated.[8]

The third strategy these men employed was rationalization. They reasoned that beating their wives is not abusive or injurious. Here are some
examples:

I never beat my wife. I responded physically to her.

[Did you injure your wife?] Not really. Pinching does leave bruises and I
guess, slapping. I guess women bruise easily, too. They bump into a door
and they bruise.

These people told her that she had to get all of these orders of protection
and stuff like that because I was going to kill her. . . . I mean, I'd yell at her
and scream, and stuff like that, and maybe I'd whack her once or twice,
you know, but I wasn't going to kill her. That's for sure.[9]

These quotes demonstrate the acute break with reality that abusers
reach in their pervasive attempt to deny any responsibility. Christian leaders
must recognize this dynamic, lest they become seduced by the abusers' lies
and enable victim blaming. Abusers must be held to the highest levels of
accountability. Nothing short of complete ownership of their abusive behavior should be accepted by their family or churches; anything less contributes
to their abuse and justifies their sin.

Justifying the wicked is considered an abomination to God (Proverbs
17:15 ESV). When Nathan the prophet confronted King David for his evil
abuse, he held him fully accountable for his actions. He did not entertain
a discussion of how Bathsheba was partially responsible for bathing on the
roof or how the servants were somewhat to blame for bringing Bathsheba
to David when they knew he was having a midlife crisis. Nathan boldly
declared, "You are the man!" David responded without qualification: "I have
sinned against the LORD" (2 Samuel 12:7, 13).

Conversely, David's predecessor, King Saul, gives one of the clearest
examples in all of Scripture of the extremes to which abusers will go to

---

8. Ptacek, "How Men Who Batter," 251, 254.
9. Ptacek, "How Men Who Batter," 252–53.

avoid taking responsibility for their sins. Saul attempted to kill his own son Jonathan to cover up his own foolishness, but the people prevented Saul from doing so (1 Samuel 14:44–45). Saul later assaulted David with a deadly weapon and repeatedly attempted to kill him (18:11). The turning point in Saul's life occurred when God commanded him to destroy the evil Amalekites and to save nothing, not even livestock (15:3). Saul partially obeyed by attacking and defeating the Amalekites, but he kept the choicest spoil and did not kill their king as he was commanded. The amazing part of the story is that when Samuel came to Saul after the battle, Saul greeted him by declaring that he had carried out the Lord's command—a bold distortion he actually seemed to believe. Abusers can get so caught up in their deception that they lose touch with reality.

When Samuel confronted Saul with the facts, he cleverly explained that they had destroyed everything as God commanded, except for the best livestock, which they planned to offer to the Lord as a sacrifice (1 Samuel 15:15). Notice the way abusers use religion to justify their sins. Samuel confronted Saul with his disobedience, telling him he had done an evil thing. Samuel asked, "Why did you not obey the LORD? Why did you pounce on the plunder and do evil in the eyes of the LORD?" (15:19). Saul insisted that *he* had obeyed, but that the people had disobeyed: "But I did obey the LORD," but "The soldiers took sheep and cattle from the plunder" (15:20–21). At this point, Saul resorted to blame shifting, one of the favorite tactics of abusers.

Only after being persistently confronted with the facts of his disobedience did Saul acknowledge his sin. Even then, he was more concerned about saving his reputation than about the way he had sullied God's honor and reputation. Saul pleaded, "I have sinned. But please honor me before the elders of my people and before Israel" (1 Samuel 15:30). After this incident, Samuel refused to see Saul again. However, he did grieve Saul's tragic moral decline (15:35). Saul's pervasive denial of responsibility is characteristic of most abusers. Those responsible for protecting minors and other vulnerable people must recognize the insidious nature of denial and courageously expose it.

Bold Deceitfulness

Closely connected with the abuser's unwillingness to own their destructive behavior is bold deceitfulness—a "skill" abusers need in order to maintain their innocence, avoid the discomfort of changing long-established patterns of behavior, escape the painful consequences of their actions, and assuage their own nagging consciences. Families, congregations, and secular leaders often find the audacity and persuasiveness of abusers' deceitfulness to be overwhelming. Abusers are masterful at manipulating words and actions to confuse, confound, and put others on the defensive.[10]

There are biblical examples of such bold deceit, particularly in 2 Samuel 11. After David took sexual advantage of Bathsheba, the unmistakable physical evidence (her pregnancy) signaled his sinful behavior. Instead of repenting of his sin and taking the appropriate steps of correction and restitution, David sought to cover his tracks by bringing Bathsheba's husband home from battle to have sexual relations with his wife (11:5–6). David deceitfully pretended to have called Uriah home so David could get news of the battle and honor Uriah. We read, "David asked him how Joab was, how the soldiers were and how the war was going" (11:7). This was a sham, of course. David was fixated on his own welfare, not the people's. When David sent Uriah home and encouraged him to have sexual relations with his wife, he sent him a gift (11:8).[11] The irony is that David had already stolen a most precious gift from Uriah. What astonishingly bold deception—showering gifts and kindness on the very man whose wife you have impregnated!

When Uriah's loyalty to his soldiers prevented him from sleeping with his wife, David plied him with wine to get him drunk, thinking it would serve as the necessary disinhibiting aphrodisiac. When that failed, David took advantage of Uriah's godly character. Knowing full well that Uriah was fiercely loyal to God and to the king, David had Uriah carry the very sealed message containing instructions for his own murder.[12] The message read, "Put Uriah out in front where the fighting is fiercest. Then withdraw from him so he will be struck down and die" (2 Samuel 11:15). Abusers are cunning, and they deceitfully prey on the very virtues of those they abuse,

---

10. See Dan Allender and Tremper Longman, *Bold Love* (Colorado Springs: NavPress, 1992), 236. Hannah Arendt describes the incredible way Nazis used "language rules" both to camouflage their brutal actions and to program their own executioners. For instance, the word for "murder" was replaced by "to grant a mercy death." The code words for "execution" were "final solution," "evacuation," and "special treatment." The soldiers were programmed for their task by being told, "We realize that what we are expecting of you is superhuman," when in reality their orders were "superhumanly inhuman" (Arendt, *Eichmann in Jerusalem*, 85–86, 105–8).

11. David enjoined Uriah to go home and "wash his feet." On this phrase being a euphemism for sexual relations, see Gale A. Yee, "Fraught with Background: Literary Ambiguity in II Samuel 11," *Interpretation* 42, no. 3 (1988): 245.

12. Ronald Youngblood notes the similarity of David's three-phase, increasingly ruthless plan to deal with his "problem" to the abusive plan used earlier by an Egyptian pharaoh, who first oppressed the Israelites with forced labor. When that didn't work, the pharaoh commanded the Hebrew midwives to kill newborn Hebrew males. When that didn't work, he ordered all Egyptians to drown newborn Hebrew male children (Frank E. Gaebelein, ed., *The Expositor's Bible Commentary*, vol. 3 [Grand Rapids: Zondervan, 1993], 932–33). As abusers become more desperate, they often become more ruthless and deceptive.

counting on the fact that their victims will not act treacherously, even as they are. The message David sent to his general, Joab, was equally deceitful, orchestrating Uriah's death in battle in such a way that it would appear to be an accident.

Finally, David's feigned response to the news of Uriah's death reflects hardened, calculated deceit, as David said, "Don't let this upset you. [Literally, 'Do not let it be evil in your sight']; the sword devours one as well as another. Press the attack against the city and destroy it" (2 Samuel 11:25). The wickedness of this response is as obvious as it is deceptive. People on both sides *do* get killed in battle, but solders are killed by the enemy, not by their own king. Joab did need to resign himself to the vagaries of war—but not to the venalities of his king. Redoubling their efforts was irrelevant. Defeat in the previous battle was not the result of military failure by the general but moral failure by the monarch. All reality had been veiled by David's fog of deception, but the fog lifted in the very last statement of chapter 11 of 2 Samuel: "But the thing David had done displeased the LORD." Those who deal with abusers must have the courage and wisdom to see through the smoke and speak truth.

One of Celestia's earliest clients was a three-year-old who had been referred by a local pastor. This girl came home from Sunday school one day and told her parents about a man at church who had touched her private parts. It turned out that a longtime elderly member of the church, a grandfather figure to most of the children, had fondled her in the church office while others were coming in and out of the office. He was so deceitfully clever that he was able to abuse this girl while appearing to be reading to her as she sat on his lap. The boldness of this abuser's deceit was seen in the fact that one week after the church confronted him, contacted the police, and forbade this man from having any contact with the church's children, he visited another church less than a five-minute drive from this one and offered to serve in their children's ministry. Celestia and the church leaders were stunned by his bold deceit!

Finally, we should note that often an abuser's deception extends far beyond their victims. Some of the most dangerous abusers are able to lead a double life year after year, gaining great admiration in their community and churches, even from their professional colleagues, all the while committing remarkably wicked acts that no one but their victims would believe they were capable of. Perhaps the clearest example of the extent to which abusers can deceive is Dr. Larry Nassar. In 2017, Nassar pled guilty to numerous sexual abuse and child pornography charges and was sentenced to 175 years in state prison and sixty years in federal prison. More than 350 women and one man have accused Nassar of abusing them over a period of twenty-four years (most of the victims' abuse couldn't be prosecuted due to statute of limitations restrictions).

Nassar was an icon in the sports medicine world. He treated most of the US female Olympic gymnasts, taught in the College of Medicine at Michigan State University, authored six research papers on the treatment of gymnastics injuries, and was considered one of the country's leading sports physicians. His deception was so convincing that numerous abuse allegations over many years were discounted by university, law enforcement, and sports authorities. Most of his victims were abused during "medical treatments," often while the girls' mothers were in the room. Nassar actually deceived the medical community into believing that his abuse, which involved inserting his fingers into the girls' vaginas, was a legitimate medical procedure. A chilling case study in deception is found in a 2014 interview conducted with Nassar by MSU detective Valerie Obrien and in a subsequent 2016 interview where Nassar used a stunning variety of tactics to (unsuccessfully) deceive the detective, including:[13]

- Feigning compassion by crying.
- Misleading by emphatically affirming the importance of integrity:
    "Trust is sacred."
- Attempting to garner credibility by repeatedly asserting that the girls' "misunderstanding" regarding his medical treatments "hurt me."
- Offering a rational explanation and false ownership for what happened:
    "The girls misunderstood the exam because I must not have explained it well enough ahead of time," and "maybe I was distracted and didn't explain it right."
- Shifting responsibility onto the victims:
    "Why didn't they complain or say they were uncomfortable at the time? I'm trusting them to tell me if I'm hurting them,; that is the only way I can know."

Tragically, a quarter-century of deception created monstrous harm to hundreds of young women and their families, damaged the entire gymnastics

---

13. The 2014 interview can be found on the internet at www.youtube.com/watch?v=mgLdFqea1io. The 2016 interview can be found at www.youtube.com/watch?v=GAW4IsWUxGY.

community, led to the resignations of the entire eighteen-member board of USA Gymnastics, as well as those of the MSU president and director of athletics, and led to the largest settlement by a university for a sexual abuse case ($500 million to 332 alleged victims). The stakes are very high when abusers can successfully deceive.

Harsh Judgmentalism

In spite of—and because of—their own destructive behavior, unrepentant abusers are judgmental and harsh toward others. This pompous religious platform allows them to maintain the "high moral ground" and deflect attention from themselves. This strategy creates a moral facade that perpetuates their denial of responsibility. This harsh judgmentalism is a godless method for deflecting their own shame. Instead of facing the shame of their immoral behavior, which is a gracious, God-given emotion to call us to repentance, they displace their healthy shame and show contempt for the innocent. Abusers become quite sophisticated at this technique, for it is generally developed over long periods of time. Eric Leberg notes this tendency in child molesters:

> Because the offender is still minimizing his guilt, he will desperately try to maintain secrecy through verbal taunts and accusations that sidetrack all meaningful discussion . . . Thus, he will remember the number of times that the wife refused his demands for sex, the times she got intoxicated, or the times she didn't clean the house to his satisfaction or forgot his birthday wishes or left her dirty socks on the floor. He'll remember the times the children fought, disturbed his sleep, came home late, did poorly in school, wasted their allowance, spilled milk during dinner . . . To each of these events he will attach some value judgment that, although it may be absurd, again deflects the discussion away from his sexual abuse of his child or children.[14]

The tendency of abusers to harshly judge others is well attested in Scripture. King David was sleeping with the very woman he stole from his most faithful servant, whose loyalty he rewarded by murdering him. When cleverly confronted with his sin, David expressed great outrage that a rich man would steal a lamb from his poor neighbor, not recognizing his own sinful act in the prophet's story. In fact, David's moral outrage was

---

14. Leberg, *Understanding Child Molesters*, 65–66.

so great that he said the rich man deserved to die (2 Samuel 12:5), even though stealing was never deemed a capital offense in the Torah. Rather, the Torah prescribed restitution for theft, not death (Exodus 22:12).[15] On the other hand, murder, rape, and adultery with a married woman were all capital offenses.[16] Thus, David's response to the rich man who stole a sheep evidences an ironically harsh judgment from one who had committed and continued to cover up not one but multiple capital offenses.

The intensity with which abusers maintain their hypocritical judgmentalism is often ferocious. The more counselors and family members try to confront an abuser's sin, the more aggressive they become in identifying and scrutinizing the sins, mistakes, and weaknesses of others.

Shaun grew up in an affluent, religious home in the Deep South. As an adolescent, he took advantage of his prestige and wealth, developing a callous disregard for women once he obtained what he wanted from them. In college he started going to church again, as it afforded him ample opportunity to meet attractive and often naive young women. Shaun began to date a shy student named Beth, who had little social experience. He pressured Beth into having sex early in their relationship. Once this happened, his disrespect for her became palpable, and he began to ridicule her for not being able to meet his needs. He demanded that she clean his house and do his laundry. He constantly joked about the anatomies of other women and accused Beth of sinful jealousy when she asked him to stop. She felt trapped and guilty about their sexual relationship and, against her better judgment, told nobody about her struggles, eventually agreeing to marry him.

Once they were married, Shaun's abusive behavior intensified. He repeatedly threatened Beth physically and put his fist through a wall in an effort to intimidate her. His escalating use of pornography and his repeated online affairs caused him to make twisted, abusive sexual demands of Beth. He raged at her for not being a godly wife and for not responding to his leadership by meeting his sexual needs. Shaun's verbal, physical, and spiritual abuse intensified.

Eventually, after their third child was born, Beth decided she could no longer endure her abusive marriage. With the help of a Christian

---

15. Restitution for the stealing of sheep was expressly said to be fourfold (Exodus 22:1), as it was for stealing other goods and for extortion (Leviticus 6:1–5; Luke 19:8; cf. 2 Samuel 12:6).

16. Murder was a capital offense (Genesis 9:6; Numbers 35:33), and David was ultimately responsible, not just for Uriah's murder, but for the murder of other unnamed soldiers with him (2 Samuel 11:24). He was also guilty of adultery with (or rape of) a married woman, both of which were capital offenses (Deuteronomy 22:22, 25).

psychologist and a godly neighbor who was a retired medical missionary, Beth began to gain the strength to set appropriate boundaries around her husband's destructive behavior. She separated from Shaun and insisted he get counseling. Shaun wrote the following letter to Beth after she, her pastor, and the psychologist insisted Shaun not contact her directly:

> I believe the reason you are so angry and bitter toward me is not because I was such a horrible person but because you got into a relationship you didn't want to be in in the first place. You felt pressured to get married, and you got married. This isn't my fault . . .
>
> If you actually loved me, a lot of the bitterness and resentment you have inside you would not be there. Love covers a multitude of sins. Beth, you did some pretty horrible things to me as well. Please don't forget that you called me every name in the book. You swore at me. You've hit me dozens of times. You've withheld sex from me. You refused to get close to me, and you leave every time life gets tough . . . I have done nothing a little forgiveness won't take care of . . . You refuse to help me overcome my sin. That is why I have fallen.

Clearly, Shaun placed the blame for his marital abuse squarely on Beth's shoulders—she was to blame for their problems, including his sexual sin; she was to blame for being bitter. In fact, his letter ends with a demand that she become more Christlike. Shaun offers a chilling example of the harsh judgment that abusers often exhibit.

Abusers' judgmentalism greatly compounds the damaging effects of abuse. Abuse creates toxic shame that makes victims feel they are worthless, defective, and responsible for the abuse. In some cases, even the anticipation of abuse can launch this self-blame. For instance, in 1 Kings 18:9, godly Obadiah thought he was about to be murdered by King Ahab, so he asked Elijah what sin he had committed such that he was about to be abused. In reality, God had spoken through the prophet Elijah to declare he would send a severe drought on the land as judgment for Ahab's wickedness in leading the people into idolatry (16:29–17:1). After several years of severe drought, when Ahab saw Elijah, the first words out of his mouth were, "Is this you, you troubler of Israel?" (18:17). In fact, Ahab's harshness had no basis in reality. Ahab himself was the troubler of Israel. In this case, Elijah was mature enough not to accept Ahab's judgmental blame. Most abuse victims are not as spiritually mature as this seasoned prophet, and their abusers' judgmentalism compounds their soul damage.

Calculated Intimidation

Because abusers' lives are built around twisting reality, avoiding consequences, and engaging in behavior that brings temporary relief to their inner
torment, they typically cannot face the reality of their destructive actions.
Abusers are desperate to keep their victims from revealing the truth. Thus,
they strategize to intimidate their victims into silence and submission, which
allows them to continue to abuse with impunity. This also creates further
damage to the victims, for it adds to their emotional trauma and intensifies
feelings of powerlessness and vulnerability.

Biblical Examples of Intimidation

The Bible contains several examples that illustrate the various kinds of
intimidation used by abusers. The most extreme is the direct promise of
severe bodily harm, as seen in wicked Queen Jezebel's threat to have Elijah
killed within twenty-four hours after he carried out divine judgment on the
priests of Baal (1 Kings 19:1–2). Sadistic sex offenders are known to tell their
victims ahead of time what horrible things they plan to do to them, as this
type of intimidation brings them perverse pleasure.[17]

Sometimes opaque threats are just as traumatizing as direct threats
because they create a general sense of dread. This is what King Ahab did
with the prophet Micaiah when he put him in prison after the prophet gave
a prophecy Ahab didn't want to hear. Before he left for battle, Ahab told
Micaiah and the prison guards that Micaiah was only to be given a sparse
diet of bread and water "until I return" (1 Kings 22:27), implying that a much
worse fate would befall the prophet when the king came back victorious
from battle.

One of the most common types of intimidation used by abusers is
the verbal threat of harm unless they are given what they want. The field
commander, leader of an Assyrian army infamous for its sadistic cruelty,
threatened extreme harm to the Judeans unless they gave in to him (2 Kings
18:27–35). This was no idle threat, for the Assyrians were well-known for
extreme cruelty to their enemies. Archaeologists have discovered various
ancient texts in which the Assyrians, with great braggadocio, recount the
utter destruction of cities they conquered. They graphically recorded how,

---

17. See Salter, *Transforming Trauma*, 104–16. Unlike other kinds of abusers, sadistic offenders
do not deny the victims' pain and suffering; rather, they feed off of it. It's one of the primary reasons
they intimidate—it creates even greater emotional pain and degradation for the victims.

after defeating enemy armies, they would pile up the severed heads of enemy soldiers, slaughter the defeated citizens, torture the defeated royal family, flay political leaders, and place conquered women in the royal harem.[18] Thus, the commander's threats must have been exceptionally intimidating.

The Diabolical Creativity of Intimidation

The creativity of abusers to intimidate is quite diabolical, for it is often based on a serious calculation of the victim's weaknesses, points of vulnerability, and greatest fears. We've often heard sexual abuse victims say they passively endured their fathers' abuse as long as they did because the fathers threatened to molest the younger siblings if they resisted. One sixteen-year-old serial physical and sexual abuser of adolescents told his young victims he would come back and kill their family members if they told anyone what he had done to them. Furthermore, he told these naive young children that he could see and hear through walls, so he would always know if they told anyone. Sadly, they believed him.

Several years ago in Arizona, a Christian school principal was convicted of child abuse for forcing a fifteen-year-old girl who was considering enrolling at the school to completely disrobe, bend over, and receive swats on her buttocks. At first, she refused to comply, but he threatened to give her twelve swats unless she immediately stripped. He said he wanted her to understand corporal punishment *before* she attended the school. The girl's mother, who witnessed the incident, told police she was too frightened to stop the headmaster. In fact, the mother was so intimidated that in the middle of this incident she told her daughter to "just do whatever he tells you to do, so we can get this over with." The principal was given a one-year prison sentence for abusing this teenage girl and another young boy. In the process of prosecution, it was discovered that this man had been kicked out of another school district in another state for what appeared to be physically abusive behavior. Shortly after the principal was released from prison, he moved to Europe, where he quickly opened another private religious school. No doubt he continued to intimidate parents and children, just as he had done for many years. Parents and others who care for minors must be just as strategic and determined to protect children as abusers are to intimidate them.

---

18. For a general discussion of Assyrian cruelty to those they defeated, see Georges Contenau, *Everyday Life in Babylon and Assyria* (New York: Norton, 1966), 141–57.

Types of Abusers

In addition to these general characteristics, it's helpful to note specific characteristics of several types of abusers. Entire books are written on single types or even subtypes of abusers, so the best we can do here is to give a brief overview of both sexual molesters of minors and physical abusers (of adults and children).

General Adult Child Molesters

We'll begin with some statistics from the *Fourth National Incidence Study of Child Abuse and Neglect:*[19]

- Thirty-seven percent of sexually abused children were abused by a biological parent, and another 23 percent were abused by a stepparent.[20]
- Eighty-seven percent of sexually abused children were abused by a male.[21]
- The vast majority of child sexual abuse victims are molested by someone they know (90 percent).

Child molesters come from all walks of life and are difficult to identify, even for professionals. The influences that lead a person to sexually violate a child or adolescent are complex and not entirely understood.[22] For example, a common misconception is that the majority of child molesters were sexually abused as children. Some research indicates that 20 to 35 percent of child molesters were themselves sexually abused as children or adolescents.[23]

---

19. Andrea J. Sedlak et al., *Fourth National Incidence Study of Child Abuse and Neglect (NIS–4): Report to Congress* (Washington, DC: U. S. Department of Health and Human Services, Administration for Children and Families, 2010), https://cap.law.harvard.edu/wp-content/uploads/2015/07/sedlaknis.pdf.

20. Michael Gordon and Susan Creighton found that stepfathers were disproportionately represented among paternal abusers ("Natal and Non-Natal Fathers as Sexual Abusers in the United Kingdom: A Comparative Analysis," *Journal of Marriage and Family* 50, no. 1 [1988]: 99–105).

21. On the high percentage (80–90 percent) of child sexual abusers being males, see David Finkelhor et al., "Sexual Abuse in a National Survey of Adult Men and Women: Prevalence, Characteristics, and Risk Factors," *Child Abuse & Neglect* 14, no. 1 (1990): 19–28. On female sex offenders, see Charlotte D. Kasl, "Female Perpetrators of Sexual Abuse: A Feminist View," in *The Sexually Abused Male: Prevalence, Impact, and Treatment*, vol. 1, ed. Mic Hunter (Lexington, MA: Lexington, 1990): 259–74.

22. David Finkelhor offers an excellent theoretical model to analyze the complex dynamics of child sexual abuse. He argues that four preconditions must be met for someone to sexually violate a child (*Child Sexual Abuse: New Theory and Research* [New York: Free Press, 1984], 36–46, 53–61).

23. David M. Fergusson and Paul E. Mullen, *Childhood Sexual Abuse: An Evidence-Based Perspective* (Thousand Oaks, CA: Sage, 1999), 49; see Rochelle F. Hanson, Julie A. Lipovsky, and Benjamin E. Saunders, "Characteristics of Fathers in Incest Families," *Journal of Interpersonal Violence* 9, no. 2 (1994): 155–69.

While this figure is certainly much higher than the rate of abuse experienced in the general male population, it shows there must be other factors besides personal sexual victimization that influence adults to sexually violate children. We do know that a high percentage of child molesters report they came from dysfunctional families of origin.[24] The majority of sex offenders describe their fathers as cold, distant, hostile, and aggressive; often report conflicted relationships with their mothers; experienced high rates of physical abuse; and indicate that they communicated less with their parents than did their peers.[25] Research suggests that experiencing or witnessing serious intrafamilial violence, as well as experiencing neglect, may be more influential than sexual abuse on sexual abuse victims' becoming sexual abusers themselves.[26]

Thus, the families many adult molesters come from are often emotionally and physically hurtful. They do not provide healthy emotional nurturing, respect for the individual, or modeling of healthy conflict resolution and communication skills. These negative relational experiences lead some men to distrust adult relationships and look to children and adolescents to meet their emotional and sexual needs.

Here are several other characteristics of adult child molesters. These observations can aid churches and organizations as they screen adults who volunteer to work with children and youth.

- They most often molest females.
- They are rarely family members of the victim (only 10 percent) and are most often friends or acquaintances.[27]
- When the molester is a family member, he is much more likely to molest the child repeatedly and more severely.[28]
- Stepparents are up to ten times more likely to molest than natural parents.[29]

24. Hanson, Lipovsky, and Saunders, "Characteristics of Fathers in Incest Families," 164.

25. Julie McCormack, Stephen M. Hudson, and Tony Ward, "Sexual Offenders' Perceptions of Their Early Interpersonal Relationships: An Attachment Perspective," *Journal of Sex Research* 39, no. 2 (2002): 85–93.

26. Daniel Salter et al., "Development of Sexually Abusive Behaviour in Sexually Victimised Males: A Longitudinal Study," *Lancet* 361, no. 9356 (2003): 471–76. In a study of more than seven hundred sexual offenders, Jill Levenson and Melissa Grady found that factors that most significantly predicted sexual offending included having experienced childhood sexual abuse or emotional neglect ("The Influence of Childhood Trauma on Sexual Violence and Sexual Deviance in Adulthood," *Traumatology* 22, no. 2 [2016]: 94–103).

27. Fergusson and Mullen, *Childhood Sexual Abuse*, 45–47.

28. Fergusson and Mullen, *Childhood Sexual Abuse*, 47.

29. Jessie Anderson et al., "The Prevalence of Childhood Sexual Abuse Experiences in a Community Sample of Women," *Journal of the American Academy of Child and Adolescent Psychiatry*

- Child molesters often have large numbers of victims. In one study, the molesters of girls had an average of twenty victims, while the molesters of boys had an average of 150 victims.[30]
- Child molesters are rarely caught and thus may not have a criminal record for molesting. They are, however, often guilty of committing nonsexual crimes and may have a criminal record for some of these offenses, which may indicate they are a potential sexual risk to minors. These telltale offenses include drunken driving, drug offenses, trespassing (often connected with voyeurism), shoplifting, and assault.[31]
- Research reveals that half or more of sex offenders have a history of alcohol abuse and one-third to half were high or intoxicated at the time of their offense.[32]
- Molesters, including incest offenders, often commit various kinds of sex crimes, including rape, exhibitionism, and voyeurism.[33]

Fixated Child Molesters (Pedophiles)

Some child molesters are so consistently sexually aroused by minors that they are placed in a separate category of molesters we call pedophiles (literally, "lovers of children"). These people are often called "fixated molesters" for their sexual fixation with children or adolescents. Most often this sexual attraction is to boys. Pedophiles will typically have a fairly narrow age range of sexual interest. According to some experts, pedophiles attracted to girls usually prefer girls eight to ten years old; pedophiles attracted to boys are often drawn to boys who are slightly older.[34] Some pedophiles are attracted to children of both genders.

Most pedophiles first began molesting children when they themselves

---

32, no. 5 (1993): 911–19; see also Diana E. H. Russell, *The Secret Trauma: Incest in the Lives of Girls and Women* (New York: Basic Books, 1986), 388.

30. Gene G. Abel et al., "Self-Reported Sex Crimes of Nonincarcerated Paraphiliacs," *Journal of Interpersonal Violence* 2, no. 1 (1987): 3–25.

31. Gene Abel and his fellow authors ("Self-Reported Sex Crimes") calculate that child molesters have only a 5 percent chance of getting caught. Mark R. Weinrott and Maureen Saylor document the large number of nonsexual crimes committed by child molesters ("Self-Report of Crimes Committed by Sex Offenders," *Journal of Interpersonal Violence* 6, no. 3 [1991]: 286–300); see also Salter, *Transforming Trauma*, 21–23.

32. Fleur L. Kraanen and Paul M. G. Emmelkamp, "Alcohol and Drugs in Relation to Sexual Offending," in *The Oxford Handbook of Sex Offences and Sex Offenders*, ed. Teela Sanders (New York: Oxford University Press, 2017), 144. While this may provide a partial explanation for the overcoming of inhibitions by molesters, it should never be accepted as an excuse or justification for sexual offenses against minors.

33. Salter, *Transforming Trauma*, 13–17.

34. John B. Murray, "Psychological Profile of Pedophiles and Child Molesters," *Journal of Psychology* 134, no. 2 (2000): 212.

were adolescents. Of all the types of child molesters, pedophiles are in many respects the most troublesome, for they have the greatest number of victims and their sexual proclivity toward children is often the most resistant to treatment. Many experts believe pedophiles cannot be cured—if cure means eliminating sexual desire for children.

Through self-assessment surveys and personality tests, pedophiles are often shown to be introverted, emotionally immature, and fearful of adult heterosexual relationships.[35] Thus, they turn to children for intimate relationships, for they relate much better to children than to adults. This helps us understand why pedophiles often believe they are expressing love to the children they are molesting.

Pedophiles tend to use physical force on their victims less frequently than other molesters, though they often utilize threats and psychological manipulation to keep their victims silent about the abuse. Pedophiles are extremely deliberate, patiently "grooming" potential victims in order to gain their trust and lower their inhibitions so they can have a sexual relationship with the child or adolescent without having to use physical force.[36]

Grooming

Since grooming is very commonly employed by all types of child sexual abusers, often with great effectiveness, it's essential for parents and caregivers to have a basic understanding of the grooming process. This knowledge is also important for pastoral and clinical counselors who serve sexual abuse survivors.[37] Grooming is the process by which abusers (1) gain the trust of potential victims; (2) gain access to the victim, in part by gaining the trust of the community and the potential victim's family and other caregivers; and (3) break down the victim's defenses so that they can sexually abuse the child.

Four specific stages of grooming can be described as follows:[38]

---

35. Murray, "Psychological Profile of Pedophiles," 214; see also A. Nicholas Groth, William F. Hobson, and Thomas S. Gary, "The Child Molester: Clinical Observations," *Journal of Social Work & Human Sexuality* 1, no. 1–2 (1982): 129–44.

36. Eric Leberg gives helpful examples of the calculated grooming that sex offenders, especially pedophiles, utilize (*Understanding Child Molesters*, 15–45, 139–43).

37. Molly Wolf and Doyle Pruitt found that the long-term effects experienced by CSA victims varies with the type of grooming. Specifically, threatening/violent grooming was a predictor of greater trauma severity, and verbal coercion was a significant predictor of adult sexual problems ("Grooming Hurts Too: The Effects of Perpetrator Grooming Types on Trauma Symptoms in Adult Survivors of Child Sexual Abuse," *Journal of Child Sexual Abuse* 28, no. 3 (2019): 345–59.

38. Summarized from Georgia Mae Winters and Elizabeth Jeglic, "Stages of Sexual Grooming: Recognizing Potentially Predatory Behaviors of Child Molesters," *Deviant Behavior* 38, no. 6 (2017): 724–33. For a detailed discussion of the various targets of grooming, see Anne-Marie McAlinden,

Stage One: Selecting a Vulnerable Victim

Abusers often target children who are from single-parent homes, have poor self-esteem and lack confidence (49 percent of abusers in one study looked for children with poor self-esteem[39]), have emotional or behavioral problems, are physically disabled, are physically weak or small, or have been sexually abused in the past. Child molesters are like sharks, with a finely attuned ability to smell "blood in the water," that is, to find the emotional wounds or insecurities that make the child vulnerable to being preyed on.

Stage Two: Gaining Access to the Child

The goal in this stage is to isolate the child physically and emotionally from those around them. This typically involves patiently gaining the trust of parents and caregivers. Abusers are calculated and very patient in the grooming process. Some take as long as two or three years in a new community to build trust before they begin to offend. Abusers find elaborate ways to gain the trust of the community to lower everyone's suspicions, gain trust, and have access to minors. For instance, a number of award-winning coaches and teachers of the year were subsequently convicted of child abuse. In such cases, trust is so high that numerous suspicions and reports are ignored because the abuser has so thoroughly groomed the community. Many extra-familial offenders strategize to find a warm welcome in the victim's home as a means of gaining access to the child. They may do this by offering to help single mothers with home repairs, becoming a "father figure," and so forth.

Stage Three: Developing a "Special" Trust Relationship with the Child

Abusers prey on the vulnerabilities and needs of their victims. They befriend the child, offer activities or gifts that are meaningful to the child, and create a special bond with the child, often through secrets they share (sometimes involving breaking rules or even the law, thus strengthening their "special relationship"). In this stage "the perpetrator portrays himself as a nonthreatening individual with whom the child can talk and spend time with. During this step, the offender adjusts his strategies based on the age of the child he is targeting, the needs of the child, and the child's perceived vulnerabilities."[40]

"'Setting 'Em Up': Personal, Familial and Institutional Grooming in the Sexual Abuse of Children," *Social & Legal Studies* 15, no. 3 (2006): 339–62.

39. Michele Elliott, Kevin Browne, and Jennifer Kilcoyne, "Child Sexual Abuse Prevention: What Offenders Tell Us," *Child Abuse & Neglect* 19, no. 5 (1995): 581.

40. Winters and Jeglic, "Stages of Sexual Grooming," 726.

Stage Four: Desensitizing the Child

Once trust is established, the abuser begins to desensitize the child through increasingly invasive touch and sexual messages. Touch is often initially introduced to appear accidental and then gradually increases. The abuser is measuring the extent to which they can increase touch without unduly alarming the child. This will often involve a progression of benign or "accidental" touches, tickling, wrestling, hugs, light kisses, caresses, touching near the genitals, and the like. Victims can also be desensitized through sexual descriptions and the gradual introduction of sexual humor and pornography.

Female Molesters

While female molesters are far less common than male molesters, many experts believe that the number of female perpetrators is significantly underestimated, accounting for as much as 20 percent of the sexual molestations of minors.[41] There is limited literature on female offenders, but Anna Salter notes that, given what we do know, we can place female molesters in three categories:[42]

- **Women who molest children under the age of six, usually their own children.** This is one of the largest groups of female offenders. These are women whose identities are so amalgamated with their children's that they cannot function as mothers. Rather than nurture children, as healthy mothers do, they use children to meet their own emotional and sexual needs. Tragically, these women often have sadistic tendencies and take twisted pleasure in hurting children.
- **The teacher/lover group of women who primarily molest adolescents.** They are generally emotionally needy women in their thirties who take advantage of their position of authority to build romantic relationships with vulnerable teens.
- **Women who were initially coerced into having sexual relations with children by an adult male partner.** Some of these women will go on to initiate sexual relations with their own children.

---

41. Finkelhor et al., "Sexual Abuse in a National Survey," 19–28.

42. See Anna C. Salter, *Predators, Pedophiles, Rapists, and Other Sex Offenders: Who They Are, How They Operate, and How We Can Protect Ourselves and Our Children* (New York: Basic Books, 2003), 76–79; see also Ruth Mathews, Jane Matthews, and Kate Speltz, "Female Sexual Offenders," in *The Sexually Abused Male: Prevalence, Impact, and Treatment*, vol. 1, ed. Mic Hunter (Lexington, MA: Lexington Books, 1990), 275–93.

Adolescent Molesters

Adolescent sex offenders provide a very serious challenge.[43] It is estimated that adolescents commit up to half of all child sexual abuse, and their victims tend to be younger children. It is important to note that the majority of adult sexual offenders began sexual offending before they turned eighteen.[44] Adolescent molesters are a diverse population that can be put into several different categories:[45]

- **Experimenters.** These adolescents are sexually naive eleven- to fourteen-year-olds who have little history of acting-out behavior and have a limited number of exploratory acts with children.
- **Group offenders.** These adolescents have little or no previous delinquency history but are influenced by peers to engage in sexual offenses against children.
- **Undersocialized offenders.** These adolescents exhibit chronic social isolation and lack of social skills and are motivated to molest children by a need for greater self-importance and intimacy.
- **Pseudosocialized offenders.** These adolescents appear to have good social skills and confidence but are likely to have been extensively sexually abused themselves. They molest for sexual pleasure.
- **Sexually aggressive offenders.** These adolescents typically come from an abusive and out-of-control home and have a personal history of antisocial behavior, substance abuse, and poor impulse control. They use force to molest, so as to experience the power of domination while humiliating their victims.

While there is a broad range of adolescent offenders, research reveals some common traits of adolescents who molest children:

---

43. A particularly helpful and concise resource on juvenile sex offenders is David Finkelhor, Richard Ormrod, and Mark Chaffin, "Juveniles Who Commit Sex Offenses against Minors," *Juvenile Justice Bulletin*, December 2009, Office of Justice Programs, www.ojp.gov/pdffiles1/ojjdp/227763 .pdf. See also Gail Ryan, Tom Leversee, and Sandy Lane, eds., *Juvenile Sexual Offending: Causes, Consequences, and Correction*, 3rd ed. (Hoboken, NJ: Wiley, 2010).

44. Gail Ryan, "Incidence and Prevalence of Sexual Offenses Committed by Juveniles," in *Juvenile Sexual Offending*, 11.

45. Craig S. Cashwell and Michele E. Caruso, "Adolescent Sex Offenders: Identification and Intervention Strategies," *Journal of Mental Health Counseling* 19, no. 4 (1997): 336–48, https://core.ac .uk/download/pdf/149233558.pdf.

- They tend to come from families that are rigid and emotionally disengaged.[46]
- They are significantly more likely than their nonabused peers to have experienced childhood physical abuse or neglect.[47]
- They most often molest girls.
- Early adolescence (thirteen to fourteen years old) is the peak age for adolescents to offend against younger children, whereas offenses against fellow teens surge during middle to late adolescence.
- Forty percent of sex offenders who victimize children under age six are juveniles.
- Compared to nonoffending peers, they tend to possess weak social skills, have learning disabilities, are more socially isolated, and feel powerless.[48]
- The vast majority of adolescents who molest children are males (up to 90 percent), but the females who do molest children have childhood histories of severe maltreatment, including sexual victimization, and typically molest boys.[49]

Children Who Violate Other Children

Tragically, it's common for children who have been sexually abused or sexualized by exposure to sexual activity to sexually violate other children.[50] Recent research has found that the majority (58 percent) of children who initiated sexual activity with other children had viewed sexually explicit media.

---

46. Gary P. Bischof, Sandra M. Stith, and Martha L. Whitney, "Family Environments of Adolescent Sex Offenders and Other Juvenile Delinquents," *Adolescence* 30, no. 117 (1995): 157–70.

47. Cathy Spatz Widom and Christina Massey, "A Prospective Examination of Whether Childhood Sexual Abuse Predicts Subsequent Sexual Offending," *JAMA Pediatrics* 169, no. 1 (2015), https://jamanetwork.com/journals/jamapediatrics/article-abstract/2086458.

48. Mark Chaffin, Elizabeth Letourneau, and Jane F. Silovsky, "Adults, Adolescents, and Children Who Sexually Abuse Children: A Developmental Perspective," in *The APSAC Handbook on Child Maltreatment*, 2d ed., ed. John E. B. Myers et al. (Thousand Oaks, CA: Sage, 2002), 208–9; see also Gail Ryan et al., "Juvenile Sex Offenders: Development and Correction," *Child Abuse & Neglect* 11, no 3 (1987): 385–95.

49. Judith V. Becker, "What We Know about the Characteristics and Treatment of Adolescents Who Have Committed Sexual Offenses," *Child Maltreatment* 3, no. 4 (1998): 317–29.

50. Some experts suggest it's improper to use the terms *molester* and *perpetrator* for children who initiate sexually inappropriate acts on other children because of the limited cognitive development of children, the legal inappropriateness of these terms, and the fact that such labels can do more harm than good developmentally (see Chaffin, Letourneau, and Silovsky, "Adults, Adolescents, and Children," 208–9).

The researchers conclude that this sexually explicit material was the stimulus for children to sexually act out on other children.[51]

At this juncture, a clarification is in order. At what point do sexual behaviors between children become exploitive? While many, if not most, children at one time or another engage in innocent sexual exploration ("playing doctor"), sexual behavior becomes exploitive if it:

- occurs with manipulation, intimidation, or force;
- continues in secrecy after caregivers have advised the child that their behavior is inappropriate;
- involves children of discrepant ages or developmental stages; or
- involves explicit sexual acts (attempted or simulated sexual intercourse, oral sex, and the like).

Unlike adult and juvenile sex offenders, gender is not a distinctive characteristic of children who sexually violate other children. In fact, 65 percent of preschool children who sexually violate other children are girls, though the most sexually aggressive children are males (91 percent).[52]

Domestically Abusive Men

While domestically abusive men (those who commit physical, emotional, verbal, or sexual abuse against their wives or girlfriends) are found in all ethnic and socioeconomic groups, the lowest-income households experience dramatically higher rates of domestic abuse.[53] Domestic abusers most often commit various kinds of abuse, often against multiple family members. For instance, children who witness intimate partner violence in their household in a given year are almost four times more likely to be abused themselves by those same parents/caregivers who had abused each other.[54]

Virtually all domestic abusers who physically or sexually abuse family

---

51. Cynthia DeLago et al., "Children Who Engaged in Interpersonal Problematic Sexual Behaviors," *Child Abuse & Neglect* 105 (2020): 6–8.

52. Chaffin, Letourneau, and Silovsky, "Adults, Adolescents, and Children," 209; Jane F. Silovsky, Larissa Niec, and Debra Hecht, "Clinical Presentation and Treatment Outcome of Preschool Children with Sexual Behavior Problems," paper presented at the San Diego Conference on Responding to Child Maltreatment, San Diego, CA, January 2000.

53. Callie Marie Rennison and Sarah Welchans, "Bureau of Justice Statistics Special Report: Intimate Partner Violence" (May 2000), www.ojp.usdoj.gov/bjs/pub/pdf/ipv.pdf.

54. Zelimar Bidarra, Geneviève Lessard, and Annie Dumont, "Co-ocurrence of Intimate Partner Violence and Child Sexual Abuse: Prevalence, Risk Factors and Related Issues," *Child Abuse & Neglect* 55, no. 4 (May 2016): 10–21; Sherry Hamby et al., "The Overlap of Witnessing Physical Violence with Child Maltreatment and Other Victimizations in a Nationally Representative Survey of Youth," Child Abuse & Neglect 24, no. 10 (October 2010): 734–41.

members also verbally abuse them. Scripture repeatedly calls attention to evil abusers who engage in multiple kinds of abuse, oppression, and intimidation.[55]

One of the most predictable features of domestically abusive men is that they experienced domestic abuse during childhood;[56] they learned that abuse is an acceptable way to deal with stress and frustration while not being taught practical skills of healthy communication and conflict resolution. Most abusive men are deeply wounded by their painful childhoods, which has resulted in deep insecurities.

Behaviorally, *control* is the most common characteristic of abusive men, who seem to have a pathological need to control much or all of their spouses' and children's lives. They do so through psychological manipulation, verbal abuse, and physical force.[57] They have an underlying sense of insecurity, inadequacy, and powerlessness. These men are not hypermasculine or supermacho, as is commonly perceived, but in fact tend to rate themselves as lower in masculinity,[58] exhibiting what some have called a "failed macho complex,"[59] which leads them to control and batter the one who most threatens their fragile male ego—namely, their female partner.[60]

While there are widely varying types of domestically abusive men, the following attitudes and beliefs are characteristic.[61] Note how these beliefs are mutually reinforcing and closely connected.

---

55. See, for instance, Job 24:2–12; Psalms 10:2–9, 18; 12:3–5; 64:2–8; Isaiah 3:13–15; Ezekiel 22:6–13; 45:8–9; Micah 2:1–2. Scripture often describes the co-occurrence of physical and verbal abuse: Psalms 10:7–10; 64:1–6; 73:6–9; 140:1–4; Isaiah 59:2–4; Jeremiah 9:3–8.

56. Ola W. Barnett, Cindy L. Miller-Perrin, and Robin D. Perrin, eds., *Family Violence across the Lifespan: An Introduction* (Thousand Oaks, CA: Sage, 1997), 239.

57. See Bancroft and Silverman, *Batterer as Parent*, 5–7.

58. Alan Rosenbaum, "Of Men, Macho, and Marital Violence," *Journal of Family Violence* 1, no. 2 (1986): 121–29.

59. Edward W. Gondolf and James Hanneken, "The Gender Warrior: Reformed Batterers on Abuse, Treatment, and Change," *Journal of Family Violence* 2, no. 2 (1987): 177–91.

60. Edward W. Gondolf, *Research on Men Who Batter: An Overview, Bibliography and Resource Guide* (Bradenton, FL: Human Services Institute, 1988), 7; see also David J. Livingston, *Healing Violent Men: A Model for Christian Community* (Philadelphia: Fortress, 2002), 18–21; Diane Goldstein and Alan Rosenbaum, "An Evaluation of the Self-Esteem of Maritally Violent Men," *Family Relations* 34, no. 3 (1985): 425–28.

61. Bancroft and Silverman, *Batterer as Parent*, 7–19; see also Mary Nomme Russell, *Confronting Abusive Beliefs: Group Treatment for Abusive Men* (Thousand Oaks, CA: Sage, 1995), 36–46. One influential typology proposes three types of physical male abusers in ascending order of violence: the family-only batterer, the borderline/dysphoric batterer, and the generally violent/antisocial batterer (Amy Holtzworth-Munroe and Gregory L. Stuart, "Typologies of Male Batterers: Three Subtypes and the Differences among Them," *Psychological Bulletin* 116, no. 3 [1994]: 476–97). Lundy Bancroft describes ten different types of abusive men (*Why Does He Do That? Inside the Minds of Angry and Controlling Men* [New York: Putnam, 2002], 76–105).

- **Overarching sense of entitlement.** Lundy Bancroft and Jay Silverman note that entitlement "may be the single most critical concept" for understanding the mindset of domestic abusers. The authors go on to define entitlement as "the belief that one has special rights and privileges without accompanying reciprocal responsibilities."[62] Being entitled reduces or eliminates one's sense of reciprocal responsibility to other family members, who exist to serve and not be served. If you feel you are entitled, then it is logical and justifiable, even essential, to take whatever steps are necessary, including abuse, to force family members to treat you as you deserve. Sadly, entitlement for professing Christian men is often turbocharged in a distorted, powerful manner. As one of the world's leading experts on domestic violence in religious families notes:

  > Almost all men who batter believe they are *entitled* to certain goods and services from their intimate partners, and when they do not receive what they believe they deserve, they react with angry, controlling actions. Religious men often believe that God is on their side, having preordained that men, or husbands, should be treated in a certain way and that men are invested with certain power in the family context. They believe this gives them certain rights and decision-making privileges and control to which their wives or partners are not entitled . . .
  >
  > [Therefore, they may say] 'I am in charge of my family; I am entitled to sex, care, and children from my wife; and I can punish them when they do not submit to my authority.[63]

- **Air of superiority.** A belief in one's superiority is one of the most "fundamental aspects of abusive men's belief systems."[64] This male superiority is inextricably connected to abusive men's sense of entitlement and leads domestic abusers to believe they are above any accountability for their actions, an attitude well attested in biblical descriptions of abusers.[65]

---

62. Bancroft and Silverman, *Batterer as Parent*, 7.

63. Nancy Nason-Clark et al., *Religion and Intimate Partner Violence: Understanding the Challenges and Proposing Solutions* (New York: Oxford University Press, 2018), 73. Ironically, Scripture is quite clear that godly leadership in general and a husband's family leadership in particular, is to be characterized not by entitlement or power but by servanthood and sacrificial love, Matthew 20:25–27; Ephesians 5:25–29. Furthermore, no matter how one understands biblical commands to wives to submit to their husbands, such commands are always directed at wives. There is absolutely no teaching anywhere in the Bible that husbands have a right to punish their wives or "force" them to submit.

64. Russell, *Confronting Abusive Beliefs*, 41.

65. See, for instance, Psalms 10: 6–7, 10–13; 59:2, 6–7; 94:3–7.

- **Extreme possessiveness.** Family members are viewed as owned objects, which helps explain why physical assault and homicide rates go up dramatically when women separate from their abusive husbands or boyfriends.
- **Manipulativeness.** Bancroft and Silverman note that few of their abusive clients rely solely on verbal or physical abuse to control family members; instead, they utilize high levels of deceptive manipulation.[66] Domestic abusers are often so adept at deception and manipulation, that everyone around them—family, friends, and even their own children—are confused and conned, not seeing their abuse for what it really is. Domestic abusers' deceptive manipulations cover up their abuse but also facilitate it. The psalmist eloquently describes this misleading tactic: "His talk is smooth as butter, yet war is in his heart; his words are more soothing than oil, yet they are drawn swords" (Psalm 55:21). Similarly, Jeremiah states of abusers, "Their tongue is a deadly arrow; it speaks deceitfully. With their mouths they all speak cordially to their neighbors, but in their hearts they set traps for them" (Jeremiah 9:8).[67]
- **Denial, minimization, victim blaming.** One of the most characteristic traits of domestic abusers is their obstinate unwillingness to own their abuse. They either deny it altogether, minimize its seriousness, or blame the victim—all in the face of irrefutable evidence of their guilt. The prophet Jeremiah eloquently describes the breathtaking denial of physical abusers: "On your clothes is found the lifeblood of the innocent poor, though you did not catch them breaking in. Yet in spite of all this you say, 'I am innocent; he [God] is not angry with me'" (Jeremiah 2:34–35).

Finally, we would like to summarize findings on domestically violent religious men. Nancy Nason-Clark is a Canadian sociologist who has spent much of her professional career researching domestic violence in religious communities. She is also a Christian who is deeply committed to helping the church better assist abusers and their families. Here are some of her findings regarding the characteristics of men enrolled in a faith-based batterers intervention program.[68] Of the more than one thousand abusive religious men she studied,

---

66. Bancroft and Silverman, *Batterer as Parent*, 15.
67. See also Job 20:12; Psalms 5:6; 10:8–9; Micah 6:12.
68. Nancy Nason-Clark et al., "An Overview of the Characteristics of the Clients at a Faith-Based Batterers' Intervention Program," *Journal of Religion & Abuse* 5, no. 4 (2003): 57–71.

- most were married (a much higher percentage than secular DV abusers);
- a high percentage had a history of problems in school (many had been diagnosed with learning disabilities);
- 87 percent of the men were employed (a much higher percentage than secular DV abusers), and 48 percent listed unskilled laborer as their occupation;
- 57 percent admitted to having had problems related to their use of alcohol;
- 56 percent had witnessed domestic violence in their family of origin;
- 43 percent had been the recipients of violence in their family of origin;
- 56 percent had been incarcerated for criminal offenses; and
- 24 percent admitted to a history of problems with illegal drug use.

While this research highlights the fact that men who are less educated and lower in the socioeconomic stratum have much higher rates of DV perpetration, there is evidence that lower levels of violence are just as likely to be perpetrated by well-educated and/or higher-income men as by lower-class men.[69] Thus, "we do see indications that some better-educated batterers may rely less on physical violence and draw more on sophisticated techniques of psychological abuse that they have at their disposal."[70]

Now that we've carried out an overview of the characteristics of abusers, we'll put this information into a relational/familial context in the next chapter. Because abusers rarely act in isolation, it's important to understand the characteristics of abusive families.

---

69. Gerald T. Hotaling and David B. Sugarman, "An Analysis of Risk Markers in Husband to Wife Violence: The Current State of Knowledge," *Violence and Victims* 1, no. 2 (1986): 101–24.
70. Bancroft and Silverman, *Batterer as Parent*, 27.

CHAPTER 4

Portrait of an Abusive Family

Nothing made sense to me anymore.
I knew I was young, I knew I was small. But I
was worried that I might already be ruined.

Augusten Burroughs, *A Wolf at the Table*

"Your relatives, members of your own family—
even they have betrayed you;
they have raised a loud cry against you.
Do not trust them,
though they speak well of you."

Jeremiah 12:6

A busive families—families in which abuse takes place—are identical to and yet radically different from other families. While abusive families typically blend in with all the nonabusive families in your neighborhood, they have certain distinct traits that contribute to and result from the abuse. It's imperative that we understand these traits; if we don't, we cannot properly support those we love and can ultimately create additional hurt and damage.[1]

Early in our marriage, we served in a church in the Pacific Northwest. Steve was giving a series of sermons on family life. We were young and naive and didn't understand the counterintuitive dynamics of abusive families. Thus, even as we attempted to care for our community, we ended up hurting some of the very ones we loved. Tina was a young woman in our congregation who had grown up in an abusive family. After Steve's second sermon, Tina mustered up the courage to send the following letter:

---

1. For an excellent redemptive, biblical overview of abusive families that focuses on the story of Joseph, see Andrew Schmutzer, "Joseph's Tears: Suffering from Family Toxins," in *Between Pain and Grace: A Biblical Theology of Suffering*, ed. Gerald W. Peterman and Andrew J. Schmutzer (Chicago: Moody, 2016), 177–208.

Dear Pastoral Staff,

For the past two years, I have sat through many Sunday school lessons and sermons, only to go away defeated and hurt by the assumptions you make about families. You do not understand the kind of families some of us grew up in. When you preach about family harmony, communication, resolving family conflict, and honoring your father and mother, do you have any idea how complicated and confusing these topics are for those of us who grew up in abusive families? Let me tell you a little bit about my family.

By the age of three, I was already well acquainted with family violence. My biological father abused my mother in front of me on many occasions. My mother divorced my father twice before I was three. We were a typical welfare family when my mother met and married a man twice her age. My stepfather was and is an EVIL man in every sense of the word. He beat my brothers and me until we were blobs crying on the floor. In addition, the punishment for trying to defend ourselves involved sitting on his lap while he told us why he had to molest us.

The abuse continued until I was sixteen. During this time, neighbors, teachers, and friends knew what was happening. We often stayed out of the house until well after dark to avoid a confrontation. Anything and everything—from not folding the towels correctly to walking in front of the television—would result in the cycle of beatings we went through. My mother during this whole time just watched. How could anyone just watch? Only once did she beg him to stop, which resulted in him throwing his keys and breaking her glasses. She never spoke up again. Finally, when I was sixteen, I ran away with my brothers. Only then did my mother wake up. We moved out of Idaho with only the clothes on our backs, and I have not seen him since. Even after twelve years, I still fear him, still look over my shoulder, still believe he can get to me because he is EVIL.

I realize it is hard to understand something unless you have gone through it—but please feel my pain when you speak on abuse, honoring your father and mother, forgiving those who hurt you. I'm not asking you to heal my pain, but you don't have to alienate me either.

Sincerely,

One of the abused in your congregation

Our hearts broke for Tina and for the way Steve had inadvertently hurt her. Since then, we've witnessed these dynamics in a myriad of ways and have studied them throughout Scripture. King David's family gives a remarkable glimpse inside an abusive system and sheds light on the nature of abuse itself, particularly the dynamics of rape. While this biblical text isn't a systematic assessment of abuse, it corresponds well with contemporary research on abuse and has much to teach us about abusive families.

The Story of Tamar and Amnon

Before you read on, we encourage you to read 2 Samuel 13:1–21, which describes the rape of Tamar by her half brother Amnon. For the remaining portion of this chapter, we'll outline some of the most significant characteristics of abusive families revealed in this Bible passage.[2]

The Needs of Family Members Are Expendable

The story begins in 2 Samuel 13:1 with an introduction of the key players: "Amnon son of David fell in love with Tamar, the beautiful sister of Absalom son of David." Like a well-crafted Shakespearean tragedy, this story begins by deftly introducing pregnant phrases that will soon turn sinister. The careful reader will quickly detect something amiss in this family. First of all, Absalom and Amnon are identified as sons of David, but Tamar is simply Absalom's sister. This is odd, since Tamar is the daughter of King David and Queen Maakah (3:3). Ironically, nowhere in the entire account is Tamar ever referred to as David's daughter.

In abusive families, family members are not equally valued by the parents. Especially in patriarchal families, female children are often given less protection and honor than their male siblings. It's also peculiar that the story begins by mentioning Absalom first, since Amnon was the royal prince who would succeed David on the throne and thus would normally be honored by being mentioned first. However, Absalom is probably cited first here in the broader context of 2 Samuel, because this particular story is about the quest for an heir to the throne.[3]

---

2. For an excellent practical analysis of the rape of Tamar, with an emphasis on the misuse of power, see Anna Carter Florence, "Read the Rape of Tamar, and Pay Attention to the Verbs," *Christian Century*, July 18, 2018, www.christiancentury.org/article/critical-essay/read-rape-tamar -and-pay-attention-verbs.

3. David Noel Freedman notes that the birth of Solomon precedes this section, and the account of the rape of Tamar is foundational to explaining the "fulfillment of the quest for an heir in the rise of Solomon, the fourth and the youngest of the sons to seek or claim the throne" ("Dinah and Shechem, Tamar and Amnon," *Austin Seminary Bulletin* 105, no. 2 [1990]: 60). Similarly, Andrew Hill argues that Tamar is just a pawn in the power play for the throne ("A Jonadab Connection in the Absalom Conspiracy," *Journal of the Evangelical Theological Society* 30, no. 4 [1987]: 389, www.etsjets.org/files /JETS-PDFs/30/30-4/30-4-pp387-390-JETS.pdf).

Unfortunately for Tamar, she ends up being a pawn in her family's hunger for power. This will become particularly salient in 2 Samuel 13:21 where we observe David's failure to respond to Tamar's rape. Sadly, in abusive families, *the needs of individual family members are highly expendable*. The most vulnerable members of a family can be consumed and exploited to feed the appetites of the more powerful family members.

Reality Is Difficult to Discern

We learn two other things about Tamar in this opening verse: she was beautiful, and her brother Amnon loved her. In a healthy family, these would be prescient statements of blessing and happiness. Not so for Tamar. In abusive families, *reality is difficult to discern*. Nothing is as it appears. Beauty metastasizes into pain and shame; brotherly love turns into bestial lust. What you believed to be the safest place on earth—your own family home—turns out to be the most dangerous. No wonder those who grow up in abusive families find it nearly impossible to trust their own perceptions and emotions. No wonder abuse victims are confused and feel as if they're going insane. Most are quite sane, but they live in insane families.

The Victim Is Made Responsible

While Tamar hadn't experienced it yet, verse 2 of 2 Samuel 13 tips off the reader to Amnon's true character. He was so frustrated because of his "love" for his beautiful sister Tamar that he made himself sick. While Scripture does reference healthy, romantic lovesickness (Song of Songs 5:8), that's hardly what we have here. Amnon was specifically described to be frustrated because Tamar was a virgin, and it "seemed impossible . . . to do anything to her." This probably refers to the fact that royal virgins were kept under close guard, so Amnon was not able to have sexual relations with her.

Amnon's "love" was nothing more than an incestuous *lust* he had fanned into a raging fire. The irony here is that Amnon made himself sick with his own lust for his sister, but Amnon, Jonadab, and David (with varying degrees of knowledge) all placed the responsibility on Tamar for Amnon's self-induced sickness. In abusive families, *the victim is made responsible for solving needs—even evil needs—they didn't create and could never legitimately satisfy.*

There are many modern-day Tamars. Take Sheila, for instance, who was the oldest of six children. Sheila's frail mother was often sick in bed because she was utterly overwhelmed by life. Thus Sheila was "adultified" as a young girl and became Mommy's little helper, which included being more of a mother to her siblings than her mother was. She dressed her siblings for school, prepared the meals, and created grocery lists.

Later, as Sheila reminisced on her childhood, she described herself as the model child, even though she experienced chronic neglect and intermittent beatings at the hands of her drunk father. While Sheila's role in her dysfunctional family had given her a confusing sense of potency as a young girl, it had drained her soul and was more costly than she realized at the time. When Sheila turned nine, her father began to molest her once or twice a week. He explained that her mother was not available to meet his needs, and that a man's needs must be met. Sheila tried to resist her father without success. She despised what he was doing to her. Sheila's incest and neglect programmed her from birth to take care of others at the expense of herself.[4]

The Family Appearance Is Deceptive

Amnon's lust might have eventually died out had it not been for his interaction with his shrewd adviser, Jonadab, who had inquired about his downcast countenance. Amnon described his state of depression because he was in love with the sister of his brother. The fact that Amnon did not identify Tamar as his own sister might well suggest he had already begun to depersonalize Tamar and his familial relationship with her to justify his lust.[5] In a healthy family, Jonadab would have corrected Amnon and coached him in the proper way to meet his relational and sexual needs.[6] Instead, Jonadab concocted a devious scheme for Amnon to gain physical access to his sister by pretending to be ill and asking his sister to feed him (2 Samuel 13:3–5). Jonadab was Amnon's cousin, and as a member of the family he should have been concerned for Tamar's welfare and his cousin's moral well-being.

Jonadab reveals another characteristic of abusive families. *Appearances are deceptive. The family's shiny exterior belies a dark inner reality.* "Jonadab"

---

4. Many researchers note that in abusive families, particularly in incestuous families, role reversal is very common, with one or more of the older children taking care of both a physically and emotionally frail mother and younger siblings (see Catherine Cameron, *Resolving Childhood Trauma: A Long-Term Study of Abuse Survivors* [Thousand Oaks, CA: Sage, 2000], 32); see also Judith Lewis Herman, *Father-Daughter Incest*, rev. ed. (Cambridge, MA: Harvard University Press, 2000), 78–81. This helps explain why victims of father-daughter incest are most often firstborn children (see David Finkelhor, *Sexually Victimized Children* [New York: Free Press, 1979], 129).

5. Anna C. Salter notes that those who are violent toward people they are connected to tend to distance themselves from them with their words, just as they do with their emotions (*Predators, Pedophiles, Rapists, and Other Sex Offenders: Who They Are, How They Operate, and How We Can Protect Ourselves and Our Children* [New York: Basic Books, 2003], 220).

6. Research shows that support and guidance from family members can significantly reduce abuse by fathers. See Carol Coohey, "The Role of Friends, In-Laws, and Other Kin in Father-Perpetrated Child Physical Abuse," *Child Welfare* 79, no. 4 (2000): 373–402.

means "the LORD gives generously." Sadly, enabling your cousin's incest grotesquely perverts the generosity of God. The scheme itself also epitomizes the deceptive appearance of abusive families. On the face, it appeared that Tamar was simply being asked to provide physical sustenance (food) and comfort for her sick brother. In reality, her kindness and trust would be skillfully manipulated to shatter her safety and strip her of emotional comfort for the rest of her life.

The entire royal family had a very polished, impressive appearance. Before Tamar's rape, David had sinned with Bathsheba, but he had repented and been forgiven. God blessed David and Bathsheba with another son (Solomon), whom Nathan the prophet named Jedidiah, which means "loved by the LORD" (2 Samuel 12:25, text note). Tamar and Absalom were attractive royal family members who obeyed their father, and yet Jonadab and Amnon hid their sin behind this impressive exterior.

Very significantly, immediately before the account of Tamar's rape, the writer tells us that the Israelites had secured a great victory over the Ammonites (2 Samuel 12:26–31). The Israelite general Joab carefully guarded David's appearance and reputation by asking David to lead the final assault so the city would be renamed after David and not Joab. As the chapter concludes, David's positive public persona reaches a crescendo as David is coronated with a glittering gold crown stolen from the enemy king. But as we've already seen, the royal family was not what it appeared to be.[7]

Judith Lewis Herman notes the deceptive appearance of abusive families in her insightful study of forty abusive families:

> The families in which the informants grew up were conventional to a fault. Most were churchgoing and financially stable; they maintained a facade of respectability. They were for the most part unknown to mental health services, social agencies, or the police. Because they conformed to traditional family norms, their private disturbances were easily overlooked.[8]

The Truth Is Ignored

Amnon followed his cousin's advice perfectly. He feigned illness to persuade David to send Tamar to feed him "some special bread" (2 Samuel 13:6). David fully cooperated with Amnon's fiendish plan, ordering Tamar to go

---

7. We are not disputing the fact that God had forgiven David or that God was blessing David but asserting that, based on the events that follow, the composite family appearance did not mirror the composite family reality.

8. Herman, *Father-Daughter Incest*, 71.

to Amnon's house and prepare him food. If this was all the information we had regarding David's response to Tamar, we might conclude he had been so thoroughly deceived that he bore little responsibility for her violation. David's behavioral pattern toward his children shows otherwise. In fact, David demonstrates another trait of abusive families: *vulnerable family members are not protected because no one really wants to know the truth.*

The truth is ignored. In other words, maintaining one's own emotional well-being is more important than admitting that dangerous family problems exist. As the God-ordained spiritual leader charged with the well-being of his household (Deuteronomy 6:1–9; Proverbs 1:8–9; 4:1), David should have known, at the very least, that something was wrong with Amnon, whose depression was quite evident to other family members. The fact that Amnon was the immediate heir to David's throne made it even more inexcusable that David failed to observe such wholesale moral turmoil in his own son. Amnon's character most likely had been eroding over an extended period of time. No spiritually healthy man wakes up one morning and decides he's going to rape his sister. David chose to see nothing and do nothing, and Tamar was eventually raped as a result.

David didn't want to face the painful truth about his son. After the rape, when Amnon's predatory deviancy was public knowledge, David still did absolutely nothing. His silence reverberates throughout the biblical account. There's no indication that David consoled Tamar, cautioned Absalom, or punished Amnon. He was inexcusably silent. He didn't ask because he didn't want to know. Later, when unavenged Absalom asks for Amnon to join him for sheepshearing, David allows Amnon to go, precipitating his murder (2 Samuel 13:24–29). And then, much later, when Absalom begins to steal away the hearts of the people, which ultimately results in civil war, David was oblivious to his son's growing rebellion (15:1–14). David's failure to embrace the truth of Absalom's bitterness cost the lives of at least twenty thousand soldiers (18:7), as well as his own son Absalom's life (18:14–15). In addition, David's denial led directly to ten royal concubines being publicly raped (15:16; 16:22). David didn't protect because he didn't want to be disturbed with the truth.

We've heard hundreds of stories in which palpable evidence of abuse was chronically ignored, with no questions asked. The evidence can include a wife's unmistakable facial bruises, children who cower and cry the moment a parent or older sibling walks into the room, the inexplicable discovery of a young child's bloody underwear, a ten-year-old boy who suddenly begins wetting the bed and having nightmares shortly after visiting his aunt and uncle, or a husband who gets up repeatedly in the night to go into a child's room, shuts the door, and each time afterward washes the child's sheets, leaving them folded on the dryer the next morning. In each of these instances, family members asked no questions and the abuse continued.[9] In abusive families, *truth is the enemy and those who expose it are the guilty ones.*

Family Abusers Use Various Types of Force

Amnon's ruse worked, and after sending away the servants, he gained private access to Tamar. At that point, he wasted no more time pretending to be a bedridden invalid. He grabbed Tamar and lewdly demanded sex. The language of the text highlights Amnon's abusive use of physical force to hold Tamar against her will. The Hebrew verb translated here as "grabbed" is the same one used in 2 Samuel 2:16, where Israelite soldiers "grabbed" or "seized" enemy soldiers by the head so they could stab them to death.[10]

Amnon's behavior with Tamar highlights the fact that rape survivors and other abuse victims should never be blamed for what happened to them. *Family abusers use various types of force to get their sordid way*—physical force, emotional blackmail, verbal threats, intimidation, or calculated emotional manipulation to hold victims against their will so they can abuse them.[11]

Furthermore, the effects of chronic abuse create a sense of "learned helplessness," which helps explain why chronic abuse victims often cannot just walk away from their abuser. If Amnon had chronically raped his sister, as is common in cases of incest, Tamar may have lost her ability to try to resist, even if she had a chance to do so, which would make it even easier for Amnon to abuse her.

There are many notable examples of such "passivity" on the part of chronic abuse victims. For instance, eleven-year-old Shawn Hornbeck was kidnapped by a sadistic sexual predator while riding his bike near his home in Richwoods, Missouri. He was held captive and chronically abused for

9. Diana Russell found that in cases of incest, family members are least likely to support the victim (including accepting the evidence) if the perpetrator is a member of the nuclear family (*The Secret Trauma: Incest in the Lives of Girls and Women* [New York: Basic Books, 1986], 373).

10. The Hebrew verb *chazaq* means "to fasten upon, to seize, to bind." It is used just a few verses later in 2 Samuel 13:14 to describe Amnon's being "stronger" than Tamar.

11. We've heard some pastors suggest that Tamar bore some moral guilt for the rape, based on the fact that when Amnon grabbed and propositioned her, she didn't cry out, which Deuteronomy 22:24 requires a victim to do. This assertion is absurd. The text doesn't tell us she did not cry out. What it does tell us is that, with no provocation whatsoever, Amnon forcefully grabbed Tamar and sexually forced himself on her. Furthermore, three times Tamar told Amnon, "No, don't!" (2 Samuel 13:12). Apparently, some pastors, as well as rapists ancient and modern, still do not believe that "don't" means "don't."

more than four years. Though his captor eventually gave him a cell phone and allowed him to periodically go out of the house by himself, Shawn never tried to escape, nor did he notify the authorities.

The abuse Shawn suffered had deeply shattered his sense of agency and personhood so that his abuser did not have to use the same level of power and threat to keep him under his control.[12] This same dynamic is often seen in cases of domestic abuse in which a chronically abused women stays with her abuser in spite of ongoing abuse.[13] We should note that some recent researchers argue that the learned helplessness of trauma victims is actually an "unlearned" autonomic biological response in which the brain activates as if no escape is possible.[14] Whether this is learned or unlearned helplessness, the result is the same: victims become increasingly powerless and more easily abused.

There Is No Straightforward, Healthy Communication

Amnon's sexual demand was both crass and confusing, for this was the first and only time he called Tamar "my sister" (2 Samuel 13:11).[15] As we've seen in the previous chapter, abusers manipulate with their words and actions and have little regard for the impact of their manipulation on the victim. For Tamar, *sister* should have been a term denoting a tender familial relationship that elicited steadfast loyalty, care, and protection (Genesis 34:1–31; Leviticus 18:11; cf. 1 Timothy 5:2).[16] Instead, this sister received violent defilement, contempt, and abandonment.

We see here another characteristic of abusive families: *there is no straightforward, healthy communication, and many of the verbal messages*

---

12. The psychological dynamics that kept Shawn from fleeing are explained by Kristina Sauerwein, *Invisible Chains: Shawn Hornbeck and the Kidnapping Case that Shook the Nation* (Lanham, MD: Lyon, 2008).

13. A highly influential model of the learned helplessness experienced by abused women is given by Lenore E. A. Walker, *The Battered Woman Syndrome*, 4th ed. (New York: Springer, 2017).

14. Steven Maier and Martin Seligman, "Learned Helplessness at Fifty: Insights from Neuroscience," *Psychology Review* 123 (2016): 349–67. These researchers found that this passive biological response was centered in the dorsal raphe nucleus of the brain.

15. It is significant that Amnon's sexual proposition of Tamar is identical to that given by Potiphar's wife to Joseph (Genesis 39:12), except that he adds "my sister," making it all the more confusing and manipulative. In this respect, family members have more power to hurt by their abuse than do outsiders, for one should expect tender care from those in one's own family. Diana Russell's study shows repeatedly that the least severe form of sexual abuse, such as erotic kissing by a family member, is more traumatic and damaging than violent rape perpetrated by a nonfamily member (*Secret Trauma*, 362, 365, 372).

16. *Sister* has a nonliteral usage that can have an erotic connotation (Song of Songs 4:9–10), but this metaphorical use probably draws on the tenderness implicit in a healthy brother-sister relationship. Amnon's use of *sister* is neither metaphorical (she was his blood sister) nor tender (he was her violent rapist).

are contradictory and confusing. In abusive families, messages are, at best, ambiguous and bewildering; at worst, they are demeaning and destructive. The net effect is tremendous confusion. For instance, Tamar was told by her father that her brother was sick and needed her to feed him bread. She soon found out he was morally sick and needed her to feed his lust. He called her his sister but demanded her to be his lover. Before the rape he called her his sister, but afterward he calls her "this woman" (2 Samuel 13:17). He initially offered her entrance into the most personal place in the household—his bed—but when he was finished with her, he threw her out on the street and locked the door. The ambiguity, distortion, and dishonesty of verbal messages in abusive families produce profound confusion and damage.[17]

The Victim's Response Is Often Futile

After Amnon's brash proposition, Tamar had the inner strength to offer a courageous response. The clarity and logic of her response make her rape all the more tragic. While being held against her will, she immediately spoke up and gave Amnon three "don'ts" in 2 Samuel 13:12 (don't force me; don't do what isn't done in Israel; don't do such a wicked thing) and three "ands" in verse 13 (and it would disgrace me so I'd have to get rid of my reproach somehow, and you will become a public fool, and the king won't deny your request if you ask him for my hand in marriage).

The three "don'ts" emphasize the moral impropriety of forced sexual intercourse—it violates the sacred law of God.[18] The first two "ands" emphasize the terrible consequences of such a sin (disgrace and shame for Tamar, social ostracism for Amnon), and the final one suggests an alternative, nonsinful course of action (marriage with the king's consent).[19] All of

---

17. Florence Rush insightfully illustrates the ambiguous, confusing messages that cloud reality for abuse victims by referencing the 1944 Ingrid Bergman film *Gaslight* (*The Best-Kept Secret: Sexual Abuse of Children* [Englewood Cliffs, NJ: Prentice-Hall, 1980], 81–82).

18. The Hebrew word translated "force" (*anah*) indicates sexual intercourse—often referring to forced sexual intercourse that violates the law of God (Genesis 34:2; Deuteronomy 22:29; Judges 19:24; Ezekiel 22:10–11). This leads to the second "don't": "Such a thing should not be done in Israel" because it is a violation of God's law. The "disgrace" mentioned in the first "and" ties this together. P. Kyle McCarter Jr. (*II Samuel* [New York: Doubleday, 1984], 322–23) notes that the term for "wicked thing" (*nebala*) is often translated "folly," but here it conveys the idea of a "sacrilege," for it refers to "a violation of the sacred taboos that define, hedge, and protect the structure of society . . . *Nebala* is used especially of sexual misconduct, including rape (Judges 20:6, 10), promiscuity (Deuteronomy 22:21), adultery (Jeremiah 29:23), and homosexual assault (Judges 19:23)." These violations have far-reaching individual and societal consequences.

19. It's impossible to know whether Tamar was suggesting a course of action she truly believed King David would follow and one she would have cooperated with—or whether she was bluffing to avoid being raped. While marriage between a half brother and half sister was expressly condemned in the Torah (Leviticus 18:9, 11; 20:17), some commentators argue there's no way to know if the law

Tamar's statements were accurate, with one exception. She warned that if Amnon proceeded to rape her, he would experience social ostracism. In a just society, Amnon *would* have faced severe social consequences for his sex crime, but nothing in the text suggests this happened. The terrible irony is that Amnon's sinful actions resulted in *Tamar's* social ostracism. As is so often the case in our fallen, unjust world, abuse victims often suffer far worse consequences than do their perpetrators.

Tamar's response was logical, wise, and in harmony with God's standards. Her tragic story illustrates that *the victim's response is often futile.* The calamity here is that when abuse victims rise above the dizzying waves of distorted and pernicious verbal messages and gather the courage to speak the truth, their words often fall on deaf ears. *Abusers rarely respond to reason, which is why it's vital for families and churches to focus on listening to, empowering, and protecting abuse victims.* Reasoning with unrepentant abusers most often enables more abuse.

Several years ago, a pastor asked for our advice. He and other church leaders had been working with a couple who were having severe marital problems. The husband had been asked to leave two previous churches for being contentious, domineering, and verbally abusive to church members and to his own family. When this man didn't get his way, he would threaten, intimidate, and humiliate his wife and children. There was evidence suggesting the man had even been hitting his wife and children. Two different Christian counselors who had worked with the couple advised the wife to separate from her husband, believing he posed an immediate threat to his family. The wife had asked the husband to move out until he got counseling and dealt with his abusive anger. The husband refused to leave.

The pastor was convinced this person was a dangerous, abusive man and wanted our help in writing a detailed position paper responding to the husband's biblical arguments. He and the other church leaders hoped that by confronting the abusive husband with thorough, sound biblical teaching, the man would see the light. Unfortunately, chronic abusers have "hearts of stone" that only God can penetrate. They don't respond to logical persuasion.

The apostle Paul understood the fact that stone-hearted sinners cannot be reasoned with. He instructed his colleague Titus that after someone has rejected a clear presentation of the truth, they must simply be removed to

---

was in practice at this time, especially in royal families that may have felt the normal rules didn't apply to them. They might have argued, for instance, that Sarah and Abraham were married siblings (Genesis 20:12). McCarter contends convincingly that the use of "brother" and "sister" six times in 2 Samuel 13:1–14 emphasizes that this is incest as well as rape (*II Samuel*, 328).

protect the rest of the spiritual family: "Warn a divisive person once, and then warn them a second time. After that, have nothing to do with them. You may be sure that such people are warped and sinful; they are self-condemned" (Titus 3:10–11). Steve advised this pastor to go ahead and gather the biblical data for the good of this wife and for the church's education but to put 90 percent of his energy into protecting the abused woman and her children. Following our conversation, the pastor and his leadership team wrote an excellent biblical summary on marriage, anger, and the servant leadership God requires of husbands. Sadly, this abusive man rejected all additional attempts by the church to persuade him. Tragically, his response was predicted in Scripture.

Power Is Used to Exploit

In contrast to Tamar's courageous, well-reasoned objections, Amnon used his brute strength to ravage his sister: "Since he was stronger than she, he raped her" (2 Samuel 13:14). The Hebrew text makes crystal clear the brutality of his act, for it literally says, "he forced her and laid her." *In abusive families, power is used to exploit.*

While this may seem like an obvious point, it bears noting that in abusive families, power is used in creative ways to exploit. For instance, one major study of incest victims revealed that half of the women who had experienced sexual abuse by their fathers had also been physically battered by their fathers or in some cases by both parents. Another 25 percent of these women had been severely disciplined as children, which in many cases might have been abusive as well.[20] Similarly, Judith Lewis Herman concludes from her study of abusive families that "one of the most significant distinguishing characteristics of the incestuous fathers was their tendency to dominate their families by the use of force. Half of the informants reported that their fathers were habitually violent"[21]—that is, they physically abused family members.

In abusive families, nonphysical power is used to exploit as well. This can include psychological/emotional manipulation (shaming, threatening to reveal ugly secrets if they don't get what they want, threatening a family member with divine punishment, and the like); social coercion (threatening to tell other family members how horrible the victim is, threatening to cut the victim off from the rest of the family, and the like); and financial

---

20. Cameron, *Resolving Childhood Trauma*, 35.
21. Herman, *Father-Daughter Incest*, 73.

coercion (threatening to force the victim—or anyone who protects them—out on their own, cutting off finances, and the like).

Stated or perceived financial intimidation is a particularly significant force in many abusive families. Research shows that girls with mothers who are sick or minimally educated are at much higher risk of incest at the hands of their fathers or stepfathers—largely because these mothers, who are especially vulnerable and financially dependent on their husbands, find it extremely difficult to protect their daughters from abuse.[22] Additionally, abusive husbands are typically quite skilled at exploiting their wives' vulnerability.[23]

Both emotional and financial intimidation help explain the findings of a recent research study. This study showed that two of the most significant factors in predicting whether a mother will believe and protect a child who discloses intrafamilial sexual abuse are (1) the age of the mother when she had her first child and (2) the mother's relationship with the perpetrator.[24] Mothers who had their first child at a young age tend to be more emotionally and financially vulnerable than mothers who had their first child when they were older. And mothers of abuse victims are far more likely to experience emotional and financial pressure and deprivation if the perpetrators are the husbands than if the perpetuators are non-spouses.[25]

The Family Is Emotionally Unstable

Immediately after Amnon raped his sister, his lovesickness was suddenly transformed into intense hatred. The text says that "Amnon hated her with intense hatred. In fact, he hated her more than he had loved her" (2 Samuel 13:15). This dynamic of "love" that morphs into hatred can seem strange to those who don't understand abuse.[26] It is, however, common and illustrates the instability of abusive families.

---

22. Finkelhor, *Sexually Victimized Children*, 144, 211–12.

23. A number of researchers have noted that fathers and stepfathers who commit incest often take advantage of their wives' powerlessness (and much of their powerlessness is financial); see, for instance, Russell, *Secret Trauma*, 363–67; Herman, *Father-Daughter Incest*, 72–73, 78–79.

24. Denise Pintello and Susan Zuravin, "Intrafamilial Child Sexual Abuse: Predictors of Postdisclosure Maternal Belief and Protective Action," *Child Maltreatment* 6, no. 4 (2001): 349–50.

25. This finding helps explain why victims of extrafamilial abuse consistently receive more support from family members than do victims of intrafamilial abuse; see Ann N. Elliott and Connie N. Carnes, "Reactions of Nonoffending Parents to the Sexual Abuse of Their Child: A Review of the Literature," *Child Maltreatment* 6, no. 4 (2001): 314–31.

26. The rabbis were so puzzled by this verse they imaginatively postulated that Amnon hated Tamar because, when he had sexual relations with her, he hurt himself by becoming tangled in her pubic hair (Babylonian Talmud, b. Sanh. 21a).

In Amnon's case, his actions clearly show he didn't really love Tamar in the first place, though the extent of his newfound hatred was no doubt exacerbated by his guilt and shame. Thus, emotional instability can both contribute to and result from abuse.[27] In abusive families, love and hate often dwell side by side. Abuse victims, especially incest victims, are often given special treatment, attention, and "love" by the abuser.[28] As with so many other dynamics in an abusive family, this experience is confusing and contributes to a distrust of one's own emotions.

Barbara is a twenty-nine-year-old nurse with three small children and lives in a New England mill town.[29] She volunteered to share her personal account of growing up in an abusive family in order to encourage others with similar experiences. Barbara grew up as the oldest of six children in a North Carolina working-class family. Her father had gone to Princeton but was drafted before he could graduate. He was a proud man who disdained the South and anyone with a Southern accent, including his own wife.

Barbara's father physically, sexually, and verbally abused his family for twenty years and sadly began fondling Barbara when she was just three years old. The sexual abuse continued until she was well into adolescence. Barbara articulately described the confusing emotional climate of her abusive home, where she and her other family members experienced the disconcerting mix of love and kindness, abuse and rage—all from the same man. Even at the age of twenty-nine, Barbara still feared her father, acknowledging that she had been deeply impacted by his abuse. She began by describing her father on a positive note:

> He always appeared the family man. He was affectionate. He used to take us fishing. When he was being a father, I suppose he did as well as anyone. He was giving and fun, and we enjoyed his company. But when he was drinking he was certainly very different . . .
>
> We were always afraid of him . . . We always knew that there were certain things that had to be done, or else. The "or else" was usually physical. He would beat us. But I was exempt from much of it. It's like there were

---

27. For this reason, some have described life in an abusive family as constantly walking on eggshells to keep the peace and avoid setting off the abuser (see Lynn Heitritter and Jeanette Vought, *Helping Victims of Sexual Abuse* [Minneapolis: Bethany House, 1989], 72–73).

28. An especially articulate account of this dynamic is given by Diana E. H. Russell ("The Making of a Whore," *Violence Against Women* 1, no. 1 [1995]: 77–98).

29. Barbara's story, along with excellent commentary on it, is told by David Finkelhor (*Sexually Victimized Children*, 185–214).

two families because I was different. I was different in many ways, but I was definitely my father's pet . . .

I had a bond with my father, which may have been a source of strength even though he was my [sexual] pursuer most of the time. But still I think that bond is important: *to have someone that's looking out for you even if they are beating you at the same time* . . .

My father showed my mother a lot of affection around us. When the family was together, he would love her, he would kiss her, and they would appear to be a happy couple. He would express good feelings about her . . . But when he was drinking, they would fight. I've seen him hit her and throw her against the wall . . .

At the time I definitely felt that if I didn't comply [sexually], I would be hurt. He had hit me and knocked me around. I wasn't totally free of what was going on with the other kids. I got less than the others, probably because I was a good kid. I guess I always did what he told me, *and I was always the favorite child.*[30]

Barbara described her father as loving and affectionate but also as abusive. She felt he looked out for her, even though he beat her. She felt she was his favorite, even though she was his victim. Clearly, Barbara continued to be confused about her father and his treatment of her.

The Victim Is Shamed, Blamed, and Demeaned

Tragically, Amnon's abusive behavior did not stop with the rape. After his lust was satiated, hatred welled up in his heart, and he ordered Tamar to "get up and get out!" (2 Samuel 13:15). Tamar refused to leave, arguing that to send her away was more evil than the rape itself. Amnon's response was to order the servants to "get this woman out of my sight" (verse 17) and bolt the door.

While it seems strange to modern readers that a woman would want to stay with her rapist, we must put Tamar's actions in their historical context. In an ancient patriarchal culture that placed great emphasis on sexual purity and honor, a young woman who had lost her virginity, even through rape, would have few chances of marriage. Without marriage, a woman would have little chance of supporting herself and would thus leave her with no social and financial future. She would also be unable to have children, which

---

30. Finkelhor, *Sexually Victimized Children*, 187, 191, 193, 201, emphasis added.

was the single most important role of women in Jewish culture. For this reason, Old Testament law mandated that when a man raped an unmarried woman, he had to pay a dowry and marry her and could never divorce her.[31] Thus, Tamar cried out that Amnon's second act was a greater wrong than the first, for in kicking her out and not marrying her, he was destroying her future.[32]

Amnon thus showed great disdain for Tamar by declaring, in essence, that she wasn't worthy to be married to *anyone*, not even to her rapist. The manner in which Amnon threw out Tamar was also demeaning and abusive—ordering a servant to remove Tamar, a princess. Furthermore, she was no longer viewed as his sister but as "this woman."[33] All this adds up to another sad characteristic of abusive families: *abuse victims are shamed, blamed, and demeaned.*[34]

The characteristics of abusive families are seen not only in nuclear families but also in spiritual families (churches and religious organizations) and social families (schools, close-knit communities, and the like). Churches and communities often shame, blame, and demean abuse victims. Several years ago, Celestia began working with a troubled teenage client. After a few sessions, the girl shared that she had gone to a shopping mall and met some local teen boys, who offered her a ride home. She was flattered and accepted their offer. Instead of taking her home, however, they took her into the desert and gang-raped her. Eventually, they let her go and threatened her with great harm if she told anyone what had happened. She had the courage to tell the authorities and to press charges against the boys. When the principal of the conservative Christian high school she attended heard

---

31. Exodus 22:16–17 and Deuteronomy 22:28–29 address the sexual seduction of a nonengaged virgin. If a man raped an *engaged* woman, he was to be stoned to death, but nothing punitive was to be done to the woman (Deuteronomy 22:25–26)—which seems to imply that if an engaged woman is raped, her fiancé will go through with the wedding.

32. See Dominic Rudman, "Reliving the Rape of Tamar: Absalom's Revenge in 2 Samuel 13," *Old Testament Essays* 11, no. 2 (1998): 332–33. Joyce G. Baldwin argues that the bolting of the door reinforces this message, for once Tamar was thrown out and the door bolted, "she knew deep down that the door to marriage was bolted against her for good" (*1 and 2 Samuel* [Downers Grove, IL: InterVarsity, 1988], 249).

33. Mary J. Evans suggests that the Hebrew phrase rendered "this woman" (*zot*) is very demeaning and could be translated "this thing" (*1 and 2 Samuel* [Peabody, MA: Hendrickson, 2000], 963–64). Supporting this rendering is the derogatory use of the equivalent masculine term "this fellow" (*zeh*) in 1 Samuel 10:27.

34. See Herman, *Father-Daughter Incest*, 36–49. In the case of Tamar, amazingly (and with no coherent textual justification), Pamela Tamarkin Reis blames Tamar for being raped, for she argues that Amnon and Tamar's sexual intimacy was consensual and was encouraged by Tamar's flirtatiousness ("Cupidity and Stupidity: Woman's Agency and the 'Rape' of Tamar," *Journal of the Ancient Near Eastern Society* 25 [1997]: 43–60).

about the incident, he expelled her from school. He stated that only a slut would allow such a thing to happen to her—and they didn't want sluts in their Christian school.

Family Members Are Isolated and Lack Intimacy

The unmitigated tragedy of Tamar's story was revealed in her response to being thrown out of Amnon's house. She tore her long robe—the kind worn by virgins—and put ashes on her head, put her hands on her head, and wept bitterly (2 Samuel 13:19). All of these actions were cultural signs of grief, for from this time on, Tamar would have no social future and would be isolated from society (see 20:3). While Tamar, like all abuse victims, experienced many destructive consequences from the abuse, this text highlights one in particular—long-term social isolation. Tamar was part of an abusive family in which family members offered little or no real intimacy.

King David didn't really know his children. He didn't realize Amnon's moral struggles or the danger David had brought on Tamar by sending her to his house. Once he found out his son was a rapist, he was angry, but he never seemed to have confronted Amnon or consoled Tamar (2 Samuel 13:21). Later when Absalom avenged Tamar's rape by having Amnon murdered, David was comforted and longed to go to Absalom, but he refused to speak to Absalom or to see him (13:37–39; 14:24). Even though David loved Absalom, the only way Absalom could get his father's attention was to manipulate a response by setting the commanding general's field on fire (14:28–33). In short, the family members in this ancient abusive family knew little or nothing of healthy intimacy; they were isolated from the very family members to whom they should have been closest. Sadly, this dynamic is very common, for *abusive families are characterized by social isolation and a lack of intimate relationships.*[35]

Those who grow up in abusive families may have many people around them, but they are perpetually lonely. Tamar was socially isolated for the rest of her life, for after her rape and expulsion, "Tamar lived in her brother Absalom's house, a desolate woman" (2 Samuel 13:20). One abuse survivor put it this way: "I had a fantasy of myself screaming inside a block of ice.

---

35. Many researchers note the social isolation of abusive families, both as a cause and as a result of abuse (see Lucy Berliner and Diana Elliot, "Sexual Abuse of Children," in *The APSAC Handbook on Child Maltreatment*, 2nd ed., ed. John E. B. Myers et al. [Thousand Oaks, CA: Sage, 2002], 57; Diane DePanfilis, "Social Isolation of Neglectful Families: A Review of Social Support Assessment and Intervention Models," *Child Maltreatment* 1, no. 1 [1996]: 37–52). Edward W. Gondolf notes the social isolation of physically abusive husbands and their wives (*Men Who Batter: An Integrated Approach for Stopping Wife Abuse* [Holmes Beach, FL: Learning Publications, 1985], 131–32).

People were walking right by, but no one saw or heard me. I wanted so much for someone to melt the ice."[36] Because those who grow up in abusive families often experience chronic isolation and loneliness, and because as divine image bearers they long for intimate relationships, they often end up in promiscuous or otherwise unhealthy relationships.[37]

A Strict Code of Silence Is Enacted

The biblical story now shifts to Absalom, who, upon seeing Tamar's visible grief, makes several incredible statements (2 Samuel 13:20). He first asks her if she has been with Amnon. Some interpreters take this as evidence that Absalom and Jonadab were working in concert, and that Absalom had been in on the rape plan all along—which would have given him an excuse to kill Amnon so he could become heir to the throne. We believe Absalom's treatment of Tamar suggests, rather, that he loved her and had not actively conspired with her rape but had passively conspired by ignoring warning signs of Amnon's devious intentions.[38] After all, abusive families aren't intimate, don't know each other well, and don't protect vulnerable family members because they don't really want to know the truth.

Absalom next issues a well-meaning but dreadful injunction: "Be quiet for now, my sister; he is your brother." The basis for keeping quiet about the abuse is that the abuser was the victim's brother. This points to another characteristic: *abusive families enact a strict code of silence, especially if the abuser is a family member.*

For millennia, families have closed ranks and maintained the strictest code of silence when they find out a family member is abusing another family member, particularly if the abuse is sexual. This silence may be due to the fact that, in most cultures, incestuous sexual abuse brings more severe legal and social consequences than do other forms of abuse. Family members often find it difficult to believe a fellow family member could commit such a terrible act. In other instances, the abuser has so much power that other family members fear the consequences if they are held liable for family abuse.

---

36. Quoted in Cameron, *Resolving Childhood Trauma*, 32.

37. This may explain, for instance, why nonperpetrating mothers of incest victims are often abuse victims themselves (see Herman, *Father-Daughter Incest*, 107–8). It may also explain why women who grow up witnessing domestic violence in their own homes are considerably more likely to end up in physically abusive relationships (see Richard J. Gelles, "No Place to Go: The Social Dynamics of Marital Violence," in *Battered Women: A Psychosociological Study of Domestic Violence*, ed. Maria Roy [New York: Van Nostrand Reinhold, 1977], 60).

38. Phyllis Trible notes that Absalom's words to Tamar are the only kindness she experiences in this entire episode (*Texts of Terror* [Philadelphia: Fortress, 1984], 51). Absalom also permanently took Tamar into his home and cared for her (2 Samuel 13:20) and named his own daughter after her (14:27).

Thus, for a variety of reasons, families place tremendous explicit and implicit pressure on victims of intrafamilial sexual abuse to stay quiet.[39]

This conspiracy of silence is one of the most characteristic dynamics of abusive families and is documented in much of the literature on abuse. For instance, in Diana Russell's landmark study of sexual abuse, her probability sample included 930 women, with 648 cases of sexual abuse before the age of eighteen. Of these, only thirty cases (just 5 percent) were reported to the authorities. Of the women who were sexually abused by a family member, only 2 percent of the cases had been reported to the authorities.[40] While Tamar's family might not have listened to her report, the truth should have been told, for covering up such horrible sin has grave consequences for the victim and for the entire family. The Bible repeatedly condemns covering up, overlooking, or relabeling evil (see Psalm 74:8–9; Isaiah 5:20; Micah 2:6–11).

Healthy Emotions Are Denied and Distorted

Absalom's final command to Tamar is probably also well-meaning but equally dreadful. He said, "Don't take this thing to heart" (2 Samuel 13:20)— that is, do not worry about or pay undue attention to the rape. Absalom may well have been trying to comfort Tamar, knowing he intended to get revenge on her rapist. But how could a rape victim not take to heart one of the most violating, damaging events that could ever occur to her? How could she not pay attention to an event that had dramatically and permanently shattered her life? In fact, Tamar's dramatic actions (putting ashes on her head, tearing her dress weeping) were most appropriate expressions of grief over a tremendous loss.

Absalom's request is in keeping with the characteristics of abusive families, for *abusive families deny and distort proper healthy emotions.* Abusive families pressure victims to go numb and not express appropriate grief and anger, and the abusers don't express proper emotions either. Other than lust disguised as love, the only emotions Amnon expressed were anger and disgust, and they were directed at the gracious sister he had raped. There is no biblical hint that Amnon had any appropriate emotions (compassion, sorrow, remorse,

---

39. See Carol E. Barringer, "The Survivor's Voice: Breaking the Incest Taboo," *NWSA Journal* 4, no. 1 (1992): 4–22; see also Cameron, *Resolving Childhood Trauma*, 241.

40. Reported in Russell, *The Secret Trauma*, 85–87. Other experts assert that at least 90 percent of incest cases go unreported (see Herman, *Father-Daughter Incest*, 223). More recently, Benjamin Saunders et al. conducted local and national surveys of childhood abuse victims and found that in the local study (Charleston, South Carolina), only 5.7 percent of the 139 abuse incidents had been reported to the authorities, and only 12 percent of the 699 sexual abuse incidents in the national study had been reported ("Child Sexual Abuse as a Risk Factor for Mental Disorders Among Women: A Community Survey," *Journal of Interpersonal Violence* 7 [1993]: 189–204).

and the like) toward Tamar.[41] This dynamic helps us understand why abuse victims have such a hard time experiencing healthy, appropriate emotions.

The Wrong Ones Are Protected

King David's response offers a final insight into abusive families. After hearing of Tamar's rape, David was "furious" (2 Samuel 13:21). What is confusing is that this sovereign monarch was very angry, and yet he said and did absolutely nothing. David's ambiguous response is explained in some of the Hebrew manuscripts, which add the following to this verse: "but [David] did not curb the excesses of his son Amnon; he favored him because he was his firstborn."[42] In other words, David was angry that Tamar was raped, but because Amnon was the firstborn golden boy, David protected him and not Tamar. Even though God's law dictated that Amnon should either be cut off from the people for committing incest (Leviticus 20:17) or be forced to marry Tamar for raping her (Deuteronomy 22:28–29), David insisted on protecting the abuser—which unveils another characteristic: *in abusive families, the wrong ones are protected.*[43]

We could give countless examples of how families, churches, and denominations protect abusers instead of victims and potential victims. One of the most egregious recent examples of such misdirected protection is the sexual abuse scandal in the Roman Catholic Church in America, particularly in Boston, Massachusetts. An investigative team of journalists with the *Boston Globe* won a Pulitzer Prize for the book *Betrayal*, which documents how scores of Catholic priests, particularly in Boston, molested thousands of children for decades, while the church's top leadership (including cardinals) knew of the abuse, systematically covered it up, and tenaciously protected the abusive priests.[44] In this book, the authors give overwhelming evidence that

41. The problem with abusers is not just that they lack positive emotions but that they don't have the appropriate ones at the appropriate times. For example, in Lenore Walker's widely accepted cycle theory of violence, there are three phases of domestic violence: (1) tension buildup, (2) acute battering incident, and (3) kindness and contrite, loving behavior. While the third phase may appear to be an appropriate expression of healthy emotions, it is not, for these emotions are based on denial and manipulation (*Battered Woman*, 91–99).

42. This additional clarifying sentence, which is left out of the Masoretic (Hebrew) text, is found in the Septuagint and in the Dead Sea texts (4QSam). P. Kyle McCarter convincingly argues that the Masoretic text reflects scribal error, for the scribe's eye must have skipped from the *wl'* at the beginning of the last passage to the *wl'* at the beginning of verse 22 (*II Samuel*, 319–20).

43. For example, the seventy-two incest survivors in Catherine Cameron's study were abused by over two hundred different family members, and yet not one of these perpetrators was ever charged with a sex crime. Clearly, the families these incest survivors grew up in were highly committed to protecting perpetrators, not victims (*Resolving Childhood Trauma*, 268).

44. See The Investigative Staff of the Boston Globe, *Betrayal: The Crisis in the Catholic Church* (Boston: Little, Brown, 2002). For a similar account written by an investigative reporter who is Catholic,

the leadership of the Catholic Church misused their spiritual authority to silence abused children and their parents through direct injunctions, veiled threats, secret settlements, sealed records, and patent lies and deception.

Tragically, this pattern seems to have occurred in other parts of the country as well. Some of the worst offenses were reported in New Mexico, where abusive priests were sent to a treatment program at the Paraclete Center. After that, they were sent to area churches, where reportedly many of them continued to molest. One attorney intimately familiar with the situation described the incongruity of the royal treatment the abusive priests received at the treatment center in contrast to the church's disregard for the victims:

> I can tell you what the atmosphere was [at the Paraclete Center]. They flew in fresh fish and special food items and they went on hikes in the mountains and they were released over the weekend into the local parishes, where they continued to abuse children . . . There is not a single shred of evidence that anyone gave one whit about the victims.[45]

Protecting abusers at the expense of the vulnerable is also a serious problem for Protestants. One of the most dramatic recent examples was exposed in 2019 when the *Houston Chronicle* and *San Antonio Express-News* published a six-part "Abuse of Faith" investigative report documenting widespread sexual abuse and cover-up in churches of the Southern Baptist Convention, the world's largest Protestant denomination.[46] The journalists found that almost four hundred church leaders and volunteers sexually abused some seven hundred children or adolescents over a twenty-year period. They found that some predatory abusers were hired by churches even after being convicted and serving prison time for sex crimes. Protecting sexual abusers appears to be such a problem throughout the evangelical world that some have referred to it as an "epidemic of denial."[47] Sadly, in both ancient Israel and the modern church, abusers, instead of their victims, are often protected.

see Jason Berry, *Lead Us Not into Temptation: Catholic Priests and the Sexual Abuse of Children* (Chicago: University of Illinois Press, 1992).

45. Quoted in Staff of the Boston Globe, *Betrayal*, 174.

46. The investigative reports are available at "A Chronicle Investigation: Abuse of Faith," *Houston Chronicle*, www.houstonchronicle.com/local/investigations/abuse-of-faith.

47. Joshua Pease, "The Sin of Silence: The Epidemic of Denial about Sexual Abuse in the Evangelical Church," *Washington Post*, May 31, 2018, www.washingtonpost.com/news/posteverything /wp/2018/05/31/feature/the-epidemic-of-denial-about-sexual-abuse-in-the-evangelical-church.

Tragically, in abusive families and churches, abusers are protected, while innocent, vulnerable victims are not.

A Final Word of Hope

God works in and through abusive families. The biblical account of Tamar's rape ends as it began, highlighting the abuse and family dysfunction that would destroy numerous lives and threaten the entire nation. But God was not finished with this flawed family; and he is not finished with our flawed families. Centuries later, one of Tamar's relatives, the "seed of David," would come to break the curse and bring justice and healing to the nations (Isaiah 11; 42:1–9; Revelation 22:16)! As David and Diana Garland note:

> The stories of families in the Bible are raw and uncensored, bitter reminders of how awful family life can become . . . Our families and the families in ancient Israel are flawed by dismemberment, physical and emotional violence, infidelity, petty jealousies, and mean-spiritedness. They are far from perfect. Yet it is exactly in those flawed places that the Spirit of God moves and where we can catch a glimpse of grace."[48]

Conclusion

We can now summarize what Tamar's rape by her brother teaches us about the primary characteristics of abusive families:

- The needs of individual family members are highly expendable.
- Reality is very difficult to discern.
- The victim is made responsible for solving needs they didn't create and could never legitimately satisfy.
- The family's shiny exterior belies a dark inner reality.
- Individual family members are not protected because no one really wants to know the truth.
- Family abusers use force to get their sordid way.
- There is no straightforward healthy communication, and many of the verbal messages are contradictory and confusing.
- The victim's response is futile.

---

48. David and Diana Garland, *Flawed Families of the Bible: How God's Grace Works through Imperfect Relationships* (Grand Rapids: Brazos, 2007), 13–14.

- Power is abused to exploit.
- Abusive families are emotionally unstable.
- The victims are shamed, blamed, and demeaned.
- Members are isolated and lack intimacy.
- A strict code of silence is enacted.
- Abusive families deny and distort proper healthy emotions.
- The wrong ones are protected.
- God works in and through broken, abusive families

Now that we've examined the nature of abuse and the profiles of abusers and abusive families, we're ready to move on to part 2, where we'll examine the specific effects of abuse.

PART 2

The Effects of Abuse

In order to present an accessible and effective abuse healing model, we must have a comprehensive understanding of abuse's effects. Many of these effects are so counterintuitive that they baffle even the experts. However, in the past fifteen years we've seen some major breakthroughs in our understanding of abuse. The ACEs (adverse childhood experiences) study is one of the most fascinating and significant of these.[1]

Dr. Vincent Felitti was chief of the department of preventive medicine for Kaiser Permanente in San Diego in the early 1980s. For five years, Kaiser had directed weight loss clinics, and in spite of the participants' success in losing weight, the groups experienced a 50 percent dropout rate. Felitti was baffled by this attrition rate because most of the dropouts had lost significant weight; thus the clinic was quite successful helping the participants do exactly what they had signed up to do—lose weight. Felitti was curious and began conducting exit interviews, and as he did a clear pattern emerged: these dropouts were normal weight at birth and did not gain weight gradually over the years, which would be a more typical pattern. Rather, they abruptly gained weight at a particular time in their life, and then their weight stabilized.

As Felitti investigated further, he discovered that the vast majority of dropouts had experienced sexual abuse and their weight gain had begun shortly after the abuse. Felitti recounts that he was given very little training

---

1. For a basic overview of ACEs and relevant literature, see "Adverse Childhood Experiences (ACEs)" on the Centers for Disease Control and Prevention website, www.cdc.gov/violenceprevention/aces/index.html.

on abuse in medical school, yet the dramatic connection between childhood abuse and adult health astounded him. This initial finding regarding adult obesity prompted Felitti to devise a major (one of the largest of its kind) study of childhood trauma and later adult health and well-being. It was called the "adverse childhood experiences" study.

The researchers studied 17,421 adults from 1995 to 1997 and then conducted fifteen years of follow-up. The original study focused on three types of childhood abuse (physical, sexual, emotional) and five types of family dysfunction (exposure to domestic violence, household mental illness, incarcerated family member, parental separation or divorce, household substance abuse). An additional two ACEs were eventually added (emotional and physical neglect), creating a total of ten ACEs. In the original study, Felitti found that two-thirds of the adult population in the US had experienced one or more ACEs and one in eight had experienced four or more.[2] The ACEs research demonstrated not only how prevalent child trauma is, but how impactful it is on long-term physical, mental, and social health.

The ACEs findings are both startling and revolutionary. Childhood abuse and other forms of trauma have dramatic lifelong impact on virtually every aspect of physical, mental, and social health. For instance, ACEs scores are strongly tied to seven of the ten leading causes of death. The original study found that people with an ACEs score of four or more are 390 percent more likely to have the serious respiratory disorder COPD (chronic obstructive pulmonary disease) than those with a score of zero. Those who have an ACEs score of four or more are also 460 percent more likely to be currently depressed than those with a score of zero. As ACEs scores increase so do the tragic outcomes. For instance, those with an ACEs score of six are 4,600 percent more likely to have used illicit IV drugs than those with a score of zero. Children with an ACEs score of four or more are thirty-two times more likely to exhibit learning or behavioral problems in school.[3]

Before we explore the effects of abuse, we want to address an important issue—namely, to what extent are abuse survivors responsible. The best way to begin is with a story.

Our Mending the Soul trauma training team filed into a tiny, muggy

---

2. Vincent J. Felitti, "The Relation Between Adverse Childhood Experiences and Adult Health: Turning Gold into Lead," *Permanente Journal* 6, no. 1 (2002): 44–47.

3. Nadine Burke Harris, "How Childhood Trauma Affects Health across a Lifetime," filmed September 2014 in San Francisco, TEDMED event, TED video, 15:50, www.ted.com/talks/nadine _burke_harris_how_childhood_trauma_affects_health_across_a_lifetime; see also Nadine Burke Harris, *The Deepest Well: Healing the Long-Term Effects of Childhood Adversity* (New York: Houghton Mifflin Harcourt, 2018).

chapel on the outskirts of Beni in the Democratic Republic of the Congo. We were visiting a residential center of a Christian organization called CEPIMA, a French acronym for "Centre for the Protection of the Destitute and Mentally Ill." We were not prepared for the overwhelming, widespread effects of trauma in this war-torn region, and yet the faith and courage and joy of the CEPIMA's staff rivaled the suffering. It was stunning.

> Joy is a mystery because it can happen anywhere, anytime, even under the most unpromising circumstances, even in the midst of suffering, with tears in its eyes.
>
> Frederick Buechner,
> *The Hungering Dark*

As honored guests, we were seated in a row of dusty plastic chairs at the front of the crowded chapel. Residents and staff pushed closely together on narrow wooden benches clearly excited to have *wazungu* (white) visitors. After a few brief introductions, they began to sing and dance. Congolese worship, if you have not experienced it, is a high-energy, whole-body expression. It's ethereal and beautifully unforgettable.

And then we saw her. An emaciated girl, perhaps nine or ten, crouching in front of us. She stared, with arms half-raised, as if frozen in time, tremoring. We wept upon seeing her. After the service, Mama Abia, the founder of CEPIMA, told us her name was Neema, which, ironically, means "grace" in Swahili. We asked to pray with the patients, and Mama Abia led us to the residential section where, one by one, we had the privilege of hearing each person's story and provided whatever emotional and spiritual comfort we could offer. When we visited Neema, she couldn't communicate and didn't seem to realize we were in the room.

Mama Abia told us a bit of Neema's story. Several months earlier, she had been attacked with machetes and gang-raped by militia members. Abia reported that this little girl, who had until the attack been a well-mannered, joyful child who loved going to church, was almost instantly transformed into an utterly different person, unrecognizable to her family and friends. After the attack, she became highly promiscuous, sleeping with multiple men in her village. She was angry, emotionally disconnected, and anxious. She kept deteriorating until she could no longer function or even care for herself. Abia believed these promiscuous relationships, including the shaming response from her village, were every bit as psychologically damaging as the initial attack and gang rape.

Neema's story illustrates many aspects of abuse trauma—the potency and complexity of its effects, its counterintuitiveness, the power of shame, and the critical role of community. We will explore each of these in subsequent portions of the book. Her story also raises critical questions about the effects of trauma and personal responsibility. More specifically, to what extent was Neema responsible for being rebellious and promiscuous? Should Neema's healing process include having a CEPIMA counselor instruct her to ask God to forgive her for her rebellion, anger, anxiety, and sexual sin? Stated differently, to what extent are abuse victims morally responsible for the effects of their abuse?

These are not merely academic questions. Some evangelical authors are highly critical of abuse healing models that place an emphasis on understanding and responding to the effects of abuse. In particular, these models are viewed as misguided and harmful ways that minimize sin. For instance, one author denies that he is an abuse victim, in spite of the fact that he acknowledges growing up in a home with alcoholic parents who abused him. His rationale for this denial is that "Scripture never addresses me as a victim, only as a sinner."[4] Another author tells the story of a girl who had been sexually abused and went on to develop an eating disorder, as well as that of a combat veteran who was struggling to hold down a job, and describes them as permanent victims who refused to take responsibility for their actions. The author goes on to say that we must not encourage abuse survivors "in the name of sympathy, to abdicate their duties toward God. Simply being a victim determines nothing."[5]

If for the sake of argument we accept that simply being a victim determines nothing, does it follow that being a victim means nothing? Surely not. While Neema was more than an abuse victim, she was no less than a victim. And her victimization had profound consequences. Robust abuse trauma healing requires abuse effects to be understood and mitigated.

Furthermore, abuse survivors certainly need to confess their own sins and obey God. But is it really as neat and tidy as these authors suggest? Is it always clear exactly which sins the abuse survivor needs to confess? Neema's story, like so many abuse survivor's stories, strongly suggests otherwise. How do the effects of abuse and the survivor's moral responsibility relate

---

4. Jim Owen, *Christian Psychology's War on God's Word: The Victimization of the Believer* (Stanley, NC: Timeless Texts, 2004), 113. Owen also belittles counseling models that factor the impact of abuse trauma into healing as "victimization therapy" (97–112). In addition to his inaccurate reductionism that Scripture solely views people as sinners (contra Psalm 8), it is hard to know where to begin in responding to Owen's denial that Scripture ever addresses individuals as abuse victims. Given the fact that abuse/oppression and their destructive impact are addressed in hundreds of passages of Scripture in which abuse victims cry out to God over their abuse and God responds regarding the abuse they are experiencing (see particularly the books of Job, Jeremiah, Lamentations, Habakkuk, and dozens of lament psalms), one wonders what to him would qualify as "Scripture addressing an abuse victim."

5. Mark Chanski, *Manly Dominion (in a Passive-Purple-Four-Ball World)* (Merrick, NY: Calvary, 2004), 22.

to one another? What follows are some helpful principles for survivors and their mentors.

Most often, abuse survivors should begin their healing journey with a primary focus on the abuse they have suffered. As we will see in chapter 5, one of the most powerful and universal effects of abuse is shame. Shame clouds our ability to see ourselves and others clearly, causing survivors to blame themselves for others' sins. Spiritual and emotional health comes from accurately identifying and confessing our own real sins. Erroneously owning others' sins destructively distorts the truth. It does not strengthen but rather imperils our intimacy with God.

Furthermore, abuse trauma produces emotional blunting/numbness and relational disconnection, making it difficult to hear or interpret accurately our conscience and the voice of the Holy Spirit. Thus, most abuse survivors are not ready to understand, feel, or deal with the sins they have committed until they've understood, felt, and dealt with the abuse sins they've experienced.

While Scripture clearly teaches that all humans, including abuse victims, are sinners (Psalm 143:2; Romans 3:23), it does not follow that the abuse victims' "sins" are always clearly identifiable. Only God can discern the human heart. Only he can accurately weigh a person's true motives. Based on differing internal motives and beliefs, an act that is sinful for one person may not be sinful for another person (Romans 14:1–23). Furthermore, an action can be unwise and unhealthy without being intrinsically sinful. Little Neema's promiscuity was certainly unwise and unhealthy, but it is far from clear that she had the cognitive ability or the emotional stability for it to be sinful. Counselors who quickly focus on identifying the abuse survivor's sins run the serious risk of distorting reality and heaping additional toxic shame on the survivor.

Recently, after we conducted a training on sexual abuse, one of the attenders, a director of a large ministry to at-risk women, confided that she had been sex trafficked twenty years earlier when she was an adolescent. She stated that while being trafficked she had done many "bad things," and for twenty years she has struggled to know how to understand and deal with the things she had done. We encouraged her to recognize that some of abuse survivors' "bad actions" are forced on them by the abuser (directly and indirectly); thus, while being "bad," they are not necessarily sinful. It is exceedingly difficult for humans to determine at what point a sex-trafficked girl who has been brainwashed, beaten, and threatened by a pimp is sinning when she has sex with customers. We reminded her that in a context of confession of sin, David declares that God is compassionate toward his children, delights in forgiving, and understands their vulnerabilities (Psalm 103:13–14). We advised her to articulate honestly her struggle to God, asking him to show her any real sin she had not confessed, to ask him to help her receive and feel his forgiveness for real sins confessed, and to give his wisdom in understanding her past "bad actions" (James 1:5).

Even when a sexual abuse survivor's behavior preceding or subsequent to their abuse does seem to be sinful, we must maintain a rigid separation between discussions of their sin and their abuser's sin. Otherwise, we implicitly or explicitly make the victim partially responsible for the abuse, inappropriately devalue the gravity of the abuser's sin, and/or inappropriately inflate the comparative moral gravity of the victim's behavior.

For example, one evangelical writer asserts that the woman is often partially responsible for date rape by dressing immodestly and making poor choices (such as inviting her date to her dorm room), and thus she "may also be sinful, contributing to the man's desire to sin."[6] She concludes that it's wrong to say the woman bears no responsibility for the date rape and if we are going to be "helpful" to the woman, we should hold her accountable for the way she "contributed" to the rape. In addition to reflecting gross ignorance of the dynamics and impact of sexual assault, this writer has perversely distorted the victim's and the abuser's behaviors by making the victim partially responsible for what Scripture classifies as one of the worst kinds of sin imaginable. Furthermore, she has harmfully placed the rapist's and their victim's "sins" on the same plane (rape being irrefutably sinful while the morality of poor judgment and dress are highly subjective, depending on one's knowledge and motives).

Scripture does not lump abuse (physical or sexual) into the same mix with all other sins, for abuse is one of only a handful of capital offenses in Mosaic law and is an abomination uniquely hated by God and categorically worse than most other sins (Deuteronomy 22:25–26; Psalm 11:5; Proverbs 6:16–17).[7] I liken this author lumping together the "sins" of poor judgment/

---

6. Beth Impson, *Called to Womanhood: The Biblical View for Today's World* (Wheaton, IL: Crossway, 2001), 143.

7. While there is an "absolute" quality to sin in that *all sin is wrong* and separates us from a holy God (Romans 6:23; Galatians 3:10; James 2:10), God does not view or respond to all sin as if it were the same (1 John 5:16–17). Some sin reflects a greater perversion from the creation order and results in greater and more destructive consequences, and hence some sins are cited as those God hates (Psalm 11:5; Proverbs 6:16–19) or as abominations (Leviticus 18:22; 20:13; Deuteronomy 7:25–26; 12:31; 18:9–12). Hence, God promises much greater punishment for some sins than for others (Matthew 11:24; Luke 12:10, 47–48). Thus, Cornelius Plantinga observes "all sin is equally wrong but not all sin is equally bad" (*Not the Way It's Supposed to Be: A Breviary of Sin* [Grand Rapids: Eerdmans, 1995], 21).

immodesty with rape—and making the former a contributing and guilt-producing cause of the latter—to a child who gets impatient and angry. Let's assume the child is old enough to know better and is truly acting in a spoiled and sinful manner by stomping her feet because she didn't get her way. So in response to her tantrum, her father flies into a rage and punches her in the face, breaking her jaw and knocking her unconscious, which causes long-term neurological damage. Now is it really "helpful" and appropriate to "hold the child accountable" for the sin of anger and for her "contribution" to her father's abuse? Rubbish! No woman is responsible for being raped any more than a child is responsible for being beaten, regardless of their actions. And there is a qualitative difference between a temper tantrum and a vicious beating, just as there is between poor judgment / immodest dress and rape.

Similarly, when it comes to inappropriate post-abuse behavior on the part of the abuse survivor, Scripture does not lump the victim's sin into the same category as their abuser's. For instance, Jesus says, "If anyone causes one of these little ones—those who believe in me—to stumble, it would be better for them to have a large millstone hung around their neck and to be drowned in the depths of the sea" (Matthew 18:6).[8] Jesus clearly places the greatest judgment not on the "little one's" sin but on the one who damaged them in such a way as to cause them to stumble morally. And abuse is surely one of the most malignantly effective means of spawning a host of long-term sin struggles, thus causing "one of these little ones to stumble."

It is vital to foster a sense of humility-driven compassion as we assess our own or others' unhealthy behavior. Abuse trauma creates great internal damage and pain, which makes various kinds of destructive behavior very enticing, and healthy behavior very confusing and difficult. Much of the impetus for destructive behavior is not evident to abuse survivors—they are often just reacting to situations through the grid of their trauma effects, including traumatic fear, shame, and cognitive distortions, in a way that seems like the best, or only, way to meet their needs. Humans are prone to being deceived and led astray![9]

---

8. The millstone referred to here (*mulos*) was the heavy upper millstone weighing hundreds of pounds that was turned by an ox or donkey. Jesus was not speaking of a purely hypothetical act, for this horrible form of punishment was on occasion used by the Romans (Josephus, *Antiquities* 14.450–15.10; 1 Enoch 48:9).

9. It is important to recognize that Scripture uses numerous Greek and Hebrew terms to describe various aspects of sin (Millard Erickson, *Christian Theology*, 3rd ed [Grand Rapids: Baker, 2013], 517–28). One category of sin (being deceived or led astray) is expressed in the New Testament with the *planao* word group (Ephesians 4:14; Revelation 2:20; 12:9) and in the Hebrew Scriptures with the *shagah/shagag* word group. While Scripture commands believers to not allow themselves to be led astray, and hence we cannot use this as an excuse to sin (Mark 13:5; John 3:7), those who sin defiantly,

Judith Lewis Herman gives a classic example of the way sexual abuse survivors engage in destructive behavior that is triggered by the abuse, often as a misguided, even subconscious attempt to regain a sense of power and control. Sharon Simone, an incest survivor, recounts how she suddenly made the link between her high-risk behavior and her childhood sexual abuse:

> For a couple of months, I had been playing chicken on the highway with men, and finally I was involved in an auto accident. A male truck driver was trying to cut me off, and I said to myself in the crudest of language, there's no f——ing way you're going to push your penis into my lane. Like right out of the blue! Boom! Like that! That was really strange.
>
> I had not been dealing with any of the incest issues. I knew vaguely there was something there and I knew I had to deal with it and I didn't want to. I just knew I had a lot of anger at men. So I let this man smash into me and it was a humongous scene. I was really out of control when I got out of the car, just raging at this man. I didn't tell my therapist about it for about six weeks—I just filed it away. When I told I got confronted—it's very dangerous—so I made a contract that I would deal with my issues with men.[10]

The complexity and deep pain of sexual abuse trauma should activate in us great compassion, gentleness, and humility for people from hard places. For instance, given the chronic shame, emotional distress, and intrusive memories that most abuse survivors live with daily, it is tragically predictable that many adult survivors may numb their pain with illegal drugs or alcohol and become alcoholics and addicts.[11] Seeing someone destroy their life through alcohol addiction should break our hearts and humble us regarding

with their eyes wide open (Numbers 15:30–31; Deuteronomy 29:19; Isaiah 22:12–14), are dealt with differently in Scripture than those who sin through ignorance or deception (Numbers 15:27–29; Luke 12:47–48; 1 Timothy 1:13).

10. Quoted in Judith Lewis Herman, *Trauma and Recovery*, rev. ed. (New York: Basic Books, 1997), 40.

11. For a survey of several studies showing the greatly increased risk of alcohol and drug dependency for sexual abuse survivors, see Anna C. Salter, *Transforming Trauma: A Guide to Understanding and Treating Adult Survivors of Child Sexual Abuse* (Thousand Oaks, CA: Sage, 1995), 239–40. One major study of adults in treatment for alcohol dependency found that almost 60 percent of the participants reported lifetime abuse (Christopher Rice et al., "Self-Reports of Physical, Sexual and Emotional Abuse in an Alcoholism Treatment Sample," *Journal of Studies on Alcohol* 62 [2001]: 114–23). In one study of middle-aged adults (mean age forty years) who had a court documented history of childhood abuse or neglect, the abuse survivors were found to be one and a half times more likely than the control group to have used illegal drugs the previous year, used a great number of illicit drugs, and had more substance abuse related problems, than the control group (Cathy Spatz Widom, Naomi R. Marmorstein, and Helene Raskin White, "Childhood Victimization and Illicit Drug Use in Middle Adulthood," *Psychology of Addictive Behaviors* 20 (2006): 394–403.

our own sinful tendencies. Who am I to say that if I lived with the pain the alcoholic sexual abuse survivor lives with and lacked the social support system I've enjoyed all my life, I would have made better choices than they have? There but by the grace of God go I![12]

Finally, in the process of healing, it is essential that abuse survivors accurately identify and honestly confess their sin to God. Much of the literature, be it Christian or secular, has little to say about this process. This may well be due to the difficulty of survivors owning sin that is not theirs to own. But this is a major oversight with serious consequences. Sin is not a trivial matter. It shatters shalom and brings death and destruction. From Genesis to Revelation, the Bible chronicles the devastation and pain that sin brings on individuals, nations, and the human race.

Thus, survivors must grapple not just with how they have been sinned against but with how they have sinned against others. We are all victims of sin and perpetrators of sin. One of the most helpful ways in which survivors can engage in the process of dealing with their sin is to ask God to show them how in their woundedness they developed unhealthy and sinful patterns of behavior. If survivors do not eventually own what is theirs to own, their growth and healing will be crippled, and eventually stop all together. Furthermore, survivors who do not fully deal with their own sin become much more likely to harm others. As Cornelius Plantinga wisely notes, "Victims victimize others, who then send their own vengeance ricocheting through the larger human family. Nobody is more dangerous than a victim."[13]

In summary, it is generally unwise to begin the abuse healing process with a focus on the survivors' own sins. Most often survivors are not ready to self-assess accurately. At the same time, it is essential that survivors eventually and thoroughly address their own unhealthy and sinful choices and patterns. Such ownership is essential for spiritual health, intimacy with God, and true healing.

Clearly, abuse in all its forms has a complex, dramatic impact on survivors and all those around them. In the following three chapters, we will unpack some of the most significant effects of abuse. We will roughly organize this in three categories: psychological impact (shame), biological impact (the traumatized brain), and social/spiritual impact (disconnection).

---

12. This declaration is often attributed to the sixteenth-century English Reformer John Bradford, though the apostle Paul voiced something very similar: "For I am the least of the apostles and do not even deserve to be called an apostle, because I persecuted the church of God. But by the grace of God I am what I am" (1 Corinthians 15:9–10).

13. Plantinga, *Not the Way It's Supposed to Be*, 57.

CHAPTER 5

Shame

"You looking good."
"Devil's confusion. He lets me look good long as I feel bad."
Toni Morrison, *Beloved*

The difference between guilt and shame is
very clear—in theory. We feel guilty for what
we *do*. We feel shame for what we *are*.
Lewis Smedes, *Shame and Grace*

I live in disgrace all day long,
and my face is covered with shame.
Psalm 44:15

Years ago, Steve served as a college pastor near a large state university. We met thousands of college students during his tenure there, but Mary Beth was one of the most memorable. Bill, one of our graduate students, had invited Mary Beth to church, and she finally agreed to visit.

After Steve met Mary Beth, he understood why Bill had worked so hard to reach out to her. She was neatly dressed and attractive but was so painfully shy and withdrawn it almost hurt to look at her. Mary Beth never made eye contact. Days later, Steve and Bill invited Mary Beth to lunch at the Student Union cafeteria. She reluctantly agreed. As soon as they sat down, Mary Beth informed them she wouldn't be coming back to church, as it had been an enormous mistake for her to visit. Steve assumed she had some objections to Christianity or to his lesson and began to prepare for a defense of the faith.

However, before he could respond, she slammed a verbal line drive into the outfield. She began to apologize profusely, for contaminating the church's sanctuary with her presence. She described herself as an "evil person" and felt it was important that we knew. She told Steve and Bill she would never come back. They tried to assure her that everyone in church is a sinner and struggles in different ways—that God loves her more than she can possibly imagine. As the conversation continued, it became clear their words penetrated no farther than a fist-sized rock would penetrate the armor of an M1 tank.

We were baffled by Mary Beth's utter inability to accept God's love until later that week when Bill connected the dots. Mary Beth had been molested for years by her stepbrother and was saturated with shame and self-loathing. She was severely anorexic and had been hospitalized several times during the previous year. Compulsive exercise had permanently damaged her knees, but she relentlessly continued to jog miles and miles every day. When Mary Beth looked in the mirror, she saw a fat, wicked woman who deserved to suffer for the sexual acts that had been perpetrated against her. Her sexual trauma had permeated every cell in her body with destructive shame. We desperately longed to help Mary Beth experience God's healing, but in spite of calls and invitations, we never saw her again.

The Nature and Characteristics of Shame

We're convinced that shame is the most powerful human emotion—overwhelming, directing, and transforming all other emotions, thoughts, and experiences.[1] For instance, no matter what encouragement or validation Mary Beth received from her friends, pastors, or doctors, no matter what she felt or experienced, her conclusion was always the same: she was a filthy, fat girl who deserved to suffer. Her toxic shame effectively hijacked all other internal and external voices.

Once a pernicious shame virus has infected our mental hard drive, it's extremely difficult to remove because it filters out all helpful thoughts and feelings that could be used to remove it. For example, when abuse victims like Mary Beth experience sensory pleasure (touch, pleasant music, and the like), they typically feel guilty. This toxic pairing of guilt with pleasure reinforces and strengthens their core shame-based belief that they are disgusting and dirty.

This is true for positive accomplishments as well. For example, when Mary Beth received an A in one of her courses, instead of accepting that the

---

1. John Bradshaw argues that shame is the "master emotion" because when it is internalized, all other emotions are bound by it (*Healing the Shame That Binds You* [Deerfield Beach, FL: Health Communications, 1988], 55). Shame is a profoundly influential emotion because, as Gershen Kaufman points out, it is intrinsic to one's development of personal identity (*The Psychology of Shame: Theory and Treatment of Shame-Based Syndromes* [New York: Springer, 1989], 16–19).

good grade gave evidence of her academic skills and hard work, her shame acted as an emotional parasite. It sucked all the healthy nutrients out of the experience by twisting her hard-earned A into harsh self-judgment about all the times in her life she didn't get As. Thus, her shame reasoned, she probably didn't deserve the A in the first place and was given such a grade because the instructor felt sorry for her.[2] With toxic shame, all experiences, including positive accomplishments, indict and assault God's beautifully created self.

While shame is universally and profoundly experienced, it is seldom understood. For instance, there's very little scholarly consensus on what constitutes shame.[3] Nonetheless, here is our definition: *shame is a deep, painful sense of inadequacy and personal failure based on the inability to live up to a standard of conduct—one's own or one imposed by others.* Regardless of the subjectivity, fickleness, or rationality of the standard that was violated, if it's a standard that we or others who are important to us value, it will produce shame. Because shame is connected with one's failure to live up to an important standard of conduct, shame creates a sense of disgust toward oneself. Thus, shame makes us want to hide from others and even from ourselves.[4] Longtime Fuller Theological Seminary professor Lewis Smedes paints a clear picture of what shame feels like:

> To begin with, shame is a very heavy feeling. It is a feeling that we do not measure up and maybe never will measure up to the sorts of persons we are meant to be. The feeling, when we are conscious of it, gives us a vague disgust with ourselves, which in turn feels like a hunk of lead on our hearts
>
> Almost everybody feels shame sometimes, like an invisible load that weighs our spirits down and crushes out our joy. It is a lingering sorrow.[5]

---

2. The catch-22 here is obvious: If bad things happen to me, it's my fault (which shows I'm a bad person). If good things happen to me, it's not because of me (so good things do *not* show that I'm a good person). Candice Feiring, Lynn Taska, and Michael Lewis describe this shame dynamic in terms of internality (the self is the cause) versus externality (something outside of me is the cause). Their research shows that an internal attributional style for negative events is one of the three most influential factors that lead to shame in abuse victims ("A Process Model for Understanding Adaptation to Sexual Abuse: The Role of Shame in Defining Stigmatization," *Child Abuse & Neglect* 20, no. 8 [1996]: 769).

3. An excellent overview of secular models and definitions of shame is given by Paul Gilbert, "What Is Shame: Some Core Issues and Controversies," in *Shame: Interpersonal Behavior, Psychology, and Culture,* ed. Paul Gilbert and Bernice Andrews (New York: Oxford University Press, 1998), 3–38. For a survey of theological models of shame, see Stephen Pattison, *Shame: Theory, Therapy, and Theology* (New York: Cambridge University Press, 2000), 189–228.

4. Sandra D. Wilson highlights the relational disconnection shame produces. She says shame is "the strong sense of being uniquely and hopelessly different and less than other human beings" (*Released from Shame,* rev. ed. [Downers Grove, IL: InterVarsity, 2002], 23).

5. Lewis B. Smedes, *Shame and Grace: Healing the Shame We Don't Deserve* (San Francisco: HarperSanFrancisco, 1993), 5.

Healthy Shame

While shame is a painful emotion, it is not necessarily an unhealthy one. In fact, shame is a divine gift, but a gift that Satan often distorts so it becomes destructive and deadly. The critical difference between healthy and unhealthy (toxic) shame is the relationship between shame and guilt. Guilt is a moral/legal state that results from having violated the law, thus rendering one liable to a penalty. Shame is the painful emotional response to the perception of being guilty.[6] Thus, healthy shame is an appropriate response to an actual violation of the law of God. It is a divine gift because it signals that something *is* dreadfully wrong, that we are not living up to our created design, and that we are alienated from our loving, holy Creator (Romans 2:14–15). As Anthony Hoekema notes, "The very greatness of man's sin consists in the fact that he is still an image-bearer of God. What makes sin so heinous is that man is prostituting such splendid gifts . . . The corruption of the best is the worst."[7]

A man without shame stops at no vice.

Procopius,
in *Day's Collacon*

The point is that healthy shame is based on our unique dignity as God's image bearers. No matter how much we've sinned, healthy shame is a gracious call to correction and cleansing so we can be what the Lord of the universe meant us to be. Even some secular philosophers have argued for the positive role that healthy shame (and its counterpart "honor") can play in motivating virtue, particularly altruism and concern for others. Western cultures that lack a healthy sense of shame are experiencing a destructive "epidemic of shamelessness" reflected in selfishness, moral cowardice, and "rampant individualism."[8] In other words, healthy shame sounds an internal foghorn that we are headed toward the jagged rocks. It is a gracious call to repentance, correction, and moral growth.[9]

---

6. Our definitions are theologically grounded and shouldn't be confused with definitions given by psychologists who use different terminology. For example, Michael Lewis distinguishes between shame and guilt by arguing that shame, not guilt, is most damaging, for guilt is an alterable negative emotion related to one's behavior, whereas shame is a fixed negative emotion related to one's being (*Shame: The Exposed Self* [New York: Free Press, 1992]).

7. Anthony A. Hoekema, *Created in God's Image* (Grand Rapids: Eerdmans, 1986), 85.

8. Tamler Sommers, *Why Honor Matters* (New York: Basic Books, 2018); see also Kwame Anthony Appiah, *The Honor Code: How Moral Revolutions Happen* (New York: Norton, 2010).

9. Thus, I strongly disagree with Karen A. McClintock, who asserts in the context of sexual behavior that chronic shame is never helpful, for it eats away at one's sense of well-being (*Sexual Shame: An Urgent Call to Healing* [Minneapolis: Fortress, 2001], 21–22). Similarly, pastoral theologian Stephen Pattison, based on his erroneous assertion that humans are not alienated from God because of their sin, argues that the God of historic orthodox Christianity is, in many ways, a destructive, "shame-generating monster" (*Shame* [New York: Cambridge University Press, 2000], 241). It is a fool's paradise to have a sense of well-being when one's moral condition has created guilt and condemnation. Jeremiah

Unhealthy/Toxic Shame

Unhealthy or toxic shame, on the other hand, never redeems; instead, it corrodes and destroys. For the recipient, toxic shame often feels similar to healthy shame, but it is based on lies and distortions about God, our sin, our worth, and our redeemability. The distortions may be subtle or outrageous, but the result is the same: toxic shame perverts our sense of dignity as divine image bearers—convincing us that we're bad and unforgiveable and thus alienating us from those who love us and driving us toward those who don't. Even when we really *have* sinned against God, toxic shame gives a false interpretation of our sin that strips away all hope. Lewis Smedes describes well the way toxic shame distorts reality:

> [Unhealthy] shame can be like a signal from a drunken signalman who warns of a train that is not coming. The pain of this shame is not a signal of something wrong in us that needs to be made right. Our shame is what is wrong with us. It is a false shame because the feeling has no basis in reality. It is unhealthy shame because it saps our creative powers and kills our joy. It is a shame we do not deserve because we are not as bad as our feelings tell us we are. Undeserved shame is a good gift gone bad.[10]

The worst aspect of toxic shame is that it isolates us from God, from others, and even from ourselves. Since we are made for relationship with our Creator and with those made in his image, isolation is a debilitating result of shame. Since toxic shame convinces us that we're defective, irredeemable, and unlovable, it makes sense that we try so hard to hide from others. In their song "Creep," the group Radiohead articulates the shame-soaked message that one is permanently defective and hopelessly different from other normal people. The singer compares himself to a friend and bemoans the fact that the friend is beautiful and special, while he is defective in body and soul. He repeats his futile desire to be special, to belong, and to be noticed by others and declares, "But I'm a creep, I'm a weirdo, what the hell am I doin' here?" This is the essence of shame's distorted messaging: *I'm permanently defective. I'm just a creep and a weirdo who will never belong, and even when I do, I don't deserve it.*

---

condemned those who tried to heal Israel's moral sickness superficially by crying out, "Peace, peace" when there was no peace (Jeremiah 6:14). Jeremiah instead asked God to cause shame to fall on the people so that they would feel the weight of their sin and repent (Jeremiah 3:11–13, 25; 8:11–12).

10. Smedes, *Shame and Grace*, 37.

Shame and Abuse

Shame is a soul eating emotion.

Carl Gustav Jung

The exact manner in which abuse creates long-term damage is complex and inadequately understood. Some researchers have turned their attention to the precise mechanisms by which children adjust to the trauma of abuse. They have found that shame, not the severity of the abuse, has the greatest effect on adjustment one year after the abuse.[11] In other words, feelings of shame mediate (act as the intermediary agent for) the emotional trauma of the abusive event.[12] Shame resulting from childhood abuse has also been shown to be strongly associated with adult revictimization and adult depression.[13]

In a broken world, all humans experience shame, but the dynamics of abuse are such that abuse victims' lives literally revolve around shame. Abuse produces shame, then the more shame abuse victims feel, the more long-term damage they experience—and the cycle goes on and on until it is disrupted. It's as though the corrupt things an abuser does penetrates below a victim's skin, perverting their soul. Most survivors feel haunted by the very things they hate and fear, like an alien parasite they cannot remove.

Nothing generates clouds of toxic shame like abuse, and because shame doesn't evaporate with time, survivors need a concerted strategy for understanding and eliminating shame in order to be set free from its toxic power. Why does abuse create such vast amounts of toxic shame? There are several reasons.

Shame Is Transferred from Abusers

Survivors inherit toxic shame from their abusers and the family that enables them. Abusive families (or other unhealthy systems such as churches, schools, and the like) use shame to manipulate and control others, which

---

11. Candice Feiring, Lynn Taska, and Michael Lewis, "Adjustment Following Sexual Abuse Discovery: The Role of Shame and Attributional Style," *Developmental Psychology* 38, no. 1 (2002): 87.

12. See Candice Feiring, Lynn Taska, and Michael Lewis, "The Role of Shame and Attributional Style in Children's and Adolescents' Adaptation to Sexual Abuse," *Child Maltreatment* 3, no. 2 (1998): 130.

13. Bonnie L. Kessler and Kathleen J. Bieschke, "A Retrospective Analysis of Shame, Dissociation, and Adult Victimization in Survivors of Childhood Sexual Abuse," *Journal of Counseling Psychology* 46, no. 3 (1999): 335–41; see also Bernice Andrews, "Bodily Shame as a Mediator between Abusive Experiences and Depression," *Journal of Abnormal Psychology* 104, no. 2 (1995): 277–85.

hides abuse and enables abusers to harm and keep harming others.[14] As we noted in our examination of the characteristics of abusers, abusers consistently shift blame to their victims, are deceitful, and exhibit harsh judgmentalism. These behaviors largely result from the abusers' own shame—both toxic and healthy—that they are unwilling to own and address. *When an abuser doesn't take responsibility for their own sin, the victim is the one to carry it.* The abuser transfers their shame to the victim.

When the victim is a child, this transfer of shame is even more damaging, since children are most vulnerable. Children don't have the cognitive or emotional resources to ferret out the truth and cannot reject the undeserved shame that abusive parents pile on them. Pastoral counselor Richard Frazier explains the way abusive parents' shame is absorbed by their vulnerable children: "A child is emotionally unable to refuse, modify, or detoxify a parent's abusive projections. The power differential is too great and the projections too toxic and overwhelming. Furthermore, the child actually lives in the emotional world and fantasy life of the parent. This is the child's reality."[15]

Given these characteristics of abusers, along with the debasing nature of abuse itself, it is understandable that abuse victims come to believe they are disgusting and deserve to be abused.

During the time the first edition of this book was written, several police officers in our community discovered a seven-year-old boy named Isaac who had been locked in a closet laden with urine and feces for six months. His parents reportedly had denied him food for up to a week at a time. When discovered, Isaac weighed only thirty-six pounds and was so malnourished that he was losing his hair and could barely stand.

Officer Ben Baltzer, who found the boy, said that when he interviewed the parents, they acted as if Isaac deserved the treatment he had received. Isaac's mother reported that she didn't like his attitude and thus he was being punished.[16] One of the authorities interviewed about the case said Isaac should make a full physical recovery, but his emotional healing will take years. In particular, this little boy will need extensive support to overcome the toxic shame that was transferred from his evil parents.

---

14. See Wilson, *Released from Shame*, 60–65. Two insightful books that can help parents learn to avoid shame-based parenting are Sandra D. Wilson, *Shame-Free Parenting* (Downers Grove, IL: InterVarsity, 1992), and Jeff VanVonderen, *Families Where Grace Is in Place* (Bloomington, MN: Bethany House, 2010).

15. Richard T. Frazier, "The Subtle Violations—Abuse and the Projection of Shame," *Pastoral Psychology* 48, no. 4 (2000): 322.

16. Carlos Miller and Katie Nelson, "Phoenix Parents Charged after 'Tortured' Boy, 7, Found in Closet," *Arizona Republic*, June 10, 2003, https://groups.google.com/g/alt.true-crime/c/Gzz3B1Nd3_k.

A Child's Natural Defense

A second and closely related reason abuse victims have large amounts of shame is that absorbing undeserved shame is a natural defense mechanism for children who have been abused by their parents or caregivers. It's much easier for abused children to conclude that they are bad and defective than to accept the fact that their parents, who are all-powerful and beyond the scope of the child to change, are evil and their parenting is defective.

Children possess a God-given intuitive desire and expectation to be nurtured and loved by their parents, which reflects the relational aspect of the image of God. Psychological research on attachment theory has shown that the security of a child's attachment with their parents is of utmost long-term importance for the child's healthy development. In fact, the need and desire for love and nurture from parents is so great that if parents are abusive instead of loving, children resort to various psychological defense mechanisms to cope. They may deny the abuse, dissociate, or blame themselves (absorb toxic shame). Judith Lewis Herman explains this dynamic:

> When it is impossible to avoid the reality of the abuse, the child must construct some system of meaning that justifies it. Inevitably the child concludes that her innate badness is the cause. The child seizes upon this explanation early and clings to it tenaciously, for it enables her to preserve a sense of meaning, hope, and power. If she is bad, then her parents are good. If she is bad, then she can try to be good. If, somehow, she has brought this fate upon herself, then somehow she has the power to change it. If she has driven her parents to mistreat her, then, if only she tries hard enough, she may someday earn their forgiveness and finally win the protection and care she so desperately needs.[17]

Thus, abused children are put in an extremely difficult emotional bind, for they are dependent on one or more abusive adults. As a defense against the powerlessness and vulnerability that come from acknowledging that their parents are evil, they instead blame themselves. In essence, they absorb their abuser's guilt and shame. The abused child's erroneous conclusion that their guilt and defectiveness are the causes of the abuse is further

---

17. Judith Lewis Herman, *Trauma and Recovery: The Aftermath of Violence—From Domestic Abuse to Political Terror*, rev. ed. (New York: Basic Books, 1997), 103; see also Kaufman, *Psychology of Shame*, 32–35, 66–67; Dan B. Allender, *The Wounded Heart: Hope for Adult Victims of Childhood Sexual Abuse*, rev. ed. (Colorado Springs: NavPress, 1995), 67.

strengthened by the abusive parent's destructive verbal messages. This complex defense mechanism, combined with the abusive parent's shaming messages, helps explain why shame is so deeply entrenched in abuse victims.

Susceptibility to Shameful Behavior

Shame corrodes the very part of us that believes we are capable of change.

Brené Brown, *I Thought It Was Just Me*

The damage and emotional starvation suffered by abused children make them much more susceptible to destructive, often sinful behavior, which can in turn create more shame. In other words, Satan takes advantage of the impact of abuse to entice people into meeting their needs in inappropriate ways that become very destructive. This does not justify harmful or sinful behavior, but we must understand this dynamic if we are going to effectively support traumatized people.

Some Christians are so concerned to uphold the doctrine of human depravity that they fail to recognize that abuse victims who are already saturated with shame are not motivated to repent by having their noses rubbed in their sin.[18] In fact, they often get entangled in destructive patterns because their shame convinces them that they're bad and thus unredeemable.[19]

Lucy, a beautiful middle-aged woman who was in vocational Christian ministry for many years, illustrates the manner in which abuse generates shame and emotional hunger, which leads to destructive behavior, which in turn creates more shame and further reinforces the destructive core belief of worthlessness. As a young girl, Lucy was molested by various adult men, including her stepfather, her pastor, and a family friend. Then, in her teenage years, when her abusive stepfather found out she was sexually active outside the home, he labeled her a "worthless whore."

Lucy describes the insidious damage and confusion created by the sexual and emotional abuse and the resultant shame that led to her shame-induced destructive behavior:

---

18. Note, for instance, the contrast between the harsh, judgmental way the Pharisees responded to "sinners"—which only served to intensify their shame—and the way Jesus drew sinners to repent of their sins by treating them with outrageous love and grace (see Matthew 9:9–13; Luke 7:36–50; 19:1–10; John 8:1–11).

19. Lewis Smedes notes a strange paradox: "Some shamed people do shameful things to prove to themselves that they are not ashamed to be what they are ashamed of being. They act out their shame with a fury in the hope that if they flaunt their shame they will convince themselves that they deserve it" (*Shame and Grace*, 94). Thus, shamed people, in essence, create self-fulfilling shame prophecies.

Just about every man I had contact with as a young girl eventually wanted sex. Older men told me they loved me and wanted to take care of me. I actually thought they meant it. I was so needy and in need of love—a father's love—that I accepted whatever I could get. When they left, I felt so abandoned and so ashamed that I had believed them. So I felt that it simply had to be *me*. This didn't happen with my friends, so it must be me. It's interesting that I was very smart. I was an A student. I was very talented—I danced, did ballet and jazz, sang, and played the piano. But I always felt it didn't matter what I could do; it was my body that people were interested in. That's where my worth was. I had the feeling that I somehow "owed" sex to men.

The drinking began when I was very young, prior to being a teenager. I remember the first time I tasted alcohol. The feeling was, "I'm finally okay." The feelings of fear and longing and self-consciousness and unhappiness left . . . for that small amount of time. It was an escape from my feelings. It changed my reality for a while. As I got older, the alcohol allowed me to do things I would not have done sober. Then as the guilt and shame over what I had done overwhelmed me, I either drank more or I took Valium to quell the feelings of disgust and shame.

It's such a vicious cycle. The abuse sets up the worthless feelings, the worthless feelings set up the need to escape, the need to escape sets up the destructive behavior and/or addictions, the behavior sets up the need to escape and hide in the addictions, and the addictions lead to more destructive behavior, which sets the entire cycle into motion again.

Lucy found Christ as a young woman, but she lived several more years of compulsive promiscuity and alcoholism before she was able to truly experience the love and grace of God, find strength and direction from Scripture, and overcome her destructive lifestyle.

We believe this cycle of abusive treatment—shame, sinful destructive behavior, and more shame—is foundational to Jesus' treatment of the Samaritan woman in John 4:7–39. The fact that the Samaritan woman came to draw water in the middle of the day strongly suggests she was a social outcast, because water was normally drawn at sunset and in the company of others. While Jesus didn't overlook her sexual sin (4:17–18), he didn't start there. Rather, he met her where she was and treated her with the love and grace her shame-filled soul craved.[20] He saw a vulnerable

---

20. Joanna and Alister McGrath note the importance of affirming those who are emotionally beaten down and have little self-esteem, as this is what Jesus modeled. They clarify, however:

woman engulfed with shame, who was trying to fill her soul by means of sinful sexual relationships. Knowing this, Jesus appealed to her inner longings by offering her "living water" that would quench her deepest thirst (4:10–14).

The most amazing aspect of the Samaritan woman's conversion is the account she gave to her fellow Samaritans. She testified to Christ by saying that he was the One who "told me everything I ever did" (4:39)—a profound indication that Jesus had offered grace to a shame-filled sinner. She had tasted enough of the grace of God that she could allow her sins to be exposed, first to Christ and then to her community.

Nature of Our Sexuality

Men who have not been violated don't understand what it is like to have the edges of your body blurred—to feel that every inch of your skin is a place where fingers can press, that every hole and orifice is a place where others can put parts of their bodies. When your body stops being corporeal, your soul has no place to go, so it finds the next window to escape.

Rene Denfeld, *The Enchanted*

The nature of sexual abuse itself adds to a survivor's shame. Our genitals are the most intimate and personal part of our bodies. Any inappropriate exposure, let alone contact with one's genitals, results in deep shame, which may explain why some of the Hebrew words for "shame" used in the Old Testament refer to the external genitals.[21] This isn't because the genitals are inherently shameful, but rather because they are so personal that they have a profound capacity to incite shame when inappropriately exposed.

Furthermore, as noted in chapter 2, sex is the most powerful bonding activity one can engage in. Sexual sin forms a unique bond that creates damage beyond that brought about by any other bodily activity (see 1 Corinthians 6:18). Thus when one is violated sexually, it invariably results in tremendous shame.

"Affirmation of people does not mean leaving them where they are; it means meeting them where they are—wherever that may be, and however distasteful that may be—and moving them on in love" (*The Dilemma of Self-Esteem: The Cross and Christian Confidence*, rev. ed. [Wheaton, IL: Crossway, 2002], 147). It should be noted that Alister McGrath is a world-renowned theologian, Christian apologist, and Oxford professor. His comments on self-esteem are deeply rooted in Scripture.

21. The Hebrew words *cherpa* and *qalon*, which most often mean "reproach" or "shame," have a literal usage of "pudenda," that is, the external genital organs, especially of females.

Symptoms of Shame

Shame manifests itself in diverse and contradictory ways. For instance, hair-trigger anger as well as servile passivity, debilitating depression as well as frenetic overachievement, arrogance as well as inferiority, can all result from destructive shame.[22] Hence, it's helpful to list some of the most significant characteristics of shame:[23]

- **Chronic low self-esteem.** Shame-filled people do not accept their God-given worth. They feel inferior to others, inherently flawed, and unalterably defective.
- **Chronic low-grade depression.** Those who view themselves as permanently inferior and defective develop a sense of hopelessness that often leads to depression.
- **Insecure and jealous.** Feelings of inferiority and worthlessness create great insecurity, which leads in turn to jealousy of others. When others succeed or are complimented, it triggers insecurity in a shame-filled person.
- **Prone to compare and compete.** Shame-filled people constantly compare themselves to others and must compete to stay ahead.
- **Unable to accept criticism.** Because shame-filled people reject themselves, they assume everyone else rejects them as well. Even constructive criticism triggers self-rejection and is perceived as a wholesale attack. Shame-filled people cannot separate who they are from what they've done.
- **Quick to deflect blame onto others.** Insecurity and self-rejection cause shame-filled people to flinch from accepting blame for their mistakes. Thus they constantly blame others for their own failures.
- **Feel like they don't belong.** Shame-filled people feel as though they are defective and different from the rest of the world. In their minds, other people are "normal" but they are different and do not belong.
- **Self-focused.** Shame-filled people are so insecure they constantly focus on themselves. They overinflate their place in life. All comments are interpreted as being about them. If they are in a group, they assume everyone is looking at them. Thus they are unable to freely love and serve others.

---

22. The complex symptomatology of shame is largely the result of what John Bradshaw calls "feeling conversion," in which individuals convert shameful feelings into other feelings that are more acceptable (*Healing the Shame*, 77).

23. Most of these characteristics are covered in Marie Powers, *Shame: Thief of Intimacy* (Ventura, CA: Gospel Light, 1998), 19–21.

- **Insecure and superficial.** Since shame-filled people are insecure about what's on the inside, they rigidly control what others see on the outside. They deeply fear that others will discover the truth about their inner defectiveness, and so they're desperate to create the appearance that everything in their life is okay.
- **Addiction struggles.** Chronic shame is extremely painful and often leads to compulsive or even addictive behavior, which can temporarily anesthetize emotional pain. Shame can often lead to alcoholism, sexual addiction, and eating disorders.
- **Long for but also fear intimacy.** Shame-filled people long for intimacy but are deeply afraid their defectiveness will be exposed. Thus they tend to sabotage relationships as they begin to get intimate.
- **Hypercritical of others.** Shame-filled people project their shame onto others by being hypercritical. They cannot accept God's grace for themselves, nor can they extend God's grace to others.
- **Emotionally disconnected and/or dishonest.** Because shame-filled people are full of painful negative feelings, they detach from their own feelings. They don't know what they really feel. Emotions they find unacceptable are transformed into more acceptable emotions. For instance, a shame-filled man often has a hard time admitting he is disappointed or fearful, so he'll act angry instead.
- **Shallow.** Because shame-filled people intensely dislike themselves, they do not engage in healthy reflection or introspection. They constantly hide from others, so they're typically unable to offer more than a shallow, surface-level conversation or relationship.
- **Exhausted.** Living a shame-filled life is tremendously draining. Great energy is expended to keep up a facade so that one's real self is never exposed. Shame strips people of hope and joy and leaves them exhausted and spent.

The Biblical Meaning of Shame

While the secular literature on abuse frequently discusses shame, it is typically ignored in the biblical/theological literature.[24] Similarly, pastors

---

24. For instance, one of the most respected academic biblical encyclopedias, *The Anchor Bible Dictionary*, has no entry under "shame" or "honor." Of all the New Testament writers, Paul most fully develops the concept of shame, using sixteen different Greek terms for shame or aspects of shame in his letters and eight terms for honor. Yet, a widely respected dictionary on Paul has no entry for "shame" or "honor" (*Dictionary of Paul and His Letters*, ed. Gerald F. Hawthorne, Ralph P. Martin, and Daniel G. Reid [Downers Grove, IL: InterVarsity, 1993]). The past twenty-five years has seen renewed interest in

rarely, if ever, preach sermons on shame, though sermons often trigger shame—especially for abuse victims. The failure of the biblical community to address the doctrine of shame is most curious, since it's such a profound human experience and since Scripture has so much to say about it. The English word *shame* and related terms (*ashamed, reproach, humiliate, nakedness*) appear approximately three hundred times in Scripture. These uses are translations of approximately ten different Hebrew and seven different Greek root words.

The basic biblical concept of shame is emotional humiliation due to sin, which results in human or divine disgrace and rejection. Shame in Scripture carries similar connotations to its modern usage—a painful emotional sense of guilt, unworthiness, and disgrace due to one's failure to live up to a standard.

Furthermore, as does the psychological literature, the Bible speaks of the debilitating effects of shame—it breaks the heart and makes one emotionally sick (Psalm 69:20). But unlike secular psychological descriptions of shame that define it purely in terms of subjective human experience, biblical shame is ultimately defined by the character of God. Hence, the Greek and Hebrew words used in the Bible for shame sometimes refer not to human emotions but to *behavior* that is intrinsically shameful.[25] Thus, the key to overcoming shame is more than simply learning to love and accept oneself; it is to discern God's perspective on one's shame and guilt and to let his perspective drive and reshape one's thoughts, actions, and, ultimately, one's feelings.

Biblically, shame is not just an emotional or psychological reality but a judicial one as well, for human emotional experience is not always concordant with one's spiritual condition. For instance, the Bible repeatedly speaks of hard-hearted evildoers, who are guilty but lack an appropriate sense of shame (Jeremiah 3:3; 6:15; 8:12). Likewise, the Bible speaks of the righteous, who are unjustly shamed by their abusive enemies (Psalms 22:6; 69:7–9, 19–21; Jeremiah 15:15). Biblical shame, especially in the Psalms and the

---

the biblical concepts of shame and honor. See, in particular, David deSilva, *Honor, Patronage, Kinship and Purity: Unlocking New Testament Culture* (Downers Grove, IL: InterVarsity, 2000); Jayson George and Mark Baker, *Ministering in Honor-Shame Cultures: Biblical Foundations and Practical Essentials* (Downers Grove, IL: InterVarsity, 2016); Jerome Neyrey, *Honor and Shame in the Gospel of Matthew* (Louisville, KY: Westminster John Knox, 1998); Te-Li Lau, *Defending Shame: Its Formative Power in Paul's Letters* (Grand Rapids: Baker Academic, 2020).

25. Thus, one of the three primary meanings for *aischune* (shame) is "a shameful deed, which one commits" (Walter Bauer et al., *A Greek-English Lexicon of the New Testament and Other Early Christian Literature*, 3rd ed. [Chicago: University of Chicago Press, 2000], 30). Throughout Scripture, shame is associated with intrinsically indecent or disgraceful behavior committed by someone: Judges 19:24 (violent, sexual "outrageous thing"); Jeremiah 11:13 ("shameful god Baal"); Romans 1:27 (sexual "shameful acts"); Ephesians 5:4 (verbal "obscenity"); Titus 1:11 ("dishonest [disgraceful] gain").

Prophets, is often connected with God's judgment on unrepentant sinners, who often do not feel guilty or shameful.[26] Thus, the Bible treats shame as a common painful response to sin. But due to the warping effect of sin on the heart and mind, shame is not necessarily a reliable emotion. The Bible is quite clear that humans do not always feel shame when they are guilty, and they are tempted to feel shame when they are not guilty.

Satan's Fourfold Strategy for Enhancing Shame

> When evil enters the world, do you think it comes with horns and cloven feet, billowing some foul stench?
>
> Zia Haider Rahman, *In the Light of What We Know*

Satan's work in the world has been compared to a burglar who breaks into a jewelry shop in the middle of the night. Instead of stealing the items in a jewelry case the thief merely swaps the price tags. Cheap costume jewelry is given a ridiculously high price tag, while a diamond necklace is priced at a pittance. In a similar manner, Satan cannot create a new world, but he can rearrange the price tags. In the case of shame, he overinflates and underinflates the appropriate value of shame, based on guilt. Hence, humans attach more shame than they should to certain behaviors (especially those that God has forgiven), while attaching less than they should to other behaviors (especially those that have not been repented of).[27] Let's consider the various ways Satan plots to pervert truth in order to drive people away from God.

Deny or Ignore Guilt

Abusers minimize or completely ignore their guilt so that they don't feel painful, appropriate shame. Zephaniah proclaimed judgment on evil, physically violent men who had no sense of shame (Zephaniah 1:9; 3:1, 5).

---

26. See Psalm 71:13; Isaiah 7:20; Jeremiah 46:24–25; Daniel 12:2. This concept is also seen in the Septuagint with the *aischuno* word group, which most often has God as the subject and refers to the shame he brings in judgment (Gerhard Kittel, ed., *Theological Dictionary of the New Testament*, vol. 1 [Grand Rapids: Eerdmans, 1964], 189). Since physical exposure is a great source of psychological shame, God promises to strip and expose unrepentant sinners in judgment, thus shaming them for their evil (Ezekiel 23:25–29; Hosea 2:3). Hence, the Hebrew word *ervah* literally refers to nakedness, but it is often associated with shame that both leads to and results from divine judgment (Isaiah 3:17; Ezekiel 16:22–23; Habakkuk 3:13; Zephaniah 2:14; 3:5).

27. Dan Allender explains this shame confusion in terms of depravity and longings: "We ignore the issue of depravity and feel shame about our longing for what God intended us to enjoy" (*Wounded Heart*, 68).

Jeremiah also excoriates evil, ruthless abusers (Jeremiah 2:34; 7:6, 9) who were so hardened they could neither feel shame nor even blush (Jeremiah 6:15; 8:12). The inability to feel shame for real guilt helps explain the repeated prayer in the Old Testament that God would cover evil people—especially physical abusers—with shame (Psalm 35:4; 40:14; Jeremiah 3:25). Biblically, we can affirm that "shamelessness is the grossest immorality."[28]

Modern authorities on abuse perpetrators note this same dynamic, and report that abusers rarely have remorse for their actions.[29] One of the most dramatic examples of this failure of remorse is seen in the interviews French journalist Jean Hatzfeld conducted with perpetrators of the Rwandan genocide. Almost none of the interviewees took full responsibility or expressed remorse for their actions. As one of the genocide perpetrators stated, "In prison and on the hills, everyone is obviously sorry. But most of the killers are sorry they didn't finish the job. They accuse themselves of negligence rather than wickedness."[30] This failure of remorse explains why in one study of incarcerated sex offenders, 70 percent were not interested in participating in treatment programs.[31] The twisted logic goes like this: "If I do not feel shame, I am not really guilty; if I am not guilty, there is nothing to fix." Thus, failure to feel shame keeps sinners from being driven to the God who forgives guilt and lifts shame.

A jarring example of an abuser with no shame is professional boxer Mike Tyson. In 1992, Tyson was convicted and given a six-year prison sentence for raping a beauty pageant contestant. In a subsequent interview with Fox News reporter Greta Van Susteren in 2003, Tyson declared that he did not rape the woman but that she has so victimized him that "she put me in that state, where . . . now I really do want to rape her."[32] Tyson also indicated he'd like to rape the woman's mother. A few weeks after doing the interview, Tyson was again arrested for physical assault. This illustrates how lack of shame takes away a God-given restraint on sin, so that those who have no shame pollute the land with their flagrant evil (Jeremiah 3:1–3).

---

28. Christopher Flander and Werner Mischke, *Honor, Shame, and the Gospel: Reframing Our Message and Ministry* (Littleton, CO: Carey, 2020), xxii.

29. See Judith Lewis Herman, *Father-Daughter Incest*, rev. ed. (Cambridge, MA: Harvard University Press, 2000), 232.

30. Quoted in Jean Hatzfeld, *Machete Season: The Killers in Rwanda Speak* (New York: Picador, 2006), 163.

31. Reported in J. Stephen Wormith, "A Survey of Incarcerated Sexual Offenders," *Canadian Journal of Criminology* 25, no. 4 (1983): 384.

32. Quoted in Fox News, "Tyson: 'I Really Do Want to Rape Her,'" January 13, 2015, www.fox news.com/story/tyson-i-really-do-want-to-rape-her.

Take Others' Guilt

The most common manner in which abuse shame is distorted is when victims feel shame for their abusers' guilt. Children instinctively take their abusers' guilt. For instance, Antwone Fisher, whose memoir was made into an inspirational motion picture, experienced years of severe abuse of every kind before finally being abandoned to the streets by his foster parents. In his memoir, he reveals that a female neighbor first began to sexually molest him when he was three years old. He recounts the incident and his own reaction in which he innately blamed himself for the abuse:

> She has on the worst monster face you ever saw. Only this I didn't make up in my mind. It's too terrible to be true. But it is true.
>
> Then she's finished. Her voice lays empty as she says, "Where your clothes at? Put some clothes on." She sounds like it's my fault I don't have clothes on. She dresses, tosses my clothes at me, and says, "Go on outside in the shade and play. I think they makin' mud pies out there."
>
> For a second Willenda smiles. But then her face flashes a warning. She doesn't need to tell me in words. I know what it says—never, never, never tell, or something more horrible than you can even imagine will happen to you.
>
> And it wasn't really the fear of her punishing me that kept me from telling anyone all those years. It was the unspeakable shame I felt about what went on with her in the basement, and my unspeakable shame that maybe it was my fault.[33]

As we noted earlier, abuse victims also feel shame because abusers strategically shift the blame to their victims. In the biblical world, abusers (especially military and political leaders) would maim or disfigure their enemy so they'd experience long-term shame for the abusers' actions (Judges 1:6–7; 1 Samuel 1:2; 2 Samuel 10:4–5). Tamar is a tragic example of a sexual abuse victim whose life was ruined because of the shame she experienced due to her rape. Amnon was guilty, but in essence she bore his guilt and shame (2 Samuel 13:13–20).

Abuse victims can learn, by God's grace, to reject the guilt and the ensuing shame they don't deserve. For example, the apostle Peter instructed his audience of Christians who were experiencing persecution—including verbal and physical abuse—"If you suffer as a Christian, do not be ashamed

---

33. Antwone Quenton Fisher, *Finding Fish: A Memoir* (New York: HarperCollins, 2001), 44.

[accept the shame], but praise God that you bear that name" (1 Peter 4:16).[34] In other words, abuse victims can learn to reject their abusers' guilt and not take on their guilt and shame.

Reclaim Forgiven Guilt

If I were to read or hear about a local homebuilder who was offering to give a brand-new 10,000-square-foot mansion in a luxurious gated community, free of charge, along with full membership to the most prestigious country club in the area, to any criminal convicted of multiple felonies who calls their toll-free number, I would assume this ad was a tasteless joke. Criminals deserve a prison cell, not a mansion. Their crimes deserve social stigma, not country-club prestige.

It's hard for us to accept the fact that God offers to remove all of our guilt and the stigma of sin and replace it with present and eternal blessings; all freely given as a free gift apart from earning his favor through good deeds. The good news is that God's forgiveness comes to us through faith in Christ (Romans 3:21–24; Philippians 3:9). We all have sinned, so we don't deserve God's favor and blessing, and yet this is exactly the meaning of grace—*undeserved favor*.

Here's the truth that is challenging to believe: when God removes the guilt of sin, it is completely and utterly removed (Psalm 103:8–12). The beauty of the gospel of grace is that God saves not the beautiful but "the lame" and "the exiles"—turning their shame into honor (Zephaniah 3:19). Satan, the accuser, wants to keep believers from experiencing the joy of their salvation. He wants them to reclaim forgiven guilt—to continue to feel a sense of shame for sin that God has already forgiven. Abuse victims are particularly vulnerable to this satanic strategy and must resist it fiercely.

Take on Others' Harsh Judgment

A final way Satan distorts the truth regarding shame is getting us to define ourselves based on others' erroneously low view of us. Shame is the rejection and disgrace that others place on us because they find us unacceptable. Anyone who has endured middle school understands the destructive power of social shame. Several of the Hebrew words for shame in the Old Testament highlight this aspect of shame.[35] One term comes from a root

---

34. There are repeated references in 1 Peter to the verbal abuse being experienced by Christians (1 Peter 2:12; 3:16; 4:4, 14). But the verb used in 1 Peter 2:20 (*kolaphizo*) clearly refers to physical abuse—literally, beating.

35. "Honor and dishonor represent the primary means of social control in the ancient Mediterranean world" (Craig A. Evans and Stanley E. Porter, eds., *Dictionary of New Testament Background* [Downers Grove, IL: InterVarsity, 2000], s.v. "Honor and Shame").

that means "to emit a sound," and refers to scornful whispering.[36] Another word for shame comes from a word whose meaning is "to wound," but figuratively it means "to taunt or insult."[37] Another term for shame or disgrace comes from a root (*qalon*) that means "the lowering of another's social position."[38]

Many passages of Scripture speak of the unwarranted shame and dishonor that others heap onto the vulnerable or the shame that comes from physical and verbal abusers that is injected into the innocent (1 Samuel 20:34; Nehemiah 4:4; Psalm 22:6). Abuse victims are especially susceptible to the effects of social shame, for harsh judgment from others can strengthen their flawed belief that they are defective and worthless.

Lucy, the woman whose story of abuse and alcoholism we shared earlier, demonstrates the potency of this aspect of shame. By the time Lucy was a teenager, she had been molested by several male authority figures in her life, including her stepfather. She had no healthy sense of boundaries or intimacy, and she became sexually active with her boyfriend. When her abusive stepfather found out she was having sex with her boyfriend, he told her she was a worthless tramp who so disgusted him that he ordered her not to use the hallway near his room so he wouldn't have to hear or see her. Lucy said this incident did more to infuse her with a sense of utter worthlessness than did the sexual abuse itself. Satan used the contemptuous, demeaning comments of Lucy's evil stepfather to drive her further away from healthy relationships.

Strategy for Overcoming Destructive Shame

Since shame is such a pervasive, destructive force, a brief strategy for overcoming destructive shame is in order.

Experience Authentic Community

If we can share our story with someone who responds with empathy and understanding, shame can't survive.

Brené Brown, *Daring Greatly*

---

36. The Hebrew word *shimtsah* means "shame or scornful whispering; derision" (Exodus 32:25) and comes from *shemets* ("to emit a sound").

37. The Hebrew word *kalam* is used by various Old Testament writers to indicate shame or reproach and often indicates social shame (Numbers 12:14; Judges 18:7; Ruth 2:15; 1 Samuel 20:34; 2 Samuel 10:5; Isaiah 50:7).

38. R. Laird Harris, Gleason L. Archer Jr., and Bruce K. Waltke, eds., *Theological Wordbook of the Old Testament*, vol. 2 (Chicago: Moody, 1980), 799.

Shame is relational. Its power comes from the fact that God has made us relational beings who long for intimacy—to know and be known—because God himself is a relational being (Father, Son, and Spirit in an eternal love relationship). Humans are conceived, develop, and grow in relationship with others. This is why we're hurt most deeply in relationships and can only heal in relationships.[39] While it is true that our most foundational relationship is with God, we are made to experience God's love through each other. It's very difficult for survivors to receive shame-eradicating love from God until they begin to experience shame-eradicating love from another person.

> Through simply touching, more directly than in any other way, we can transmit to each other something of the power of the life we have inside us. It is no wonder that the laying on of hands has always been a traditional part of healing or that when Jesus was around, 'all the crowd sought to touch him' (Luke 6:19). It is no wonder that just the touch of another human being at a dark time can be enough to save the day.
>
> Frederick Buechner,
> *Whistling in the Dark*

Survivors often feel that if others really knew the truth about what they've experienced, people would be disgusted and want nothing to do with them. Thus they hide and allow no one to discover the shame of their abuse. In essence, shame-filled people expect others to be as disgusted with them as they are with themselves. This is a lie, of course, but the only way to eradicate this lie is experiential, not cognitive.

The survivor must risk entering into genuine—honest and real—relationships with at least one or two safe people. Curt Thompson astutely notes the challenge and power of healthy relationships. He argues that healing shame must include "the counterintuitive act of turning toward what we are most terrified of." And it is "in the *movement toward another*, toward connection with someone who is safe, that we come to know life and freedom from this prison."[40]

We are convinced that one of the best ways to facilitate healing community for abuse survivors is through small support groups led by well-trained facilitators. The need for community-based, free trauma support prompted MTS to create a ten-chapter workbook, as well as a number of other resources to train and equip mentors and small group facilitators.[41]

---

39. Secular literature also emphasizes the importance of community in overcoming the shame of abuse. See Bradshaw, *Healing the Shame*, 119–31; Herman, *Trauma and Recovery*, 214–36; Christine A. Courtois, *Healing the Incest Wound: Adult Survivors in Therapy* (New York: Norton, 1988), 244–74.

40. Curt Thompson, *The Soul of Shame: Retelling the Stories We Believe about Ourselves* (Downers Grove, IL: InterVarsity, 2015), 35, italics in original.

41. Celestia Tracy, *Mending the Soul Workbook for Men and Women*, 2nd ed. (Phoenix, AZ: Mending the Soul Ministries, 2015). The workbook can be ordered on the MTS website (www.mending

In these small, peer-led groups, facilitators model healthy vulnerability through briefly sharing their own abuse story first.[42] MTS facilitators are trained to keep the group safe and on track, practicing healthy relational interactions. In hearing others' stories, participants learn that they're not alone, nor are they shamefully "abnormal." As participants begin to share their story, they *experience* love, acceptance, and empathy in the context of the very things that previously caused them to hide in shame.

This is powerfully transformative! Authentic safe community is hard to find, yet it is God's design for the church (Acts 2:41–47). In healthy community, we're seen for who we really are, we confess our sins (James 5:16), we're emotionally honest about our joy and sorrow (Romans 12:15), we give and receive love (Romans 16:16), we meet each other's needs (Acts 2:45; Galatians 6:2), we pray for each other (James 5:16), and we patiently help each other grow (1 Thessalonians 5:14). And perhaps most significantly for healing shame, safe authentic community is the place where utmost honor (respect, dignity, value—the antitheses of shame) is given abundantly to each other (Romans 12:10; 1 Peter 2:17).[43] As survivors experience authentic community, they can increasingly recognize and reject shame-based lies and learn to embrace the truth of who they are and what God designed for them to experience in relationship with others!

Accept the Creator's Verdict: God Delights in His Children

The grace of God means something like: Here is your life. You might never have been, but you are because the party wouldn't have been complete without you. Here is the world. Beautiful and terrible things will happen. Don't be afraid. I am with you. Nothing can ever separate us. It's for you I created the universe. I love you.

There's only one catch. Like any other gift, the gift of grace can be yours only if you'll reach out and take it.

Maybe being able to reach out and take it is a gift too.

Frederick Buechner, *Wishful Thinking*

---

thesoul.org). Facilitator resources can be found at www.mendingthesoul.org/facilitator-resource-center. An online "Basic Facilitator Training" can be found at www.mendingthesoul.org/learn.

42. On the power of vulnerability in the face of shame, see Brené Brown's TED talks "The Power of Vulnerability" (www.youtube.com/watch?v=psN1DORYYV0) and "Listening to Shame" (www.youtube.com/watch?v=iCvmsMzlF7o).

43. For a discussion of specific ways churches can help sexual abuse survivors heal toxic shame, see Steven Tracy, "Abuse and Shame: How the Cross Transforms Shame," in Flanders and Mischke, *Honor, Shame, and the Gospel*, 108–12.

Survivors suffer overwhelming shame because of their abuse. One of the key steps to shedding this toxic, undeserved presence is to let God, not the abuser, define one's worth. It is surely one of Satan's greatest perversions when we ingest toxic shame and conclude that we're worthless. That is an evil lie straight from the pit of hell! God is imaged uniquely in each of us. Frederick Buechner says it this way:

> Whatever you *do* with your life—whatever you end up achieving or not achieving—the great gift you have in you to give to the world is the gift of who you alone are: your way of seeing things, and saying things, and feeling about things, that is like nobody else's. If so much as a single one of you were missing, there would be an empty place at the great feast of life that nobody else in all creation could fill.[44]

We are God's sons and daughters and our worth is proved by the fact that our Creator and Judge of the universe allowed his own precious Son to experience every form of abuse so we could have an eternal love relationship with him.

Cling to your Creator's verdict. If you have put your faith in Jesus as your Lord and Savior (Romans 10:9–10), God declares that your sins are completely forgiven—removed as far as the east is from the west (Psalm 103:12). He declares that nothing can separate you from his love (Romans 8:38–39); that he chose you for salvation before the creation of the world, based not on your innate goodness but on his rich grace (Ephesians 1:4–7); that all who put their faith in Christ have been justified. This means that when your Creator looks at you, he doesn't see your sin but rather the righteousness of Christ.[45] Thus, God does not look at you with disgust but with delight (Zephaniah 3:17). Even when you stumble and fall into sin, he disciplines out of his love; he does not punish out of disgust (Hebrews 12:6–11).

Choose today to rely on your Creator's proclamation—he delights in you![46] Many have been helped by compiling a list of biblical descriptions

44. Frederick Buechner, *The Clown in the Belfry: Writings on Faith and Fiction* (San Francisco: HarperSanFrancisco, 1992), 65.

45. This is what justification means—Christ's righteousness imputed to sinners (Romans 3:24–26). See John Stott, *The Cross of Christ* (Downers Grove, IL: InterVarsity, 1986), 182–92; Anthony A. Hoekema, *Saved by Grace* (Grand Rapids: Eerdmans, 1989), 172–84.

46. On how believers can learn to cultivate a deeper sense of God's love for and delight in them, see Brennan Manning, *Abba's Child: The Cry of the Heart for Intimate Belonging*, rev. ed. (Colorado Springs: NavPress, 2015); Brennan Manning, *The Ragamuffin Gospel*, rev. ed. (Colorado Springs: Multnomah, 2005); Robert Wicks, *Touching the Holy: Ordinariness, Self-Esteem, and Friendship*, rev. ed. (Notre Dame, IN: Ave Maria, 2007). Wicks astutely contends that the critical question of spiritual

about the truth of who they are and what they possess in Christ, and then prayerfully meditating on these truths: I am God's child, united with Christ, forgiven, reconciled to God, and blessed with every spiritual blessing in Christ. On these truths I stand.[47]

Clarify Ownership

Satan jumbles up shame so that perspective is lost with regard to what one should and should not feel shame for. Hence, when we work with survivors, we suggest creating a shame history that chronicles the times and events that produced high levels of shame. Once this is done, we invite them to ask three questions about each shameful event: (1) What do I need to own and confess? (2) What do I need to release? (3) What do I need to make right?

The first two questions involve personal responsibility: Who was responsible for what? Abuse survivors must *not* own their abuse. Subsequent choices, however, are a different matter. With God's help, a person begins to clarify which shameful events they *are* responsible for (such as numbing pain by getting drunk, acting out their abuse by abusing others, and so forth), and which ones they are *not* responsible for. Once ownership (responsibility) has been clarified, it's time to release unhealthy shame by handing it back to the abuser—described in the next step—or by specifically confessing the sins they *are* responsible for (1 John 1:9). Confession doesn't maintain one's salvation, but rather strengthens one's walk with God and a sense of God's forgiveness.[48]

Question three involves restitution. Unhealthy restitution is a counterproductive attempt to earn God's favor, but properly done, healthy restitution is a biblical concept that highlights ownership of both one's sin and the damage it has caused (Exodus 22:1–15; Leviticus 6:5; Deuteronomy 22:28–29). Restitution may involve making a long overdue apology, offering to pay for counseling for someone you've deeply damaged, or even writing a symbolic letter to someone who can no longer be contacted. Biblical restitution flows naturally from the experience of God's grace (Luke 19:1–8).

---

health is not whether we believe God loves us but whether God *likes* us. Similarly, Henri Nouwen develops the importance of growing in our sense of being God's beloved (*Life of the Beloved: Spiritual Living in a Secular World*, rev. ed. [New York: Crossroad, 2002]). His comments on how our brokenness relates to "belovedness" is particularly helpful for abuse survivors (85–103).

47. See, for instance, Steven and Celestia Tracy, appendix B, "The Father's Love Letter," in *By His Wounds: Trauma Healing for Africa* (Phoenix, AZ: Mending the Soul Ministries, 2014).

48. Anthony Hoekema notes, "When we commit a grave sin, we lose our consciousness of forgiveness; we lose our sense of peace with God. When we confess our sins to God, he awakens our sense of forgiveness and revives our assurance that we have been justified once for all" (*Saved by Grace*, 181).

Hand Shame Back to the Abuser

It's immensely empowering to hand shame back to your abuser. Theologians rarely discuss this concept, but it's a frequent biblical theme. Biblical writers often asked God to shame their abusive enemies.[49] Most likely, this meant asking God to do two things: (1) cause the abuser to be engulfed with shame to push them toward repentance, and (2) bring utter destruction on unrepentant abusers.

Asking God to utterly destroy unrepentant abusers is not an unchristian prayer.[50] We long for justice because God is a God of justice. When we experience injustice, we cry out, "That's not fair!" because it is not the way things are supposed to be. In fact, the Bible tells us that the prospect of God's full and final justice on unrepentant evil people is what allows us to endure injustice in this life without becoming bitter (2 Timothy 4:14; 1 Peter 2:23). Christians are not to seek revenge, not because it's an inappropriate desire, but because they don't have the power or authority to properly exact justice on abusers. Paul admonished the Roman believers not to take revenge on their enemies but to let God do it for them (Romans 12:19). His retribution will be perfect and inescapable. Thus, it's biblical to pray that abusers will be filled with shame so that they repent and that they'll be punished and destroyed if they do not.

Abuse survivors can apply this principle by writing down the names of their unrepentant abusers. They can then regularly pray over the list, asking God to engulf these individuals with shame so that they'll either repent or experience divine judgment if they refuse to repent.

Reject Toxic Shame and Replace with Truth

In a fallen world, we can never stop people from shaming us, but we can refuse to accept the shame they hand us. This step requires discipline and a tenacious commitment to biblical truth. With God's help, we can choose to reject the shame that abusers and others keep trying to give us. Christ is our perfect example, for even though in his public torture and execution on a cross he experienced the greatest shame imaginable in ancient culture,[51]

---

49. See Psalms 35:4–8, 24–26; 40:14; 69:19–28; 70:2; 71:13; 83:13–17.

50. Praying for God to judge unrepentant abusers may seem to be at odds with Jesus' command to love one's enemies (Luke 6:27–35), but Jesus' message and ministry repeatedly intertwine both divine love for sinners and divine judgment on the unrepentant (see Willard M. Swartley, "Luke's Transformation of Tradition: *Eirene* and Love of Enemy," in *The Love of Enemy and Nonretaliation in the New Testament*, ed. Willard M. Swartley [Louisville, KY: Westminster John Knox, 1992], 165–71).

51. On the social ignominy and shame attached to crucifixion in the ancient Roman world, see Martin Hengel, *Crucifixion* (Philadelphia: Fortress, 1977).

he focused on God and chose to disregard—to ignore—the shame created by his abusers (Hebrews 12:2).[52] He clarified the truth about who he was and deliberately rejected the illegitimate shame that others placed on him.

The first step in rejecting toxic shame is to recognize and understand the dynamics at play. Often, we're so conditioned to simply accept shame from others that we don't question it. When others treat us shamefully, we tacitly assume they must be right—we *must* deserve it. Of course, this is an incorrect assumption. It's particularly challenging to reject inappropriate shame from family members because we are conditioned to accept their judgments.

Healing toxic shame requires skillful analysis of shame messages and rejection of the shame we don't deserve.[53] For instance, Jonathan, whose abusive father tried to kill both him and his closest friend David, was shamed by his father for protecting David. Saul cursed Jonathan, called him a bastard,[54] and accused him of bringing shame on the family (1 Samuel 20:30). In truth, it was rebellious Saul who had shamed the family (15:28–35). Just because you're told by a parent that you're a bastard does not make you one. Survivors can learn to reject illegitimate shame.

It's helpful to record the implicit and explicit shame messages you've received and prayerfully reflect on the lies embedded in each one. Replace the lies embedded in these toxic messages with truths found in God's Word. What God says about us is our truth about ourselves—always. Rewrite the truths on cards and in your journal. This is an empowering way to meditate on and absorb God's living, healing words that help refute the shame embedded in these shame messages. Satan cannot create anything, so he goes after the best of what God has created. And that best is you and the ways in which you uniquely image God. Reject the shame and claim God's truths! As you practice this principle, it will get easier.

Now that we've assessed the psychological impact of shame, we'll transition to the next chapter, where we discuss the neurobiological impact of abuse.

---

52. The Greek phrase here (*aischunes kataphronesas*) is best translated as "disregarding the shame." Similarly, in Isaiah 50:6–8, God's righteous servant, who is physically abused by evil persons, is not disgraced—does not absorb the shame—because of his determination to accept God's vindication and reject the verdict of his abusers.

53. While I disagree with John Bradshaw that constructive criticism has little value (see Proverbs 12:1; 27:5–6), he does point to helpful ways to deal with unjustified criticism (*Healing the Shame*, 209–13).

54. Ronald F. Youngblood notes that the Today's English Version's "you bastard" and the New Jerusalem Bible's "you son of a rebellious slut" are vulgar but capture the Hebrew (*1 and 2 Samuel*, vol. 3 in *The Expositor's Bible Commentary*, rev. ed. [Grand Rapids: Zondervan, 2009], 209).

CHAPTER 6

The Traumatized Brain

The body knows things a long time before the
mind catches up to them. I was wondering
what my body knew that I didn't.

Sue Monk Kidd, *The Secret Life of Bees*

She is pillaged, plundered, stripped!
Hearts melt, knees give way,
bodies tremble, every face grows pale.

Nahum 2:10

B y all accounts, Elizabeth was a delightful, well-adjusted fourteen-year-old. She was actively involved in church youth group, well respected by her peers, and an A student. Yet her comfortable, safe world was shattered in one night when a homeless religious zealot named Brian David Mitchell quietly broke into her home, crept into her room, held a knife to her throat, and, after threatening to kill her and her family unless she cooperated, led her into the woods. Elizabeth's sister Mary Katherine, who shared the same room, witnessed the abduction while pretending to sleep.

During and immediately after the kidnapping, Mary Katherine stayed frozen in fear and waited several hours before notifying her parents of the abduction. When the police arrived Mary Katherine reported not recognizing the kidnapper, and yet spontaneously, four months later, she was able to recall his voice and correctly identified Elizabeth's abductor as "Immanuel," the homeless handyman who had worked on the Smart family's property just days before the kidnapping.

After abducting Smart, Mitchell led her at knifepoint several miles up the mountain, a difficult night hike that took several hours. They eventually arrived at the hidden camp of Mitchell and his wife, Wanda Barzee. Later that same day, Mitchell "married" Elizabeth and proceeded to rape her, something he would do daily, sometimes multiple times a day, for the next nine months. Elizabeth later recounted that in a mere matter of seconds, she experienced devastating trauma that resulted in stark terror, emotional numbness, loss of sense of time, shame, and despair.[1]

On the first day of Elizabeth's capture, Mitchell padlocked a lengthy chain to her leg, which prevented her from escaping; six weeks later the chain was removed. It was no longer needed. During the nine months of Elizabeth's captivity, she was so transformed by her trauma that she repeatedly thwarted would-be rescuers. Four different times, she, Barzee, and Mitchell were stopped and questioned by law enforcement authorities. The first three times police questioned the trio, Elizabeth was utterly passive and did not ask for help. Officials and witnesses later recounted that she was "zombie-like," and that when asked if she specifically needed help, "there was nothing, just blank stares."[2]

Finally, on March 11, 2003, witnesses reported seeing Mitchell and possibly Elizabeth in Sandy, Utah. Police immediately responded and found the trio. For forty-five minutes, the officers interviewed Elizabeth, who repeatedly, adamantly, and "petulantly" denied who she really was.[3] The final break came after an officer showed her an Elizabeth Smart missing person poster and said, "Tell us you're Elizabeth Smart." She responded with, "Thou sayest," evidencing the impact that Mitchell's bizarre religious brainwashing had had on her.[4]

How can one make sense of this account? This story, like all abuse accounts, is comprehensible only when we understand the impact of trauma on the brain. Such knowledge is essential for family members and caregivers, as well as abuse survivors. One of the most consistent and tragic effects of abuse is seen when survivors deduce there is something deeply wrong with them, that they are "abnormal," "crazy," or "weak" because of confusing symptoms such as powerlessness, "freezing," emotional numbing, impaired memory, panic attacks, nightmares, and distorted beliefs. Quite the contrary: these are *normal* responses to *abnormal* events.

---

1. For Elizabeth's own account, see Elizabeth Smart, *My Story* (New York: St. Martin's, 2013).

2. Maggie Haberman and Jeane MacIntosh, *Held Captive: The Kidnapping and Rescue of Elizabeth Smart* (New York: Avon, 2003), 237, 240.

3. Haberman and MacIntosh, *Held Captive*, 299.

4. For a fascinating comparison of Elizabeth's abuse and its impact and Brian David Mitchell's childhood abuse and its impact, as well as the unique resources Elizabeth had that most survivors don't experience, see Lucinda A. Rasmussen, "Victim and Victimizer: The Role of Traumatic Experiences as Risk Factors for Sexually Abusive Behavior," *Israel Journal of Psychiatry and Related Sciences* 49, no. 4 (2012): 270–79, https://cdn.doctorsonly.co.il/2013/03/06_-Victim-and-Victimizer.pdf.

History of Trauma Research

The English word *trauma* is a transliteration of a Greek word that means "physical wound," and is used in Luke 10:34 to refer to the physical injuries the Good Samaritan treated. In modern usage, *trauma* can also refer to internal, nonphysical wounds. Psychologically, *trauma* refers to emotional distress resulting from catastrophic life events that are overwhelming and create a sense of fear and vulnerability to harm.[5]

While an almost limitless spectrum of experiences can be traumatic, including illness, loss of loved ones, natural disasters, vehicular accidents, and abuse, deliberate human-caused trauma is by far the most traumatic. It is more personal and in a very real sense more diabolical. Being struck unconscious by lightning is traumatic and can be life-threatening, but we don't have a personal relationship with lightning. It is an "act of nature," and it occurs due to physics. In contrast, if you were knocked unconscious by your parent or a friend, you would experience *much* higher levels of trauma. For instance, one study found that males who had been raped were seventeen times more likely to develop PTSD (posttraumatic stress disorder) than males who had experienced a natural disaster.[6]

In the past few decades, much insightful research has enlarged our understanding of trauma, particularly its biological effects.[7] However, modern trauma research actually began in the late nineteenth century when the French neurologist Jean-Martin Charcot began a formal study of the disorder called hysteria.[8] The word *hysteria* comes from the Latin word for

---

5. Charles Figley defines trauma as "an emotional state of discomfort and stress resulting from memories of an extraordinary, catastrophic experience which shattered the survivor's sense of invulnerability to harm" (*Trauma and Its Wake: The Study and Treatment of Post-Traumatic Stress Disorder* [New York: Brunner/Mazel, 1985], xviii).

6. Rachel Yehuda, "Post-Traumatic Stress Disorder," *New England Journal of Medicine* 346 (2002): 108–14, see table 2 on p. 110.

7. The body of literature on the neurobiology of trauma is vast, but here are a few resources we have particularly benefited from: J. Douglas Bremner, "Traumatic Stress: Effect on the Brain," *Dialogues in Clinical Neuroscience* 8, no. 4 (2006): 445–61; Jim Hopper, "Neurobiology of Trauma & Sexual Assault," lecture at Tufts University, July 2015, www.youtube.com/watch?v=dwTQ_U3p5Wc; Jamie Marich, *Trauma Made Simple: Competencies in Assessment, Treatment and Working with Survivors* (Eau Claire, WI: PESI, 2014); David J. Morris, *The Evil Hours: A Biography of Post-Traumatic Stress Disorder* (New York: Houghton Mifflin Harcourt, 2015); Babette Rothschild, *Revolutionizing Trauma Treatment*, vol. 2 in *The Body Remembers* (New York: Norton, 2017); William M. Struthers, Kerryn Ansell, and Adam Wilson, "The Neurobiology of Stress and Trauma," in *Treating Trauma in Christian Counseling*, ed. Heather Gingrich and Fred Gingrich (Downers Grove, IL: InterVarsity, 2017), 55–77; Bessel A. van der Kolk, *The Body Keeps the Score: Brain, Mind, and Body in the Healing of Trauma* (New York: Viking, 2014).

8. In outlining the history of trauma research, we've drawn heavily on Judith Lewis Herman, *Trauma and Recovery: The Aftermath of Violence from Domestic Abuse to Political Terror*, rev. ed. (New

"uterus" and was thus believed to be an exclusively female psychological disorder characterized by bizarre symptoms such as extreme fear or anxiety, loss of memory, convulsions, extreme emotional excitability, and physical or emotional paralysis. Charcot's careful investigation led him to conclude that hysteria's origins were psychological.

Two other notable physicians, Sigmund Freud and Pierre Janet, also began studying hysteria at that time and came to similar conclusions—namely, that hysteria is caused by psychological trauma. Shortly before the twentieth century began, researchers discovered that symptoms of hysteria could be relieved when women disclosed their traumatic memories and the feelings associated with them and put them into words. This treatment became the cornerstone of modern psychotherapy.

After doing extensive case studies with women in Vienna, Freud reached the conclusion that hysteria was most often the result of a particular kind of trauma, specifically sexual abuse.[9] Before long, however, Freud shrank back in horror at the implications of his conclusion. The women he analyzed were consistent in their accounts of sexual abuse, so Freud had to somehow account for their stories and symptoms. He reasoned that surely well-mannered, upper-class men would not commit incest with their daughters, so he dismantled his theory of the origins of hysteria. He reasoned instead that these women had invented fantasies of sexual relations with their fathers.[10]

This was the basis for Freud's famous Oedipus complex theory in which young children are said to innately desire erotic relations with their opposite-sex parent. Thus, he reasoned, women who suffered hysteria were ultimately to blame for their symptoms. It was all in their heads! Sadly, Freud, like many others, decided it was easier in the end to blame the victims instead of the perpetrators.

While Freud and many of his fellow researchers reversed their theories and blamed women's fantasies, not trauma, for hysteria, political events

York: Basic Books, 1997), 10–28. J. David Kinzie and Rupert R. Goetz offer an excellent summary of the history of trauma research ("A Century of Controversy Surrounding Posttraumatic Stress Stress-Spectrum Syndromes: The Impact on DSM-III and DSM-IV," *Journal of Traumatic Stress* 9, no. 2 [1996]: 159–79).

9. Sigmund Freud developed this theory most fully with the publication of *The Aetiology of Hysteria* in 1896 (included in *The Standard Edition of the Complete Psychological Works of Sigmund Freud*, ed. James Strachey [Stanford, CA: Meridian, 1997]).

10. Various writers have documented Freud's dramatic reversal in his theory of hysteria, including Judith Lewis Herman, *Father-Daughter Incest*, rev. ed. (Cambridge, MA: Harvard University Press, 2000), 7–12; J. M. Masson, *The Assault on Truth: Freud's Suppression of the Seduction Theory* (New York: Farrar, Straus, and Giroux, 1984); Florence Rush, *The Best-Kept Secret: Sexual Abuse of Children* (New York: McGraw-Hill, 1980), 80–104.

in the twentieth century would undermine their chauvinistic theories.[11] During World War I, thousands of soldiers were withdrawing from battle lines due to hysteria-like symptoms (amnesia, physical or emotional paralysis, uncontrolled weeping, inability to speak), even though they didn't appear to be physically injured. One military psychologist coined the term *shell shock* to describe these symptoms, assuming that these soldiers were suffering from neurological damage caused by being too close to exploding artillery.

Further exploration was done and revealed that most of the men suffering from shell shock hadn't been subjected to artillery or other explosions after all; they had, however, experienced psychological trauma from war. Sadly, a few medical authorities persisted in arguing that these soldiers were moral invalids and cowards who should be dishonorably discharged. Thankfully, the research continued on for decades, exploring the nature and origins of hysteria and shell shock, until a new consensus finally emerged in the mid-twentieth century: these trauma symptoms were *not* the result of moral weakness; *anyone* subjected to high levels of psychological stress could develop long-term symptoms.[12]

It is often easier for people to validate the reality of long-term psychological harm experienced by soldiers exposed to combat than to validate the psychological harm experienced by abuse victims. Research on stress and PTSD does show, in fact, that the trauma effects of abuse and combat are strikingly similar. For instance, in one study of eight survivor groups, the group with the highest stress response symptoms was Vietnam combat veterans; the group with the second highest symptoms was victims of sexual assault.[13]

Furthermore, ten stressor variables that increase PTSD were identified. Vietnam veterans typically experienced nine out of ten of these stressors; victims of physical or sexual abuse also experience most of these.[14] And all other forms of relational trauma can create long-term trauma damage. For instance, various studies show that fifty years *after* combat or POW

---

11. Pierre Janet was the only major nineteenth-century researcher who continued to maintain that hysteria was the result of trauma. His views were unpopular but are now widely accepted and foundational for much of current trauma theory.

12. See Kinzie and Goetz, "A Century of Controversy," 171; see also Richard A. Kulka et al., *Trauma and the Vietnam War Generation: Report of Findings from the National Vietnam Veterans Readjustment Study* (New York: Brunner/Mazel, 1990), 268–70.

13. John P. Wilson, W. Ken Smith, and Suzanne K. Johnson, "A Comparative Analysis of PTSD among Various Survivor Groups," in *Trauma and Its Wake*, 142–72.

14. Wilson, Smith, and Johnson, "Comparative Analysis of PTSD," 149–53.

imprisonment, many veterans still experience severe trauma symptoms.[15] Child abuse survivors exhibit similar long-term harm. For instance, a study of adults who had experienced childhood abuse revealed that one-third met the criteria for lifetime PTSD.[16] Prolonged or repeated trauma in particular, whether chronic childhood abuse, chronic domestic violence, or prison camp incarceration, can produce such long-term and pronounced damage that many experts argue it deserves a new diagnostic category.[17]

Basic Neurobiological Impact of Trauma

My emotions were bigger than my body, and thus, my mind slipped. Wavered. Traveled to someplace I now understand is tantamount to psychosis, but at the time, it just seemed like I'd entered a room filled with night water.

Lidia Yuknavitch, *The Misfit's Manifesto*

The reason that trauma, whether experienced by a captured pilot in a POW camp or a disempowered wife in a well-appointed kitchen, can have such profound and long-lasting impact is simply this: trauma alters the brain. And if those changes persist over time, long-term deleterious impact is inevitable. The psalmist affirms God's intricate handiwork of the human brain and nervous system by declaring that we are "fearfully and wonderfully made" (Psalm 139:14).

Let's begin with a simple neurobiological overview (see figure 3). While an adult brain weighs a mere three pounds, it is "the most complex known structure in the universe," directing the function of our entire body through the nervous system.[18] The brain and spinal cord compose the "central nervous system," and the nerves that enervate all other organs compose the "peripheral nervous system." The peripheral nervous system, in turn,

---

15. See Wybrand Op den Velde et al., "Current Psychiatric Complaints of Dutch Resistance Veterans from World War II: A Feasibility Study," *Journal of Traumatic Stress* 3, no. 3 (1990): 351–58; Nancy Speed et al., "Posttraumatic Stress Disorder as a Consequence of the POW Experience," *Journal of Nervous and Mental Disease* 177, no. 3 (1989): 147–53.

16. Cathy Spatz Widom, "Posttraumatic Stress Disorder in Abused and Neglected Children Grown Up," *American Journal of Psychiatry* 156 (1999): 1223–29, https://ajp.psychiatryonline.org/doi /pdf/10.1176/ajp.156.8.1223.

17. Judith Lewis Herman argues for the existence of a form of posttraumatic disorder in survivors of prolonged or repeated trauma she calls "complex PTSD" ("Complex PTSD: A Syndrome in Survivors of Prolonged and Repeated Trauma," *Journal of Traumatic Stress* 5, no. 3 [1992]: 377–91).

18. Catherine Zuckerman, "The Human Brain, Explained," *National Geographic*, October 15, 2009.

has two subdivisions: (1) the somatic (related to the body), which controls voluntary movement, and (2) the autonomic, which controls involuntary systems such as hormone production, heartbeat, and digestion.

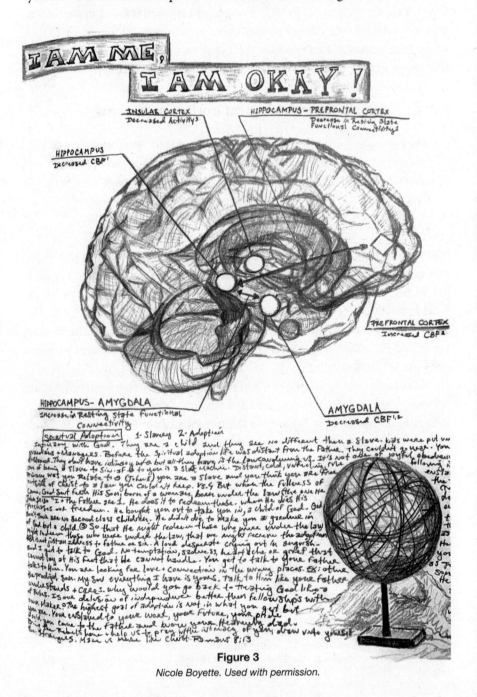

Figure 3

Nicole Boyette. Used with permission.

Our nervous system facilitates very complex exchanges between the various parts of the brain and organs. For instance, the thalamus in the center (core) of the brain functions as a relay station, receiving data (nerve impulses) from elsewhere in the body and relaying them on to the relevant portion of the brain. The hypothalamus, in the core of the brain, also communicates vital messages to the body. It does this by releasing hormones (its own and ones it stimulates to be released from the pituitary gland) into the bloodstream. These hormones, in turn, stimulate various physiological processes that govern a wide variety of activities, including emotions, reproduction, respiration, digestion, and stress responses.

The cerebrum is the largest part of the brain and is found in two hemispheres that perform the "higher" functions: it processes and interprets data from our five senses, controls speech and reasoning, and regulates emotion, memory, and learning. The cerebrum contains the prefrontal cortex, which directs the "executive" function of the brain, including analyzing, planning, self-monitoring, self-assessing, and self-control. Surprisingly, this "higher" functioning part of our brain makes up only 30 percent of what is contained in our skull.[19]

The brain is intricately wired to identify and respond to stressors and potential threats, adapting its response based on past experiences. The brain's primary goal is to return one's body to a healthy state of functioning (homeostasis). Thus, moderate levels of stress are actually beneficial because they stimulate the body to grow resiliency. Unfortunately, certain stress is so great that it overwhelms the brain, preventing it from returning to a healthy functioning state.

The brain's stress response is particularly guided by what is called the HPA axis—the hypothalamic-pituitary-adrenocortical systems—which automatically stimulates action in response to perceived danger and releases powerful, quick-acting hormones that prepare the body to facilitate safety. The amygdala, part of the limbic system, is the brain structure that plays a pivotal role in processing fear and emotion. When sensory data (information from the five senses) is received that suggests danger, this sensory data is sent to the amygdala, which in turn activates the HPA axis—the "fight or flight" response. This response is so rapid that the amygdala launches a somatic reaction to potential danger before a person has a conscious sense of threat.

Furthermore, the chemicals released in the stress response impede the functioning of the prefrontal cortex, the part of the brain that facilitates

---

19. See Van der Kolk, *Body Keeps the Score*, 55.

reasoning, decision making, and memory. This HPA override of our higher cognitive processing is obviously beneficial, as it immediately moves us out of harm's way. In many situations, the additional time needed to assess, evaluate, and problem-solve would increase risk.

This same cognitive override, however, can also work against trauma victims, because they usually blame themselves for not being able to think clearly enough to escape the danger, for not being able to give a coherent account of the trauma, or for having hazy memories of the traumatic event itself. For instance, it is normal for people in the midst of an HPA trauma threat response to be unable to remember their home address, phone number, or the location of the door out of their home. Such cognitive blocks have nothing to do with intelligence or dishonesty.[20]

A personal account of the amygdala's stress response occurred when Steve worked on a cattle ranch in southern Arizona. Early one morning, as he reached into a thick clump of green beans, he suddenly jerked back his hand and found his heart racing. He had no idea why. He hadn't *chosen* to jerk his hand away and obviously hadn't commanded his heart to beat twice its normal pace. In actuality, his involuntary muscle contractions were precipitated when his amygdala sensed danger before his prefrontal cortex could process the information. It was a disorienting experience. Within seconds, he saw a six-foot Mojave rattlesnake coiled up asleep at the bottom of the bush. Immediately the snake woke and angrily struck at him several times. Sensory data from Steve's eyes and possibly fingertips (to this day he doesn't know if he actually touched the snake) had been sent to the amygdala, which immediately sprung his body into protective action. For several weeks afterward, Steve continued to startle when he saw "snakelike" sticks on the ground. Finally, his brain and nervous system returned to a calm, homeostasis, and this rattlesnake episode became little more than a sensational story to tell!

However, some events are so stressful that they overwhelm the neurological system such that the brain cannot return to homeostasis. If the stress symptoms persist for more than a month, they lead to a condition called posttraumatic stress disorder (PTSD),[21] in which the traumatic event

20. More specifically, neuroimaging studies reveal that trauma causes the amygdala to be hyperresponsive and the medial prefrontal cortex (which controls decision making and retrieval of long-term memory) and the hippocampus (which plays a major role in learning and memory) to be hyporesponsive and thus diminishes their capacity (Lisa M. Shin and Israel Liberzon, "The Neurocircuitry of Fear, Stress, and Anxiety," *Neuropsychopharmacology* 35 (2010): 169–91.

21. Using the DSM-5 criteria, lifetime risk for PTSD is 8.7 percent (American Psychiatric Association, *Diagnostic and Statistical Manual of Mental Disorders, Fifth Edition* (Washington, DC:

precipitates intrusive symptoms (nightmares and flashbacks). emotional numbing, hyperarousal (rapid breathing, heart palpitations, and the like), negative changes in cognitions and mood, and extreme avoidance of all trauma reminders.[22]

In summary, virtually everyone who experiences a traumatic event suffers stress afterward. For some, the stress symptoms lessen with time and the memory of the traumatic event is stored as an unfortunate event belonging to the past; for others, however, the memory and emotions connected with the trauma begin to take on a life of their own. Then as the trauma is replayed over time, the distress increases.[23] In essence, the amygdala is the body's "alarm system" that activates when danger is perceived. Thus when the brain is too overwhelmed to return to normal functioning, the amygdala launches threat responses prematurely and repeatedly. The body's alarm system can't shut off!

It is essential to understand that *fear based on perceived threat, not actual injury or the reality of threat,* is what drives the body's stress responses. The role of fear, even in the absence of any physical injury whatsoever, in creating long-term neurological harm can be clearly seen in the effects of the Chowchilla school bus kidnapping in 1976. This story also illustrates the manifold impact of the traumatized brain.

On a summer afternoon in Madera County, California, three men kidnapped a busload of twenty-six children ages five to fourteen, along with their bus driver, as they returned from a swim outing at the fairgrounds. The victims were driven around for eleven hours before being entombed inside a moving van buried in a rock quarry. After sixteen hours underground in an eight-by-sixteen-foot space, the victims dug their way out and were found in a remote park nearby. The survivors were taken to a nearby hospital, where they were all pronounced to be in good physical condition.

American Psychiatric Publishing, 2013), 276. Several population studies of trauma and PTSD suggest that, based on various risk factors, approximately 25 percent of those exposed to an extreme stressor event will develop full-blown PTSD. See Bonnie L. Green, "Psychosocial Research in Traumatic Stress: An Update," *Journal of Traumatic Stress* 7, no. 3 (1994): 345; Bessel A. van der Kolk, "The Psychological Consequences of Overwhelming Life Experiences," in *Psychological Trauma*, ed. Bessel A. van der Kolk (Washington, DC: American Psychiatric Publishing, 1987), 10–12.

22. *Diagnostic and Statistical Manual*, 271–72.

23. See Bessel A. van der Kolk and Alexander C. McFarlane, "The Black Hole of Trauma," in *Traumatic Stress: The Effects of Overwhelming Experience on Mind, Body, and Society,* ed. Bessel A. van der Kolk, Alexander C. McFarlane, and Lars Weisaeth (New York: Guilford, 1996), 7–9. Babette Rothschild also notes the way trauma is reexperienced in those with PTSD. She places particular emphasis on the somatic (body) symptoms (*The Body Remembers: The Psychophysiology of Trauma and Trauma Treatment* [New York: Norton, 2000], 6–7).

They were warmly welcomed home and supported by their community; the entire ordeal had lasted less than forty hours.

In spite of the brevity of the experience and the lack of physical injury, the psychological effects on the children were devastating. Lenore Terr conducted an extensive study of twenty-five of the twenty-six kidnapped children five to thirteen months after the ordeal and did a follow-up study four years after that.[24] The latter study revealed that, even five years after being kidnapped for less than forty-eight hours, all twenty-five children continued to exhibit posttraumatic stress symptoms, including somatic disturbances, nightmares, and extreme anxiety. Most of the children continued to experience profound embarrassment and humiliation for the extreme vulnerability they felt during the kidnapping. Thirteen suffered from an irrational fear that a fourth kidnapper was still at large, though there was never any evidence supporting this. Almost five years after the kidnapping, twenty-three of the children suffered from severe pessimism, believing their futures would be greatly limited, and twelve children continued to suffer from nightmares about dying.[25]

Other studies of long-term effects reveal similar findings.[26] Even short-term trauma that produces little or no physical injury can create long-term emotional and psychosomatic damage.

Three Primary Brain Effects of Trauma

Judith Lewis Herman identifies four primary trauma effects: hyperarousal, intrusion, constriction (numbing), and disconnection.[27] (We will address disconnection in the next chapter.) All four of these trauma effects have a neurobiological basis that is well-documented in scientific research, particularly through the use of brain scans.

While the Bible was obviously written in a prescientific era, it is signif-

---

24. See Lenore C. Terr, "Children of Chowchilla: A Study of Psychic Trauma," *Psychoanalytic Study of the Child* 34 (1979): 547–623; Lenore C. Terr, "Chowchilla Revisited: The Effects of Psychic Trauma Four Years after a School-Bus Kidnapping," *American Journal of Psychiatry* 140, no. 12 (1983): 1543–50.

25. In fact, terrifying nightmares of dying increased over time. In the initial study, only five children reported these, whereas twelve reported them in the second study four to five years after the kidnapping (Terr, "Chowchilla Revisited," 1547–48).

26. See Henk M. van der Ploeg and Wim Chr. Kleijn, "Being Held Hostage in the Netherlands: A Study of Long-Term Aftereffects," *Journal of Traumatic Stress* 2, no. 2 (1989): 153–69.

27. See Herman, *Trauma and Recovery*, 35–73. For the characteristics of trauma observable in children, see Lenore C. Terr, "Childhood Traumas: An Outline and Overview," *American Journal of Psychiatry* 148, no. 1 (1991): 12.

icant that various passages describe somatic responses to fear that are virtually identical to the ones identified by modern trauma researchers. These include heart palpitations, muscle trembling, quivering lips (Habakkuk 3:16; Nahum 2:10), nightmares and shaking (Job 4:13–14), altered blood flow resulting in pale skin (Daniel 5:6), muscle weakness and dry mouth (Psalm 22:15), mental confusion (Mark 16:8), and emotional constriction (Genesis 45:26 ESV).

Hyperarousal

Hyperarousal, as the name suggests, is a condition in which the nervous system is perpetually aroused long after the traumatic event has ended.[28] This results in chronic hypervigilance and anxiety,[29] increased heart rate, sleeplessness, irritability, high startle response, and nausea.

What is particularly disconcerting about hyperarousal is that a seemingly endless number of events or experiences can unexpectedly and often subconsciously remind the brain of the trauma event and trigger a physiological response. For example, a woman walking down the street may suddenly experience a panic attack. Her heart begins to race and she feels nauseous for no apparent reason. A particular cologne's scent, a stranger's face, or even a color in a store window may have subconsciously reminded her brain of the man who abused her when she was a child, alerting her body to respond as though she were in immediate danger. Hyperarousal triggers are quite complex and may bear no obvious or logical connection to the trauma one has experienced. This makes hyperarousal even more frustrating for survivors, tempting them to shut down emotionally and disconnect so they won't experience these symptoms.

Amy is a beautiful, accomplished professional artist and is one of our most effective Mending the Soul facilitators. She delights in guiding others through the same healing path she has walked. Amy sketched this image (see figure 4) to make visible the terror she experienced as a child. Her childhood abuse happened suddenly and without warning and was perpetrated by a man her family loved and trusted. Amy's mother was the "safe" parent and yet didn't believe her attempts to disclose:

---

28. On the neurobiology of hyperarousal, see Shin and Liberzon, "Neurocircuitry of Fear, Stress, and Anxiety."

29. On the research noting the correlation between anxiety disorders and abuse, see Anna C. Salter, *Transforming Trauma: A Guide to Understanding and Treating Adult Survivors of Child Sexual Abuse* (Thousand Oaks, CA: Sage, 1995), 171–75.

Figure 4: Terror

My mom is back and we're safe. We share with her what happened. She doesn't seem to believe us. Why? She thinks I'm spinning a tall tale, which I was known to do, but this is real. This really happened. This man who I think was Papa Jerry hurt us. Why doesn't she believe me? She does nothing. We go to bed. I pull the sheet over my whole body and tightly wrap the edges under my arms and feet. I can't breathe . . . If I don't move a muscle and lie still, then no one will know I am here. I am invisible. I feel safe.

Intrusion

The traumatic incident becomes encoded in a confusing form of memory, which pushes spontaneously into consciousness by means of *intrusion*—both as flashbacks during waking states and as traumatic nightmares during sleep.[30] Eighty to 90 percent of PTSD patients report insomnia, and 50–70 percent report nightmares.[31] Flashbacks tend to be quite vivid, highly emotional, and decontextualized—that is, they tend to be fragments of traumatic memories that lack a larger, more coherent context.[32] With both forms of intrusion, the trauma memory of the past continues to haunt the present—thus abuse victims relive the past trauma over and over again until the past is adequately integrated with the present. Intrusive memories are profoundly traumatic, for they often have all the vividness and emotional intensity of

30. John N. Briere, *Child Abuse Trauma: Theory and Treatment of the Lasting Effects* (Thousand Oaks, CA: Sage, 1992), 21. Briere notes that these nightmares are typically one of two types: (1) graphic and realistic dreams of the original abuse or (2) symbolic representations of the original abuse trauma, involving themes of violence, violation, and danger. The first type appears soon after the abuse and often decreases in frequency over time, whereas the second type is both a short-term and long-term trauma effect.

31. Erin Koffel, Imran S. Khawaja, and Anne Germain, "Sleep Disturbances in Posttraumatic Stress Disorder: Updated Review and Implications for Treatment," *Psychiatric Annals* 46, no. 3 (2016): 173–76.

32. Tania Storm, Marianne Engberg, and Christian Balkenius, "Amygdala Activity and Flashbacks in PTSD: A Review," *Lund University Cognitive Studies* 156 (2013): 6.

the original trauma and yet, like hyperarousal triggers, often bear no obvious or logical connection to the trauma one has experienced.[33]

Timmy was a small boy who was fondled by a male neighbor. In therapy he was asked to write a letter indicating what he wanted to happen to his abuser. His letter poignantly illustrates the link between intrusion (nightmares), hyperarousal (fear and nausea), and a desperate desire to regain power and safety:

> I feel that he should go to jail until he dies because I think that whoever touches children should be punished as worse as you can and that he should die. Because I hate him. It makes me afraid of other men. It makes me afraid to go to bed sometimes because I don't want to dream about him. He makes me cry every time I think about him. And his name now makes me want to puke.

Another aspect of intrusion is compulsive reexposure to or reenactment of the trauma. This behavior is a subconscious attempt to overcome the powerlessness experienced during and after the original trauma. Because reenactment doesn't bring a survivor the sense of mastery and power they desperately need, it can easily become compulsive, increasingly dangerous, and harmful.[34]

Children often act out (reenact) their abuse over and over again in play. Gabriel, age seven, came into counseling because of a severe stutter he developed after witnessing his father commit suicide. During the first six weeks of play therapy, Gabriel would begin each session by elaborately setting up a train set. He would then tie his father to the tracks and pretend to run over him with the train. His play was silent and repetitive and had a robotic, purposeful feel. He knew what he needed to do in order to integrate his trauma and gain a sense of mastery over his powerlessness as he witnessed, frozen in time, the death of a father he loved dearly. It was unspeakable. If his father had to die, then instead of helplessly standing by and watching, he would be the one in control.

---

33. See Ron Zaczek, *Farewell, Darkness: A Veteran's Triumph over Combat Trauma* (Annapolis, MD: Naval Institute Press, 1994), 160–63. Bessel A. van der Kolk and Alexander C. McFarlane note that, over time, "triggers for intrusive traumatic memories may become increasingly more subtle and generalized; what should be irrelevant stimuli may become reminders of the trauma" ("The Black Hole of Trauma," in *Traumatic Stress*, 10).

34. Diana Russell gives a lucid account of this dynamic in her detailed case study of a South African woman who as a young girl was chronically abused by her grandfather ("The Making of a Whore," *Violence Against Women* 1 [1995]: 77–98).

As Gabriel continued in counseling and began to face and integrate his grief in the form of fear, rage, and dark, traumatic memories, his stuttering dramatically improved. During his last session, he was asked to draw one more picture (see figure 5). He threw himself into the task! Gabriel's

Figure 5

dinosaur picture depicted healthy resolution as he acknowledged ongoing fear but healthy mastery over it. His dinosaur (intrusion) still came into his room at times, but now, when it did, Gabriel would jump up, grab it by the tail, and fling it "all the way to New York." Gabriel had integrated his trauma enough to move from subconscious reenactment to a connected sense of mastery.

Another example of reenactment is when adolescent teens who have been sexually violated as children become highly promiscuous in a subconscious attempt to regain a sense of control. We counseled a young faith leader who had been raped as an adolescent by her sister's former boyfriend. After the rape, this boy would watch her house at night and repeatedly break into her bedroom when her family was away. She felt powerless to stop him. At the time, she did not feel safe enough or have enough support to tell anyone. Within a year, this young woman had become wildly promiscuous. She described walking into a room full of people and deciding which man she would seduce that night into having sex with her. Through counseling, she was able to make connections between her childhood sexual abuse and her subsequent destructive, sexualized patterns. She began to heal as she went to the source of her pain and integrated the original traumatic memories, which gave her a healthy sense of control over the very act that had made her feel so powerless.

Constriction/Numbing

> As we grow older, the riveting, dis-empowering feelings that grabbed us during moments of our abuse do not change with knowledge, awareness, or new experiences. They are locked inside until we return to release them.
>
> Jeanne McElvaney, *Spirit Unbroken: Abby's Story*

Constriction or "numbing" is a somatic, cognitive, and emotional response to trauma. Emotionally, constriction involves an internal shutting down of feelings so that, instead of feeling pain, one simply feels nothing. Externally, it has been described as a "reduced responsiveness to the outside world."[35] Emotional numbing can take place at the time of the trauma itself, in which time seems to slow down, pain subsides, and a state of detached calm reigns.

Numbing can also be experienced as pulling away from one's feelings and even one's own self (sometimes called "dissociation").[36] Abuse survivors, especially those who experienced chronic or severe abuse, often describe dissociation by recounting that during the abuse it felt as though they had left their body and were somewhere in the room, watching what was happening to them. Elizabeth's Smart's "zombie-like" appearance when she was questioned by a police officer is a classic manifestation of severe constriction or dissociation.

Numbing can also take place long after the original trauma, when abuse survivors shut down all feelings (pleasurable and painful). No feelings seem preferable to painful and confusing feelings.

Emotional numbing is complex—it can be a conscious choice or an automatic response to extreme stress.[37] For some survivors, emotional numbing proves insufficient to ease their distress, so they resort to drugs and alcohol to chemically numb their pain.[38] While numbness or dissociation at the time of the trauma can provide immediate emotional protection, over the long haul it comes at a high price. One abuse expert wisely observes, "Dissociation . . . does not take the abuse away; it takes the person away."[39]

Another aspect of constriction is physical and involves immobility or "freezing." Trauma expert Peter Levine argues that the freeze response is "the single most important factor in uncovering the mystery of human trauma." He insightfully sees the actual physical freeze as paradigmatic of the way in which the energy of trauma is "frozen" and "remains trapped

35. Ronnie Janoff-Bulman, "The Aftermath of Victimization: Rebuilding Shattered Assumptions," in *Trauma and Its Wake: The Study and Treatment of Post-Traumatic Stress Disorder,* ed. Charles R. Figley (New York: Brunner/Mazel, 1985), 16.

36. It should be noted that dissociative disorders involve more than just impairment of emotion. They are also characterized by disruption or impairment of normal consciousness, memory, identity, motor control, and perception (see *Diagnostic and Statistical Manual,* 291).

37. Joyanna L. Silberg notes that the exact etiology of dissociation is unclear, but it is "likely a complex interaction of psychobiological, familial, and cultural processes" ("Fifteen Years of Dissociation in Maltreated Children: Where Do We Go from Here?" *Child Maltreatment* 5, no. 2 [2000]: 127).

38. See Salter, *Transforming Trauma,* 239–40. A large study of adults being treated for alcohol dependency revealed that almost 60 percent of the participants reported lifetime abuse (Christopher Rice et al., "Self-Reports of Physical, Sexual and Emotional Abuse in an Alcoholism Treatment Sample," *Journal of Studies on Alcohol* 62, no. 1 [2001]: 114–23). Richard A. Kulka et al. discovered that almost 40 percent of male Vietnam combat veterans have a lifetime prevalence of alcohol abuse or dependence (*Trauma and the Vietnam War Generation,* 274–75).

39. Salter, *Transforming Trauma,* 246.

in the nervous system where it can wreak havoc on our bodies and spirits" until it's released.[40]

Freezing results from the exact same HPA (hypothalamic-pituitary-adrenocortical) hormonal response as "fight or flight," and some experts argue that of the three responses, it is the most common. Mary Katherine Smart's inability to get out of bed to report her sister's abduction is a clear example of trauma freeze. Freezing can be experienced on a wide continuum—from extreme physical weakness, to immobility, to physical paralysis, to loss of consciousness. In cases of extreme trauma, freezing involves physical numbing and reduced sensitivity to pain. Again, it is essential to recognize that the freeze response is *autonomic and biological, diminishing or crippling a survivor's ability to feel or otherwise protect themselves*—diabolically leaving the abuser with all the potency.

Disrupted Memory

Another confusing aspect of constriction is *memory disruption*.[41] Our memory is complex and involves several different parts of the brain. It is also not static. It develops and is consolidated over the course of time. There are four types of memory—two are conscious (explicit memory) and two are subconscious (implicit memory). Mary Katherine's delayed recollection of the kidnapper's voice is a stark example of the mutable nature of memory in general and trauma memory in particular. How trauma impacts memory is one of the most misunderstood aspects of emotional numbing.

- **Explicit memory** is the conscious recall of past events or facts and involves two categories: (1) *declarative memory*, which involves the recollection of data such as the location and operating hours of a restaurant and the like, and (2) *episodic or autobiographical memory*, which is far richer and includes chronology, context, and a measure of emotional coloring.
- **Implicit memory** strongly guides and influences our lives, but these aren't memories we can consciously recall, as they sit just under the surface of our consciousness. Our implicit memories are separated

40. Peter A. Levine, *Waking the Tiger: Healing Trauma* (Berkeley, CA: North Pacific, 1997), 16, 19.

41. Some of the best works on the impact of abuse on memory are Jennifer J. Freyd, *Betrayal Trauma: The Logic of Forgetting Childhood Abuse* (Cambridge, MA: Harvard University Press, 1996); Peter Levine, *Trauma and Memory: Brain and Body in a Search for the Living Past* (Berkeley, CA: North Atlantic Books, 2015); Charles L. Whitfield, *Memory and Abuse: Remembering and Healing the Effects of Trauma* (Deerfield Beach, FL: Health Communications, 1995); Linda M. Williams and Victoria L. Banyard, eds., *Trauma and Memory* (Thousand Oaks, CA: Sage, 1999).

into two categories: (1) *procedural memory* (motor memory) such as that used in riding a bike and (2) *emotional memory*, which is highly somatic (experienced in the body).

Emotional memory is what abuse survivors experience during hyperarousal—they are experiencing their brain's memory of what their bodies felt like during the trauma. When the amygdala senses fear, released hormones (particularly dopamine and norepinephrine) inhibit the hippocampus, impeding its ability to encode explicit memory.

Trauma memories are largely emotional memories encoded as intense bodily sensations. They tend to be fragmentary and lack a broader context and time sequence. In other words, the trauma memories are still in the abuse victim's brain but aren't stored as a unitary whole that can be recalled as a historical event; rather, they're stored as fragments of sensations, which can then trigger severe trauma symptoms, even if the person has a very limited recollection of the traumatic event.[42]

Thus, it's not surprising when rape victims struggle to recount various details of their attack. They have gaps in their memory and cannot accurately recount a detailed chronology for the rape.[43] Furthermore, severe trauma can also impair one's short-term memory capacity in general, even decades after the trauma.[44] Abuse survivors have intense emotional memories but weak episodic memories, making their experiences difficult to understand or share with others.

Not only does trauma impair memory of the past, but it also creates cognitive distortions regarding the future. These are often quite dramatic. We saw in the case of the children kidnapped in Chowchilla, that five years after the kidnapping, twenty-three of the children suffered from severe pessimism, believing their futures would be greatly limited. Other studies

42. See Bessel A. van der Kolk and Rita Fisler, "Dissociation and the Fragmentary Nature of Traumatic Memories: Overview and Exploratory Study," *Journal of Traumatic Stress* 8, no. 4 (1995): 511–12, 519–20. On the negative impact of trauma on autobiographical memory in general, see Miyuki Ono et al., "A Meta-Analytic Review of Overgeneral Memory: The Role of Trauma History, Mood, and the Presence of Posttraumatic Stress Disorder," *Psychology of Trauma: Theory, Research, Practice, and Policy* 8, no. 2 (2016): 157–64.

43. For an excellent practical discussion of the impact of trauma on memory as applied to the Brett Kavanaugh Supreme Court hearings, see Jim Hopper, "How Reliable Are the Memories of Sexual Assault Victims?" *Scientific American*, September 27, 2018, https://blogs.scientificamerican.com /observations/how-reliable-are-the-memories-of-sexual-assault-victims.

44. Isabelle Blanchette et al., "Long-term Cognitive Correlates of Exposure to Trauma: Evidence from Rwanda," *Psychological Trauma: Theory, Research, Practice, and Policy* 11, no. 2 (2019): 147–55; Vida Mirabolfathi et al., "Affective Working Memory Capacity in Refugee Adolescents," *Psychological Trauma: Theory, Research, Practice, and Policy*, advance online publication, February 10, 2020.

have shown that abuse survivors catastrophize the future and anticipate that they will experience much worse things in the future than the painful things they've experienced in the past.[45] Thus, it is essential for abuse survivors and their caregivers to be aware of the challenge of viewing the world and the future realistically and to focus on reorienting their minds based on the promises and character of God.

The most extreme form of impaired memory is *amnesia*, in which survivors have no conscious memory of the traumatic events. The past few decades have seen considerable debate regarding the possibility and accuracy of repressed memories,[46] but it is simply irrefutable that extreme trauma can cause partial, as well as complete, blockage of memories. In other words, abuse can deaden not only one's feelings but also one's knowledge of the truth.

Lenore Terr, an expert on childhood trauma, has done extensive case studies of seven adults who had repressed memories of childhood abuse for years—abuse that was later confirmed—and her studies demonstrated that abusive trauma can create complete memory blockage that may last for decades. While she found that memories of abuse can be subject to corruption and are occasionally false, it was rare for spontaneously recovered abuse memories to be substantially false.[47]

One of the most powerful scientific validations of the reality and frequency of repressed abuse memories was conducted by Linda Meyer Williams. She obtained the records of 206 women who as children had received hospital treatment after being sexually assaulted. She was able

---

45. David Rubin, "Schema-Driven Construction of Future Autobiographical Traumatic Events: The Future Is Much More Troubling Than the Past," *Journal of Experimental Psychology* 143, no. 2 (2014): 612–30.

46. The False Memory Syndrome Foundation (FMSF), founded in 1991, has been particularly vocal in proclaiming that childhood abuse rarely, if ever, results in repressed memories. In reality, there is no "false memory syndrome." David Calof documents the defamatory, destructive tactics used by the FMSF against psychologists and researchers identified with abuse and trauma treatment ("Notes from a Practice Under Siege: Harassment, Defamation, and Intimidation in the Name of Science," *Ethics and Behavior* 8, no. 2 [1998]: 161–87). Stephanie J. Dallam notes the way the FMSF and some of its leaders have justified abuse and enabled abusers ("Unsilent Witness: Ralph Underwager and the FMSF," *Treating Abuse Today* 7, no. 1 [1997]: 27–39).

47. Lenore Terr notes several aspects of false memories: (1) they can be planted by suggestions from outside agents, such as parents or counselors; (2) they more commonly come when someone is receiving help from a counselor who works exclusively with abuse victims; and (3) they will not create the cluster of trauma symptoms that are caused by actual childhood abuse (*Unchained Memories: True Stories of Traumatic Memories, Lost and Found* [New York: Basic Books, 1994], 159–62). The last point is the most important in determining the historical veracity of abuse memories, for false trauma memories do not have the same kind of collective emotional and somatic effects that real ones do.

to set up interviews with 129 of these women seventeen years after the abuse had taken place. The research method was rigorous. The interviewers didn't know anything about the circumstances of the women's abuse; they simply asked questions about their memories of abuse and recorded them. Williams found that 38 percent had no recollection of the abuse they had experienced seventeen years earlier.[48] Other studies of contact abuse and neglect also confirm this finding. A significant percentage of those who experience childhood abuse will experience partial or total memory loss of the abuse.[49]

Traumatic amnesia is relatively rare for those abused in adulthood and for those who suffer a single-event (onetime) trauma. It is most often experienced by children, because they typically have the greatest sense of powerlessness, are most dependent on their abuser—especially if the abuser is an adult—and have the fewest cognitive skills to make sense of the abuse. In fact, after studying survivors of childhood incest, one abuse researcher concluded that "massive repression [of memory] appeared to be the main defensive resource available to patients who were abused early in childhood and/or who suffered violent abuse."[50] Sadly, some childhood abuse is simply too overwhelming for a child to deal with.

The Faces of Trauma

The following verbal and visual images—all of which resulted from the trauma of abuse—further illustrate various aspects of the traumatized brain, particularly emotional constriction and powerlessness.

---

48. See Linda Meyer Williams, "Recall of Childhood Trauma: A Prospective Study of Women's Memories of Child Sexual Abuse," *Journal of Consulting and Clinical Psychology* 62, no. 6 (1994): 1167–76. It's highly unlikely that these women had not actually forgotten the abuse but rather were simply too embarrassed to mention it to the interviewers, since 68 percent of the women who had no memory of the documented abuse told of other sexual assaults they had experienced.

49. Cathy Spatz Widom and Suzanne Morris conducted a study of 653 individuals with a child-hood history of officially documented physical, sexual, and neglect abuse. Some twenty years after the abuse, they interviewed these individuals and found that only 64 percent of the women who had been sexually abused recalled being abused, and only 16 percent of the men recalled being sexually abused ("Accuracy of Adult Recollections of Childhood Victimization, Part 2: Childhood Sexual Abuse," *Psychological Assessment* 9, no. 1 [1997]: 42). Of those with documented histories of childhood physical abuse, 40 percent reported not remembering being abused (Cathy Spatz Widom and Suzanne Morris, "Accuracy of Adult Recollections of Childhood Victimization, Part 1: Childhood Physical Abuse," *Psychological Assessment* 8 [1996]: 418).

50. Judith L. Herman and Emily Schatzow, "Recovery and Verification of Memories of Childhood Sexual Trauma," *Psychoanalytic Psychology* 4, no. 1 (1987), 11; see also Freyd, *Betrayal Trauma*, 9–11.

Jilian—The Reality of Powerlessness

Jilian's college pastor referred her to counseling after she began exhibiting out-of-control, self-destructive behavior that developed shortly after sexual abuse. In her first few sessions, Jilian had a difficult time talking about her feelings with her counselor, but she was able to powerfully convey

them through expressive art. Here is a self-portrait Jilian created early in her healing (see figure 6).

It's dark, foreboding. Exposed. Jilian is being sucked into a vortex that threatens to engulf her vulnerable and exposed body. The pull is much stronger than she is, highlighting her helplessness. A black chain holds her securely, just above the abyss. She described the chain as representing her parents' steady love and faith, which was the only thing keeping her from complete self-destruction.

For her counselor, the remarkable part of this family was that Jilian's parents were high-profile faith leaders in the community, and yet they could see past their daughter's sexual misbehavior, to her needs—extending love, understanding, and grace, which proved in the end to be greater than the downward pull of her shame. Today this talented and compassionate woman is a respected licensed social worker, serving trauma survivors in a community-based setting where she uses her story to set others free.

Figure 6

Brianna—The Danger of Numbing

Brianna came to counseling when she was twelve years old. She had not experienced physical or sexual abuse, but years of chronic emotional neglect by her alcoholic mother and emotionally paralyzed father had taken a heavy toll. In addition to her experience of neglect, her parents had divorced a few years earlier, and she silently blamed herself. Her loving stepmother brought her into counseling because she was exhibiting sexually precocious behavior at school.

Figure 7: This is me on the outside

Figure 8: This is me on the inside

As part of her initial evaluation, Brianna drew herself as a smiling, beautiful girl on a stage, "making people laugh" (see figure 7 on page 169). She described herself as entertaining her family and friends in the seats below. The therapist was intrigued by this depiction and asked Brianna if she always felt this way, as the drawing appeared artificial and contrived. Brianna shook her head soberly, turned the picture over, and began to draw again. Initially, she seemed to be drawing the same portrait, but new details made this one dramatically different. In this second picture, she drew her face saturated with sad, dark emotions (see figure 8 on page 170). Small images depicting abandonment and traumatic memory obscured her facial features. In this picture, so contradictory to the first, she stood utterly alone in the darkness—no smile, no friends, no lights, no applause.

How could a young, gifted girl perceived by her family as sweet and innocent be so sexually aggressive on the playground that school officials threatened expulsion unless she received professional counseling? Why would a young girl, in a span of less than twenty minutes, draw two strikingly antithetical self-portraits? The answer is that the trauma Brianna had experienced in her short eleven years of life had caused her to begin to split. She had developed two radically different personas. One was the acceptable, happy, public self everyone loved and applauded; the other was the hidden, troubled self no one clearly saw or understood.

Brianna was successfully able to dissociate (internally pull away) from her pain and loneliness to such an extent that she fooled everyone around her, including herself. In essence, Brianna learned to live by dying to her inner truth. But numbing and denying feelings, longings, and memories don't eradicate them; they just become more deeply buried, more influential, and less comprehensible.

After several months Brianna's family discontinued her counseling. They felt it was "making her worse." Tragically, three years later, Brianna showed up again in her counselor's office. She had been sexually victimized in a nine-month-long relationship with her thirty-five-year-old tennis coach. No one knew. Brianna's story illustrates the way abuse creates shame, emotional constriction, and powerlessness, which greatly increases one's vulnerability to increasing levels of harm. Trauma must be dealt with or it will reproduce itself.

Abby—The Death of Desire

Abby illustrates how emotional constriction resulting from abuse can strangle healthy desires. As a survivor of chronic neglect and spiritual abuse, she articulately described to me the gradual process of dying to desires:

Growing up in a large, blended family with a severely disabled sibling, constant financial struggles, and frequent moves, there was no shortage of disappointment. My parents would tell me they were sorry and wished it could be different, but the unspoken message was, "But it's not okay to feel sad about it."

That shame message taught me early on that desire was a dangerous thing. I was an intense, driven child with great initiative and sky-high dreams. My dreams served as an escape from reality. In my late teens, however, the harshness of my reality became stronger than my dreams. Escape mechanisms only work for a period of time until, like a drug, one needs something stronger. When dreams couldn't provide an escape any longer, I turned to deadness.

Soon after high school, my parents convinced me to turn down a college scholarship and stay home to support the family physically and financially. I convinced myself it was actually what I wanted to do. At first, I was happy. It was all in a spiritual context, and I felt like the family hero. I worked several jobs and was able to earn quite a bit of money. Every time my family had a financial crisis, they asked me for money, which soon turned into many thousands of dollars. Saying no was not an option. That meant an hour lecture from Scripture telling me how selfish I was.

Eventually I became depressed. I stopped my pursuits and hobbies because I knew I could never pursue them anyway. I saw that there was no way out, and I felt trapped forever. I eventually reasoned that desire was my real enemy. I thought to myself, *If I don't desire, then I can't be disappointed.* I was desperate to escape my misery, and I distinctly remember choosing to die to desire.

A few years ago, I began to realize just how dead I was. One Sunday after church, I saw a woman talking to a young mother and her baby. As the woman reached out to hold the baby, I could see tremendous desire and expression on her face. My next rush of thoughts shocked me. *Why would anyone feel excited about holding a baby?* I instinctively backed away. Strong desires felt threatening to me. Then I felt scared.

Until then, deadness had been an attractive solution, a shelter to the relentless, unending pain in my heart. But was this the consequence? I had always loved children! How could I feel so turned off by someone who was excited about holding a baby? That night, I learned that my deadness was a choice and that it was sin because it affected other people. It clashed with the very nature of what God had designed me to be.

Today, desire versus deadness is still one of my biggest struggles.

It often feels like desires and passions are dangerous things that should be avoided at all costs. Yet God continues to work on me and show me more and more ways to repent. I know he can't use an Abby who is dead, so I'm willing to keep changing, even though it's painful.

"Hope deferred makes the heart sick, but a longing fulfilled is a tree of life" (Proverbs 13:12). Hope is a prerequisite for life. Abby's story highlights the role of choice in healing. She courageously identified the wounds that precipitated her choice to numb and deaden herself to desire so she could open them to the healing touch of God through others in her life. She chose life!

Johnny—Death to Hope

Johnny sought counseling because he was failing in school. He demonstrated no motivation and showed visible signs of depression.[51] Johnny experienced considerable traumatic stress as a result of his parent's emotional neglect and his father's harsh, physically abusive methods of punishment. In therapy, he drew a picture of a dejected, lonely boy with his hands in his pockets (see figure 9). He repeatedly drew himself alone, outside the circle of friends and family. The boy in the picture had no feet, evidencing an inability to act—probably reflecting Johnny's feelings of powerlessness. The caption read, "Here I am, just standing there." Clearly, this was a boy who had become dead to hopes, dreams, and relationships.

Figure 9

Hope

We're created with the capacity to live life abundantly (John 10:10); to experience deep joy and delight in God and his creation (Psalm 34:8).[52] Jesus is

---

51. Depression is a common symptom of both physical and sexual abuse and is particularly associated with the latter. Anna Salter notes that "depression appears to be found more often in adult survivors of child sexual abuse than any other symptom (*Transforming Trauma*, 165).

52. The best treatment of this concept is John Piper, *Desiring God: Meditations of a Christian Hedonist*, rev. ed. (Sisters, OR: Multnomah, 1996). Piper's thesis is that the noblest, most godly

truth incarnate (John 14:6), and life comes to those who face their pain and embrace God's Word as their absolute truth—about themselves, others, and their future (John 8:32–45; 14:6). When we deaden ourselves to the truth, we are ultimately declaring that God is not big enough for the real world in which we live.[53]

Christianity is rooted in the proclamation that the risen Jesus gives hope to the world (Matthew 28:5–10). God is the omnipotent (all-powerful) healer of the universe; nothing is too hard for him (Genesis 18:14). He delights in giving strength to the destitute (Isaiah 40:9–31). In short, God made us in his image so we could be fully alive, offering the world a visible picture of who God is. Abuse happens in relationship, and thus healing can only happen in relationship. We're made to know and be known. Abuse threatens to maim and destroy the very purposes for which we were created.[54] We must not let that happen!

As we were typing the final words of this chapter, Jumah Patrick, one of Mending the Soul's African directors, called with an update from the Democratic Republic of the Congo. He had just finished a trauma training for three hundred Christian leaders in Ituri Province, a region that currently has some of the worst conflict in all of East Africa. During the training, armed rebels stormed the city Jumah was in, while Congolese soldiers and local militia chased the rebels. Jumah and his trainees watched as a full-scale firefight unfolded around them. Within an hour, fifteen people were killed, and finally all the rebels had fled or been shot. Jumah described this as one of the most terrifying events he has ever experienced.

During the attack, Jumah froze in fear and literally thought he was having a heart attack. He couldn't think rationally or move in a normal way (classic neurobiological responses to trauma). That night, he had a vivid nightmare of a woman attacking him with a knife. He woke up the next morning anxious and exhausted, but he put into practice some of the very strategies we teach to stabilize trauma symptoms: (1) to lower his intense anxiety, he went to the bathroom and bathed his head in cold water. This mild sensory shock helps stop hyperarousal and turn off the brain's alarm;

---

motivation for all human behavior is pleasure. All of life should be driven by the prospect of experiencing joy and delight in God.

53. Dan Allender states this well: "Denial is an affront to God. It assumes that a false reality is better than the truth. It assumes that God is neither good nor strong enough" (*Wounded Heart*, 202).

54. Alistair McFayden argues that abuse is so damaging because it threatens to distort the abuse survivor's experience of enrichment, life, and abundance that come from our Creator, who wants to bless his creation (*Bound to Sin: Abuse, Holocaust, and the Christian Doctrine of Sin* [Cambridge: Cambridge University Press, 2000], 238.

(2) he began deep breathing and remembered the "square breath" model—inhale, hold, exhale, hold (all for four seconds each). Repeat four times. He began to calm down and relax; (3) he pulled out his journal and did an expressive art exercise we teach to traumatized children who are having nightmares;[55] and (4) when he awoke the next morning, he organized a small group of pastors to talk through their feelings and the trauma effects they had experienced. They made the invisible visible and drastically reduced their symptoms.

Jumah was exhausted but able to function again; he was no longer overwhelmed. While he knew he would have to do more work to recover from this terrifying experience, he had an activated and effective healing plan. Trauma happens to us, and we have no choice—healing is something we choose that not only mends our individual brokenness but positively changes our relationships as well. Our traumatized brains can mend! In chapter 8, we will flesh out our trauma healing model.

In this chapter, we focused on the internal impact of abuse, but abuse has an impact that reaches far beyond the individual survivor. In the next chapter, we'll address the fourth primary effect of abuse as we seek to understand how trauma disconnects us from our most important relationships.

55. Celestia Tracy and Kayla Tracy, *My Journal for the Good and Hard Stuff* (Phoenix, AZ: Mending the Soul Ministries, 2018), 51–52.

CHAPTER 7

Disconnection

What had been created in a state of desperation had become
permanent. The isolation itself had been a guarantee
that nothing would ever rock my existence again.

Linda Olsson, *The Memory of Love*

One of the most blasphemous consequences of injustice,
especially racist injustice, is that it can make a child
of God doubt that he or she is a child of God.

Desmond Tutu, *No Future without Forgiveness*

My friends and my companions avoid
me because of my wounds;
my neighbors stay far away.

Psalm 38:11

Ingrid is an articulate forty-year-old accountant who works for a Christian publishing company. She is highly regarded by her coworkers and gets excellent performance reviews. While working for a Christian organization has been very positive for her, it hasn't erased the dramatic impact of her childhood abuse. Most of her coworkers would be astounded to know how much shame and isolation she experiences every single day. Ingrid was never beaten, physically neglected, or raped, and yet the abuse she did experience was astoundingly destructive. When Ingrid shared her story with me, I was struck by the way her abuse had shattered her relationships, leaving her feeling isolated and hopeless. She described her abuse and its impact:

When I was a child, my mother was an alcoholic and extremely unstable. She wasn't a happy drunk. She was the kind of drunk who would pick a fight with my dad and end up crying and talking to me about her sex life. From the time I was seven, she was very sexually explicit when talking to me about my dad or about other guys she found attractive. At their drinking parties, she would flirt shamelessly with all the men. But when I became an adolescent and found pleasure in attracting boys of my own, she would call me a slut.

My mother had insatiable intimacy needs that she has used me to fill all my life. Up until I was in high school, she would make me sleep in her bed when my dad was out of town. She would spoon with me and kiss me on my neck while she rubbed her body up and down my back. Whenever she found the opportunity, she would touch my clothed breasts (up to and including this past Christmas). From the time I was fifteen, I just tried to stay out of the house as much as possible. My skin crawls every time my mother touches me.

My dad, on the other hand, was my "safe" parent. He was completely uninterested in me or anything I did and let my mother rule the house. I think he wanted to be a good father, but he didn't know how to protect us from her. Because he was uncomfortable with any show of emotion whatsoever, we experienced extreme levels of emotional neglect. As long as we kept the conversation light and everyone acted happy, he was fine. I haven't had any major trauma in my life. My parents took relatively good care of us, provided a nice house, took us on vacations, and bought us things when we wanted them. Even so, the abuse and neglect I experienced left me with a deep-rooted shame that I will probably never fully recover from.

The worst part, though, is that I picked up where my parents left off. I've abused myself in ways far worse than my parents ever did. For as long as I can remember, I've had this little voice inside me that cries, *Something is wrong here!* I have a sense of mournful sadness and a feeling of utter worthlessness. I have never felt like a woman or an adult. My life is a giant mistake, and I'm wasting precious oxygen. I loathe myself and have thought about suicide at least once a day for the past twenty years, because I believe it would be best for everyone concerned if I just went away.

I spend every minute of every day feeling like no one loves me and that society in general is deeply disappointed with my mere presence. I want more than anything else to be completely invisible. I have sabotaged most of my personal relationships. The only friends I still have are the persistent ones who don't take it personally when I don't call them. Ever.

It is nearly impossible for me to believe that God loves me, even though I want him to. Most of the time I feel like he couldn't possibly have chosen me to be one of his children, and I won't be surprised if I die and find out my name isn't written in the Book of Life. I don't reach out

to him for help because I'm convinced he wouldn't be interested. I love
my family beyond words, but I find it hard to accept their love in return
because I don't think I deserve it. It's so hard, in fact, that up until recently,
I became enraged inside when my daughter would pick up my hand and
kiss it while we were driving in the car.

It's mentally and physically exhausting to constantly fight the lies
that I've believed for so long that they have become my truth. I don't know
what, if anything, is left of the person I started out to be.

The Relational Impact of Sin and Abuse

The genocide pushes into isolation those it could not push into death. Some
people have lost their taste for kindness.

Bertha Mwanankabandi, Rwandan genocide survivor, *Life Laid Bare*

Why would a woman like Ingrid, who has a loving husband, a devoted
daughter, and numerous close friends, pull away from the very people who
mean the most to her? Why is she triggered with rage by her daughter's
affection? After hearing several years of teaching and preaching on the love
of God, why would she continue to believe she wasn't saved or that she was
an exception to God's love? Why would a bright, talented woman have no
clear sense of who she is?

While the specific relational effects of abuse vary based on the type
and severity of abuse,[1] the simple fact is that most abuse produces profound
long-term relational impairment. Research clearly shows that survivors are
much more likely to be in unhealthy relationships in which they are revictimized, have a harder time making social adjustments, and have a much
more difficult time establishing relational trust than those who have not
been abused.[2] Additionally, abuse survivors are more likely to experience
divorce or separation.[3]

---

1. Pamela C. Alexander, "The Differential Effects of Abuse Characteristics and Attachment in the
Prediction of Long-Term Effects of Sexual Abuse," *Journal of Interpersonal Violence* 8, no. 3 (1993): 346–62.

2. David DiLillo and Patricia J. Long, "Perceptions of Couple Functioning among Female
Survivors of Child Sexual Abuse," *Journal of Child Sexual Abuse* 7, no. 4 (1999): 59–76; Liz Grauerholz,
"An Ecological Approach to Understanding Sexual Revictimization: Linking Personal, Interpersonal,
and Sociocultural Factors and Processes," *Child Maltreatment* 5, no. 1 (2000): 5–17; Gina P. Owens
and Kathleen M. Chard, "Cognitive Distortions among Women Reporting Childhood Sexual Abuse,"
Journal of Interpersonal Violence 16, no. 2 (2001): 178–91; David A. Wolfe et al., "Factors Associated
with Abusive Relationships among Maltreated and Nonmaltreated Youth," *Development and
Psychopathology* 10, no. 1 (1998): 61–85.

3. Reported in David Finkelhor et al., "Sexual Abuse and Its Relationship to Later Sexual

The debilitating effects of abuse on relationships are apparent not only in adults but also in children. Research shows that abuse leaves its mark sooner rather than later as children and adolescents who have been abused are more distrustful and isolated and have fewer intimate friendships than their nonabused peers.[4]

Abuse creates further isolation for survivors because of the discomfort people feel around abuse survivors. Typically, nonvictims don't want to be reminded of the unpleasant aspects of the world. They are uncomfortable facing overwhelming evil and more prone to distance themselves from the damaging effect that abuse has on those around them, thus distancing themselves from even the subject of abuse and victims of abuse.

The relational impact of abuse is so substantial and consistent that disconnection from other people is considered one of the primary effects of trauma.[5] When victims disconnect from others, they cannot enter into intimate relationships because they keep others at a safe distance. We noted in chapter 2 that a major aspect of being made in God's image is that humans cannot thrive apart from intimate relationships—relationships where we're safe and connected and known for who we really are. Those of us who've experienced nurturing intimacy have the capacity to offer it to others. Unlike animals, humans simply cannot thrive in isolation. We're designed by our Creator to bond with others; we have a deep ache to know and be known, to love and be loved.

Connection is our most fundamental human drive and helps explain the potency of sexual addiction, for instance, where one is driven to compulsively connect with others while at the same time is relationally hiding because of the effects of early abuse and ever-spiraling shame. Thus, one of the greatest tragedies of sin in general and abuse in particular is that it undermines and shatters intimate relationships, which often leads to nefarious compulsions and addictions that confound and confuse us and those who love us.

Satisfaction, Marital Status, Religion, and Attitudes," *Journal of Interpersonal Violence* 4, no. 4 (1989): 384, 392; Diana E. H. Russell, *The Secret Trauma: Incest in the Lives of Girls and Women* (New York: Basic Books, 1986), 118–19.

4. See Candice Feiring, Saul Rosenthal, and Lynn Taska, "Stigmatization and the Development of Friendship and Romantic Relationships in Adolescent Victims of Sexual Abuse," *Child Maltreatment* 5, no. 4 (2000): 317–19; Suzanne Salzinger et al., "The Effects of Physical Abuse on Children's Social Relationships," *Child Development* 64, no. 1 (1993): 169–87; Jeffrey G. Parker and Carla Herrera, "Interpersonal Processes in Friendship: A Comparison of Abused and Nonabused Children's Experiences," *Developmental Psychology* 32, no. 6 (1996): 1025–38.

5. See Judith Lewis Herman, *Trauma and Recovery: The Aftermath of Violence—From Domestic Abuse to Political Terror*, rev. ed. (New York: Basic Books, 1997), 51–73.

Genesis 1–3 offers a dramatic example of this. The creation account eloquently describes the dazzling way God designed humans for intimacy. In Genesis 2:18, we're told it was not good for Adam to be alone, so God made a helper to complement him as his equal.[6]

When God created the woman Adam longed for, God took her from Adam's rib, suggesting the most intimate kinship or connection possible between a man and a woman. Moses described the relationship of the man and the woman as a "one flesh" relationship—a relationship so intimate that Adam and Eve enjoyed complete physical and emotional oneness. They were naked in each other's presence without the slightest twinge of shame (Genesis 2:25). Their physical nakedness was surely indicative of complete openness and transparency with each other. Strikingly, this is the only Old Testament passage in which physical nakedness is unambiguously positive.[7] The creation account ends with a shout of delight over the intimacy that Adam and Eve enjoyed as God's divine gift.

However, the celebration was abruptly shattered the moment they sinned (Genesis 3:6–13). All of the natural intimacy Adam and Eve had previously enjoyed reversed. Instead of delighting in each other's bodies in an ongoing celebration of love, they covered their genitals in shame;[8] instead of mutually ruling over creation as intimate allies, Adam shifted blame onto Eve, attacking her for his failure; instead of continuing in an unending dance of intimacy with God, they hid from him in the bushes.

Sin disrupts the safety and mutuality of intimacy, turning lovers into enemies and allies into adversaries. Abuse, more than any other type of sin, has a particularly menacing effect on relationships. By definition, abuse is the misuse of one's power to harm another person. Abuse is a frontal assault on another person's worth and dignity, and hence it can cripple one's ability to experience healthy relationships.

---

6. The Hebrew word used here for "helper" (*ezer*) does not connote inferiority. This term is used twenty-nine times in the Hebrew Scriptures, and in every other usage except for one, it is used of God himself. The phrase "helper suitable for him" indicates the woman corresponded to Adam and complemented him as an intimate equal.

7. See Victor P. Hamilton, *The Book of Genesis: Chapters 1–17* (Grand Rapids: Eerdmans, 1990), 181. Hamilton notes three major uses of *nakedness* in the Old Testament, but all three are connected with some form of humiliation.

8. The fact that Adam and Eve used fig leaves showed how desperate they were to overcome their shame, since fig leaves are rough in texture and would have been quite irritating, particularly in the genital region. Victor Hamilton suggests that Adam and Eve used fig leaves because they were the largest leaves in the garden (*Book of Genesis*, 191).

Three Dynamics Leading to Disconnection

Abuse fractures relational intimacy in three ways. Think back to our discussion in chapter 5 about shame's powerful role in disrupting intimate relationships. Because shame makes victims feel utterly defective and worthless, it propels them to hide not only from God and themselves, but from others as well. Reread Ingrid's story at the beginning of this chapter and highlight her statements that are laced with shame. In these brief paragraphs, you'll clearly see the connection between shame and isolation as it is—a devolving, destructive cycle.

Shattered Assumptions

Abuse shatters many of the false assumptions that give us security, such as bad things don't happen to good people; God doesn't allow evil people to harm the innocent; if I pray, abuse will stop; people are basically good; and the like. Abuse causes people to feel unsafe, fearful, and powerless, and because of it, the world is increasingly viewed as hostile and dangerous. Doesn't this brief discussion help you understand why survivors feel safer when they avoid vulnerability, stay out of intimate relationships, maintain overt or covert control, and enjoy fierce independence? Judith Lewis Herman describes the effects of shattered assumptions:

> Traumatized people feel utterly abandoned, utterly alone, cast out of the human and divine systems of care and protection that sustain life. Thereafter, a sense of alienation, of disconnection, pervades every relationship, from the most intimate familial bonds to the most abstract affirmations of community and religion. When trust is lost, traumatized people feel they belong more to the dead than to the living.[9]

Jeremiah, a godly prophet with a difficult assignment from God, illustrates the way abuse shatters assumptions and creates relational disconnection. He had the dubious task of telling a rebellious people—whom he knew would not listen—that God was sending an inescapable divine judgment (Jeremiah 1:19; 11:6–13). When Jeremiah delivered God's dire message to the high priest and other religious leaders, he was physically and verbally abused (20:1–2, 10). Jeremiah knew intellectually that God was all-powerful, just,

---

9. Herman, *Trauma and Recovery*, 52.

and worthy of praise (20:11–13), yet the effects of his abuse caused him to pull away from God, believing that God had deceived him (20:7). Jeremiah went on to curse the day he was born and the man who reported his birth to his father (20:14–18). Abuse shatters our assumptions about life and tempts us to pull away defensively from God and others.

Mistrust

Shattered assumptions lead naturally to mistrust, which is one of the most consistent consequences of abuse. Relational trust is the cornerstone for intimacy. All forms of abuse create mistrust, though sexual abuse, particularly incest—one of the greatest imaginable forms of betrayal—often produces the greatest level of mistrust and significantly increases various trauma effects.[10]

Abuse victims' mistrust is often so pervasive that it outweighs other types of consequences. David Finkelhor, based on his extensive research with child sexual abuse victims, makes this observation:

> [Abuse] victims report that the lasting trauma of incest is not so much sexual as emotional. The scar that stays the longest is a deep inability to trust others, particularly men. They find themselves suspecting other motives, feeling that they are being used. They have a hard time opening up or getting close, because they fear all men want from them is sex.[11]

Trauma victims' mistrust often involves far more than mistrust of their abusers. In fact, abused children often feel significantly more anger and mistrust toward the nonabusive parent for not protecting them than they do toward the abusive parent. For instance, women who in childhood were molested by their fathers often report much more anger toward their mothers than their fathers. They are also able to recall some positive memories of their abusive fathers but virtually none of their mothers.[12] Abuse victims' mistrust is often globalized, infecting and undermining every relationship.

Tineal illustrates this dynamic. A children's choir director had sexually abused her over a twelve-month period. In therapy, she drew a two-framed

10. See Pamela M. Cole and Frank W. Putnam, "Effect of Incest on Self and Social Functioning: A Developmental Psychopathology Perspective," *Journal of Consulting and Clinical Psychology* 60, no. 2 (1992): 174–84; Christine A. Courtois, *Healing the Incest Wound: Adult Survivors in Therapy* (New York: Norton, 1988), 111, 215–16; Jennifer J. Freyd, *Betrayal Trauma: The Logic of Forgetting Childhood Trauma* (Cambridge, MA: Harvard University Press, 1996), 3–11.

11. David Finkelhor, *Sexually Victimized Children* (New York: Free Press, 1979), 214.

12. See Judith Lewis Herman, *Father-Daughter Incest*, rev. ed. (Cambridge, MA: Harvard University Press, 2000), 30–31, 81–89, 184.

picture of herself behind bars (see figure 10). In the first frame, she is turned away. She is bleeding from a knife stuck in her back. This symbolizes the horrible betrayal she had experienced by a "man of God" who was supposed to protect her but instead violated her. Her hands are tied behind her back and a heavy ball and chain traps her leg, powerfully illustrating her sense of powerlessness. In the second frame, she stands alone, stoically staring out from behind the bars, hiding the knife and her bloody wound. Ironically, the prison bars cover her mouth.

The betrayal she experienced from one man—and the subsequent mistrust—had led to isolation from all others. The sad irony is that when Tineal drew this picture, her abuser was actually the one isolated behind bars in a state prison, and yet she was the one who felt isolated and imprisoned. Her journey out of the bondage of powerlessness began by speaking her truth in a safe relationship. Only then could the knife be identified, disclosed, and removed, and her wound washed so she could begin to heal.

Figure 10

Numbing/Constriction

> She feels gutted, with nothing inside of her and nothing to say, cannot think anything, cannot feel anything. If there is sorrow inside of her, she can't tell. She feels like something has been pulled out of her guts, roots and all, some alder tree, and where it was before, a nauseous emptiness, but that is all she can feel, no sorrow, nothing.
>
> Gabriel Tallent, *My Absolute Darling*

Since one of the primary trauma effects is numbing—shutting down emotionally—it's easy to see how survivors often experience little or no relational intimacy. Numbing means that abuse victims don't feel anything, whether it's pain or pleasure. They don't feel their own feelings, and thus they can't recognize or embrace the feelings of others. In shutting down to avoid pain, abuse survivors miss out on love. As C. S. Lewis so eloquently notes, those who shut down their emotions to avoid pain pay an astronomical price for their emotional safety:

To love at all is to be vulnerable. Love anything, and your heart will certainly be wrung and possibly be broken. If you want to make sure of keeping it intact, you must give your heart to no one, not even to an animal. Wrap it carefully round with hobbies and little luxuries; avoid all entanglements; lock it up safe in the casket or coffin of your selfishness. But in that casket—safe, dark, motionless, airless—it will change. It will not be broken; it will become unbreakable, impenetrable, irredeemable . . . The only place outside Heaven where you can be perfectly safe from all the dangers and perturbations of love is Hell.[13]

Relational intimacy is built on emotional connection and risk-taking. To form intimate relationships, one must first be aware of one's own feelings. Emotional constriction causes trauma victims to be estranged from their past and the significant emotions connected to it. Hence, they cannot enter into deep relationship with others because their deepest self is locked away. Furthermore, emotional constriction makes it all but impossible for them to enter into the pain and feelings of others. Just as healthy marital sexual intimacy requires physical nakedness, so relational intimacy requires emotional nakedness (honesty and transparency).

Scripture gives both mandates and models for emotionally connected relationships. We see it, for instance, in the example and admonitions of the apostle Paul, who had deeply intimate relationships with his colleagues and those he shepherded. He admonishes believers to "rejoice with those who rejoice; mourn with those who mourn" (Romans 12:15); "carry each other's burdens" (Galatians 6:2); be "like-minded, having the same love, being one in spirit" (Philippians 2:2); and to look to "the interests of the others" (Philippians 2:4).

Sandy illustrates the dynamics and dangers of shutting down. She grew up in a neglectful, emotionally abusive family. While Sandy's mother found cathartic relief in sharing with her daughter the graphic details of her sexual and marital struggles, Sandy found these conversations extremely painful and emotionally paralyzing. Hence, in counseling Sandy drew a picture of one of these conversations with her mother (see figure 11), where she illustrated herself in adultlike clothes and makeup, but with the proportions of a small child, her face rigid and tense. She is talking on the phone to her mother, who is yelling at her. Sandy is tuned out as she externally agrees

---

13. C. S. Lewis, *The Four Loves* (New York: Harcourt Brace Jovanovich, 1960), 169.

with her mother, saying, "Uh-huh," over and over, but internally is saying, "Shut up" and "Goodbye."

In her home, Sandy was not allowed to express her pain or say anything negative to, or about, her mother. She was not allowed to set limits around her emotional needs. Her real voice was silenced. Thus she had learned to shut down her painful feelings while outwardly agreeing with others even as they hurt her. Sadly, Sandy's family didn't alter this pattern, and she remained shut down. By middle adolescence, she was sexually promiscuous and was eventually abused by multiple boys. She continued to respond positively to the very behavior that hurt her.

Figure 11

In the song "Easier to Run," the group Linkin Park describes the way abuse, shame, shutting down, and isolation are connected. They describe a dark secret that's been kept locked away from everyone. They tell of wounds so deep they can't be seen, wounds of shame, wounds ignored until they're forgotten. They sadly confess that it's easier to run, to exchange the pain for something numb. They sum it up with this powerful line: "It's so much easier to go than face all this pain here all alone."[14]

Sabotaging the Most Important Relationships

> You can outrun what is running after you, but not what is running inside of you.
>
> Rwandan proverb

Numbing pain and running from your past are understandably tempting, but these behaviors don't work. Trauma cannot be left behind or erased—it must be faced and dealt with. When you run from the past, you die to the future because all your important relationships are successfully sabotaged. And the insidious part is that when you're numb, you can't even feel the damage.

---

14. Linkin Park, "Easier to Run," track 6 on *Meteora* (Warner Bros. Records, 2003).

God

Surprisingly, few formal studies have been conducted on the spiritual impact of abuse. However, those that have been done reveal that abuse seriously undermines religious faith. The first national random sample survey in the United States of sexual abuse showed that sexual abuse victims are far more likely to be nonpractitioners of religion than those who had not been abused.[15] In her large-scale study of incest victims, Diana Russell found there was no significant correlation between religious upbringing and incest victimization, but there was a striking relationship between incest victimization and adult religious practice. She found that 56 percent of adult Catholic and Protestant incest victims had defected from their religious faith.[16]

The impact of abuse on one's relationship with God is seen in three typical responses: rejecting, withdrawing, and cowering. While these responses look very different, the end result is eerily similar. Intimacy with God is shattered.

Rejecting

This is the response of abuse victims who conclude that God does not exist. Given the evil they've experienced, some survivors simply reject the notion that there is a personal, transcendent God with whom they can have an intimate relationship. We believe this is the least common but most extreme spiritual response to abuse.

In a stunning and terrifying account of the Holocaust that won a Nobel Peace Prize for literature, Elie Wiesel recounts receiving and witnessing unimaginable abuse in Nazi concentration camps in Auschwitz and Buchenwald. Wiesel was a young teen when one day, he and all the other prisoners were forced to watch the Nazis hang three fellow prisoners. One was a small boy who, because he was so light, slowly choked to death for more than a half hour while Elie and the others were forced to watch. Wiesel recalls a prisoner asking, "Where is God now?" Wiesel's internal voice responded, "Where is He? Here He is—He is hanging here on this gallows."[17] For some abuse survivors, God died with their abuse.

One need not experience the extreme murderous abuse of Nazi con-

---

15. Finkelhor et al., "Sexual Abuse and Its Relationship," 382.

16. Russell, *Secret Trauma*, 119–21. The adult religious defection rate for women with no incest history was 32 percent. The most dramatic differences were found among Catholics, with twice as many Catholics who experienced incest defecting from the church as Catholics who did not experience incest.

17. Elie Wiesel, *Night* (New York: Avon, 1969), 76.

centration camps to reject God. The band Everclear articulates the way nonlethal abuse can also cause abuse victims to reject God. In their song "Why I Don't Believe in God," they specifically point to childhood physical abuse and abandonment by a mentally ill mother for their loss of faith. At the end of the song, they proclaim, "I wish I believed like you do . . . In the myth of a merciful god."[18]

Rejection of God as a consequence of abuse isn't limited to adults and adolescents, as it often begins in childhood. Wesley was molested by another boy when he was six, and then he began to initiate sexual behavior with other children. In therapy he drew a picture of what he felt when he did this (see figure 12). He said the picture was of his heart. He drew himself as a child with tears running down his cheeks. He was engulfed in blackness, alone, and believed God had vacated his heart. When Celestia asked him for a title for his drawing, he hurriedly scribbled, "Where's God when I'm scared?"

As a young boy, Wesley had already begun to experience the horror of alienation from God, whom he believed had not been there when he was molested or when Wesley was molesting others. Thankfully, Wesley received emotional and spiritual support early in his development so that the lies he believed about God could be exposed and replaced with truth.

Figure 12

18. Everclear, "Why I Don't Believe in God," track 12 from *So Much for the Afterglow* (Capitol Records, 1997).

Withdrawing

Withdrawing and cowering are the most common and insidious spiritual responses. Survivors who withdraw still believe God exists, but they don't believe they can trust him. Instead, they withdraw from him so they feel less vulnerable to being misused. They may reason that God did not stop their abusers from violating them, in spite of the Bible's testimony that God will protect his children (Psalm 27:1–3; 91:1–14).

Since survivors have experienced betrayal and harm from those with more power, God is particularly frightening to them because he is said to be *all*-powerful. And when the abuser is the victim's father or spiritual leader, mistrust and withdrawal from God are even more understandable, because children project their experience with their earthly father onto God, their heavenly Father. They often reason that if their earthly father, who had limited power, abused them, then God, their omnipotent heavenly Father, might well do the same. Thus, a survivor minimizes their vulnerability to an unsafe God by withdrawing from him and not completely surrendering to him.

Linda Katherine Cutting, a highly accomplished concert pianist and music professor, tells of growing up in a highly religious, abusive home. Her father was a minister, who chronically abused his children physically, sexually, and spiritually. Both of Linda's brothers committed suicide, and as an adult, Linda suffered a nervous breakdown, completely losing her ability to perform music. In a stunning display of denial, Linda's father never acknowledged his evil behavior and continued to work as a minister in New England.

As a result, Linda lost any sense of a safe relationship with God. She eventually became a Quaker and felt much more comfortable in a church with no pulpit, no cross, no preacher, and no emphasis on human religious authority. Sadly, through her minister father's abuse, these had become the very things that triggered her withdrawal from God. She recounts, "In my father's church, he always had the final word. At the end of each week, on the day after the beatings, he offered absolution. We could ask our Father in heaven through our earthly father to forgive us our sins. 'Our Father who art in heaven,' we'd begin. But as long as our father was leading it, the words seemed tainted."[19]

Withdrawal from God is often a subconscious response. Many abuse victims believe in God and do all the things Christians are supposed to do.

---

19. Linda Katherine Cutting, *Memory Slips: A Memoir of Music and Healing* (New York: Harper-Collins, 1997), 165.

They worship, tithe, pray, and serve in their church—all out of religious duty, not heartfelt affection or delight. Their relationship with God is cognitive behavioral, transactional, not intimate. They've emotionally withdrawn from God but cannot feel it. They don't really trust him. In fact, their religious service is a hollow substitute for an intimate, real relationship with God.

Cowering

Jesus don't want me for a sunbeam.

Nirvana, "Jesus Doesn't Want Me for a Sunbeam"

A third spiritual response to abuse is to cower before God. This response may involve mistrust, but the emphasis here is not so much on something being wrong with God as on everything being wrong with oneself. Cowering is a shame-based response in which survivors feel they are so defective that God will never really love or accept them. They believe that God exists and that he probably loves some people, but not them. They are too defective.

In one sense, cowering is a reliving of the abuse. Just as survivors cower before their abuser and believe they deserved the abuse, so they cower before God and come to believe they deserve to be rejected by him. This is precisely what Ingrid articulated in her story when she confessed, "It is nearly impossible for me to believe that God loves me, even though I want him to. Most of the time I feel like he couldn't possibly have chosen me to be one of his children, and I won't be surprised if I die and find out my name isn't written in the Book of Life."

As with other aspects of abuse, cowering is intensified if the abuser was the victim's father. Linda Cutting testifies to her own cowering response to her minister father's abuse:

> The thing that's kept me spiritually alone all of these years was somehow equating God with my father's church and, most of all, with my father . . . In Sunday school we used to sing "Jesus loves the little children, all the children of the world." It listed the colors "red and yellow, black and white." For some reason I never felt I was on the list. I'd sing as loud as I could, so that God would hear my voice, and I'd look over at the mural of Jesus gathering the children into his loving arms and wish I could be one of them.[20]

---

20. Cutting, *Memory Slips*, 156.

Spouse

Since God intended the husband-wife relationship to be the most intimate of all human relationships (it alone is to be a "one flesh" relationship), abuse damage is often seen most acutely in marriage. Marriage should involve the greatest level of long-term trust, for in a healthy marriage, couples share that which is most precious—their bodies, their wealth, their homes, their children, and their dreams. Sadly, many survivors have experienced such profound betrayal that they conclude, "If I couldn't trust my family, whom can I trust? No one is trustworthy."[21] This can then become a self-fulfilling prophecy as abuse survivors refuse to trust even a loving spouse, and their marriage crumbles.

There are many specific ways in which the damage of abuse impacts marriage and creates isolation from the survivor's spouse. *Abuse affects a couple's ability to communicate.* In one study, 23 percent of abuse survivors reported they had no meaningful communication with their partners, whereas only 6 percent of nonabused adults said this.[22] Abuse survivors often have a difficult time confiding in others, including their spouses—due in part to a difficulty trusting others and possibly also because childhood abuse survivors are conditioned to keep secrets, which can become an ingrained pattern into adulthood.

Abuse survivors' difficulties with marital communication are often the result of residual shame. Shame-filled people hide—they don't bare their souls, not even to their spouses. For survivors of physical and verbal abuse, conflict avoidance is a huge factor that affects marital intimacy. These individuals learned as children to avoid conflict at all costs, for conflict was inherently dangerous. Hence, they became conditioned to avoid any perception of disagreement, even in a safe relationship. Thus real communication becomes virtually impossible, because the moment potential conflict is perceived (no matter how mild), the survivor shuts down emotionally and verbally, and genuine communication ceases.

Sexual intimacy is one of the most important ways married couples reenact their marriage vows and express and strengthen their intimacy as a couple.[23] Sadly, *abuse survivors, especially female sexual abuse survivors,*

---

21. Cited in Courtois, *Healing the Incest Wound,* 111; see also Clark E. Barshinger, Lojan E. LaRowe, and Andrés T. Tapia, *Haunted Marriage: Overcoming the Ghosts of Your Spouse's Childhood Abuse* (Downers Grove, IL: InterVarsity, 1995), 206–8.

22. P. E. Mullen et al., "The Effect of Child Sexual Abuse on Social, Interpersonal and Sexual Function in Adult Life," *British Journal of Psychiatry* 165, no. 1 (1994): 39.

23. For more on this, see Steven R. Tracy, "The Marriage Mystery," *Christianity Today* (January 7, 2002), 63.

are particularly prone to sexual dysfunction in marriage.[24] Interestingly, childhood sexual abuse does not have the same impact on adult men, for overall it is not an accurate predictor of adult male sexual dysfunction.[25] For men, childhood emotional abuse seems to have the greatest impact on adult sexual health.[26]

For women, there are many factors in childhood sexual abuse that may help lead to adult sexual dysfunction. To begin with, sexual relations with even a loving husband can prompt trauma body triggers that evoke memories and sensations of childhood abuse. Any number of marital behaviors or experiences, from a hug in the middle of the night to the actual position of intercourse, can trigger childhood sexual trauma. Also, since sexual abuse creates distrust, the most intimate physical act—sex within a context of relational intimacy—can be too intimate to be enjoyed. Furthermore, a female sexual abuse victim often develops great dissatisfaction about and even antipathy toward her body and its sexual urges. Her abuser's interest in her body was the source of great pain, so her body's healthy, autonomic arousal can become her enemy.

Even victims of nonviolent sexual abuse may struggle with accepting sexual pleasure, for in the process of being abused, they experienced the ambivalence of sexual pleasure that happened in the context of shame and revulsion. Thus, nonabusive sexual pleasure becomes connected with prior abuse and shame, so the adult survivor is automatically repulsed by and seeks to shut down all feelings of sexual pleasure. This dynamic helps explain why female sexual abuse is especially related to the inability to achieve orgasm in adulthood.[27]

A final way abuse inhibits marital closeness is by undermining the sense of self, thereby causing victims to feel worthless, powerless, and inferior to

24. See Katarina Oberg, Kerstin Fugl-Meyer, and Axel R. Fugl-Meyer, "On Sexual Well-Being in Sexually Abused Swedish Women: Epidemiological Aspects," *Sexual and Relationship Theory* 17, no. 4 (2002): 329–41; Carey S. Pulverman and Cindy M. Meston "Sexual Dysfunction in Women with a History of Childhood Sexual Abuse: The Role of Sexual Shame," *Psychological Trauma: Theory, Research, Practice, and Policy* 12, no. 3 (2020): 291–99; David B. Sarwer and Joseph A. Durlak, "Childhood Sexual Abuse as a Predictor of Adult Female Sexual Dysfunction: A Study of Couples Seeking Sex Therapy," *Child Abuse & Neglect* 20. no. 10 (1996): 963–72. Sarwer and Durlak report that up to 95 percent of female survivors of penetration sexual abuse experience adult sexual dysfunction.

25. See Johann F. Kinzl et al., "Sexual Dysfunction in Males: Significance of Adverse Childhood Experiences," *Child Abuse & Neglect* 20, no. 8 (1996): 759–66; Cindy M. Meston, Julia R. Heiman, and Paul D. Trapnell, "The Relation between Early Abuse and Adult Sexuality," *Journal of Sex Research* 36, no. 4 (1999): 385–96; David B. Sarwer, Isiaah Crawford, and Joseph A. Durlak, "The Relationship between Childhood Sexual Abuse and Adult Male Sexual Dysfunction," *Child Abuse & Neglect* 21, no. 7 (1997): 649–55.

26. See Meston, Heiman, and Trapnell, "Relation between Early Abuse and Adult Sexuality," 385.

27. Oberg, "On Sexual Well-Being," 339.

others. This is most evident when female abuse victims are unable to set healthy boundaries, make appropriate requests of their partners, or expect to be treated with respect. This helps explain why women who experience violence in childhood are more likely to marry violent men.[28] Furthermore, women who have experienced violence in childhood or in their marriage are at risk of developing trauma bonds with violent men. They become so conditioned to being physically abused and develop such cognitive distortions that they come to believe an abusive relationship is quite acceptable. It must surely be what they deserve.[29]

In short, when abuse undermines a woman's sense of self, it keeps her from being able to function as an equal partner in marriage. She is underequipped to craft a deeply intimate relationship. A woman can only be the complementing helper God intended (Genesis 2:18) when she perceives herself as her husband's complete equal. Only then can a married couple experience soul-satisfying intimacy.

Family and Friends

Abuse fractures intimacy not only with one's spouse but with other family members as well. Children who grow up in abusive families are traumatized and shamed. They aren't consistently loved and nurtured and don't learn healthy conflict resolution skills. Hence, all relationships in abusive families are weakened.

Girls who experience incest from their fathers often report intense conflict with their mothers and siblings, who resent the special attention they are being given by their father.[30] Boys who have been abused tend to externalize their pain and often express a desire to hurt their siblings and/or peers.[31] Girls tend to internalize their anger and abuse damage. This most

---

28. See Suzanne Prescott and Carolyn Letko, "Battered Women: A Social Psychological Perspective," in *Battered Women: A Psychosociological Study of Domestic Violence*, ed. Maria Roy (New York: Van Nostrand Reinhold, 1977), 72–96; Bessel A. van der Kolk, "The Compulsion to Repeat the Trauma: Re-enactment, Revictimization, and Masochism," *Psychiatric Clinics of North America* 12, no. 2 (1989): 393–95.

29. See Don Dutton and Susan Lee Painter, "Traumatic Bonding: The Development of Emotional Attachments in Battered Women and Other Relationships of Intermittent Abuse," *Victimology* 6, no. 1 (1981): 139–55; Alytia A. Levendosky and Sandra A. Graham-Bermann, "Trauma and Parenting in Battered Women: An Addition to an Ecological Model of Parenting," *Journal of Aggression, Maltreatment & Trauma* 3, no. 1 (2000): 25–35.

30. See Herman, *Father-Daughter Incest*, 114–16.

31. David Finkelhor, "Early and Long-Term Effects of Child Sexual Abuse: An Update," *Professional Psychology: Research and Practice* 21, no. 5 (1990): 326, https://calio.org/wp-content/uploads/2014/05/Early_and_long-term_effects_of_child_sexual_abuse-An_update.pdf.

often results in depression, which can also impair relationships with siblings.[32] In short, abuse isolates family members from each other.

Kay grew up in a very religious and sterile, neglectful family. Her mother hadn't dealt with her own childhood abuse, so she was completely disconnected from her own feelings and thus from her children's. Kay's father worked hard to financially provide for his family but was emotionally disconnected as well. Kay grew up in a beautiful home where her physical needs were met, yet she was emotionally starved. In therapy, she drew a picture of her family (see figure 13).

Figure 13

Even though this family lived in the same house, everyone is in their own black box, with interior walls disconnecting them from each other. Kay described the blackness coming from her father, who offered no intimacy with anyone in their family, particularly with her mother.

The impact of abuse is especially salient in the abuse survivor's relationship with their children. One of the key abuse dynamics that negatively affects parenting is shame. We see this dynamic in Ingrid's story, which we shared at the beginning of this chapter:

---

32. Depression is the most commonly cited symptom reported by adults molested as children, and it is considerably more common in children who have been sexually abused (see Lucy Berliner and Diana M. Elliott, "Sexual Abuse of Children," in *The APSAC Handbook on Child Maltreatment*, ed. John E. B. Myers et al. [Thousand Oaks, CA: Sage, 2002], 59–60).

I love my family beyond words, but I find it hard to accept their love in return, because I don't feel like I deserve it. It's so hard, in fact, that up until recently, I became enraged inside when my daughter would pick up my hand and kiss it while we were driving in the car.

Ingrid's shame and unarticulated belief in her own unworthiness triggered rage when her daughter expressed tenderness and affection. Ingrid didn't feel worthy of love, so she would instinctively and aggressively reject it from her own child. This shame/rejection dynamic created a recursive cycle that continued to get worse until there was intervention.

As a result of this shame, abuse-surviving mothers are often guilt-ridden and unable to set healthy limits on their children's behavior. Due to the emotional impact of abuse, particularly numbing (constriction), these moms can be distant and emotionally unavailable to their children or overly emotionally indulgent; either way, they struggle with boundaries.

At a more extreme level, parents may visualize their abusers in their own children—when, for example, a child's physical appearance, personality, or behavior resembles that of the parent's abuser. For instance, a mother may become hostile toward a son who looks like her ex-husband who had beaten her. A father, without consciously realizing it, may become cold and neglectful toward his daughter who has his abusive mother's personality.

Abuse can also dramatically impact peer relationships. Consider these important research findings:

- Children who have been physically abused tend to be more aggressive, experience more conflict, have lower peer status, and show less positive reciprocity with other children than their nonabused peers. In fact, one of the most extensively documented consequences of child physical abuse is heightened aggression, especially toward peers.[33]
- Abused children may have as many friends and the same frequency of contact as do their nonabused peers, but they experience more conflict, especially during play, and enjoy less intimacy in their peer friendships.[34]

---

33. See Salzinger, "Effects of Physical Abuse," 169–87; Steven M. Alessandri, "Play and Social Behavior in Maltreated Preschoolers," *Development and Psychopathology* 3, no. 2 (1991): 191–205; Mary E. Haskett and Janet A. Kistner, "Social Interaction and Peer Perception of Young Physically Abused Children," *Child Development* 62, no. 5 (1991): 979–90; David J. Kolko, "Child Physical Abuse," in *APSAC Handbook on Child Maltreatment*, 32.

34. See Parker and Herrera, "Interpersonal Processes in Friendship," 1034–35.

- Neglected children tend to be less aggressive toward peers than physically or sexually abused children, but they also tend to be more passive and withdrawn and have fewer friendships.[35]
- Sexually abused children tend to be more aggressive than their non-abused peers and are particularly characterized by increased sexual behavior with or toward other children.[36]

Sexualized behavior often continues and even increases as the child gets older. One of the most notable characteristics of opposite-sex relationships among adolescent and adult survivors of sexual abuse is increased sexual activity and promiscuity, often leading to revictimization.[37] In terms of dating relationships, adolescent abuse survivors report significantly more verbal and physical abuse toward and from their partners.[38] Due to self-blame and shame, survivors of sexual abuse are also less confident in establishing same-sex friendships, which are important developmentally for overall relational skill building.[39]

Reconnecting and Healing

Because we're made in God's image, the good and bad news is that we're profoundly impacted by our relationships with other humans. When people misuse their power and abuse, tremendous long-term damage is created. Abuse damage is particularly evident in abuse victims' relationships because abuse creates shame, mistrust, and emotional constriction, all of which undermine relationships. Abuse isolates victims.

The good news is that *healthy* relationships have tremendous power to nurture the soul and the body. Healthy relationships heal the deepest wounds. To be overcome, childhood trauma must be acknowledged in judgment-free relationships. When a person describes their traumatic experience to a safe person, they are able to construct a story about what

---

35. See Martha Farrell Erickson and Byron Egeland, "Child Neglect," in *APSAC Handbook on Child Maltreatment*, 7–8.

36. J. Adams et al., "Sexually Inappropriate Behaviors in Seriously Mentally Ill Children and Adolescents," *Child Abuse & Neglect* 19, no. 5 (1995): 555–68; see also Berliner and Elliot, "Sexual Abuse of Children," in *APSAC Handbook on Child Maltreatment*, 60.

37. Catalina M. Arata, "From Child Victim to Adult Victim: A Model for Predicting Sexual Revictimization," *Child Maltreatment* 5, no. 1 (2000): 30–31; Courtois, *Healing the Incest Wound*, 107–8; Meston, Heiman, and Trapnell, "Relation between Early Abuse and Adult Sexuality," 385–96.

38. Wolfe, "Factors Associated with Abusive Relationships," 61.

39. Feiring, Rosenthal, and Taska, "Stigmatization and the Development of Friendship," 317–19.

they've experienced and thus find a way to overcome.[40] This approach is very empowering and begins to build relational trust, one interaction at a time.

The essential role of relationships in trauma healing is strongly affirmed by leading abuse expert Bessel van der Kolk:

> Everything about us—our brains, our minds, and our bodies—is geared toward collaboration in social systems. This is our most powerful survival strategy, the key to our success as a species, and it is precisely this that breaks down in most forms of mental suffering . . .
>
> Social support is a biological necessity, not an option, and this reality should be the backbone of all prevention and treatment.[41]

The potency of human relationships to heal is an expressly biblical concept. It was a tender relationship with his new bride that healed and comforted Isaac after his mother's death (Genesis 24:67). It was David's intimate relationship with his friend Jonathan that helped him endure King Saul's murderous abuse (1 Samuel 19–20). It was Barnabas and the disciples at Damascus who took the risk to love and disciple Saul, the very man who had been persecuting Christians (Acts 9:1–30). Shortly before the apostle Paul (the man formerly called Saul) was executed, it was Timothy and Luke who brought him help and comfort when others had abandoned him (2 Timothy 4:9–17).

God designed the church, the body of Christ, to be *the* matrix in which healing and sanctification take place. Believers are to love, restore, and care for each other because they're all part of the same spiritual body through Christ.[42] This is a particularly powerful principle for those who've experienced abuse by family members because, in spite of what one has experienced from their physical family, God has given a spiritual family of brothers and sisters, and fathers and mothers who are to love and nurture and help heal one another's wounds. We are created and directed to love each other in such a way that we find our way to God. We grow and heal in the presence of love, and love is never wasted.

Romans 12 forms the basis for Mending the Soul's mentor's creed.

---

40. See Johann Hari, *Lost Connections: Why You're Depressed and How to Find Hope* (New York: Bloomsbury, 2018), 193–97.

41. Bessel van der Kolk, *The Body Keeps the Score: Brain, Mind, and Body in the Healing of Trauma* (New York: Viking, 2014), 166–67.

42. See Acts 2:41–47; Romans 12:4–5; 12:13–15:2; 1 Corinthians 12:12–27; Galatians 6:1–2; Ephesians 4:7–16; Philippians 2:1–4.

In this chapter, Paul writes, "In Christ we, though many, form one body, and each member belongs to all the others" (verse 5). That means that if you have been abused, I've been abused; if you're weeping, I weep; if you're rejoicing and celebrating, I am too. We matter in each other's lives. We're connected.

There are two principles that come into play as we encourage survivors to reconnect with others. *First, friends and family members of abuse victims must recognize the critical role they play in preventing and healing abuse damage.* Their response to abuse will largely affect the extent to which the abuse will create long-term damage. For instance, parents' and caregivers' harsh, disbelieving, or apathetic responses to a child's abuse disclosure can be as or more damaging than the original abuse, whereas supportive responses can mitigate abuse damage.[43]

This principle is true for adult survivors of abuse as well. One of the strongest findings in a large-scale study of female sexuality and abuse was that women who were raped as adults were far less likely to destructively seek to control their sexual desires (shut down, and the like) if they had felt very close to at least one immediate family member in childhood.[44] In another study of adult rape survivors, the reported length of time required for recovery was directly related to the quality of intimate relationships the women experienced in the present. Survivors who had supportive, stable relationships with spouses or partners recovered more quickly than those who did not.[45]

Friends and family members of survivors must be strong, gracious, and patient, recognizing that shattered trust is rebuilt very slowly. In the early stages of recovery, abuse survivors often lash out most severely at their closest allies. It is in relationship to you that a survivor will learn to trust, as long as they're not successful in pushing you away. In those moments,

---

43. Leonard T. Gries and David S. Goh studied twenty-one children who had been placed in foster care because of parental abuse. The reaction of the foster parents to the children's disclosure of abuse was identified as the most salient feature connected with the children's subsequent emotional functioning ("Positive Reaction to Disclosure and Recovery from Child Sexual Abuse," *Journal of Child Sexual Abuse* 9, no. 1 [2000]: 29–51). Caregivers' reactions to disclosures have long-term consequences as well. In a study of sixty-six adults who had been sexually abused as children and disclosed the abuse during childhood, Thomas A. Roesler found that the reaction of the family members to the disclosure had a mediating effect (positive and negative) on adult emotional well-being, specifically on scores assessing general trauma, posttraumatic stress disorder, and dissociation ("Reactions to Disclosure of Childhood Sexual Abuse: The Effect of Adult Symptoms," *Journal of Nervous and Mental Disease* 182, no. 11 [1994]: 618–24).

44. Gail E. Wyatt, Michael D. Newcomb, and Monika H. Riederle, *Sexual Abuse and Consensual Sex: Women's Developmental Patterns and Outcomes* (Thousand Oaks, CA: Sage, 1993), 187.

45. Ann W. Burgess and Lynda L. Holmstrom, "Adaptive Strategies and Recovery from Rape," *American Journal of Psychiatry* 136, no. 10 (1979): 1278–82.

it's helpful to remember that much of the survivors' rage is displaced anger at their abuser.

The second principle is that abuse victims must, with God's strength, learn to develop safe, intimate relationships.[46] They must learn to resist the temptation to hide and pull away, to give God and the healthy people he puts into their lives a chance to love them, and then once they've let love in, to give it to others, in spite of the fact that they will be hurt again. They must resist distrusting God and good, safe people because of what an evil, unsafe person has done to them.

Lori Tapia describes the lessons she learned as she healed from incest. In particular, she notes the way God healed her sexuality and her marriage after several years of complete shutdown, isolation, and rage:

> Contrary to what many of us have believed all our lives, "Grace Happens" ... All our hard work and perseverance in the flow of God's presence had paid off. The fruits have been profound: joy, hope, true faith, and yes ... great sex! Not only did genuine intimacy become possible for me—it even became enjoyable ...
>
> As I look back ... learning to trust has been the most important task for me. I didn't know how. Step by excruciating step, I learned to trust [my husband] more each time ...
>
> This process has convinced me of the capacity of the human heart to respond to persistent love. I believe we want terribly to believe that love is real and that we are loved. Maybe we've just never seen it lived out. Or maybe we have, but our souls were so wounded that we could not receive it. At some point I had to choose to believe. The payoff has been worth the risk.[47]

Lori's comments set the stage for the final section of *Mending the Soul.* In the next three chapters, we'll map out a path so that those ravaged by abuse can experience emotional, spiritual, and relational healing.

---

46. For a biblical theology of relationships and a practical guide to relational healing and growth, see Steven and Celestia Tracy, *Forever and Always: The Art of Intimacy* (Eugene, OR: Wipf & Stock, 2011).

47. Cited in Barshinger, LaRowe, and Tapia, *Haunted Marriage*, 206–7.

PART 3

The Healing Path

I am the LORD, *who heals you.*

Exodus 15:26

Then I will compensate you for the years
That the swarming locust has eaten,
The creeping locust, the stripping locust,
    and the gnawing locust—
My great army which I sent among you.
You will have plenty to eat and be satisfied,
and you will praise the name of the LORD *your God,*
Who has dealt wondrously with you;
Then My people will never be put to shame.

Joel 2:25–26 NASB

M y pieces are coming back together." This vivid expression of healing was shared with Celestia by a beautiful Ugandan mother who was grieving the traumatic and sudden loss of her baby girl. "I feel it now." Her words reminded us of a long-standing Japanese art form called *kintsugi* in which the beauty of a ceramic dish is enhanced after it has been broken and placed in an artisan's hands (see figure 14).

For the Japanese, beauty can be found in broken things, as the cracks and repairs are important events in the life of an object. Because of *kintsugi*, the value and beauty of a piece of ceramic art are increased by the gold seams that illuminate the breaks rather than hiding or disguising them.[1] In some Japanese art books this art form is referred to as "flawed beauty."

Figure 14
iStock.com/Marco Montalti

The Hebrew prophet Isaiah declares, "We are the clay, you are the potter; we are all the work of your hand" (Isaiah 64:8). God takes the broken pieces of our story and mends them together in ways that create even more beauty than was there before. He is the gold epoxy that provides the miraculous repair (see figure 15). Every part of our story is important and nothing can be left behind. Every piece matters.

Frederick Buechner puts it this way:

My story is important not because it is mine, God knows, but because if I tell it anything like right, the chances are you will recognize that in many ways it is also yours. Maybe nothing is more important than that we keep track, you and I, of these stories of who we are and where we have come from and the people we have met along the way because it is precisely through these stories in all their particularity, as I have long believed and often said, that God makes himself known to each of us most powerfully

---

1. Christy Bartlett, *Flickwerk: The Aesthetics of Mended Japanese Ceramics*, Herbert F. Johnson Museum of Art, Cornell University, Ithaca NY, June 28–August 10, 2008, http://annacolibri.com /wpcontent/uploads/2013/02/Flickwerk_The_Aesthetics_of_Mended_Japanese_Ceramics.pdf.

and personally. If this is true, it means that to lose track of our stories is to be profoundly impoverished not only humanly but spiritually.[2]

May we listen to our lives and trust our Creator with the brokenness so that our beauty can be restored. In the remaining section, we'll unpack God's *kintsugi* and the role we each play in being a little bit of the gold. As the apostle Paul beautifully expresses, "In Christ we, though many, form one body, and each member belongs to all the others" (Romans 12:5).

Figure 15: In the Potter's Hands
Nicole Boyette. Used with permission.

A little girl named Latisha gives us keen insight into the damage of abuse and the necessity of healing. She was sexually abused by a man the family trusted and, as a result, was behaving sexually toward other children. Latisha painted this watercolor heart to describe the invisible damage and her inner pain (see figure 16). The vivid image ran on the paper, revealing unhealed, oozing wounds. Latisha punctuated her painted heart with black and gray holes, which powerfully illustrated her own victimization and the

---

2. Frederick Buechner, *Listening to Your Life* (San Francisco: HarperSanFrancisco, 1992), 321–22.

ways her sexual abuse had sexualized her behavior toward other children: *These are the holes in my heart. The black holes are the bad things he did to me; the gray holes are the bad things I have done. If you don't help me tape these holes, Satan will crawl in!*

Latisha was a sweet Christian girl who felt tremendous guilt for her sexualized behavior. This smart little girl intuitively knew that the soul damage of her abuse had to be healed, or else Satan would use it to generate more damage to herself and to those she loved.

In the following chapter we'll unpack a trauma healing model for "taping" the holes in one's heart.

Figure 16

CHAPTER 8

MTS Healing Model

As my sufferings mounted, I soon realized that there were
two ways that I could respond to my situation: either to
react with bitterness or seek to transform the suffering
into a creative force. I decided to follow the latter course.

Martin Luther King Jr., "Suffering and Faith," in *Christian Century*

He has sent me to bind up the brokenhearted,
 to proclaim freedom for the captives
 and release from darkness for the prisoners,
 to proclaim the year of the LORD's *favor . . .*
 to comfort all who mourn.

Isaiah 61:1–2

We met Lance at an Anglican church in England and were impressed
by his confidence, drive, and life experiences. He was delightful to
spend time with and entertained us with lively stories of childhood adventures. Lance's father had been a career military officer who had been stationed in various bases around the world. He explained that his parents left
the military twelve years earlier to serve as missionaries for a Christian relief
agency in Asia. Lance spoke of his parents, especially his father, in glowing
terms, and gave the distinct impression that his father was a combination of
Hudson Taylor, Chuck Yeager, and John Wayne.

A year later, we were privileged to meet Lance's parents, Don and Mindy,
when they came to England for a conference, and were surprised to find Don
to be quite nervous and reclusive; Mindy was even more puzzling. She was
obviously talented and dedicated, as was evidenced by her recent promotion.
And yet when we tried to talk with her, she was emotionally flat and so
disconnected that we struggled to maintain a five-minute conversation.

Tragically, the next time we saw Mindy was at Don's funeral, where

Lance's family reported that Don had suffered a fatal allergic reaction to medication his doctor had prescribed. The vicar performing the memorial service spoke eloquently of Don's faithful spiritual service and of Mindy's strength. Following the service, Mindy reinforced the vicar's homily by reassuring everyone that she was fine, that God was good and still in control. It all seemed rather surreal.

A week after the service, we were shocked to hear the real story. Don did not die peacefully from an allergic reaction; he was murdered in a prison cell, where he had been placed the day before for molesting the four-year-old son of a local political official. Worse yet, a further investigation revealed that Don had been molesting young boys for years and that the relief agency had received numerous allegations of Don's serial molestations. When a report came into the agency, they would just move him to another team in a new location.

Mindy knew. Don kept apologizing, repeatedly promising to stop, and she kept believing his promises. Clearly, Mindy was surviving her painful marriage by denying Don's abuse and patently refusing to process her anguish and anger. She had been groomed as a young child to survive difficult things by simply denying their existence. Mindy's father was an abusive alcoholic who died when she was a girl. Tragically, she passed this defense of denial on to her son, who would in turn, perhaps, pass it on to his son.

Lance's response to his father's murder was striking. He denied everything ugly by continuing to assert what a wonderful father Don had been. Lance, like his mother, reassured us that he was trusting the Lord and doing just fine. Minutes after the memorial service concluded, Lance returned to work. "My father was a great man!" was the last thing he said on his way out the door.

Lance found it impossible to face the truth and the pain of his father's abuse, so he molded the facts and his feelings into something more manageable and sanitary. Predictably, an assiduous refusal to face brokenness was exactly how his mother and the relief agency had dealt with the horror of Don's sin. It did not eradicate ugliness, but instead drove it deeper underground, where it grew in the dark.

Facing Brokenness: Compelling Reasons to Look at One's Painful Past

The past is never dead. It's not even past.

William Faulkner, *Requiem for a Nun*

Some Christians argue that we don't need to grieve a painful past to move victoriously into the future. Looking at past pain is said to be little more than an exercise in blame shifting, which only creates destructive bitterness.[1] Others suggest that revisiting one's painful past only serves to perpetuate the pain: "Why stir up the past? It can't be changed. Just focus on the present."

We often hear Christian leaders misread Philippians 3:13–14 to prove these points ("But one thing I do: Forgetting what is behind and straining toward what is ahead, I press on"). Ironically, facing the reality and impact of our painful past is emphasized in Philippians 3. We know that Paul can't be instructing his readers to put the past behind them and forget it because just a few verses earlier, he gave a detailed account of his own past (3:1–7), including his previous abuse of Christians (3:6). It must have been painful for Paul to reflect on the fact that he had persecuted Christians, but he didn't shrink back from honest self-examination and confession.[2]

It's also clear that Paul had reflected deeply enough on his past that he could identify unhealthy, harmful beliefs and emotional responses that needed to change. Most specifically, he came to realize that his preconversion behavior, including his abuse of Christians, was grounded in the misconception that he could gain God's favor through strict adherence to the law. It was Paul's harmfully misdirected attempt at self-righteousness apart from Christ that provided the immediate context of "forgetting what is behind" in Philippians 3:13.[3] Paul had a clear grasp of the scope of his sinful past, the lies that had fueled his sin, and exactly what he needed from God to help him change. We cannot put the painful past behind us—our abuse and the abuse perpetrated against us—until we have fully integrated it.

There are at least five reasons believers must face their brokenness to become spiritually and emotionally healthy.

A Way to Find Security and Love

Christ is in suffering, and if we want to know he's near, we must go to our wounds. He is the man of sorrows who is well acquainted with grief (see figure 17). "He was despised and rejected by mankind, a man of suffering,

1. See Ed Bulkley, *Only God Can Heal the Wounded Heart* (Eugene, OR: Harvest House, 1995), 59, 83–108, 117.

2. This isn't the only time Paul is candid about his past. In two different speeches recorded by Luke, Paul chronicles his preconversion past (Acts 22:3–6; 26:4–14), including his shameful persecution and abuse of Christians some twenty years earlier. In Acts 22:4, Paul readily acknowledged, "I persecuted the followers of this Way to their death, arresting both men and women and throwing them into prison."

3. See Thomas R. Schreiner, *Paul: Apostle of God's Glory in Christ* (Downers Grove, IL: InterVarsity, 2001), 46, 122–23.

and familiar with pain . . . Surely he took up our pain and bore our suffering . . . and by his wounds we are healed" (Isaiah 53:3–5).

Figure 17: By His Wounds, oil on canvas
James Van Fossan. Used with permission.

In MTS's trauma-care model, a survivor is first helped to connect intrapersonally—to integrate their body, heart, and mind—before connecting to the heart of God. In this sacred space where pain is faced and felt and understood, the Spirit of God is there: speaking, prompting, convicting, affirming, comforting, and mediating the retrieval and healing of painful memories.

It is here that vulnerable and honest connections take place within oneself and in relationship with others. In time, as each wound is tended and integrated, Christ becomes all the nearer and dearer. He knows the humiliation of abuse, having hung naked on a splintered cross, publicly shamed by the very ones he gave his life to save. His power and goodness to heal flips the power of evil. In time, Christ can become your secure base, the one you will trust most of all.[4] And his words about you will become your new identity: *I am fearfully and wonderfully made!* (Psalm 139:14).

Go boldly to your wounds and you'll find him there.

A Way to Express Faith

Facing brokenness is a breathtaking act of faith in the living God, while refusing to face brokenness denies his existence, power, and goodness. Because denial of pain comes so naturally, it is rarely labeled as sinful. Nor can we easily recognize how much it dishonors the God who made us and loves us. Scripture declares God to be the God of truth (John 14:6) and the Lord

---

4. Social scientists note the importance of role of "secure attachments"—healthy, trusted human relationships—for health and for trauma healing. See Bruce D. Perry and Maia Szalavitz, *The Boy Who Was Raised as a Dog and Other Stories from a Child Psychiatrist's Notebook* (New York: Basic Books, 2006); Diane Poole Heller, *The Power of Attachment: How to Create Deep and Lasting Intimate Relationships* (Boulder, CO: Sounds True, 2019). Since God is our creator, a secure attachment with him is our most important attachment.

of history who *will* ultimately triumph over all human evil (1 Corinthians 15:25–26; Revelation 20:7–15). Scripture declares that nothing—not natural disaster, abuse, or demonic powers—can separate us from the love of God (Romans 8:38–39).

Thus refusal to face the truth about our brokenness is no trivial matter. Dan Allender puts it succinctly: "The denial is an affront to God. It assumes that a false reality is better than truth. It assumes that God is neither good nor strong enough to help during the recall process. Ultimately, the choice to face past [abuse] memories is the choice not to live a lie."[5]

Stated positively, as we refuse to deaden ourselves to the truth and pain of our past, we throw ourselves into the arms of the only One who can heal us. This is why Jesus pronounces a blessing on those who mourn (and keep on mourning); they are the ones who will experience divine comfort (Matthew 5:4).[6] As long as we minimize ugliness, we short-circuit a divinely ordained means of grace, limiting God's power and sufficiency in our lives. It's only as we stand naked and broken before him, refusing to ease our pain with lies, that we can fully taste his sweetness.

Repeatedly, the psalmist admonishes us to cry out to the Lord in our brokenness so that we can taste God's power and beauty: "The LORD is close to the brokenhearted and saves those who are crushed in spirit" (Psalm 34:18). "This poor man called, and the LORD heard him; he saved him out of all his troubles" (34:6). "How long must I wrestle with my thoughts and day after day have sorrow in my heart? How long will my enemy triumph over me? Look on me and answer, LORD my God. Give light to my eyes, or I will sleep in death . . . But I trust in your unfailing love; my heart rejoices in your salvation" (13:2–3, 5). Such bold prayers are predicated on courageous honesty about one's pain and woundedness.

A Way to Freedom that Only Truth Brings

> Above all, don't lie to yourself. The man who lies to himself and listens to his own lie comes to a point that he cannot distinguish the truth within him, or around him, and so loses all respect for himself and for others. And having no respect he ceases to love.
>
> Fyodor Dostoevsky, *The Brothers Karamazov*

---

5. Dan B. Allender, *The Wounded Heart: Hope for Adult Victims of Childhood Sexual Abuse*, rev. ed. (Colorado Springs: NavPress, 1995), 202.

6. The beatitude in Matthew 5:4 uses a present participle in the Greek (*penthountes*), indicating ongoing mourning.

Telling the truth about our lives is the only way to identify and extinguish shame's destructive lies and correct the distorting effects of evil. Anna Salter states this point well: "Those negative parts of the self that remain totally hidden will remain totally shame-based. Darkness produces good mushrooms, but poor flowers."[7]

In particular, the vast majority of survivors inappropriately blame themselves for their abuse, which in turn creates numerous emotional and relational problems.[8] This dynamic often begins in childhood, for abused children are dependent on their parents and long for a close relationship with them. So they instinctively minimize and take responsibility for the evil of the abusive parents.[9] The lie that the child is responsible for the parents' abuse is perpetually reinforced by the abusive parents' blame shifting.

This destructive distortion of reality continues on into adulthood and explains why adult survivors of childhood abuse make statements such as, "My father didn't really molest me; he just touched me inappropriately at times." "Overall, my parents took pretty good care of me." "My home wasn't nearly as bad as others." "No wonder my parents got so angry with me; I was a hard child to raise." These self-protective statements serve to lessen the painful acknowledgment that their parents did not love them as they should have. They also perpetuate destructive shame by minimizing the reality of their parents' evil behavior and by removing responsibility for it. God calls us to walk in the truth (John 8:31–32; Ephesians 4:25; Titus 1:1) and promises freedom on the other side. The apostle Paul writes, "Whenever anyone turns to the Lord, the veil is taken away. Now the Lord is the Spirit, and where the Spirit of the Lord is, there is freedom" (2 Corinthians 3:16–17).

A Way to Wholeness

Facing the painful truth of one's past is necessary to mitigate and heal the ongoing effects of trauma—to find the shattered fragments and bring them back together again. We noted in chapter 6 that unresolved past trauma

---

7. Anna C. Salter, *Transforming Trauma: A Guide to Understanding and Treating Adult Survivors of Child Sexual Abuse* (Thousand Oaks, CA: Sage, 1995), 262.

8. See James A. Chu, *Rebuilding Shattered Lives: The Responsible Treatment of Complex Post-Traumatic and Dissociative Disorders* (New York: Wiley, 1998), 82.

9. See Judith Lewis Herman, *Trauma and Recovery: The Aftermath of Violence—From Domestic Abuse to Political Terror*, 2nd ed. (New York: Basic Books, 1997), 105; Charles L. Whitfield, *Memory and Abuse: Remembering and Healing the Effects of Trauma* (Deerfield Beach, FL: Health Communications, 1995), 32.

often intrudes into the present through hyperarousal, intrusion, and numbing (constriction). These trauma effects are complex and involve involuntary responses to conscious and subconscious stimuli. Left unaddressed, post-traumatic symptoms may continue for years, even decades, until the trauma is faced.

Out of sight is not out of mind. Just because one has been able to repress past trauma doesn't mean it is no longer embedded in the brain and the body. As one trauma expert notes, "[Unresolved] trauma continues to intrude with visual, auditory, and/or other somatic reality on the lives of its victims. Again and again they relive the life-threatening experiences they have suffered, reacting in mind and body as though such events were still occurring."[10]

One of the axioms of trauma therapy is that healing from long-term trauma effects requires survivors to face the reality of the trauma and the way it impacts them (their brokenness).[11] Hence, the goal of facing our brokenness is not to wallow in the past but to reclaim it in such a way that it loses its destructive grip on the present. In short, trauma symptoms are not healed by ignoring past trauma, but rather by facing, processing, and reinterpreting the trauma.

A Way to Vibrant Intimacy

Facing the truth and pain of our past is necessary in order to experience healthy, dynamic relationships. We must be honest about others' sins against us and the ways we sin against others in order to experience nurturing relationships in the present. As we relate in an appropriate manner with abusive people—setting boundaries, reconciling only when they have repented, and so forth—we minimize the risk of additional abuse to ourselves and others, and we increase the likelihood that they will be convicted of their sin. For instance, as Mindy kept denying the reality of Don's sexual abuse and the pain and loss she felt, it powerfully enabled Don to continue to molest children.

---

10. Babette Rothschild, *The Body Remembers: The Psychophysiology of Trauma and Trauma Treatment* (New York: Norton, 2000), 6.

11. See Claire Burke, *Counseling Survivors of Childhood Sexual Abuse*, 2nd ed. (Thousand Oaks, CA: Sage, 2000), 42–43; Catherine Cameron, *Resolving Childhood Trauma: A Long-Term Study of Abuse Survivors* (Thousand Oaks, CA: Sage, 2000), 211–35; Katherine Steele and Joanna Colrain, "Abreactive Work with Sexual Abuse Survivors: Concepts and Techniques," in *Application of Treatment Strategies*, vol. 2 in *The Sexually Abused Male*, ed. Mic Hunter (Lexington, MA: Lexington, 1990), 1–55.

Breaking the Cycle of Abuse

One of the hard realities of abuse is that victims are far more likely to be revictimized than those who've never been abused.[12] Many different dynamics cause survivors to be more vulnerable, including shame that creates a sense of unworthiness, making it difficult to set boundaries or have relationships with healthy people; learned helplessness that grows out of the powerlessness of victimization to challenge others' hurtful behavior; and emotional numbing (constriction), which limits one's ability to "feel" internal signals warning that another person is unsafe. Healing these unhealthy effects requires abuse survivors to face their brokenness, for only then will they begin to come alive, overcome shame, and feel and respond appropriately to their emotion.

While writing the original manuscript, we read a grim news story about these dynamics.[13] A young couple was honeymooning at an upscale Scottsdale resort when in the middle of the night, they reportedly got into a fight, at which time the groom beat and strangled his new bride to death. The groom fled to Las Vegas, leaving his wife's lifeless body in their wedding bed. The police eventually tracked him down and charged him with second-degree murder. The embedded irony of this crime is that the day the couple flew to Arizona to begin their honeymoon was the same day the groom was to appear in a Michigan court on charges of domestic violence against this same woman he had just married.

While it's inconceivable that a woman would marry a man who only a month before had been arrested for assaulting her, it is consistent with the fact that when we have not faced the pain of past abuse, we aren't able to think or feel in a healthy manner and thus are unable to establish and maintain healthy relationships. Abuse begets more abuse until the dangerous cycle is stopped.

Additionally, parents who themselves were victims of childhood abuse compromise their ability to protect their own children unless they have dealt forthrightly with their painful past.[14] While we must be careful not to blame mothers for their husbands' abusive behavior, many researchers note that

---

12. See Angie C. Kennedy et al., "Cumulative Victimization as a Predictor of Intimate Partner Violence Among Young Mothers," *Psychology of Violence* 7, no. 4 (2017): 533–42; Terri L. Messman and Patricia J. Long, "Child Sexual Abuse and Its Relationship to Revictimization in Adult Women: A Review," *Clinical Psychology Review* 16, no. 5 (1996): 397–420; John J. Potterat et al., "Pathways to Prostitution: The Chronology of Sexual and Drug Abuse Milestones," *Journal of Sex Research* 35, no. 4 (1998): 333–40.

13. Emily Bittner, "Hotel Guest Heard the Fatal Fight," *Arizona Republic* (September 12, 2003).

14. See Mary Elizabeth Collins, "Parents' Perceptions of the Risk of Child Sexual Abuse and Their Protective Behaviors: Findings from a Qualitative Study," *Child Maltreatment* 1, no. 1 (1996): 53–64.

the wives of incestuous men are often described by their daughters as weak and sickly, with no sense of power or boundary setting with regard to their abusive husbands. This is often due in part to their own histories of physical or sexual victimization, which they haven't fully faced or overcome.[15]

In essence, parents who were maltreated as children can be trapped in a long-term victim role that prohibits them from acting with the courage, strength, and insight required to protect their own children. Sadly, denial of one's own victimization increases the likelihood of victimization in the next generation. Anna Salter brilliantly describes how a mother's denial can put her own children at risk:

> The impact of denial will often affect not only the survivor's life, but her attitude toward any molested child with whom she comes into contact. Her own children are particularly at risk, given that she is likely to identify with them and project her defenses onto their situation. If she dissociated during her own abuse, she may dissociate upon evidence of her child's. If she did not report her own, she may equate reporting with public shame and be furious at her child for reporting. If she insisted that her own abuse was not abuse and that her perpetrator was not really a sex offender, she may mislabel and rationalize her child's abuse. If she denied the impact of her own abuse, she may follow suit one generation later.[16]

In summary, healthy relationships are the reward for those who courageously face their painful past and do the hard work of healing.

Biblical Examples

The story of Joseph models the importance of boldly facing the damage of abuse. After God miraculously delivered Joseph from prison and gave him an exalted position in the Egyptian government, Joseph did not deny his painful past. Rather, he honestly faced the abuse he had suffered fifteen years earlier. Neither did he repress his emotional pain, but instead, fully entered into the ache of his brothers' betrayal and distrust by weeping bitterly (Genesis 45:2; 50:15–19).

---

15. See Judith Lewis Herman, *Father-Daughter Incest*, 2nd ed. (Cambridge, MA: Harvard University Press, 2000), 72–73, 88–91; Diana E. H. Russell, *The Secret Trauma: Incest in the Lives of Girls and Women* (New York: Basic Books, 1986), 362–68; Anne M. Gresham, "The Role of the Nonoffending Parent When the Incest Victim Is Male," in *Sexually Abused Male*, vol. 2, 171–72.

16. Salter, *Transforming Trauma*, 232–33.

Joseph went on to carefully orchestrate events to force his brothers to come to grips with their abuse (Genesis 42:21–22; 43:33–34; 44:16). Joseph didn't execute his plan (hiding a cup in Benjamin's grain sack and accusing his brothers of stealing, forcing them to leave Benjamin behind) simply to torment them; rather, he sought to push them toward dealing with their past shameful choices so there could be genuine reconciliation. As Old Testament scholar Andrew Schmutzer notes, "[This] is not Joseph's revenge, but the brothers' needful 'cleaning,' after twenty-two years of hiding a toxic family secret."[17] Personal and familial health requires honesty and courage to face the truth of the past.

Similarly, the apostle Paul didn't deny or repress the reality of the way a man named Alexander had harmed him, but he was honest about how he had been hurt. Paul warned Timothy, "Alexander the metalworker did me a great deal of harm. The Lord will repay him for what he has done. You too should be on your guard against him" (2 Timothy 4:14–15). Sadly, this is seldom done in religious systems. In being honest about how he had been painfully mistreated, Paul was able to protect Timothy.

Godliness requires that we face the truth of our past. It is only then that shame and distortions can be healed and healthy relationships established. When we choose to feel, we heal and the intergenerational cycle of abuse is replaced with an intergenerational cycle of healing.

MTS Healing Model

The graphic in this section gives a visual framework for the six stages of healing that will be explained further in this and the remaining two chapters of *Mending the Soul*. The bottom tier of the model represents the most unhealthy, destructive state. Here we find the greatest amount of hiding and deception. In this domain, one is thoroughly disconnected in all relationships—with God, self, and others—which is often reflected in abusive and/or addictive patterns.

Health increases as one moves upward toward wholeness, demonstrated by deepened intimacy and maturity in all three dimensions: emotional, spiritual, and relational. In the remaining portion of this chapter, we will focus on emotional healing (reconnection with self), in chapter 9 on spiritual healing (reconnection with God), and in chapter 10 on relational healing (reconnection with others).

---

17. Gerald W. Peterman and Andrew J. Schmutzer, eds. *Between Pain and Grace: A Biblical Theology of Suffering* (Chicago: Moody, 2016), 194.

Emotional Honesty/ Health	Relational Honesty/ Health	Spiritual Honesty/ Health

Reconnecting
Healthy Intimacy

• Emotionally open and present • Empathic • Honest about feelings • Connected to body	• Authentic • Vulnerable • Compassionate • Connected to others	• Vibrant soul care • Love-driven service • Intimately connected to God • Focused on own sin

Stage 6: Live Your Redemptive Purpose

Stage 5: Love Radically Out of a Truth-Infused Identity

Stage 4: Identify Distortions and Reclaim Your Original Design

Stage 3: Reconnect the Past with the Present—Tell your Story

Stage 2: Choose to Face the Truth and Feel

Stage 1: Stabilize and Establish Safety

Hiding/Abusive/Addicted
Disconnected from self, God, others

• Emotionally numb • Robotic • Disconnected from body • Depressed and anxious • Angry • Lonely	• Hide past • Deny weakness • Isolate • Fiercely independent • Superficial • Deceptive	• Self-righteous • Arrogant • Indifferent to suffering • Hypocritical • Shame-driven service • Judgmental • Focused on others' sin

Emotional unhealthiness is evidenced by constricted feelings and disconnection from the body. Because religious people are conditioned simply to "do the right thing," they can be some of the most emotionally unhealthy people, being driven by dispassionate, robotic behavior in which individuals go through the motions of spiritual and domestic duty but lack genuine passion and joy. Thus as people learn to face their pain, they'll grow in emotional health that gradually replaces emotional deadness with vibrancy. The healthier you are and the more healing you experience, the more you'll experience the full range of emotions. The healthy person is able to acknowledge and respond to the uncomfortable feelings of their heart in real time. Since God himself feels and expresses a vast range of emotions, we as his image bearers should too.

This doesn't mean the ultimate goal of recovery is simply to feel, but learning to feel again is an appropriate and necessary early stage of healing. As we grow in emotional health, we *will* feel more, and as we do, we'll increasingly be able to recognize what our emotions are telling us about the state of our soul and our relationships.[18] Healthy people are connected to their body and soul and have the capacity to talk, feel, and deal with their positive and negative experiences. Their emotions are trusted and responded to in appropriate ways.

Manuel's Story

Manuel offers a helpful example of the progression from emotional deadness to emotional health. He was a successful physician who sought Steve's counsel after his affair with a nurse had been exposed. Manuel, who had engaged in repeated affairs, was ashamed but had no idea why he was stuck in such a destructive pattern. In his first few counseling sessions, he presented emotionally flat. With a dull voice Manuel described himself as depressed and wasn't sure he intended to stay in his marriage.

However, Manuel persevered through counseling and slowly began to face the reality of his behavior and connect the dots back to his early childhood pain. In short, he began to feel and listen to his heart. In time, he began to weep, not just because he was separated from his wife and three children, but because he had never felt like a real man during the duration of their fifteen-year marriage. He realized that his father's physical and verbal abuse had created deep insecurities regarding his masculinity, and that

---

18. See Dan B. Allender and Tremper Longman, *The Cry of the Soul: How Our Emotions Reveal Our Deepest Questions about God* (Colorado Springs: NavPress, 1994), 13–27.

getting drunk and having affairs were his subconscious attempts to bolster his fragile male ego. Through counseling he explored how his abusive father had fractured his trust in God, who seemed just as whimsical and unsafe as his father had been.

As Manuel began to face the impact of his father's abuse on his perception of God and himself, an internal light switched on. For the first time, he recognized that when he felt contempt toward others, he was ultimately projecting his own insecurities about his competence and worth onto them. As he stopped pulling away from his pain, he could stop pulling away from his wife and God. Instead, he learned to go directly to his heavenly Father with these insecurities and ask forgiveness for his cruelty to others. He began to recognize feelings of fear and distrust and repent of his attempts to bargain with and control God and others. Eventually, Manuel learned to share his true self, including his insecurities, with a small circle of trusted friends. These vulnerable, authentic connections began to give him a taste of real intimacy, the kind he had always longed for but could never find in alcohol, pornography, or affairs.

As Manuel cultivated his inner life, he learned to hear the faint stirrings of his heart and to respond to what they were telling him. One breakthrough came as he watched an elderly couple in a park share a cookie. He wept as he described this couple in the sunset of their life enjoying such a simple pleasure together. It stirred new longings in his heart to experience more of God's gifts and helped him realize how much he had missed by numbing his emotions.

In that one year, Manuel experienced more joy and intimacy than he had known in his previous forty years of life. He also experienced more sorrow, but his emotional pain no longer drove him to destructive addictions but instead to his heavenly Father and accountability partners. Manuel still mourns the losses subsumed within the reality of having an abusive father, but in coming alive and facing his brokenness, he was no longer driven by the destructive power of his father's abuse. By God's grace, he was set free.

A Healing Journey: One Stage at a Time

Over the past seventeen years since writing the first manuscript for *Mending the Soul*, we've come to more fully appreciate how healing is not a destination but rather a journey, and that our best contribution to the world will come from our wounds. As you face them and let God heal them, you'll help others do the same.

Grieving your losses is a respectful and honest response to pain. Moving into and through your painful feelings is like walking through a dark tunnel chiseled through an enormous mountain. As you walk into the tunnel, shadows obscure your view, but if you keep going, you'll emerge into the light on the other side. The important thing is to keep going—keep your pain moving—and you'll be surprised by the joy and hope you find. There's no amount of brokenness that cannot be mended and redeemed by Jesus' love and healing power. You'll get there, one step at a time.

The following six stages offer a simple framework for the messy business of healing. These stages are roughly but not strictly sequential. As one begins a particular stage, the previous stage or stages must often be solidified and incorporated into the next one. We move up and down a healing staircase as we learn to respond to life's pain in healthier ways. In time, these newly acquired skills and practices will become comfortable healing rhythms—a lot like taking satisfying, deep breaths that contribute to heart and brain health.

Stage 1: Stabilize and Establish Safety

> We have escaped like a bird
> 	from the fowler's snare;
> the snare has been broken,
> 	and we have escaped.
> Our help is in the name of the LORD,
> 	the Maker of heaven and earth.

Psalm 124:7–8

Safety

Healing begins once emotional, relational, physical, and spiritual safety have been established, and this takes time. It is the first necessary stage of healing.[19] It's common to think of safety in purely physical terms, but the other dimensions of safety—emotional, psychological, and spiritual—are just as important. The painting shown here (see figure 18) was commissioned during a time of military conflict in the Democratic Republic of the Congo and gifted to our MTS training team. It illustrates how faith

19. See Herman, *Trauma and Recovery*, 155–74; Bessel A. van der Kolk and Alexander C. McFarlane, "The Black Hole of Trauma," in *Traumatic Stress: The Effects of Overwhelming Experience on Mind, Body, and Society*, ed. Bessel A. van der Kolk, Alexander C. McFarlane, and Lars Weisaeth (New York: Guilford, 1996), 17–19. Some therapeutic models identify self-care as the first step in healing from abusive trauma (Chu, *Rebuilding Shattered Lives*, 78–80). While self-care is a broader category than establishing safety, establishing safety is a central aspect of self-care.

leaders have the ability to establish emotional and spiritual safety for abuse survivors, even when they can't fully provide physical safety.

In the painting, the pastor is lovingly teaching his congregation a biblical model of trauma care that helps them understand and mourn the abuse in their community (see Hosea 4:6). He has created a "safe place" in the church where his people can find refuge, comfort, and support, even though there is ongoing violence outside the church walls. This painting is precious to us and hangs in a prominent place in our offices, where we enjoy it daily as a hope-infused reminder of the potent healing power we have in a survivor's life.

Figure 18: "Then I will give you shepherds after my own heart, who will lead you with knowledge and understanding" (Jeremiah 3:15).
Unknown artist, given as a gift by the Community of Baptist Churches in Central Africa (CBCA leaders) in Goma, Democratic Republic of the Congo

It's difficult for those who haven't lived with an abusive husband or parent to appreciate the emotional and psychological toll of chronic abuse. Imagine the child who goes to bed every night wondering if this will be the night her father will fondle her. Imagine the wife who hypervigilantly waits for her drunk husband to come home in a blind rage. Imagine the child who can't sleep at night because that's when Mom gets high and abusive. Even though the abuse happens for a brief fraction of time, the abused child or battered spouse is constantly on alert—hypervigilant and anxious. Thus parents and church leaders must be particularly sensitive to the need for survivors to have a safe environment in which they can begin to heal; where they can regain that crucial sense of power and control over their lives that abuse strips them of.[20]

As helpers we must ask questions, not presume to know. A survivor knows what feels emotionally, relationally, and spiritually safe to them. We cannot know this for someone else. Safe people ask good questions and then believe what they hear—which acknowledges and validates any abuse of power. Relational trauma shatters trust in previously trusted people and places. So of course it takes time to establish therapeutic trust between two people. Be patient with the process and those you're helping. Healing takes the time healing takes.

While God can and does use suffering to build character, there is no virtue in enduring avoidable suffering.[21] We emphasize this because one of the bigger obstacles to the ability of domestically abused Christian women to find safety is church leaders' fear that encouraging a wife to pursue separation from an abusive husband may lead to divorce.[22]

It's important to note that Scripture teaches that we should avoid abuse and seek safety whenever possible; thus, helping establish safety for the abused has a strong biblical basis. Jesus repeatedly avoided physical assault and sought safety by hiding (John 8:59), by maintaining physical separation from his abusers (Matthew 12:14–15; John 11:53–54), and by eluding them (John 10:31, 39). Other godly individuals in the Bible, such as David and Paul, also repeatedly fled from abusers (1 Samuel 19:12; 27:1; Acts 9:22–25; 14:5–6; 17:8–10, 14).

The Bible also frequently instructs those in positions of power to

---

20. See Lundy Bancroft, *Why Does He Do That? Inside the Minds of Angry and Controlling Men* (New York: Berkley, 2002), xxii–xxiii; John N. Briere, *Child Abuse Trauma: Theory and Treatment of the Lasting Effects* (Thousand Oaks, CA: Sage, 1992), 23–27, 69–73.

21. Scripture is replete with affirmations of the myriad ways God redeems and uses suffering to deepen Christian character and bring about a greater good. See, for instance, Genesis 50:20; Job 42:5; Isaiah 53:4–12; Acts 14:22; Romans 5:3–5; 8:18–30; 2 Corinthians 4:16–18; Colossians 1:24; James 1:2–4; 1 Peter 1:3–9. Ajith Fernando offers one of the best practical, biblical overviews of how God positively uses suffering in the life of the believer (*The Call to Joy and Pain* [Wheaton, IL: Crossway, 2007]; see also Timothy Keller, *Walking with God through Pain and Suffering* [New York: Riverhead, 2013]).

22. Nancy Nason-Clark, "Christianity and the Experience of Domestic Violence: What Does Faith Have to Do with It?" *Social Work & Christianity* 36 (2009): 386–87. We should note that a growing number of evangelical theologians, including conservative evangelicals such as Wayne Grudem and John Frame, believe not just sexual but other forms of abuse provide biblical grounds for divorce. David Instone-Brewer, drawing heavily on Exodus 21:1–11, convincingly argues this position in *Divorce and Remarriage in the Bible: The Social and Literary Context* (Grand Rapids: Eerdmans, 2002). We affirm his conclusion that abuse gives biblical grounds for divorce.

ensure the safety and protection of those who are vulnerable (Psalm 82:3–4; Proverbs 24:11–12; Isaiah 1:17). Scripture is clear that godly leaders advocate for the abused. They are a voice for the voiceless, and they "defend the rights" of the vulnerable (Proverbs 31:8–9). God pronounces great blessings on those, particularly leaders, who protect the vulnerable and abused (Jeremiah 22:3–5) and pronounces severe judgment on those who fail to do so (Isaiah 5:6–9; Ezekiel 22:25–31).

Furthermore, protection of and care for the vulnerable and abused are cited in Scripture as examples of supreme godliness. For instance, when Job's "friends" asserted that he was suffering because God was punishing him for sin, Job, in his summary defense, cites his protection and care for the vulnerable as the quintessential evidence of godliness:

> I rescued the poor who cried for help,
>   and the fatherless who had none to assist them.
> The one who was dying blessed me;
>   I made the widow's heart sing . . .
> I was eyes to the blind
>   and feet to the lame.
> I was a father to the needy;
>   I took up the case of the stranger.
> I broke the fangs of the wicked
>   and snatched the victims from their teeth.
>   Job 29:12–13, 15–17 (see also Micah 6:8; James 1:27)

God unabashedly calls leaders—church, family, and societal—to provide safe, healing spaces for abuse victims. Tragically, the robust biblical mandate for leaders to protect and care for the abused stands in stark contrast to the experience of many survivors and their advocates. A 2019 study sponsored by Lifeway Christian Resources found that one in ten Protestant churchgoers under thirty-five have left a church because they believed sexual misconduct was not taken seriously.[23]

In our twenty-five years of supporting thousands of abuse survivors worldwide and their families and churches, we have found that survivors are all too often not protected and given safety. To informally quantify this dynamic, Mending the Soul anonymously surveyed in 2019 fifty-two adult

---

23. Kate Shellnutt, "1 in 10 Young Protestants Have Left a Church Over Abuse," *Christianity Today*, May 21, 2019, www.christianitytoday.com/news/2019/may/lifeway-protestant-abuse-survey-young-christians-leave-chur.html.

child sexual abuse survivors and parents of sexually abused children. Our goal was to give church leaders deeper insights into the experiences and needs of survivors. While we heard about many positive ways families and churches helped abuse victims, it was the decided exception. For instance, 61 percent of the respondents indicated they had disclosed the abuse to their families, but they were more than twice as likely to be disbelieved as believed. And the majority of those who reported the abuse to their churches were not believed or supported.

In summary, it is critically important to offer the highest levels of safety to abuse victims. To do that well, we must carefully listen and attune our responses to their felt safety needs.

Stabilization

Helping a survivor feel safe in their body by stabilizing overwhelming trauma symptoms is essential to healing. Once survivors know how to remember the past without becoming overwhelmed by it, they're ready to begin integrating past painful experiences with the present.

The most important tools for this stage of healing are psychoeducation, caregiver modeling of attention to safety (such as self-compassion/care), self-care, and skill building. In this stage, the survivor learns how to recognize, anticipate, and manage their trauma symptoms. Stabilization work (psychoeducation and symptom stabilization) will decrease a survivor's self-loathing and confusion and move them out of a victimized posture toward a place of agency and volition. Even though they did not choose trauma, they are now equipped to choose their response to it and manage the overwhelming symptoms that were previously outside of their control. *This is enormously empowering.* As a result, survivors learn that they're magnificently created to survive as smart and resourceful beings, which brings a renewed sense of hope.[24]

Once trauma symptoms are understood as perfectly normal reactions to abnormal traumatic events, each symptom can be experienced differently. During stabilization, a survivor learns that symptoms usually represent either a deeply encoded somatic memory or an attempt to solve a challenge or danger a survivor faced earlier.[25] Understanding and addressing trauma symptoms guides a survivor to the memory encoded within it. In chapter 6 we learned that trauma memories are encoded sensorially, not linguistically,

---

24. See Jeremiah 29:11, God's message of hope to traumatized Israelite exiles.
25. See Janina Fischer, "The Work of Stabilization in Trauma Treatment," paper presented at the Trauma Center Lecture Series, Boston, 1999, p. 3, https://janinafisher.com/pdfs/stabilize.pdf.

and thus a survivor can be triggered by seemingly benign sensory triggers, such as a certain kind of lighting, time of day, seasonal change, color, or smells.

The trauma symptom can guide a survivor back to original wounds. Once the wound is identified and healed, the body doesn't need the symptom anymore. During this phase, survivors are helped to normalize the feelings, such as distrust, they've pathologized in the past. A survivor learns, *I'm not crazy but I am traumatized*. Trauma symptoms are a sign that the body is doing what it was designed to do in the face of unnatural acts against it. The survivor learns that their body is actually working to protect them and has a beautiful built-in defense system against harmful acts that God never intended a human to endure.

Trauma symptoms become overwhelming when they do not subside and the body does not return to homeostasis. At this point, the survivor begins to think and feel something is wrong with them. In reality, understanding what the symptoms are trying to do and subsequently learning to monitor, control, and manage them is where the survivor's power lies in overcoming hopelessness and helplessness.

Mindfulness

There is much discussion in current trauma literature on the role of mindfulness in trauma healing.[26] The term *mindfulness* is used in widely varying ways by its proponents, but in the academic literature it normally refers to practices that allow a person to focus on the present while connecting to their inner state, thoughts, and sensations. It often involves meditation and deep breathing, as well as other forms of relaxation. Research has shown mindfulness to be quite effective in reducing the short and long-term effects of trauma.[27]

It should be noted that mindfulness does have historic roots in Buddhism, though this is by no means a necessary connection. Ironically, some Buddhists have argued that "secular" mindfulness practices are often safer for trauma survivors than those commonly practiced by Western

---

26. A variety of practical stabilizing exercises are found in Jennifer Sweeton, *Trauma Treatment Toolbox: 165 Brain-Changing Tips, Tools & Handouts to Move Therapy Forward* (Eau Claire, WI: PESI, 2019).

27. Lori Kachadourian et al., "Mindfulness as a Mediator between Trauma Exposure and Mental Health Outcomes: Results from the National Health and Resilience in Veterans Study," *Psychological Trauma: Theory, Research, Practice, and Policy* 13, no. 2 (2021): 223–30; Sarah Krill Williston et al., "Mindfulness Interventions in the Treatment of Posttraumatic Stress Disorder," *Professional Psychology: Research and Practice* 52, no. 1 (2021): 46–57; Dave Treleaven, *Trauma-Sensitive Mindfulness: Practices for Safe and Transformative Healing* (New York: Norton, 2018).

Buddhists.[28] In reality, the content and context of truly Christian mind-fulness is starkly different from Buddhist mindfulness. In Christian mindfulness, the goal is not detachment from the world but healing through heightened attachment to Christ and grounding in his Word. Rather than emptying their minds, Christians attune their mind to God and his remarkable attributes, his creation, and his promises.

Secular and Buddhist mindfulness places an emphasis on nonjudgmentalism regarding the thoughts and sensations one experiences, replacing them with a sense of curiosity. Because most survivors struggle with feeling responsible for their abuse and few abusers take responsibility for their abusive behavior, it makes sense why a nonjudgmental posture is, in the right context, very helpful in the early stages of healing.

Curiosity about the origin of trauma symptoms and triggers is vital to healing as well. We know that historic Christianity affirms the reality of objective truth revealed by God in his Word, and therefore moral and theological judgments are appropriate and necessary. At the same time, as we saw in chapter 5, abuse produces a plethora of toxic shame that causes survivors to misinterpret their experiences and inappropriately blame themselves. Furthermore, survivors often believe the trauma symptoms they're experiencing evidence the fact that they're abnormal or otherwise defective. Thus, particularly as it relates to the bodily sensations we begin to recognize, it is most helpful to approach them with a sense of nonjudgmental curiosity, asking God to help us more accurately understand what our bodies are trying to tell us.

Grounding and Centering

Grounding reconnects your brain to body to floor when you're experiencing high levels of anxiety, distress, or disassociation. It can be achieved simply by changing positions or focusing on the floor beneath your feet or the chair beneath your seat, while tightening and relaxing your pelvic floor muscles,[29]

---

28. Jane Compson, "Meditation, Trauma and Suffering in Silence: Raising Questions about How Meditation is Taught and Practiced in Western Contexts in the Light of a Contemporary Trauma Resiliency Model," *Contemporary Buddhism* 15, no. 2 (2014): 274–97.

29. To locate the pelvic floor area of the body while seated, place your hands beneath your bottom underneath the tailbone. Then with both hands, locate the front of the hip bones (the pointy front of your pelvis). Once you've felt a sense of this part of the body, imagine a line connecting those four points to create a three-dimensional square; this is your pelvic floor region. Actively release tension in this area by relaxing those muscles over and over. It takes practice! You will begin to notice how we constantly tighten our pelvic muscles, but when intentionally relaxed, the body sends a signal to the brain that it is in a relaxed state.

playing the hand-to-hand game with another person or a child,[30] or moving through a head-to-toe relaxation sequence—basically anything that puts you into a calm, centered, muscle-body state.[31] Ask yourself which tactile or kinesthetic sensations help you feel more present in your body? These might include taking a walk, drinking cold water, gardening, holding stones, bathing, and the like. When you're in a relaxed muscle-body state it is physiologically impossible to experience distress.

Breathing

Diaphragmatic or deep breathing calms the body by stimulating the parasympathetic nervous system that helps mediate acute stress responses. Science and spiritual expert Frank Huguenard writes:

> Of all the various functions of our autonomic nervous systems, from heart beat, perspiration, hormonal release, gastrointestinal operation, neurotransmitter secretion, etc., the breath stands alone as the only subsystem the conscious mind can put into 'manual override' and so it is through manipulation of the breath that we can recalibrate the entire system.[32]

There are several types of chest breathing that can help promote stabilization.[33]

Belly Breathing

According to the American Institute of Stress, twenty to thirty minutes of belly breathing each day will reduce anxiety and stress. Find a comfortable, quiet place to sit or lie down—in a chair, on the floor cross-legged, or lying on your back with small pillows under your head and knees. Place one hand on your upper chest and the other hand on your

30. See Steven R. Tracy and Celestia G. Tracy, *Caring for the Vulnerable Child: Welcoming Children Who Have Experienced Neglect, Abandonment and Abuse* (Phoenix, AZ: Mending the Soul Ministries, 2018), 63.

31. See Steven and Celestia Tracy, *By His Wounds: Trauma Healing for Africa* (Phoenix, AZ: Mending the Soul Ministries, 2014), 208–9.

32. Frank Huguenard, "The Vagus Nerve and the Healing Promise of the Sudarshan Kriya," Art of Living, August 1, 2019, www.artofliving.org/us-en/the-vagus-nerve-and-the-healing-promise-of-Sudarshan-Kriya. See also James Nestor, *Breath: The New Science of a Lost Art* (New York: Riverhead, 2020).

33. An excellent resource on stabilizing breathing is Sheryl Ankrom, "8 Deep Breathing Exercises for Anxiety," Verywell Mind, March 20, 2021, www.verywellmind.com/abdominal-breathing-2584115.

belly, below the rib cage. Allow your belly to relax, without forcing it inward by squeezing or clenching your muscles. Breathe in slowly through your nose. The air should move into your nose and downward so you feel your stomach rise with your other hand and fall inward (toward your spine). Exhale slowly through slightly pursed lips. Take note of the hand on your chest, which should remain relatively still. Repeat three times, one to four times a day.

Square Breathing (see figure 19)

1. Exhale to a count of four.
2. Hold your lungs empty for a count of four.
3. Inhale to a count of four.
4. Hold air in your lungs for a count of four.
5. Exhale and begin the pattern again.

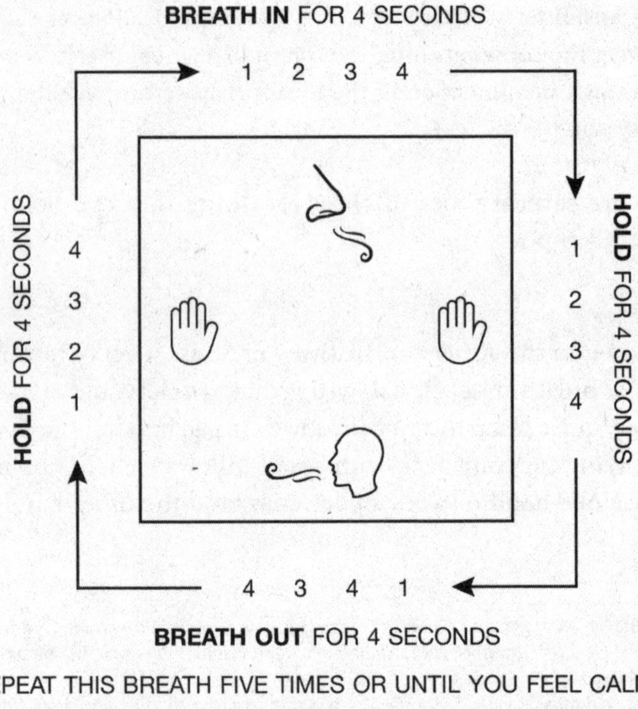

BREATH IN FOR 4 SECONDS
1 2 3 4
HOLD FOR 4 SECONDS
1 2 3 4
4 3 4 1
BREATH OUT FOR 4 SECONDS
HOLD FOR 4 SECONDS
4 3 2 1
REPEAT THIS BREATH FIVE TIMES OR UNTIL YOU FEEL CALMER

Figure 19: Square Breathing, also known as Box Breathing

Breath Prayers

Breath prayers involve repeating short prayers while focusing on your breathing, bringing your attention to the present without allowing your mind to drift to the past or future.[34] Breath prayers have a long tradition in the Christian church, particularly in the Eastern church, which developed the use of breath prayers as a way to be in constant prayer. To practice breath praying, think of a five- to seven-syllable phrase reflecting biblical truth that brings you peace: *Jesus, I belong to you; Father, be my light; Spirit, guide me in your way.* Connect your prayers to your deep breaths. If you notice your mind drifting, inhale and gently return your attention to the present.

Anchoring

Posttraumatic stress disorder symptoms involve sensory distortions in which the past intrudes on the present and the present on the past. Thankfully once intrusive symptoms (such as nightmares or flashbacks) are understood as sensory fragments about the past—and not connected to present reality—they lose their potency to frighten us. Anchoring involves techniques that connect survivors to present truth.[35] The *Mending the Soul Workbook for Men and Women* utilizes fine art and expressive art images as truth anchors for trauma survivors to secure them to comforting theological and biblical truth.[36]

Anchors can include photographs, drawings, objects, or any other image or words that feel safe to the survivor. Figure 20 is a drawing by James Van Fossan that appears in the workbook. Figure 21 is an example from the workbook of an expressive art exercise.

Figure 20: "I Will Heal Your Wounds"
James Van Fossan. Used with permission.

---

34. For an excellent explanation of Christian breath prayers, see Bill Gaultiere, "Breath Prayers with Jesus," www.soulshepherding.org/breath-prayers-with-jesus. The Soul Shepherding website has several helpful articles on breath prayers, as well as biblical breath prayer guides for purchase.

35. For a practical explanation of safe anchors for adults and children, see our adult workbook: Steven R. Tracy and Celestia G. Tracy, *A Parent's Journey to a Child's Heart* (Phoenix, AZ: Mending the Soul Ministries, 2018), 32–37.

36. Celestia G. Tracy, *Mending the Soul Workbook for Men and Women*, 2nd ed. (Phoenix, AZ: Mending the Soul Ministries, 2015).

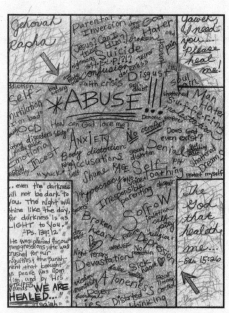

I created this cross...

during a desperate time in my healing journey, when I was truly making the transition of giving every bit of my pain to Him. I was suicidal and desperate for more of the Lord. I was desperately crying out to Him for whatever I needed. I drew a picture of the cross and put all my pain on it. Everything my abuse caused I heaved onto the Cross, as a heavy burden now off of my shoulders and safe with Jesus.

I look at this cross to remember that He died on the cross to carry these effects for me. I have many slash marks all across it to represent the stripes on Jesus' back, by which I AM BEING HEALED! As I made this picture, I almost broke the colored pencil by slash-slash-slashing the thing so much. I was healing as I did that, envisioning His healing stripes. I was brutally honest about all I had experienced and all I was feeling. This picture is very important for me to use as an...

anchor for my heart.

Figure 21

Stage 2: Choose to Face the Truth and Feel

> The tears which I had been holding back streamed down, and I let them flow as freely as they would, making of them a pillow for my heart. On them it rested.
>
> Saint Augustine, *Confessions*

This stage is inaugurated by the survivor's volitional choice to give up unhealthy defenses in order to feel and deal with the past. We've found that when a survivor feels safe and stable enough, they want to get better and will talk honestly about their pain and struggles. If they don't move into stage 2, it's usually because they don't feel safe or supported enough to do so. In this stage, a survivor expresses bold faith to begin the hard process of integrating their past with their present. In this stage, a survivor decides that it's better to face pain than to numb it, to face truth than to distort it.

This stage unfolds gradually because nobody can choose by an act of will to immediately eradicate emotional numbing or mental distortions. Even if a survivor wants to feel, they cannot simply conjure up specific feelings or establish clear perceptions of reality. In the early stages of healing, survivors rarely comprehend how deeply abuse has influenced their perceptions and feelings. Consequently, this healing stage involves *choosing to begin the journey of emotional health*. It involves a deliberate choice to no longer suppress truth and a willingness to enter into whatever feelings surface as they abandon denial and minimization of past abuse. For many, it's the most terrifying step imaginable, for they've spent their entire lives and enormous amounts of psychological energy keeping pain on the other side of consciousness.

Thus, choosing to face the truth and feel the feelings involves a deliberate act of worship based on God's trustworthiness and recognition that our innate human resources are utterly inadequate to heal. We see this in Proverbs 3:5–6 (NASB), where the writer admonishes us to "trust in the LORD with all your heart and do not lean on your own understanding. In all your ways acknowledge Him, and He will make your paths straight." As you begin to lean on God and not yourself, he promises to provide "healing to your body and refreshment to your bones" (3:8 NASB). The Hebrew word in Proverbs 3:5 for "trust" (*batah*) indicates complete reliance, which results in security and confidence.[37] It is often contrasted with the false security that comes from trusting in humans, riches, idols, military powers, religion, or one's own righteousness.[38]

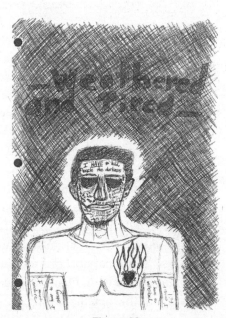

Figure 22

The following picture was drawn by an adolescent boy and poignantly expresses his emotional and spiritual condition after being exposed to sexual abuse in his church (see figure 22). It vividly illustrates both the tendency of survivors to lean on themselves and the inadequacy and futility of such a strategy. The picture is titled "Weathered and Tired." Written on the boy's face and body are various phrases that articulate drastic reliance on self for healing and protection: "I *have* to hold back the darkness." "I must endure." "I have to be strong." "I have to withstand." "I cannot fail." His heart

---

37. John Oswalt notes that *batah* is similar to the theological term *faith*, but this Hebrew word stresses the emotional aspect of trust and of feeling secure (R. Laird Harris, Gleason L. Archer Jr., and Bruce K. Waltke, eds., *Theological Wordbook of the Old Testament*, vol. 1 [Chicago: Moody, 1980], 101).

38. See Harris, *Theological Wordbook*, 102. See such Bible passages as Deuteronomy 28:52; Psalms 31:6; 49:6; 118:8; 146:3; Jeremiah 7:4; Ezekiel 33:3.

is framed with the words, "Make the hurting stop!" Sadly, no matter how much energy he puts into this effort, he cannot endure. He cannot be strong enough. He cannot hold back the darkness, nor can he heal his hurting heart. Only God can!

Denial and deadness may provide temporary relief, but they can never heal or make us feel secure. They are feeble substitutes that just make us more tired and disconnected from those who love us. Healing requires that we turn, in an act of faith, from reliance on human strategies for healing and toward God by choosing to face the truth and embrace the feelings.

Stage 3: Reconnect the Past with the Present—Tell Your Story

> Of one thing I am perfectly sure: God's story never ends with ashes.
>
> Elisabeth Elliot, *Made for the Journey*

In the past decade, there has been some pushback against a traditional trauma healing model that emphasizes telling one's trauma story.[39] Caution is in order here. Prematurely processing abuse memories can intensify trauma symptoms and mitigate against healing. Bessel van der Kolk helpfully notes, "Telling the story is important; without stories, memory becomes frozen," but "telling a story about the event does not guarantee that the traumatic memories will be laid to rest."[40] He goes on to note that the key to successfully processing memories lies in keeping the brain from being overwhelmed and going "offline."[41] Another way of saying this is this: "As important as it is to acknowledge the past, it is even more crucial for traumatized individuals to stay [bodily] connected to present time."[42] In other words, survivors must develop self-care and stabilization skills that allow the rational portions of their brain to access the past without being retraumatized by it. Once adequate self-care and stabilization skills are in place, it's time to tell your story.

One of the most effective tools to use in this third stage is a timeline that captures both positive and painful memories.[43] The *Mending the Soul*

---

39. See, for instance, Babette Rothschild, who states, "I have increasingly found the trauma therapy default mode—to process trauma memories—to be outdated and overrated" (*The Body Remembers*, vol. 2 [New York: Norton, 2017], 110).

40. Bessel van der Kolk, *The Body Keeps the Score: Brain, Mind, and Body in the Healing of Trauma* (New York: Viking, 2014), 219.

41. Van der Kolk, *Body Keeps the Score*, 220. See also Peter Levine, *Trauma and Memory: Brain and Body in a Search for the Living Past* (Berkeley, CA: North Atlantic, 2015), 63.

42. Janina Fisher, *Healing the Fragmented Selves of Trauma Survivors: Overcoming Internal Self-Alienation* (New York: Routledge, 2017), 39.

43. For an exercise in creating a timeline, see Tracy, *Mending the Soul*, 36–37.

Workbook for Men and Women encourages a survivor to place five to ten of the most significant events of their life on a timeline. These include both positive, life-giving experiences and negative, painful secrets of their past. This is a difficult step to take in the beginning but an essential one.

Many survivors, before doing their work, talk about their life story in ways that more closely resemble a "fairy tale rather than history."[44] This is because the strategies of numbing and denial that helped them survive abuse are not the same strategies they'll need to heal so they can enjoy healthy relationships. Telling your story can be done in a clinical setting with a professional counselor; with a well-trained, trauma-informed mentor; or within the safe community of a small recovery group.[45] The apostle Paul affirms the importance and efficacy of carrying each other's burdens in Galatians 6:2. If however, revisiting abuse memories becomes too overwhelming and triggers unmanageable trauma symptoms, we recommend utilizing a professional counselor to supplement the community-based support of a small group.

Constructing a family history is another helpful tool for integration. The history would include not only the abuse events themselves but also the responses of family members and caregivers to the abuse and the impact of their responses. It's important to remember that the abusive patterns you experienced in the context of your family of origin will be re-created in the next generation unless you process and heal them. The abuse survivor who goes first in a family creates a healing path for others to follow. Your healing is the best gift you can give your family!

Frederick Buechner, who grew up keeping destructive family secrets that included the suicide of his father, offers helpful guidance regarding familial honesty:

> I have come to believe that by and large the human family all has the same secrets, which are both very telling and very important to tell. They are telling in the sense that they tell what is perhaps the central paradox of our condition—that what we hunger for perhaps more than anything else is to be known in our full humanness, and yet that is often just what we also fear more than anything else. It is important to tell at least from time to time the secret of who we truly and fully are—even if we tell it

---

44. Cameron, *Resolving Childhood Trauma*, 211.

45. Peter Dale has an excellent discussion for therapists on the challenges and the process of helping clients talk about their abuse (*Adults Abused as Children: Experiences of Counselling and Psychotherapy* [Thousand Oaks, CA: Sage, 1999], 103–25). Go to www.mendingthesoul.org to find a MTS small group in your community or to train as a small group facilitator.

only to ourselves—because otherwise we run the risk of losing track of who we truly and fully are and little by little come to accept instead the highly edited version which we put forth in hope that the world will find it more acceptable than the real thing. It is important to tell our secrets too because it makes it easier that way to see where we have been in our lives and where we are going. It also makes it easier for other people to tell us a secret or two of their own, and exchanges like that have a lot to do with what being a family is all about and what being human is all about.[46]

Some abuse survivors resist constructing a family history for two reasons: (1) abusive families vigorously indoctrinate and intimidate their victims into keeping family secrets, and (2) chronicling family dysfunction and sin seems disrespectful and unimportant. However, clarifying the truth about one's family is neither inherently disrespectful nor mean, but it is necessary to reject unwarranted shame and guilt, expose lies, protect oneself and others from additional abuse, and take appropriate responsibility for our own behavior. Abuse will continue for generations until it is exposed and dealt with; only then does it stop.[47]

Unless we reflect on the truth of our families, we will repeat the dysfunction. This principle is found in psychological research literature, but, most importantly, it's biblical. The clearest example is seen in the history of the Israelite kings, most of whom were ungodly and led Israel and Judah into idolatry and evil. They had not only a broad societal influence for evil but also an immediate familial influence. For example, we read, "[King Abijah] committed all the sins his father had done before him" (1 Kings 15:3). "And [King Amon] did evil in the eyes of the LORD, as his father Manasseh had done. He followed completely the ways of his father" (2 Kings 21:20–21). Other passages highlight the intergenerational nature of family sins, noting that kings did evil according to all that their fathers (plural) had done (23:32, 37).

The rare kings who broke from the ungodliness of their fathers had to consciously assess the family history, sin, and dysfunction and, with God's help, choose to go against the family traditions and influences. King Hezekiah's father was Ahaz, a very wicked man. Hezekiah broke from the family behavioral patterns he had seen modeled and called the nation to do the same: "Do not be like your parents and your fellow Israelites, who were

---

46. Frederick Buechner, *Listening to Your Life* (New York: HarperCollins, 1992), 317–18.

47. For an excellent discussion of honoring an abusive parent, see Jennifer Greenberg, "Honoring Your Father When He's Evil," Gospel Coalition, June 18, 2021, www.thegospelcoalition.org/article/honoring-father-evil.

unfaithful to the LORD, the God of their ancestors" (2 Chronicles 30:7). Godly king Asa actually deposed his own mother from the position of queen due to her practice of idolatry—a practice she learned from her ancestors (1 Kings 15:12–13). In short, it is not unkind or ungodly to thoroughly assess the truth about one's own family.[48] It is necessary for emotional and spiritual health.

Abuse survivors need to do more than just tell the facts of the story; they need to feel the appropriate emotions as well. This is best done with the help of a safe listener who can reflect back to the abuse survivor an appropriate emotional response to the abuse story. For the survivor, the initial processing of abuse memories tends to be more factual than emotional—at least in part because abuse constricts and distorts emotions that were too terrible and overwhelming to feel at the time of the abuse. In the early stages, survivors tell their tragic stories of abuse with little or no emotion, recounting the facts of their abuse as though they were reading a weather report. Sometimes survivors even smile or laugh as they tell of being raped or beaten.

Speaking the facts is an essential first step, but healing comes as one tells their story and integrates that truth with the appropriate emotional response.[49] One of the best ways to do this is through journaling the abuse event, with the purpose of entering into the feeling associated with the past abuse.[50] In other words, survivors must reflect on the abusive event and on what they felt when it happened.

Dissociation and emotional constriction may have taken place so quickly and thoroughly at the time of the abuse that a survivor may find it nearly impossible to identify their past emotions. In this case, it may help to envision a child the same age they were when the abuse took place, and then to imagine what that child would feel if they experienced the same abuse and go on to share their reflections with a safe, empathetic listener. For instance, in the *Mending the Soul Workbook*, participants are invited to paste or draw a picture of themselves as a young child and then to respond to several prompts as they meditate on this image.[51]

---

48. Antwone Fisher, whose foster parents abused him for fifteen years and then abandoned him to the streets, eventually dealt with the hidden rage and soul damage that was destroying him. His poem "Recollections" is written to his abusive foster parents and is an excellent example of facing and telling the truth about one's abusive family (*Who Will Cry for the Little Boy?* [New York: HarperCollins, 2003], 61).

49. See Mary Ann Donaldson and Russell Gardner Jr., "Diagnosis and Treatment of Traumatic Stress among Women after Childhood Incest," in *Trauma and Its Wake: The Study and Treatment of Post-Traumatic Stress Disorder*, ed. Charles R. Figley (New York: Brunner/Mazel, 1985), 368–73; Herman, *Trauma and Recovery*, 177–78.

50. On the healing power of writing down one's trauma experiences, see Adi Duchin and Hadas Wiseman, "Memoirs of Child Survivors of the Holocaust: Processing and Healing of Trauma through Writing," *Qualitative Psychology* 6, no. 3 (2019): 280–96.

51. Tracy, *Mending the Soul Workbook*, 49.

Stage 4: Identify Distortions and Reclaim Your Original Design

I believe that each of us comes from the Creator trailing wisps of glory.

Maya Angelou, Academy of Achievement interview

Abuse distorts thoughts and perceptions about oneself, others, and God. When a child is abused, they cannot discern truth about their abuse, for they don't have the mental or emotional resources to do so. However, God calls us, his adult children, to boldly identify lies and not allow ourselves to be led astray (Mark 13:15; Titus 3:3; 1 John 3:7). It's difficult for survivors to identify shame-driven lies because they're so cleverly embedded, have often been present for years, and rarely operate at a conscious level.[52] They're difficult to identify, let alone combat. Thus, survivors need the help of others with abuse experience or professional Christian counselors to identify shame-based lies and distortions, so they can be replaced with truth.[53]

- **Common shame-based lies about God** include "I can't trust God because he didn't stop my abuse"; "God hates me"; "God is disgusted with me"; "God is punishing me for being such a horrible person."
- **Common lies about others** include "If others really knew who I am, they would reject me"; "You can't trust anyone; people will only hurt you"; "Men are all alike; all they want to do is use women"; "No decent man will ever want me."
- **Common lies about oneself** include "The abuse must have been my fault; I must have deserved it"; "I am permanently defective"; "My sexual urges show that I am disgusting and perverted"; "I don't deserve a decent guy; I would just ruin the relationship." All such lies are very damaging. Once the abuse survivor begins to identify the lies created by their abuse, the Bible can be used to challenge these lies.[54]

---

52. See John Briere, "Treating Adult Survivors," in *The APSAC Handbook on Child Maltreatment*, 2d ed., ed. John E. B. Myers et al. (Thousand Oaks, CA: Sage, 2002), 179–80.

53. A woman identified as Lydia offers several lies that were created by her abuse. She categorizes these into lies about Christ, the Holy Spirit, Satan, the church, men, women, the family, herself, and authority ("Testimony of an Abuse Survivor," in *Healing the Hurting: Giving Hope and Help to Abused Women*, ed. Catherine Clark Kroeger and James R. Beck [Grand Rapids: Baker, 1998], 71–74). See also Derek Jehu, Carole Klassen, and Marjorie Gazan, "Cognitive Restructuring of Distorted Beliefs Associated with Childhood Sexual Abuse," *Journal of Social Work and Human Sexuality* 4 (1986): 49–69.

54. Sandra Wilson offers a helpful visual that contrasts various shame-based lies with the corresponding truth (*Released from Shame*, rev. ed. [Downers Grove, IL: InterVarsity, 2002], 115). The truth that challenges shame-based lies must ultimately come from Scripture, our only sure source of truth in this life (2 Timothy 3:16–17). Once the lies and the biblical truth have been identified, the abuse survivor must learn to discipline the mind to embrace the truth and reject the lies ("We take captive every thought to make it obedient to Christ" [2 Corinthians 10:5]).

In chapter 2 we noted that being made in God's image creates powerful longings that are connected to our capacity for intimate relationships that mirror the Trinitarian relationships. When abuse fractures relational intimacy, victims' longings for relationship cause them to conclude that *they* are the problem—that something defective in them must have caused their abuse.

Integral to the relational aspect of the image of God is our sexuality as male or female. Sexual abuse perverts the beauty of our sexuality, so that normal sexual urges are given a shameful interpretation. Sadly, this is why sexual abuse victims often attach shame to marital sexual relations. Some survivors loathe their bodies because of sexual shame that causes normal bodily sensations to feel unsafe and dirty. Some survivors reject all physical pleasure and are destructive to their bodies through self-starvation or self-injury. All survivors must come to the point where they can accept that their sexuality, their bodies, and their longings for relationships, love, and affectionate touch are all majestic aspects of God's original design. Under the lordship of Christ, each is sanctified and ought to be embraced.

Mending the Soul's trauma-care model was shaped by Celestia's clinical care and our work with thousands of survivors worldwide. Consistently, we've observed a pattern: when a survivor uncovers their specific shame-based lies, they discover that those lies are direct perversions of the best of their original design. For example, a thirty-year-old single professional woman described many shameful childhood memories involving public humiliation and verbal abuse by her father when she "hammed it up" for the camera. As a child, she had an effervescent and vivacious personality easily detectable in the childhood pictures she brought to counseling. By age thirteen, her vivacious personality had completely changed. She had become reclusive and no longer tried out for cheer squads or school sports teams. By age twenty-six, she was a hundred pounds overweight and completely shut down. She couldn't keep a job due to uncontrollable angry outbursts, had never dated, and loathed her femininity—seeking to hide it as effectively as possible. What impressed Celestia the most about this woman was her underlying beauty, quick wit, and love for movement.

Celestia enthusiastically described their counseling sessions as a work of "uncovering buried treasure." Beneath the layers of shame was a cache of pure gold. As this woman began to grow and reclaim the truth of her original design, she signed up for dance classes and volunteered to direct the church play. She was tentatively unlocking a door that had been slammed shut for a very long time. One by one, she began to re-embrace those aspects of her personality and gifting that had previously been shamed out of her. She was rediscovering her best self—created by God for his glory and her joy.

Stage 5: Love Radically Out of a Truth-Infused Identity

So it is if the heart has devoted itself to love, there is not a single inch of emptiness.

Mary Oliver, "Honey Locust"

You may remember from chapter 6 that some aspects of traumatic stress surrounding the abuse are autonomic (not conscious) choices. As abused children grow into adulthood, however, the psychological mechanisms they automatically employed in childhood to cope with overwhelming trauma begin to become destructive patterns for which they must take moral responsibility. What begins as necessary childhood defenses can subtly become a crutch, and a crutch can become an idol, which is anything that we give our trust and allegiance to other than our Savior.

While only God knows precisely where the lines are drawn for any given individual, the important thing is to recognize that such lines of personal responsibility do exist and to know where that line is for ourselves. As we heal, we become more like Christ in the ways that we love those around us. Self-protection is in clear conflict with radical love.

One of the greatest ironies of a Christ-centered journey is that the path of life is the path of death to self (Matthew 16:24–25). Jesus tells us that the way to save one's life is to lose it (Matthew 10:39). In Jeremiah 17:5–8, judgment is pronounced on those who put their trust in humans instead of in God. The prophet warns that those who rely on human strength in the day of trouble will be like a scorched bush in the barren desert. They won't recognize prosperity when it comes. They will not experience life, vibrancy, or fruitfulness. This is a jolting description of those who, in the midst of pain, decide to manage it on their own terms instead of turning to their Creator:

> But blessed is the one who trusts in the LORD,
>   whose confidence is in him.
> They will be like a tree planted by the water
>   that sends out its roots by the stream.
> It does not fear when heat comes;
>   its leaves are always green.
> It has no worries in a year of drought
>   and never fails to bear fruit. (Jeremiah 17:7–8)

It is true. We *do* face overwhelming forces, and evil *is* too much for us, but this is exactly where faith comes in. Instead of trying to manage on our own terms a world that feels out of control, in faith we turn to God, recognize our spiritual poverty, and cling to Jesus as our only hope for life and health (John 6:68). God is our deliverer and redeemer (Colossians 1:13–14). Cling to his assurance that he will finish the good work he has begun in you (Philippians 1:6). Dare to hope on the basis of naked faith in Jesus Christ, who died to give abundant life to the dying (John 10:10).

Stage 6: Live Your Redemptive Purpose

> Don't bear trouble, use it. Take whatever happens—justice and injustice, pleasure and pain, compliment and criticism—take it up into the purpose of your life and make something out of it.
>
> E. Stanley Jones, *A Song of Ascents*

This one thing we know is that suffering is not meaningless in God's economy. One of the most important aspects of trauma healing occurs in the latter stages when we begin to find meaning in the pain and regain a sense of appropriate power. As Christians we believe that our power doesn't come from ourselves but from God. This is a strange concept in a world that worships power. But the God of the Scriptures—though he is mighty and all-powerful—delights in working through human weakness, using wounds and vulnerabilities to showcase his power. He delights to use Satan's evil plans as the very means of accomplishing his good purposes.

We see this clearly in the life of the apostle Paul, who had a difficult "thorn in the flesh," apparently some form of physical ailment sent by Satan to make life and ministry difficult. It was chronic and disfiguring. For three seasons, Paul asked God to remove this disability, but God said no. He specifically told Paul, "My grace is sufficient for you, for my power is made perfect in weakness." Paul responded by declaring, "Therefore I will boast all the more gladly about my weaknesses, so that Christ's power may rest on me . . . For when I am weak, then I am strong" (2 Corinthians 12:9–10).

Before Satan is destroyed forever, God works on earth through pain and loss. Though Satan still has power to harm, God is almighty and present in suffering's darkest places, actively redeeming evil. We see this principle powerfully at work in the life of Joseph. His brothers committed evil against him, but God providentially used all of those circumstances for good: "You intended to harm me, but God intended it for good to accomplish what is now being done, the saving of many lives" (Genesis 50:20).

One of the most powerful ways we see this principle at work is when trauma survivors are in time able to use their own stories to care for others who have suffered in similar ways. These caregivers have confidence and power that doesn't come any other way. This is similar to what Paul says in 2 Corinthians 1:3–4: "Praise be to the God and Father of our Lord Jesus Christ, the Father of compassion and the God of all comfort, who comforts us in all our troubles, so that we can comfort those in any trouble with the comfort we ourselves receive from God."

In northern Rwanda, we partnered with a translator who shared that fifty-two of his family members had been slaughtered in the genocide, many in front of his eyes. Today he has a powerful ministry of reconciliation and exudes joy. He found redemptive purpose in his suffering.

Similarly, Corrie ten Boom was a Dutch woman whose family was imprisoned by the Nazis for protecting Jews during the Nazi genocide. She suffered years of evil at the hands of German guards in a death camp. After she was liberated, God sent her to more than sixty countries in order to bring her story of trauma, message of healing, and forgiveness to the world. In an unforgettable way, she proclaimed two primary messages: "There is no pit so deep that God's love is not deeper still," and "God will give us the love to forgive our enemies." In God's economy, pain can always be redeemed.

Now that we've created a model for biological and emotional healing, we will in the next chapter unpack interpersonal healing, beginning with our relationship with God.

CHAPTER 9

Rebuilding Intimacy with God

And so I believe in Christ and confess him
not like some child; my hosanna has passed
through an enormous furnace of doubt.

Fyodor Dostoyevsky, *Literaturnoe nasledstvo*

Most of the verses written about praise in God's
Word were voiced by people who were faced with
crushing heartaches, injustice, treachery, slander,
and scores of other difficult situations.

Joni Eareckson Tada, *A Quiet Place in a Crazy World*

My ears had heard of you
but now my eyes have seen you.

Job 42:5

In 1880, the immortal Russian novelist Fyodor Dostoyevsky penned *The Brothers Karamazov*, a literary masterpiece described by many as the greatest novel ever written. It's a complex tale of a troubled family with a "wretched and depraved" father who is eventually murdered by one of his sons. Dostoyevsky used this novel to probe some of life's most vexing questions, particularly the question of how a good, all-powerful God could allow widespread, hideous child abuse.

In this novel, Dostoyevsky expresses many of his own spiritual struggles. Given the fact that Dostoyevsky's father had been an abusive alcoholic surgeon who was so cruel that his serfs murdered him, it's no wonder that Dostoyevsky agonized over how someone who had witnessed or experienced child abuse could ever develop intimacy with God.

Dostoyevsky employs two of the novel's main characters—rationalistic, skeptical Ivan and his idealistic, religious brother Alyosha—to articulate this dilemma. In a chapter titled "Rebellion," Ivan mercilessly presses Alyosha with the horror of rampant abuse. First, he recounts how the Turks ravaged villages, raped women, and bayoneted live babies while their mothers watched in horror.[1]

Then he tells the story of a "well-educated, cultured [European] gentleman" who sadistically beat his seven-year-old daughter with a large "rod" cut from a tree. The father was most delighted when his punishing rod had knots in it, because "it stings more," he said. He would beat the defenseless child for five to ten minutes straight, while she screamed pitifully until she gasped for air, whimpering, "Daddy! Daddy!" The father was eventually prosecuted for assaulting his daughter but was later acquitted by a jury that bought the lawyer's argument that flogging a child was "such a simple thing" and "an everyday occurrence."[2]

Ivan goes on to tell another story of an eight-year-old Russian boy, who, while playing in a courtyard, accidentally hit a general's dog with a rock and injured its leg. The general responded by setting his hunting dogs on the boy, killing him in front of his own mother. Ivan ends his discourse by boldly declaring that if the suffering of innocent children is the price, or "ticket," for a relationship with God, then he will have to pass. He issues this protest: "Too high a price is asked for harmony; it's beyond our means to pay so much. And so I give back my entrance ticket, and if I am an honest man I give it back as soon as possible. And that I am doing. It's not God that I don't accept, Alyosha, only I most respectfully return the ticket to Him."[3]

Few who have experienced abuse are as bold as Ivan Karamazov in declaring their unwillingness to relate to God. But as we noted in the previous chapter, while victims of abuse tend to respond to God in three different ways—rejecting, withholding, or cowering—the end result is quite similar: intimacy with God is shattered.

Thankfully, estrangement from God need not be final. As vehemently as Dostoyevsky protested the injustice of child abuse and as graphically as he reflected on its horrors, he eventually overcame this obstacle to his faith. In fact, as one of Dostoyevsky's biographers recounts, it was while Dostoyevsky was suffering abusive imprisonment and exile in Siberia that he had a dramatic and intimate encounter with Christ that remained with him for the rest of his life.

Dostoyevsky was arrested on political charges, convicted, and sentenced

---

1. Fyodor Dostoyevsky, *The Brothers Karamazov* (1880; repr., New York: New American Library, 1958), 219–20.

2. Dostoyevsky, *Brothers Karamazov*, 222.

3. Dostoyevsky, *Brothers Karamazov*, 226.

to die. He was forced to dig his own grave and then was ushered to the place of execution. Seconds before his execution, his sentence was unexpectedly commuted, and he was sent to prison in Siberia, where he witnessed and experienced widespread human misery. Almost a decade later, Dostoyevsky was released from prison, and rather than driving him *away* from God, these experiences drove him *to* God. His biographer summarizes the spiritual result of Dostoyevsky's experiences in Siberia: "Amidst inhuman sufferings, in a struggle with doubt and negation, faith in God was won."[4]

Fyodor Dostoyevsky demonstrates that while abuse often shatters intimacy with God, its effects need not be permanent. Even victims of severe, chronic abuse can rebuild a meaningful connection with God.

The Satanic Strategy

Satan himself masquerades as an angel of light. It is not surprising, then, if his servants also masquerade as servants of righteousness. Their end will be what their actions deserve.

2 Corinthians 11:14–15

Spiritual reconnection is a process that takes time and energy. In this section, we will discuss four foundational activities that will lead to deeper intimacy with God. To put these strategies in their proper context, we must briefly reflect on Satan's strategy. We saw in chapter 1 that abuse has been rampant throughout history largely because Satan is the most powerful evil being in the universe. He does not have God's power to create, so instead he delights in perverting the best of God's creation. He particularly enjoys distorting and destroying our faith in a good God. This was seen in the very first human sin recorded in Genesis 3:1–5.

Here's Satan's cunning, three-pronged temptation strategy:

Satan's Strategy in the Garden of Eden

Satan's Tactic	Biblical Dialogue
Question God's word	"Did God really say . . . ?"
Discredit God's word	"If you eat the fruit, you won't die."
Malign God's character	"God knows if you eat you'll become like him."

4. Konstantin Mochulsky, *Dostoevsky: His Life and Work* (Princeton, NJ: Princeton University Press, 1967), 650.

Adam and Eve took the bait, distrusted God, and shattered relationship with their loving Creator. Satan targets us in similar ways:

Satan's Strategy Today

Satan's Tactic	Internal Dialogue
Doubt God's word	"Surely the Bible doesn't teach you can't have sex with your boyfriend. After all, that's all you're good for."
Discredit God's word	"John 3:16 isn't true for you. You're too messed up for God to love you."
Malign God's character	"You can't trust God. He is either impotent or mean— or maybe both. After all, he didn't stop your father from raping you. Maybe God doesn't even exist."

Satan uses the specific effects of abuse trauma to facilitate his three-pronged spiritual disruption strategy. He especially uses emotional numbing (constriction), powerlessness, shame, and betrayal as strategic ways to disconnect survivors from God.[5] People who are emotionally constricted find it very difficult to be intimate with God or anyone else because they are shut down; those who feel powerless are understandably afraid of a powerful God, fearing he can't be trusted; those who are flooded with shame hide from God because of their perverted view of themselves and of his character; those who feel deeply betrayed withdraw from God to protect themselves and are unable to give themselves to others. God is steadfastly reaching for every survivor, yet the effects of abuse are roadblocks that must be overcome to understand and trust again in a loving God.

In view of Satan's strategy and the specific effects of abuse, the following four activities are essential.

How to Spiritually Reconnect

In repentance and rest is your salvation,
in quietness and trust is your strength.

Isaiah 30:15

5. This is similar to the list developed by Joanne Ross Feldmeth and Midge Wallace Finley (*We Weep for Ourselves and Our Children: A Christian Guide for Survivors of Childhood Sexual Abuse* [San Francisco: HarperSanFrancisco, 1990], 88–89).

Wrestling with God

The psalmists challenge us to decide how serious we plan to be about our relationship with God. And here, the greatest danger is not our questions but our silence . . . Oftentimes, we never ask God difficult questions because we are never disappointed or confused by God—and we are never disappointed because we never really expected God to do anything in the first place.

Glenn Pemberton, *Hurting with God: Learning
to Lament with the Psalms*

We were blessed to grow up in loving Christian homes and stable communities. As young adults we didn't understand physical or emotional struggles because as children, abuse and human misery were foreign to our experience. Thus, like many Westerners, we were utterly unprepared for the painful realities of life. Our Christian faith was robustly zealous, while at the same time we were blinded by our naivete.

This all began to change soon after we married when Steve's mother was diagnosed with cancer. Over the next eighteen months, she suffered terribly and almost died. Her suffering seemed senseless and unfair and didn't fit our preconceptions. Our comfortable and predictable world began to shake. And then three months later, our world turned upside down. In the middle of what was to be a five-hour getaway, Celestia suffered a catastrophic accident that resulted in six major orthopedic surgeries and hospitalizations within the next three years.[6] This inaugurated a journey of chronic pain that has marked our adult lives.

Suffering has scarred and changed us—yet God in his goodness has used every bit of it. Today we have the sacred privilege of resourcing and training faith leaders around the world to bring trauma care in Jesus' name to their people. We have borne witness to atrocity and unspeakable evil, and yet we stand and testify today that trauma does not have the final word! Over and over, we have seen God heal broken lives and, through the arduous path of healing, replace disconnection from God with intimate encounters with him.

God doesn't give all the answers to our haunting questions, but he gives himself to those who look for him in the dark. As Nicholas Wolterstorff

---

6. Since Celestia's initial accident in 1983 she has undergone 27 major surgeries because of the effects of a degenerative connective tissue disease. The trauma from these ongoing fractures and soft tissue tears have precipitated a neurological disease, CRPS, which manifests in chronic nerve pain.

astutely notes, "Instead of explaining our suffering God shares it."[7] And this redemptive journey begins with wrestling with God.

Most of us haven't been offered a theology of suffering, even though real biblical worship and practice involves "lament" in which individuals and/or groups cry out to God in their emotional distress, physical danger, and spiritual anguish.[8] Biblical worship is characterized by honest, even raw emotional language in which the speaker expresses pain, confusion, and threats—which includes both the suffering caused by their own actions or the actions of others, as well as the pain precipitated by what we perceive as God's failure to intervene in the face of evil.[9]

It is noteworthy that the entire book of Lamentations is a formal lament over the destruction of Jerusalem and the abuse suffered by God's people. In addition, 40 percent of the psalms, which in Hebrew means "praises," are lament.[10] In other words, Scripture gives us permission and a template for expressing directly to God the depth of one's overwhelming sorrow.

How do you wrestle with God? What does it involve? Celestia's description of her own spiritual journey in the first few years after her accident gives several practical insights.

A black hole of pain and despair was swallowing me because my body would not heal. I would push so hard in physical therapy that I would tear tendons and rebreak bones. My world, as I had known it, was over. I kept trying to *will* myself well because I was terrified to face a future that I could not control in a weak body I could not make strong.

I was exasperated with God because I knew he could heal me in an instant but was choosing not to. Why? I didn't understand! In my mind, this was proof that either he wasn't a very loving God or that *I* was not worth his care and protection. God was scaring me because he felt cold

---

7. Nicholas Wolterstorff, *Lament for a Son* (Grand Rapids: Eerdmans, 1987), 81.

8. Soong-Chan Rah, in his excellent work on the book of Lamentations, defines biblical lament as "a liturgical response to the reality of suffering and engages God in the context of pain and trouble" (*Prophetic Lament: A Call for Justice in Troubled Times* [Downers Grove, IL: InterVarsity, 2015], 21). On biblical lament see also Michael Card, *A Sacred Sorrow: Reaching Out to God in the Lost Language of Lament* (Colorado Springs: NavPress 2005); Scott Ellington, *Risking Truth: Reshaping the World through Prayers of Lament* (Eugene, OR: Wipf and Stock, 2008); Glenn Pemberton, *Hurting with God: Learning to Lament with the Psalms* (Abilene, TX: Abilene Christian University Press, 2002).

9. For instance, Habakkuk 1:3, 13 (ESV): "Why do you make me see iniquity, and why do you idly look at wrong . . . You who are of purer eyes than to see evil and cannot look at wrong, why do you idly look at traitors and remain silent when the wicked swallows up the man more righteous than he?"

10. Individual lament psalms include Psalms 3; 4–7; 13; 17; 22; 26; 31; 35; 39; 40–43; 52; 54–55; 58–59; 64; 69; 70–71; 77; 83; 86; 88; 109; 142–143. Communal lament psalms include Psalms 12; 44; 60; 74; 79–80; 89; 94; 126; 137.

and unmoved by my pain and broken body. He felt anything but good, which created a humiliating crisis of faith and meaning for me. This steady diet of repressed grief, anger, and shame was making me sick. I wanted to die. I had no idea how to heal myself or how to hope again.

My depression and anger eventually grew to a point where I had to start being honest about my confused and wounded heart. I was too ashamed to share honestly with anybody else, so I began talking honestly to God. He had pushed me to a place of surrender. I chose to trust him. I would lean in and surrender to the broken reality I didn't want to acknowledge.

My ongoing surgeries and the arduous, lonely months of recovery that followed provided a lot of one-on-one time for just God and me. Hmm, could this be God's woo of my heart to his? I was going to find out. As I learned to surrender and trust that God loved me, I started to heal on the inside. My surgeries have continued but so has my ever-deepening intimacy with my precious, suffering Savior. I had stopped running from my pain and chose instead to turn and face it. I soon found freedom on the other side.

It has been thirty-three years since that day, and God continues to show me the mysterious and often shocking connection between suffering and joy. God taught me that anger is a normal part of grief and a barometer for pain; that God is big enough to hold it all. As I wrestled through my questions and pain, God came in supernatural ways and wooed me to himself. He was drawing me closer—into deeper emotional and spiritual intimacy than I had ever known. In Isaiah 45:3, he promises, "I will give you hidden treasures, riches stored in secret places, so that you may know that I am the LORD, the God of Israel, who summons you by name." Where is God when you're hurting? Right outside your heart's door.

Healing is messy. And God is scary. From a human, time-bound perspective, God can be utterly confusing and downright hurtful. His actions can prompt fear and anger just as surely as they prompt love and trust. Yet he is a good God who wants nothing more than to bless his children. Over the years we have experienced shattered expectations, disrupted comfort, and uncertain outcomes, but we have also tasted more of God's goodness and sweetness than we could ever imagine.

In the beginning, as you heal and grow, you may find that your doubts, frustrations, and anger will intensify toward God. This is normal for people who have been emotionally numb and are beginning to feel again. As you continue to heal, keep your pain moving by wrestling with God. He will be there.

David, Jeremiah, Job, and Habakkuk are some of the most exemplary faith leaders described in the Bible, and yet they suffered some of the most excruciating levels of verbal, physical, and spiritual abuse. They not only show us how normal it is to have doubts about God's goodness but give us a template for how to communicate our pain to a holy God.[11] These men walked with God, followed God, and pleased God, yet their path to spiritual intimacy led through dark valleys of doubt and struggle.

Notice the following inspired statements of faith-filled believers who voiced deep frustration, disappointment, and confusion toward God:

> How long, LORD? Will you forget me forever?
>> How long will you hide your face from me?
> How long must I wrestle with my thoughts
>> and day after day have sorrow in my heart?
> How long will [you allow] my enemy [to] triumph over me?
>> Psalm 13:1–2

> My God, my God, why have you forsaken me?
>> Why are you so far from saving me,
>> so far from my cries of anguish?
> My God, I cry out by day, but you do not answer,
>> by night, but I find no rest.
>> Psalm 22:1–2

> God has turned me over to the ungodly
>> and thrown me into the clutches of the wicked.
> All was well with me, but he shattered me;
>> he seized me by the neck and crushed me.
>> Job 16:11–12

> Is it nothing to you, all you who pass by?
>> Look around and see.
> Is any suffering like my suffering
>> that was inflicted on me,
> that the LORD brought on me
>> in the day of his fierce anger? . . .

---

11. See 1 Kings 9:4; 11:4; 2 Kings 14:3; 16:2; Job 1:1, 8; Habakkuk 3:17–19.

Without pity the Lord has swallowed up
    all the dwellings of Jacob . . .
Like an enemy [God] has strung his bow;
    his right hand is ready.
Like a foe he has slain
    all who were pleasing to the eye . . .

Like a bear lying in wait,
    like a lion in hiding,
[God] dragged me from the path and mangled me
    and left me without help.

Lamentations 1:12; 2:2, 4; 3:10–11

These are raw passages that receive little attention in many Christian traditions. For some it is difficult to acknowledge that godly believers can have such dark feelings. The truth that the path to spiritual intimacy often involves deep disappointment, pain, and frustration is foreign to modern Christianity, which fixates on a more palatable religion.

One of the greatest emotional difficulties that survivors face is how to cope with shattered expectations and assumptions.[12] When one believes in a good, loving God, it is difficult to understand why God allows atrocities, why he does not intervene, and why in his justice he does not annihilate evil-doers. Those who don't believe in God experience no such spiritual turmoil.

We see this agonizing struggle in David, Job, and Jeremiah when they experienced the evil of abuse. They were devastated and frustrated because God did not act as they expected him to. But instead of withdrawing and giving up on God, they voiced their lament to him.

Elie Wiesel, a Holocaust survivor and human rights activist, said, "The opposite of love is not hate, it's indifference."[13] Thus we demonstrate our love for God when we wrestle through our pain, anger, and frustration with him until it is resolved. This is biblical worship.

Jacob's refusal to let go of the angel until God blessed him, even though it meant wrestling all night and ultimately suffering a dislocated hip, is a

---

12. For a detailed treatment of this issue, see Jeffrey Kauffman, ed., *Loss of the Assumptive World: A Theory of Traumatic Loss* (New York: Routledge, 2002).

13. Elie Wiesel, "Interview," *U.S. News and World Report*, October 27, 1986, quoting the Austrian psychologist Wilhelm Stekel (1921); see https://quoteinvestigator.com/2019/05/21/indifference.

wonderful paradigm for us to follow (Genesis 32:23–32).[14] Wrestling with
God means we refuse to give up as Job's wife demanded he do: "Curse God
and die!" (Job 2:9). We set the stage for reconnecting with God when we
value our relationship with him so much that we refuse to pretend everything is okay when it is not. We refuse to pretend we trust him when we do
not. We refuse to pretend we are happy with him when we are infuriated
by his actions. Author Philip Yancey describes the process of wrestling
with God:

> One bold message in the Book of Job is that you can say anything to God.
> Throw at him your grief, your anger, your doubt, your bitterness, your
> betrayal, your disappointment—he can absorb them all. As often as not,
> spiritual giants of the Bible are shown *contending* with God. They prefer to
> go away limping, like Jacob, rather than to shut God out . . . God can deal
> with every human response save one. He cannot abide the response I fall
> back on instinctively: an attempt to ignore him or treat him as though he
> does not exist. That response never once occurred to Job.[15]

Job repeatedly stated that he longed to plead his case before God (Job
13:3, 15; 16:21; 23:3–4). In spite of the fact that God seemed to be strangely
silent, Job kept coming to him, was not silenced by darkness, and spoke what
he believed to be true (23:17; 27:3–6). What was the result of this agonizing
process? Job himself acknowledged that, at the end of this painful ordeal,
intimacy with God was graciously restored: "Surely I spoke of things I did
not understand, things too wonderful for me to know . . . My ears had heard
of you but now my eyes have seen you" (42:3, 5). In other words, he had
moved from knowing God intellectually to experiencing God.

Similarly, the Israelite prophet Habakkuk provides us with another
biblical example of wrestling with God. Habakkuk was shocked and dis-
mayed at the perverse wickedness and violence rampant in his society.
Instead of backing away from a God who didn't seem to care about victims
of injustice, Habakkuk cried out, "How long, LORD, must I call for help, but
you do not listen? Or cry out to you 'Violence!' but you do not save? . . . The
wicked hem in the righteous, so that justice is perverted" (Habakkuk 1:2, 4).

---

14. It is significant that here God changes Jacob's name—from Jacob, which means "supplanter"
or "trickster," (Genesis 25:26), to Israel, which means "one who struggles with God." Thus, in this
historical incident, the spiritual value and propriety of wrestling with God are strongly affirmed.

15. Philip Yancey, *Disappointment with God: Three Questions No One Asks Aloud* (Grand Rapids:
Zondervan, 1988), 235, italics in original.

God's answer to this cry for justice seemed to create even more injustice (Habakkuk 1:5–11), for God told the prophet he would judge the wicked Judeans by allowing the Babylonians (who were even more brutal and wicked) to invade and conquer Judah. After hearing God's confusing answer to his complaint for justice, Habakkuk refused to back away or to deaden pain. He kept responding to God in his confusion and anguish: "Your eyes are too pure to look on evil; you cannot tolerate wrongdoing. Why then do you tolerate the treacherous. Why are you silent while the wicked swallow up those more righteous than themselves? (1:13).

At the end of his brief prophetic book, Habakkuk describes his terror over the impending judgment: "I heard and my body pounded, my lips quivered at the sound; decay crept into my bones, and my legs trembled" (3:16). Yet in the midst of his overwhelming pain—because he refused to give up—he encountered God, and God gave him hope:

> Yet I will quietly wait for the day of trouble
> > to come upon people who invade us.
> Though the fig tree should not blossom,
> > nor fruit be on the vines,
> the produce of the olive fail
> > and the fields yield no food,
> the flock be cut off from the fold
> > and there be no herd in the stalls,
> yet I will rejoice in the LORD;
> > I will take joy in the God of my salvation.
> GOD, the Lord, is my strength;
> > he makes my feet like the deer's;
> > he makes me tread on my high places.
>
> Habakkuk 3:16–19 ESV

Habakkuk was not expressing a pie-in-the-sky, sappy religiosity. He faced his fear and pain head-on and God met him in the crucible. Much like Dostoyevsky, Habakkuk developed vibrant intimacy and deep faith in God by actively wrestling with him. Wrestling with God is ultimately predicated on the conviction that he is a living, personal God who speaks to his children (John 10:27; Galatians 5:18; 1 Thessalonians 5:19). Ask God to speak to you in your pain, and you will hear his voice.

Elenore experienced indescribable, chronic childhood abuse that resulted in disrupted adult relationships with family members, friends, and God.

Her progress in counseling was sluggish, as her abuse had created some of the most intense shame and self-loathing her therapist had ever seen. In counseling, Elenore was encouraged to specifically ask God to communicate to her. She did so, and a few nights later, she had a dramatic dream that proved to be the turning point in her healing. She recorded her experience as follows:

> It was three o'clock in the morning, and I was wide-awake, thinking about all the things that had happened to me. My thoughts were interrupted by what I can only describe as a vision of God. With outstretched arms, God was beckoning me to come to him. At first I was hesitant, feeling inadequate and insignificant. But as God called out to me, my heart melted, and I finally surrendered. I was irresistibly pulled toward God. I ran toward him. God swooped me up and sat me on his lap and embraced me.
>
> I could not see God's face, but he kept embracing me, holding me, and I felt the warmth of God's love and his compassion. I found myself crying—crying for the first time—and asking God's forgiveness for being so angry with him, for doubting him, and for keeping him out of my life. God just continued to embrace me; he did not let go. Amazingly, God started to cry. God was crying with me. His tears were huge, and as they fell on me, they soothed and comforted me. The tears spoke volumes, but most of all they healed.
>
> For the first time, I had hope. I knew that things would work out. The road would be long, but God reassured me that he would never let go of me. I hung on to those words of God. I just wanted to sit in God's lap, being comforted and loved by him. I must have fallen asleep, for I woke up in the morning feeling like I could face the future with God by my side.

Elenore's experience is certainly unique in that God deals with his children individually, but it offers an intimate example of a survivor hanging on to God until he communicates his nearness and love. Her story also illustrates another essential activity for those who desire reconnection with God—namely, reimaging the fatherhood of God.[16]

Reimaging the Fatherhood of God

Until Elenore had this dream, she had fiercely resisted intimacy with God and with men. She was a highly educated professional woman who

---

16. See Feldmeth and Finley, *We Weep for Ourselves and Our Children*, 103–10.

maintained tight control in all her relationships. To Elenore, God was as dangerous as her abusive father had been. Her dream had for the first time given her a glimpse of God as a loving, safe, reparative Father. Reimaging God marked the beginning of her spiritual healing.

Abuse dangerously distorts perceptions of God's character so that survivors can't recognize, let alone embrace, their Creator. Most of the time, these distortions center around the fatherhood of God, which is a logical dynamic. At the heart of all abuse is the misuse of one's power to manipulate, dominate, and damage another human being. Since God is the ultimate power and authority in the universe, he represents a survivor's greatest fear. If human authority figures (often males) used their limited power to harm them, survivors instinctively sense that God (portrayed as male) will use his unlimited power to harm them too. At best, they sense that they must not give themselves to God because he is unsafe, just as other authorities in their lives have been unsafe.

For adult children who experienced abuse from their fathers or father figures, the problem is greatly magnified. Children develop their sense of God as a heavenly Father (Matthew 6:9, 32) from their experiences with their human fathers. Thus, people who experience abuse from earthly fathers find it terrifying to think of God as their heavenly Father.

By the same token, if mothers perpetrated the abuse, the fatherhood of God can also be problematic. In this case, the survivors do not fear that their heavenly Father will *actively* harm them but that he'll do so *passively*. Again, this is logical. If earthly fathers didn't stop abuse but allowed it to continue, then it is intuitive to conclude that one's heavenly Father must also be dangerous in his passivity. He won't intervene to protect, and thus he cannot be trusted.

In chapter 7, we mentioned Linda Cutting, who suffered chronic physical and sexual abuse from her father, which was doubly damaging to her concept of God, because her father was a minister. She tells of her spiritual decline in which she lost connection with God because of her father. She begins by reflecting on her childhood:

> I am thinking about God—how I used to pray. I have this clear memory of believing in God, even when I was little and all the bad things with my father were happening. For so many years I prayed . . . I stopped praying after Paul [her abused brother who committed suicide] died, after hearing my father say at his funeral, 'The Lord giveth and the Lord taketh away' . . .

The thing that's kept me spiritually alone all these years was somehow equating God with my father's church and, most of all, with my father.[17]

How can survivors change their image of God as an unsafe father? The first step is to identify the negative lessons their abusers taught them about fatherhood, authority, maleness and femaleness, and relationships. This is best done as a reflective journaling exercise. Once these negative messages are clearly distinguished from truth, one can consciously and deliberately embrace God as a reparative, loving Father who loathes abuse and promises to harshly judge unrepentant abusers.

For Linda Cutting, this distinction between God and her earthly father occurred in a dramatic way when she finally gathered the courage to contact the denomination that had ordained her father to inform them that he was an unrepentant child abuser. In spite of considerable evidence that could have been carefully examined, a denominational official informed her there was nothing they could do. He furthermore told Linda about a similar case in which two adult daughters had reported that their minister father had raped them for years, and in spite of the substantiation of those abuse claims, the congregation refused to remove the minister until he lost a civil suit filed by the daughters.

Linda was devastated to realize that her father's denomination would do nothing to remove him from ministry, but it did precipitate a spiritual breakthrough: "After hearing how the church responded to the minister's daughters who were raped, I see that God is not the church, God is not the National Association of Congregational Churches, and God is certainly not my father. At least not my biological father."[18] The manner in which these Christian leaders failed to challenge an abuser helped Linda recognize that not only did their choices not reflect God; the choices of her human father did not either. To the degree that she was able to separate her earthly abusive father from her heavenly Father, she was able to reconnect with God.

One of the most helpful ways abuse survivors can separate God from their earthly abusers is to understand what Scripture says about the fatherhood of God. The Bible teaches that God, as our loving heavenly Father, doesn't use his power to abuse and oppress but rather to love, protect, and nurture. Specifically, the fatherhood of God is described by the following actions:

---

17. Linda Cutting, *Memory Slips: A Memoir of Music and Healing* (New York: HarperCollins, 1997), 156.
18. Cutting, *Memory Slips*, 156.

- He faithfully feeds and cares for the birds of the sky and has infinitely more loving concern for his children (Matthew 6:26).
- He delights in giving good gifts to his children even more than a loving human father does (Matthew 7:11).
- He knows and cares when a tiny sparrow falls from the sky; thus he knows and cares infinitely more when his children suffer (Matthew 10:29).
- He so actively and passionately loves his children that no trivial detail of their lives is overlooked or ignored. He even keeps track of the number of hairs on their heads (Matthew 10:30).
- He delights in revealing truth to those who resemble vulnerable children while hiding it from the wise and powerful (Matthew 11:25–26).
- He specifically delights in being a father to the fatherless and an advocate for vulnerable single mothers (Psalm 68:5).

God as heavenly Father is a vitally important biblical image that needs to be clarified and not simply rejected out of hand.[19] John Cooper acknowledges that the fatherhood of God can be a difficult concept for those who have been abused or neglected by their earthly fathers, but he argues that it must not be eliminated. He notes the importance of the fatherhood of God for all humans, including survivors:

> It is also true that many people in our culture (and others) have difficulty relating to a Father God if they lack the experience of a good father . . . But for most people, the need, desire, and ability to relate to a father figure is still strongly present. Many people who lack good human fathers gladly and readily receive God the Father as their ultimate security and source of healing. Eliminating the heavenly Father is neither necessary nor helpful for dealing with the sins of their earthly fathers.[20]

---

19. See Francis Martin, *The Feminist Question: Feminist Theology in the Light of Christian Tradition* (Grand Rapids: Eerdmans, 1994), 265–92. Mary Daly's assault on the fatherhood of God has been influential among feminists. She reasons, "If God is male, then the male is God" (*Beyond God the Father* [Boston, MA: Beacon, 1973], 19). Rejecting the fatherhood of God hasn't helped women in general or abuse victims in particular. It has created a host of new problems. When Daly moved "beyond God the Father," she and others who followed her embraced goddess worship and lesbianism, which they erroneously found to be more affirming for women (see Carol P. Christ, "Feminist Theology as Post-Traditional Theology," in *The Cambridge Companion to Feminist Theology*, ed. Susan Frank Parsons [Cambridge: Cambridge University. Press, 2002], 79–96).

20. John W. Cooper, *Our Father in Heaven: Christian Faith and Inclusive Language for God* (Grand Rapids: Baker, 1998), 261.

As significant as the fatherhood of God is biblically and practically,[21] it is not the only biblical image used of God. Therefore, we urge survivors to enlarge their understanding of God. In the early stages of healing, it is often difficult to focus on God as Father without intrusive imagery of an abusive father. For this reason, it's important to know that there are many other biblical images of God, including those that are feminine in nature.[22] As survivors reflect on these images of God and allow them to clarify and correct distortions about God's character, they can in time embrace God as their tender, loving heavenly Father.

For instance, God's tenderness, love, and creative power are illustrated by likening him to the images in the chart below:

Image	Scripture Passage
A mother who gave birth to the world	Psalm 90:2
The one who bore and nursed Israel	Numbers 11:12; Deuteronomy 32:18
A mother whose young toddler rests against her to receive comfort	Psalm 131:2; see Isaiah 66:13
A nursing mother who has compassion on her child	Isaiah 49:15
A mother who tenderly, graciously feeds her child with nutritious milk	1 Peter 2:2–3
A mother bear that zealously protects her cubs	Hosea 13:8
A hen that shields her chicks from danger under her wings	Luke 13:34; see Deuteronomy 32:11

Jesus gives us a glimpse of the face of God: "Anyone who has seen me [Jesus] has seen the Father" (John 14:9; see also John 1:18). As we read the

---

21. Herman Bavinck argues that "Father" is the New Testament equivalent of Yahweh (*The Doctrine of God* [Grand Rapids: Baker, 1951], 263). For a broad evangelical discussion of the divine name and gender, see Alvin F. Kimel Jr., ed., *This Is My Name Forever: The Trinity and Gender Language for God* (Downers Grove, IL: InterVarsity, 2001).

22. I affirm (along with John Cooper) that Scripture overwhelmingly but not exclusively describes God in masculine language (*Our Father in Heaven*, 65–114); see also Donald G. Bloesch, *Is the Bible Sexist?* (Westchester, IL: Crossway, 1982), 66, 68, 76–77. Thus, if we are going to do justice to the biblical record and to abuse victims who have an aversion to masculine imagery, we need to recognize the feminine/maternal descriptions of God in the Bible. This doesn't mean, however, that we should refer to God as our heavenly Mother, for God is expressly called "our Father" in Scripture (and he is never called "Mother"). This is a divine title and a term of direct address. Feminine or maternal descriptions of God in the Bible occur exclusively as figures of speech, never as titles (see Cooper, *Our Father in Heaven*, 108).

Gospels and observe the acts and character of Jesus, we're helped to correct our distortions about God and masculinity that flow out of abuse. For instance, in seeing how Jesus treated women, children, social outcasts, and their powerful male abusers, survivors see what divine and human power should look like.

Jesus exhibited extravagant love and compassion toward women, children, and social outcasts. Jesus loved the vulnerable. He held children, prayed for them, and declared this about them: "Let the little children come to me, and do not hinder them, for the kingdom of heaven belongs to such as these" (Matthew 19:14). Jesus was slandered by the religious leaders of his day for eating with tax collectors and immoral sinners and declared that he came to heal the morally sick (Matthew 9:9–13; see Luke 19:1–10),[23] which was the essence of his mission.

When Jesus gazed on the destitute crowds that followed him, he looked past their sin and "had compassion on them, because they were harassed and helpless, like sheep without a shepherd" (Matthew 9:36). When Jesus was dining in the home of a religious leader, a notorious sinful woman, possibly a prostitute, entered uninvited. Jesus allowed her to scandalously kiss his feet, anoint them with costly oil, and dry them with her hair. When Simon the Pharisee criticized Jesus for allowing affection from such an openly shamed woman, Jesus harshly rebuked him and publicly praised the woman for her faith and her passionate love (Luke 7:36–50).

Repeatedly Jesus demonstrated compassion for marginalized and broken people; he healed the crippled, the blind, and the mute (Matthew 9:27–33; 15:30–31). In an outrageously chauvinistic culture that debased women, Jesus treated them with genuine respect and dignity. He allowed women to sit at his feet, receive his teachings, and travel with him in public ministry. He even chose women to be the first witnesses to his resurrected body (in a Jewish culture that didn't even allow a woman to give testimony in court).[24]

In terms of Jesus' use of power and his posture toward men who abused their influence and power, the gospel record is unequivocal. Jesus used his power to heal and liberate the oppressed and to rebuke the powerful and arrogant who acted unjustly. On several occasions, Jesus physically chased

23. Craig Keener gives an excellent, detailed explanation of why tax collectors and sinners were hated by the Pharisees. According to Keener, "sinners" likely refers to those who were blatant violators of the law (*A Commentary on the Gospel of Matthew* [Grand Rapids: Eerdmans, 1999], 292–96).

24. See Luke 8:1–3; 10:38–42; 24:1–11; John 4:7–27. On the status and treatment of women in first-century Palestine, see Tal Ilan, *Integrating Women into Second Temple Judaism* (Tübingen: Mohr, 1999); Tal Ilan, *Jewish Women in Greco-Roman Palestine* (Peabody, MA: Hendrickson, 1996); Joachim Jeremias, *Jerusalem in the Time of Jesus* (Philadelphia: Fortress, 1969), 359–76.

money changers out of the temple, for they were desecrating the house
of God while exploiting for profit the impoverished people who came to
worship God (Matthew 21:12; John 2:13–16). Jesus repeatedly healed the
sick on the Sabbath and verbally excoriated the Pharisees for their haughty
hypocrisy and poverty of compassion (Luke 6:6–11).

When his disciples argued about who was the greatest, Jesus summoned
a child and said that greatness is not about power but about becoming like
a child (Matthew 18:1–4). Jesus promises to use his power to judge all who
harm children, stating that if someone causes a little child to stumble, it
would be better if the offender had a millstone hung around his neck and
was thrown into the sea, compared to what Jesus would do to him on the
day of judgment (Matthew 18:6–10).

Jesus' posture toward the vulnerable, the outcast, and the broken stands
in stark contrast to the behavior of abusers. Jesus' posture also stands in
stark contrast to the attitudes of many modern-day faith leaders who gather
power and prestige by catering to the wealthy and powerful and fail to love
and nurture outcasts. Thus, the biblical images of the loving nature of God
as Father; of God's tender, maternal-like love and nurture; of Jesus' love for
broken sinners; and of God's judgment of abusers help survivors understand
how different their heavenly Father is from their abusers. May this awareness
draw us to—not away from—God in the midst of suffering.

Jessie's Story

As a young child, Jessie had been molested for several years by the youth
pastor in her church. A Christian counselor was recommended, who began
to meet with her regularly. As a part of the initial assessment, Jessie was
asked to create a picture of what it felt like to be her (see figure 23). Jessie tentatively picked up a brush and painted herself as a small rosebush growing
in the middle of a meadow. A menacing shadow was cast over the flower by
a giant foot suspended in midair, ready to crush her at any moment. A car
was parked nearby, and a bicycle was propped against the rosebush.

When Jessie's therapist asked her about a title for her painting, she
promptly said, "Jesus wept." She went on to explain that the rosebush "without thorns" growing by itself in an open field was her. Jessie described the
rosebush as feeling vulnerable, defenseless, and alone. The giant, illustrated
by an enormous foot, would come unexpectedly and step on her. She disclosed that the giant was her youth pastor, from whom she had no means of
protecting herself. Those in the car and on the bicycle who came faithfully
to visit, play, and tend to her were her parents and a friend who loved her.

"Jesus wept."

Figure 23

Her parents "could not see the shadow" because the giant was clever and knew when to come and how to manipulate her into silence.

Jessie's therapist was most moved by her understanding of a Savior who tenderly responded with deep compassion to her suffering. Miraculously, God had preserved this little girl's faith in a good God, probably because of the steadfast love and validating responses of her parents when she disclosed her abuse by a man the family had loved and trusted for years. They wept with her.

Our validating and nurturing responses to those who disclose abuse positively and powerfully impact healing outcomes.[25]

Understanding and Embracing the God of Scripture

Because Satan seeks to distance us from God by distorting his magnificent attributes, it's essential for survivors to clarify who God really is.[26] In a world of heinous abuse, evil, and brutality, there is little hope for any of us apart

---

25. The impact of positive or negative reactions to abuse disclosures is very significant for the psychological health and recovery of abuse victims. See Rebecca Campbell et al., "Social Reactions to Rape Victims: Healing and Hurtful Effects on Psychological and Physical Health Outcomes," *Violence and Victims* 16 (2001): 287–302; Leonard Gries et al., "Positive Reaction to Disclosure and Recovery from Child Sexual Abuse," *Journal of Child Sexual Abuse* 9 (2000): 29–51; Sarah Ullman, "Relationship to Perpetrator, Disclosure, Social Reactions, and PTSD Symptoms in Child Sexual Abuse Survivors," *Journal of Child Sexual Abuse* 16, no. 1 (2007): 19–36.

26. A helpful academic work on the person and character of God is Donald G. Bloesch, *God the Almighty: Power, Wisdom, Holiness, Love* (Downers Grove, IL: InterVarsity, 1995). Two classics on the

from the promises and loving character of God. Gary Haugen, the founder of International Justice Mission, previously worked in the civil rights division of the United States Department of Justice and directed the United Nations genocide investigation in Rwanda. He witnessed and investigated unfathomable incidents of abuse around the world. His experiences have not destroyed his faith in God but have instead pushed him to clarify his convictions. Having experienced the putrid depths of human depravity and cruelty, he declares there is still hope, but it's found only in a compassionate and just God, revealed through Jesus and on the pages of Scripture. Haugen makes this observation:

> As one who has with his own hands sorted through the remains of thousands of slaughtered Tutsi corpses, as one who has heard with his own ears the screams of boys being beaten like dogs by South African police, as one who has looked with his own eyes into the dull blank stares of Asian girls abused in brutal ways, I hope in the Word of God. For in the Scriptures and in the life of Jesus Christ, I have come to know God—my Maker, the Creator of heaven and earth, the sovereign Lord of the nations. It is through his Word that God reveals his character, and it is God's character, and God's character alone, that gives me hope to seek justice amid the brutality I witness.[27]

Those who have experienced human depravity and evil—who've lost all hope—must doggedly pursue a healing path that leads to a rediscovery of the true character of God. God's Word is the only source of truth we have to clearly understand the attributes of God, which evil has perverted. It requires courage and faith to consciously reject the distorted images of God created by abuse, perpetrators of abuse, and those who knew but failed to act or protect. The following chart will help get us started.

Embracing the Cross

Some of the most painful, vexing questions we've responded to as spiritual shepherds have come from those shattered by injustice and evil: *If God knew I was being abused as a defenseless child, why didn't he intervene?* Such questions cannot be satisfactorily answered.

---

attributes of God are J. I. Packer, *Knowing God* (Downers Grove, IL: InterVarsity, 1973), and A. W. Tozer, *The Knowledge of the Holy* (New York; Harper & Row, 1961).

27. Gary A. Haugen, *Good News about Injustice: A Witness of Courage in a Hurting World* (Downers Grove, IL: InterVarsity, 1999), 68.

Attribute	Definition/Description	Biblical support	Common distortions created by abuse	Truth about this attribute
Love	God's love is the sum total of his goodness toward his creation. It includes his compassion—mercy shown to those who are suffering	Exodus 3:7; Deuteronomy 7:7–8; Psalm 136; 145:8–9, 14–17; Hosea 11:9; Matthew 9:36; Romans 5:8; 8:31–39; 1 John 4:8–10	God loves other people but he couldn't love me. God's love must be earned. God's love is fickle and ephemeral. If I don't perform and measure up, God will no longer love me. God does not care about human suffering.	God loves his children unconditionally and eternally. Sinners are not loved by God because they are beautiful; they are beautiful because they are loved.* God is deeply grieved by human suffering.
Omniscience/ Wisdom	God knows all things actual or possible—past, present, and future	1 Samuel 16:7; Psalm 37:18; 139:1–6; Isaiah 40:12–14, 27; 42:9; Jeremiah 1:5; Ephesians 3:9–11	I can't be honest with God or his people. God is disgusted with me because he knows all of my secret sins. My abuser will never answer for their evil. No one believes my story; the truth will never come out.	God loves me in spite of knowing everything about me. God knows and cares about all of my hidden struggles. No abuse is ever hidden from God's sight or escapes his justice.
Sovereignty/ Omnipotence	God has absolute, unhindered rule over all of creation. His sovereignty is governed only by his good character.	Genesis 50:20; Psalm 103:19; Isaiah 40:26; Jeremiah 29:11; 32:27; Romans 8:28; Revelation 19:11–21	God is a heavenly despot who cannot be trusted. God is just waiting to smash me. God isn't good because he didn't prevent my abuse.	God can and will bring good out of human and satanic evil. I can trust God's work in my life. God is bigger than my abusers and the damage they created; he can heal me. God will ultimately triumph over all evil.
Holiness	God is distinct and separate from the created world. He is morally pure (separate from sin).	Leviticus 20:23, 26; Isaiah 6:1–7; 40:18–22; Habakkuk 1:13; 2 Corinthians 6:16–17; 1 Peter 1:15–16; Revelation 4:8	God is too pure to ever want someone like me as his child. I'm just a slut. God is like my abusive earthly father and cannot be trusted.	God is different from and greater than anything in creation. God has nothing in common with an abusive earthly father. God is loving and pure. God is far too pure to allow unrepentant abusers to go unpunished.

(continued)

* Martin Luther, cited in Bloesch, *God the Almighty*, 151–52.

Attribute	Definition/Description	Biblical support	Common distortions created by abuse	Truth about this attribute
Righteousness/ Justice	God is morally perfect. He always conforms to what is right (based on his perfect character).	Psalm 58:10–11; 119:137; 145:17; Romans 2:9; 8:32–34; Hebrews 10:1–18; Revelation 16:5	There is no justice in the universe. Look what my abusers got away with. Those with the most power always win by crushing the weak. God will eventually crush me. I deserve to burn in hell, and probably will.	No one can ever condemn God's children because Christ's perfect sacrifice satisfied the justice of God. God is a just judge; he will never allow unrepentant evil to go unpunished.
Faithfulness	God is absolutely loyal and dependable. He fulfills 100 percent of his promises	Psalm 25:10; 119:89–91; Hosea 11:8–9; Philippians 1:6; 1 Thessalonians 5:14, 24; 2 Thessalonians 3:2–3; Hebrews 10:23	No one can be trusted, not even God. Everyone lies. The Bible works for some people, but not for me. God won't keep being patient with me. He will eventually give up on me like everyone else has	God will *never* give up on his children. No matter how many people betray me, abuse me, or don't believe me, I can and will trust God; he *always* does what he says; I can trust his promises.
Eternality	God is free from all succession of time. He sees everything past, present, and future with perfect clarity. He has no beginning or end.	Exodus 3:14; Psalm 90:2; 102:12; Isaiah 46:10; 2 Peter 3:8; Revelation 4:8; 22:13	There is no hope; I could never have anticipated this horrible abuse, and I can't deal with it. I will never heal. I can't trust God's promises; they haven't worked yet, and they never will.	I can trust God because he is not bound by time as I am and sees the whole of my life when I can only see today. I can trust God to fulfill his promises according to his timetable, not mine. God experiences with me every trial I face and is always present: he knows, he sees, he hears, and he feels all that I am experiencing. He is writing my story and has a perfect plan for my future and healing.

God didn't explain the mystery of suffering and evil to righteous Job, and he hasn't chosen to explain it to us either. But neither has he left us fumbling in the dark. The more we listen and care for survivors, the more trauma research we read and understand, the more convinced we are that *the fullest divine response to suffering and evil is the cross of Christ.*

As we learn to appreciate and embrace the cross, we will be drawn closer to a loving God. Because God's love is infinite, we can experience an ever-deepening intimacy with him. The life of the apostle Paul provides a great example. In spite of intense and repeated persecution throughout his ministry and the physical abuse that ultimately cost his life, Paul's spiritual strength and equilibrium came from his fixation on the cross:[28] "For I resolved to know nothing while I was with you except Jesus Christ and him crucified" (1 Corinthians 2:2). "For the message of the cross is foolishness to those who are perishing, but to us who are being saved it is the power of God" (1:18).

Embracing the cross helps survivors reconnect with God in three important ways.

The Cross Declares God's Compassion for Human Sufferers

When abuse survivors wonder if God is indifferent to human suffering and misery, they need only look to the cross. The cross declares—indeed it shouts—of God's compassion in action. On the cross, Christ suffered the most excruciating physical, emotional, and spiritual torture to deliver us from the curse of sin (see figure 24). As Paul observes, "Christ redeemed us from the curse of the law by becoming a curse for us, for it is written, 'Cursed is everyone who is hung on a pole'" (Galatians 3:13). The prophet Isaiah writes a vivid description of our suffering Savior:

Figure 24: Christ as the Man of Sorrows
Artist: Jan Mostaert. Public Domain.

28. Paul endured multiple stonings, beatings, and imprisonments and was ultimately executed by the Roman authorities (2 Corinthians 11:23–33; 2 Timothy 4:6). On Paul's prison experience based on the historical setting, see Brian Rapske, *The Book of Acts and Paul in Roman Custody* (Grand Rapids: Eerdmans, 1994).

For he grew up before him like a young plant,
    and like a root out of dry ground;
he had no form or majesty that we should look at him,
    and no beauty that we should desire him.
He was despised and rejected by men,
    a man of sorrows and acquainted with grief;
and as one from whom men hide their faces
    he was despised, and we esteemed him not.

Surely he has borne our griefs
    and carried our sorrows;
yet we esteemed him stricken,
    smitten by God, and afflicted.
But he was pierced for our transgressions;
    he was crushed for our iniquities;
upon him was the chastisement that brought us peace,
    and with his wounds we are healed.
All we like sheep have gone astray;
    we have turned—every one—to his own way;
and the Lord has laid on him
    the iniquity of us all.

He was oppressed, and he was afflicted,
    yet he opened not his mouth;
like a lamb that is led to the slaughter,
    and like a sheep that before its shearers is silent,
    so he opened not his mouth.
By oppression and judgment he was taken away.

Isaiah 53:2–8 ESV

Our suffering Savior stands in stunning contrast to the dispassionate Greek gods who cavorted on Mount Olympus, utterly unaffected by human misery. Christ shows us the face of God, who passionately responded to human suffering in the most dramatic manner possible by sending his Son to die and thus redeem the effects of sin:

By oppression and judgment he was taken away;
    and as for his generation, who considered
that he was cut off out of the land of the living,

stricken for the transgression of my people?
And they made his grave with the wicked
     and with a rich man in his death,
although he had done no violence,
     and there was no deceit in his mouth . . .

He poured out his soul to death
     and was numbered with the transgressors;
yet he bore the sin of many,
     and makes intercession for the transgressors.

Isaiah 53:8–9, 12 ESV

We now have an answer to Elie Wiesel's haunting question posed as he watched a young boy slowly choke to death in a death camp: "Where is God now?" God went to the cross for you and me and is close to those who suffer.[29]

The cross assures us of God's compassion for human misery. The German pastor Dietrich Bonhoeffer, who was murdered by the Nazis, wrote from his prison cell, "Only the suffering God can help."[30] In the cross of Christ, we see a suffering God who stands ready to help those who suffer.

The Cross Connects Jesus with Our Suffering

As we saw in chapter 7, abuse isolates by shattering connections with God, others, and ourselves. Isolation is one of the most dangerous effects of abuse because it separates survivors from others who understand what they're going through; it disconnects the people who most need validation and comfort from those who are best able to give it. When isolated, survivors feel alone, unseen, and unheard. The beauty of the cross is that it connects Jesus with our suffering, most specifically the suffering produced by abuse.

The writer of Hebrews tells us that Jesus is our great high priest and urges us to go to him in prayer in order to receive mercy and grace. Our motivation is that, as a result of his earthly experiences, Jesus experientially relates to what we endure. The writer of Hebrews declares, "For we do not have a high priest who is unable to empathize with our weaknesses, but we

---

29. See Dorothee Soelle, *Suffering* (Philadelphia: Fortress, 1975), 148. I agree with J. Christian Becker that Soelle has helpful insights on suffering, but (among other departures from evangelical theology) she fails to distinguish between tragic suffering and redemptive suffering (*Suffering and Hope: The Biblical Vision and the Human Predicament* [Grand Rapids: Eerdmans, 1987], 110–12).

30. Dietrich Bonhoeffer, *Letters and Papers from Prison: The Enlarged Edition* (London: SCM, 1953), 361; see also Charles Ohlrich, *The Suffering God: Hope and Comfort for Those Who Hurt* (Downers Grove, IL: InterVarsity, 1982).

have one who has been tempted in every way, just as we are—yet he did not sin" (Hebrews 4:15).

Thus, Jesus personally understands the horrors and humiliation of abuse. He was mocked, slapped, beaten, spit on, sexually violated (publicly stripped and hung naked on a public thoroughfare), shamed, and tortured to death. Jesus also experienced the loneliness of isolation from God the Father and those he loved as he hung on a crude, splintered cross. He voluntarily came to us, walking into the vortex of evil to deliver us from the curse of sin and death. He feels our pain and is with us (see figure 25). As we "walk through the valley of the shadow of death, I will fear no evil, for you are with me; your rod and your staff, they comfort me" (Psalm 23:4 ESV).

Figure 25: My Good Shepherd
James Van Fossan. Used with permission.

Corrie ten Boom was a young Dutch Christian who was imprisoned by the Nazis because her family had sheltered Jews. She and her sister, Betsy, were eventually shipped to Ravensbrück, one of the Nazi death camps. Corrie recounts the humiliation of regular "medical inspections" in which she and the other prisoners were forced to strip naked and walk single file past a "phalanx of grinning guards." In the middle of one of these abusive ordeals, God brought to her mind the precious truth that her Savior was crucified naked. He personally understood the sexual humiliation she was experiencing.[31] This gave her comfort and strength to go on.

The Cross Breaks the Power of Evil and Seals Satan's Fate

For the abused it can feel as though evil has won and hope is lost. However, the Bible declares that, through his death on the cross and resurrection, Jesus broke the back of Satan and triumphed over evil. Paul tells the Colossian believers regarding Jesus' crucifixion that he "disarmed the powers and authorities [demonic spirits] . . . and made a public spectacle of them, triumphing over them by the cross" (Colossians 2:15). Paul's language here

---

31. See Corrie ten Boom, *The Hiding Place* (Minneapolis: World Wide Publications, 1971), 196–97.

describes a triumphal military procession in which the defeated enemy is forced to march in humiliation through the streets.[32]

John makes a similar claim about the cross's power to defeat Satan: "The reason the Son of God appeared was to destroy the devil's work" (1 John 3:8). Thus, the writers of Scripture, particularly Paul, teach that the overthrow and redemption of evil have already begun through the cross.[33] But our challenge is that, from a New Testament perspective, while the cross marks the beginning of the end for Satan and his demonic legions, God's final triumph over evil is yet to come. The crucifixion and resurrection of Jesus Christ assure us that the final triumph over evil *will* come and that through the cross it already has begun. This explains why more than half of the New Testament Greek words for *victory* (*nikao, nike*) appear in the book of Revelation, which tells of the end of the age and the final battles between the forces of God and Satan.[34]

It's remarkable that God used evil itself—the torture and murder of the Son of God by crucifixion—to triumph over evil. Theologian Henri Blocher makes this comment:

> Evil is conquered as evil because God turns it back upon itself. He makes the supreme crime, the murder of the only righteous person, the very operation that abolishes sin. The manoeuvre is utterly unprecedented. No more complete victory could be imagined. God responds in the indirect way that is perfectly suited to the ambiguity of evil. He entraps the deceiver in his own wiles. Evil, like a judoist, takes advantage of the power of good, which it perverts; the Lord, like a supreme champion, replies by using the very grip of the opponent . . .
>
> It is exactly this, the sin of sins, the murder of the Son, which accomplishes this work.[35]

Through the cross of Jesus Christ, evil and abuse secured the utter defeat of evil and abuse, which is the greatest reversal in the history of the world. We can now better understand why the cross was of such singular

---

32. This concept is conveyed in the verb *thriambeuo* ("to lead in triumphal procession").

33. See 1 Corinthians 2:6–10; 2 Corinthians 4:5–12; C. Marvin Pate, *The End of the Age Has Come: The Theology of Paul* (Grand Rapids: Zondervan, 1995), 43–70. On the cross and the conquest of evil, see John R. Stott, *The Cross of Christ* (Downers Grove, IL: InterVarsity, 1986), 231–51.

34. On the theme of the believer's victory in the book of Revelation, see Stott, *Cross of Christ*, 246–51.

35. Henri Blocher, *Evil and the Cross: An Analytical Look at the Problem of Pain* (Downers Grove, IL: InterVarsity, 1994), 132.

importance for the apostle Paul. It demonstrates God's mercy; it connects Jesus with human suffering; it breaks the back of Satan; it spells the eternal defeat of evil. The cross marks our path to reconnecting with God.

Sonia's Story

Steve was privileged to interview Sonia, a person who, like Fyodor Dostoyevsky, eventually developed a deep intimacy with God in spite of having experienced twenty years of unrelenting abuse that almost annihilated her faith. When Steve met Sonia, she was a confident, middle-aged woman who exuded love for her family, her church, and, most importantly, for her Savior.

Sonia loved sharing her story. She was born to a perverted father who was a pedophile and to a mother who was weak, powerless, and unwilling to protect her. Sonia's molestation at the hands of her father began when she was just three years old and continued for ten years. When Sonia turned thirteen, her father began selling her as a prostitute to his friends—an outrage that continued for several years. To the day he died, Sonia's father maintained his innocence. He self-righteously proclaimed that the abuse was good for Sonia. He claimed it was healthy sex education. The worst part of Sonia's story was that her father professed to be a Christian and expressed faith in Jesus Christ as his Savior.

After reading Sonia's story, it might be difficult to imagine how she could entrust herself to God as her heavenly Father. Following are some insights from her story that might encourage you:

- First of all, when she heard the gospel for the first time as a teen, she embraced the biblical truths that God loves sinners and wants to help us in the midst of our pain and that Jesus will never leave his children. She clung to these biblical truths in the dark days to come.
- Second, even as she continued to be abused, she cried out to God. While he didn't seem to immediately answer her prayers and stop the abuse, God did begin to work. He eventually gave her the strength to confront her father—and the abuse came to an end.
- Third, she worked hard not to allow her evil father to cause her to indict God or other men. She reflected on the fact that God put other men in her life who were good and pure, like her safe, nurturing husband and her uncle.

- Finally, with the help of her loving husband and a godly pastor, she eventually learned to forgive her abusive father—to let go of hatred toward him and entrust him to God. Sonia says this was the most important aspect of her spiritual healing. Once she forgave her earthly father, she could become more intimate with her heavenly Father.

Since forgiving abusers, especially unrepentant abusers, is so complex and difficult, we've devoted our final chapter to this important subject.

CHAPTER 10

Forgiveness[1]

Vengeance is like a fire. The more it
devours, the hungrier it gets.

J. M. Coetzee, *Disgrace*

Forgive as the Lord forgave you.
Colossians 3:13

The well-dressed professional woman sitting across from me had recently separated from her husband and had requested a session to discuss the moral propriety of her decision. Her therapist suggested she contact her pastor for theological and biblical insight into the marital struggles she was dealing with.

Knowing she was coming to talk about the biblical doctrine of marriage and divorce, I began by asking questions about what she was experiencing in her marriage. As I listened, I could sense that her situation had a decidedly ugly twist. As I probed deeper, she impassively acknowledged that her abusive husband had given her numerous sexually transmitted diseases over the course of several years, and that he was still persisting in his profligate behavior. She shared flatly that her husband's infidelity was a matter of public record. In fact, he openly flaunted his present mistress but still wanted to stay married to his wife. Though he refused to give up his illicit lover, he battled fiercely for his wife's loyalty not to divorce him. Repeatedly, he hurled what he knew to be the ultimate barb at her: if she really was a Christian, she was obligated to forgive him and take him back, since Jesus said we must forgive seventy-seven times (Matthew 18:21–22).

She felt trapped in an abusive marriage because of her understanding of

---

1. This chapter is a modification of an article previously published ("Sexual Abuse and Forgiveness," *Journal of Psychology and Theology* 27, no. 3 [1999]: 219–29).

Scripture and her deep desire to please God. There was no way to reconcile with her unrepentant, abusive husband. She agonized over knowing what Christian love and forgiveness really demanded of her. Did it mean she had to simply pray for her husband and overlook his immorality? Did it mean she had to lovingly welcome him back, even at the risk of contracting another potentially life-threatening STD? Further complicating matters, this woman's own family and church friends sided with the immoral husband in rejecting divorce as a moral option. They admonished her that she was obligated to forgive and reconcile.

In subsequent years, we've heard abuse victims recount similar stories over and over, illustrating the widespread confusion in the Christian community about the relationship between forgiveness and abuse. Religious leaders and even family members are often quick to tell victims they must forgive, regardless of the circumstances of the abuse or the posture of the abuser.[2] Sadly, insensitivity to the complexity of the biblical doctrine of forgiveness and ignorance of the dynamics of abuse often lead Christian leaders to inflict an abundance of additional damage on survivors of abuse.[3]

Survivors of abuse need clear direction about the biblical doctrine of forgiveness and what it means for their relational health. More specifically, they need to know what Christian forgiveness means for their relationships with their abusers, particularly if an abuser is unrepentant. This is what we seek to provide in this chapter.

In view of common misperceptions and the complexity of the issue, the best way to begin is by clarifying the nature of biblical forgiveness. One of the first problems to note when researching this topic is that much of the religious literature implores forgiveness but never clearly defines it. It is widely known that the primary Greek verb in the New Testament used to indicate "to forgive" is *aphiemi*, which in general terms conveys the idea of "letting go." Sadly, many Christian leaders who address forgiveness fall into the trap of oversimplification and *only* define forgiveness as "letting go."

What does this mean for the little girl who disclosed to us that her teenage cousin had been molesting her, as well as other neighborhood children, during the past year? Does it mean (as the molester's parents proclaimed) the

---

2. See Karen E. Gerdes et al., "Adult Survivors of Childhood Sexual Abuse: The Case of Mormon Women," *Affilia* 11 (1996): 39–60; Catherine Taylor and Lisa Aronson-Fontes, "Seventh Day Adventists and Sexual Child Abuse," in *Sexual Abuse in Nine North American Cultures: Treatment and Prevention*, ed. Lisa Aronson Fontes (Thousand Oaks, CA: Sage, 1995), 176–99.

3. See Pamela Cooper-White, *The Cry of Tamar: Violence Against Women and the Church's Response* (Philadelphia: Fortress, 1995), 253–57; Carolyn Holderread Heggen, *Sexual Abuse in Christian Homes and Churches* (Scottsdale, PA: Herald, 1993), 121–34.

girl and her parents should simply "let it go" and not notify the authorities? Does forgiveness mean this family must "let go" of their anger toward an adolescent sexual predator who brags about the number of children he has raped? Does it mean (as the extended family insists) the parents must "let go" of their refusal to bring their daughter to family functions if the teenage molester is in attendance? If forgiveness doesn't necessarily mean letting go of *everything*, then just what is it that is let go?

Harmful Models of Forgiveness

We'll move toward an explanation of forgiveness by first noting some of the most inaccurate and harmful models. For survivors of abuse, the most damaging definitions of forgiveness are those that conflate forgiveness, trust, and reconciliation and eliminate the possibility of negative consequences for the offender. Sadly, this is a common mistake. For example, in a two-volume work that received a Book of the Year award, a respected evangelical states that, by definition, forgiveness involves a restoration of trust and a letting go of all negative emotions, including fear, anger, suspicion, alienation, and mistrust.[4] As if this definition fails to be difficult enough for abuse victims, who have every reason in the world to fear and mistrust their unrepentant abusers, the author keeps reminding readers that if we don't forgive others, God won't forgive us. By this logic, virtually all abuse victims are damned by their inability to trust their abusers.

While some may contend these views are imprecise due to a practical, nonacademic writing style, other scholarly writers make similar assertions. One of the most respected academic Bible dictionaries defines forgiveness as "the wiping out of an offense from memory" so that once the offense is eradicated, "the offense no longer conditions the relationship between the offender and the affronted, and harmony is restored between the two."[5] Again, by this definition, the majority of abuse victims could not practice forgiveness.

Inaccurate and harmful models of forgiveness may provide a partial explanation for the extreme antipathy of many abuse counselors toward forgiveness. A popular abuse healing manual states this sentiment most vividly:

---

4. See David Augsburger, *Caring Enough to Forgive / Caring Enough Not to Forgive: True Forgiveness, False Forgiveness* (Ventura, CA: Regal, 1981), 18–21, 67–68.

5. John Kselman, "Forgiveness," in *The Anchor Bible Dictionary*, vol. 2, ed. David Noel Freedman (New York: Doubleday, 1992), 831.

Never say or imply that the client should forgive the abuser. Forgiveness is not essential for healing. This fact is disturbing to many counselors, ministers, and the public at large. But it is absolutely true. If you hold the belief survivors must forgive the abuser in order to heal, you should not be working with survivors.[6]

Forgiveness and Consequences

Given such strong reactions against the forgiveness of abusers, it's imperative to clarify biblical forgiveness. One of the most important observations to make is that, while the Bible does describe forgiveness as the removal or letting go of a debt (Matthew 6:12), forgiveness does not necessarily remove negative consequences for the one forgiven, nor does it automatically grant trust and reconciliation.

One of the clearest examples is found in Numbers 14:20–23, where God declares that he will forgive the Israelites for their rebellion, but that not one of the adults will enter the land he had promised them. More relevant for abuse is King David's sexual violation of Bathsheba and murder of her husband. Once David repented, Nathan declared that God had forgiven him and taken away his sin, and yet a series of harsh consequences was meted out by God ("Out of your own household I am going to bring calamity on you" [2 Samuel 12:11]). Similarly, when the prophet Hosea took back his adulteress wife, Gomer, by God's directive he forgave her, but she was to remain in seclusion for two months and forgo sexual intimacy with her husband (Hosea 3:1–5). Trust is earned. Forgiving evil does *not* eliminate all negative consequences.

The Biblical Nature of Forgiveness

In classical Greek, *aphiemi* was used widely and consistently to mean "to release." This meaning is carried over into the New Testament, where *aphiemi* is used more than 125 times and has different nuances of meaning. It is used to mean "to let go, to send away" (Matthew 13:36; Mark 4:36); "to cancel, to remit" (Matthew 18:27; Mark 2:5); "to leave" (Matthew 4:11; John 10:12); "to give up, to abandon" (Romans 1:27; Revelation 2:4); and even "to tolerate, to permit" (Acts 5:38; Revelation 2:20).

---

6. Ellen Bass and Laura Davis, *The Courage to Heal: A Guide for Women Survivors of Child Sexual Abuse* (New York: Harper & Row, 1988), 348.

Clearly, in defining forgiveness, one cannot simply appeal to the root meaning of *aphiemi* as "to let go." The only way to accurately determine the biblical meaning of forgiveness as it relates to abuse is to look at a broad range of Bible passages that deal with forgiveness and malevolent evil and then draw pertinent principles. In doing so, one will quickly observe the complexity of biblical teaching on the subject and the inappropriateness of much of the evangelical rhetoric on forgiveness.

The Complexity of Biblical Forgiveness

The biblical doctrine of forgiveness is surprisingly complex, a fact that seems to escape the notice of many Christian leaders. At first glance, many passages dealing with forgiveness appear to be patently contradictory:

- In Colossians 3:13 and Mark 11:25, believers are seemingly commanded to forgive others without qualification, whereas in Luke 17:3 (and inferentially in 2 Corinthians 2:7), forgiveness is entirely contingent on the repentance of the offender.
- In Ephesians 4:32, believers are commanded to forgive without qualification based on God's forgiveness, and yet in Hosea 1:6 and Deuteronomy 29:20 (also Joshua 24:19; 2 Kings 24:4), God himself staunchly refuses to forgive.
- Jesus and Stephen prayed that God would forgive their murderers (Luke 23:34; Acts 7:60), and yet Nehemiah and Isaiah specifically prayed that God would not forgive evil people (Nehemiah 4:5; Isaiah 2:9).
- In Matthew 18:21–35, the disciples are taught they must forgive those who sin against them in an unlimited fashion and thus manifest God's mercy, and yet in the previous paragraph (18:15–20), Jesus says those who refuse to repent of their sin are to be excommunicated and treated as Gentiles and tax collectors.

Again, in order to build a coherent model of forgiveness, it's important to draw principles from a broad range of Bible passages.

These apparent contradictions suggest one of two things: either (1) the Bible's teaching on forgiveness is patently contradictory, and a harmonious biblical doctrine of forgiveness cannot be constructed[7]—a conclusion that

---

7. John Patton makes this argument, asserting that the gospel writers misinterpreted Jesus' teachings on forgiveness and mistakenly made forgiveness a condition for entering the kingdom (*Is Human Forgiveness Possible?: A Pastoral Care Perspective* [Nashville: Abingdon, 1985], 157).

flies in the face of the biblical doctrine of the divine inspiration and authority of Scripture—or (2) forgiveness does not always mean the same thing in the Bible.

I believe the latter explanation does justice to the biblical evidence. Careful examination of the Bible's teaching on forgiveness reveals very different kinds of forgiveness described within its pages. I believe it is most accurate and helpful to recognize three different categories, or types, of biblical forgiveness that must be distinguished if we are going to do justice to the Bible's teaching.

Judicial Forgiveness

Judicial forgiveness involves the remission or pardoning of sin by God. It pictures a complete removal of the guilt of one's sin (Psalm 51:1–9), and it is available to abusers and all other categories of sinners (Psalm 32:1–5; 1 Corinthians 6:10–11). The judicial forgiveness of sin by God lies at the very heart of Christianity and the salvation experience.

God's desire is unequivocally to forgive and to heal those labeled by society as the worst—the most hopeless and worthless sinners—a prospect that was as odious in the first century (Matthew 9:9–13) as it is today. Modern society's repulsion toward abusers, particularly toward child molesters, is well-known and in many respects quite logical. I vividly remember calling a close friend to inform him that a mutual friend had been discovered to be a molester, and that he should take extra precautions to protect children from this man. Upon hearing that this man was a child molester, my friend's first words to me were, "As far as I'm concerned, Bill can't die and burn in hell soon enough."

I certainly understand my friend's visceral reaction to this shocking discovery, but as soon as we consign abusers to the ranks of the irredeemable, we distort the message and ministry of Jesus. What's more, we threaten to impale ourselves on our own sword of justice, for those of us who have never molested children are surely in need of God's mercy and his forgiveness for other kinds of malicious acts, as well as other kinds of sexual sins (Matthew 18:21–35).[8]

However, judicial forgiveness is contingent on confession (Psalm 32:5; 1 John 1:9), the acknowledgment of one's sin, and repentance (Luke 24:47; Acts 2:38; 5:31)—adopting a radically different attitude toward one's sin.[9]

---

8. See L. Gregory Jones, *Embodying Forgiveness: A Theological Analysis* (Grand Rapids: Eerdmans, 1995), 78–91.

9. See Pedrito U. Maynard-Reid, "Forgiveness," in *Dictionary of the Later New Testament and Its Development*, ed. Ralph P. Martin and Peter H. Davids (Downers Grove, IL: InterVarsity, 1997), 379–82; in contrast to Jones, *Embodying Forgiveness*, 158–59.

Since judicial forgiveness of sin is granted only by God, families and churches cannot give it. Hence, it's absurd for abuse victims to be pressured into forgiving their abusers so these abusers can go to heaven.[10]

While humans cannot offer judicial forgiveness, they can hinder abusers from finding God's forgiveness when they fail to press offenders for full ownership of their behavior or when they misplace blame for the abuse.[11] Sadly, the Christian church has quite a history of blaming the victims of abuse, especially when the abuser is a male church leader.[12] More insidiously, judicial forgiveness is hindered when churches or families press for premature reconciliation, which, in addition to reabusing the victim, often serves to validate and solidify the offender's denial of wrongdoing, thus preventing them from experiencing God's forgiveness.

Psychological Forgiveness

> You only have to forgive once. To resent, you have to do it all day, every day.
> You have to keep remembering all the bad things.
>
> M. L. Stedman, *The Light between Oceans*

Psychological forgiveness is the inner, personal category of forgiveness, and it has two aspects: (1) negatively, it involves letting go of hatred and personal revenge; and (2) positively, it involves extending grace to the offender.

Letting Go of Hatred and Revenge
Some philosophers have persuasively argued that bearing resentment against those who maliciously harm us is necessary to maintain the moral order and to maintain respect for the victim.[13] Furthermore, resentment often feels psychologically necessary for abuse victims. Letting go of resentment toward an unrepentant abuser feels like letting go of justice; it may also feel like letting the abuser win and may appear to justify their evil.

These arguments against psychological forgiveness cannot be brushed

---

10. See Holderread Heggen, *Sexual Abuse in Christian Homes and Churches*, 127.

11. See Bob Moeller, "When Your Children Pay the Price, " *Leadership* 14 (1993): 87–94; Marianne Morris, *Sins of the Father* (Boise, ID: Pacific, 1993), 104–6, 133–50, 155, 173–87.

12. See Marie M. Fortune, *Sexual Violence: The Unmentionable Sin* (Cleveland, OH: Pilgrim, 1983), 61–87; Holderread Heggen, *Sexual Abuse in Christian Homes and Churches*, 98–115; Ann-Janine Morey, "Blaming Women for the Sexually Abusive Male Pastor," *Christian Century* 5 (October 5, 1988): 866–69; Laurie Hall, *An Affair of the Mind: One Woman's Courageous Battle to Salvage Her Family from the Devastation of Pornography* (Colorado Springs: Focus on the Family, 1998), 18–19, 54–56, 190–91.

13. See Joram Graf Haber, *Forgiveness* (Savage, MD: Rowman & Littlefield, 1991), 35, 37; Jeffrie G. Murphy and Jean Hampton, *Forgiveness and Mercy* (Cambridge: Cambridge University Press, 1988), 14–34.

aside lightly. I'm clearly not equating all anger with undesirable hatred or resentment, nor am I letting go of justice. Anger can be a healthy and appropriate response to evil, for Jesus himself became very angry, particularly at those who defamed God and hurt humans made in God's image (Matthew 21:12–17; Mark 3:5). Many of the psalms contain vivid expressions of anger toward evildoers (Psalms 5; 10; 69). Abuse victims can and should be angry at abusers, whose evil also angers God. The kind of anger prohibited in Bible verses such as Matthew 5:22 is the "deliberate harboring of resentment" with a view toward personal revenge.[14] Hence, Paul in Ephesians 4:26 indicates that one can be justifiably angry but must be careful not to let this disposition turn into sinful resentment.[15]

Thus, forgiving abusers at this level means letting go of settled bitterness and rage and committing abusers to God, who is both loving and just. The way victims are able to do this is by entering into God's point of view, for all humans—abuse victims as well as abusers—are individuals for whom Jesus Christ died.[16] At the same time, God will execute justice against all evil. This approach to forgiveness overcomes the objection that letting go of resentment demeans the victim and undermines justice.

At a practical level, letting go of bitterness means letting go of the right to personally exact revenge.[17] In other words, forgiveness is letting go of my right to hurt another person for hurting me. This is a cardinal element of forgiveness. Letting go of personal retribution, however, doesn't mean letting go of justice or the desire for it. Rather, justice is intensified. By letting go of my right to take personal revenge on my abuser, I am relinquishing to God the roles of judge, jury, and executioner. His judgment toward unrepentant evil will be perfect and indomitable, making my feeble attempts at revenge appear quite puny. At the same time, in letting go of my right to hurt the offender for hurting me, I am implicitly expressing the desire that they would repent and experience God's forgiveness and healing so eternal judgment might be precluded.

Dan Allender and Tremper Longman helpfully observe that victims of

14. Robert D. Enright and Robert L. Zell, "Problems Encountered When We Forgive One Another," *Journal of Psychology and Christianity* 8, no. 1 (1989): 54–55.

15. The Greek word for "wrath" at the end of Ephesians 4:26 is *parorgismos*, which is an intensive form of anger. In this context it indicates a settled bitterness.

16. See Marilyn McCord Adams, "Forgiveness: A Christian Model," *Faith and Philosophy* 8, no. 3 (1991): 296, https://place.asburyseminary.edu/cgi/viewcontent.cgi?article=1334&context=faithandphilosophy.

17. McCord Adams, "Forgiveness," 297; see Dan B. Allender and Tremper Longman III, *Bold Love* (Colorado Springs: NavPress, 1992), 183–204; Maxine Hancock and Karen Burton-Mains, *Child Sexual Abuse: A Hope for Healing* (Wheaton, IL: Shaw, 1987), 65.

evil should be greatly heartened by God's promise to exact retribution on all unrepentant evil, and they can and should long for the day of God's judgment on their abusers if they don't confess and repent of the sin of abuse.[18] I believe this is precisely Paul's point in Romans 12:17–21, because in verse 19, the believers are told not to take personal revenge but to leave room for the wrath of God, for vengeance is a divine prerogative.[19] We personally are not to take revenge because God will someday do it, and his revenge will be perfectly just and absolutely thorough. Peter encouraged Christians facing persecution with this same truth (1 Peter 2:23; see also 2 Timothy 4:14–15).

We should also note Jesus' words about what God will do to abusers who cause children to stumble—they would be better off if a large millstone were hung around their necks and they were cast into the sea (Matthew 18:6). Interestingly, this verse appears in the same section as the famous parable of the servant who refused to forgive. Apparently, though Jesus implored his disciples to forgive those who sinned against them, he viewed this in concert with the promise that God will mete out severe judgment on those who practice evil in general and on those who harm children in particular.

Thus, in the final analysis, forgiveness is an act of faith, for when one forgives, they are trusting that God can and will bring judgment and create justice for all the wrongs committed against them.[20] By faith, we let go of our attempts to exact revenge from abusers, trusting that God will carry out precisely the right, inescapable vengeance that justice requires.

Extending Grace

It is not enough, however, simply to define psychological forgiveness in negative terms as the withholding of retribution, for there is a positive side as well. One of the Greek terms used for human forgiveness in the New Testament is *caridzomai* (2 Corinthians 2:7, 10; 12:13; Ephesians 4:32; Colossians 3:13), which means to extend grace. Thus, psychological forgiveness also involves the willingness to extend grace and goodness to those who have hurt us.

This doesn't mean victims give abusers free rein to hurt them again, for that would make a mockery of forgiveness. Rather, it means—based

---

18. See Allender and Longman, *Bold Love*, 197–200; Gordon Zerbe, *Non-Retaliation in Early Jewish and New Testament Texts: Ethical Themes in Social Contexts* (New York: Bloomsbury, 1993), 261, 292; in contrast to C. F. D. Moule, "The Christian Understanding of Forgiveness," *Theology* 71, no. 580 (1968): 437–39. Bryan Maier has excellent insights into the role of the imprecatory psalms in praying for justice (*Forgiveness and Justice: A Christian Approach* [Grand Rapids: Kregel, 2017], 81–96).

19. See John Piper, *Love Your Enemy: Jesus' Love Command in the Synoptic Gospels and in Early Christian Paraenesis* (Cambridge: Cambridge University Press, 1979), 115–19; Zerbe, *Non-Retaliation*, 241–49.

20. See Philip Yancey, "An Unnatural Act," *Christianity Today* 35 (April 1991), 36–39.

on the mercy and grace of God I have experienced—I'm willing to extend kindness even to my enemies (Matthew 5:43–47), with a view toward their own repentance and healing. For abuse victims, one of the most appropriate expressions of this type of forgiveness is simply the extending of grace through the inner desire and prayer for their perpetrators' healing.

Relational Forgiveness

Relational forgiveness is the restoration of relationship. It is synonymous with reconciliation. From a biblical perspective, this forgiveness is always desirable, though not always possible. God's desire for the human race is for healing and reconciliation, both individually with God (2 Corinthians 5:18–21) and interpersonally with other humans (Ephesians 2:11–14; Colossians 3:10–13). The late Stanley Grenz wrote extensively on the nature of the church as a community. He summarizes the twofold reconciling work of God in human history:

> In short, the vision of the Scriptures is clear: the final goal of the work of the triune God in salvation history is the establishment of the eschatological community—a redeemed people dwelling in a renewed earth, enjoying reconciliation with their God, fellowship with each other, and harmony with all creation. Consequently, the goal of community lies at the heart of God's actions in history. And God's ultimate intention for creation is the establishment of community.[21]

Though reconciliation is always the desired goal, many abusers cannot be given relational forgiveness, for they refuse to do the painful work of repentance. We must not soften the conditional force of Jesus' words in Luke 17:3: "If your brother or sister sins against you, rebuke them; and *if they repent* [emphasis added], forgive them." Jesus goes on to say that if this sinning person repents repeatedly, they are to be forgiven repeatedly.

Paul gives a similar teaching in 2 Corinthians 2:5–11, where he commanded the Corinthians to now forgive the man they had excommunicated for his brazen sexual sin (1 Corinthians 5:1–13), as the excommunication seemed to have served the desired purpose of creating the shame and loneliness that stimulated repentance.

Thus, Christians are to offer relational forgiveness when genuine repentance has occurred. Some argue that forgiveness is not given at any

---

21. Stanley J. Grenz, *Theology for the Community of God* (Grand Rapids: Eerdmans, 2000), 113.

level until the abuser repents,[22] but this approach fails to recognize that the biblical repentance demand applies to relational, not psychological, forgiveness. In other words, there are ways abuse survivors can offer forgiveness to their perpetrators that don't involve reconciliation or the establishment of a relationship.

The Greek word used in Luke 17:3 for "repents" is *metanoeo*, which is a combination of two Greek words meaning "change" and "mind." This verb was used in the first century to indicate a definitive change of mind, a substantive shift in perspective. Inextricably connected with this change of mind is a change of life direction and behavior (Acts 26:20; 2 Corinthians 12:21; Revelation 2:5, 21–22; 9:20–21), which, particularly from Luke's perspective, means a "turning away from a sinful way of life . . . in light of the forgiveness of sins and salvation, which have come in Jesus."[23] Hence, in Luke 3:8, John the Baptist admonishes his audience to "produce fruit in keeping with repentance."

Thus, the New Testament usage of repentance indicates that abusers who are to be reconciled must evidence a radical change of mind— particularly regarding their full responsibility for the abuse and for its sinful and destructive nature. Furthermore, this changed understanding must be evidenced in movement toward substantive (as opposed to superficial) changed behavior.

Let us summarize how psychological and relational forgiveness interact. In God's time and with his help, the abuse victim can learn to let go of hatred and extend appropriate grace to the perpetrator (psychological forgiveness). In this sense, the victim can only *remove the barriers* to relationship; ultimately, the responsibility for relational forgiveness lies with the abuser, who must *repent*.[24] This is the implication of Romans 12:18: "If it is possible, *as far as it depends on you* [emphasis added], live at peace with everyone."

When is relational forgiveness appropriate? Religious people are often profoundly naive regarding the dynamics of abuse, and some can become indignant if reconciliation is not granted as soon as a perpetrator confesses and asks for forgiveness. Remember, though, an apology is not a sure

---

22. See Maier, *Forgiveness and Justice*, 64–70; Marie M. Fortune, "Forgiveness: The Last Step," in *Violence Against Women and Children: A Christian Theological Sourcebook*, ed. Carol J. Adams and Marie M. Fortune (New York: Continuum, 1995), 201–6; John Wilson, "Why Forgiveness Requires Repentance," *Philosophy* 63, no. 246 (1988): 534–35.

23. Horst Balz and Gerhard Schneider, eds., *Exegetical Dictionary of the New Testament*, vol. 2 (Grand Rapids: Eerdmans, 1991), s.v. *metanoeo, metanoia*.

24. See Paul Ellingworth, "Forgiveness of Sins," in *Dictionary of Jesus and the Gospels*, ed. Joel B. Green, Scot McKnight, and I. Howard Marshall (Downers Grove, IL: InterVarsity, 1994), 241–43.

indicator of repentance, and with both physical and sexual abusers, it often serves, in the "reconstitution phase," to help them convince themselves they're good people who don't have a serious problem.[25] Clearly, counselors and church leaders must be astute with regard to the characteristics of abusers and the dynamics of abuse, so they don't confuse a manipulative confession or apology with genuine repentance.

Two experts who treat offenders highlight the potential problems with abusers' apologies:

> Sex offenders are expert at manipulating people in order to justify their abuse to themselves and to others, as well as to maintain control and protect secret wishes and plans. Offenders often apologize in order to minimize the abuse, be forgiven, and assuage any guilt. Likewise, they may want to gain sympathy from other family members or to appear remorseful in the eyes of a court, and thereby get a lesser sentence. They may want to maintain power and set up a scenario that facilitates reabuse.[26]

Once their abuse has been made public, abusers will often ask their victims to forgive them. This can be problematic. In cases of sexual abuse, particularly of minors, it's generally inappropriate for the abuser unilaterally to ask their victim for forgiveness. If the offender wants judicial forgiveness, they must take that up with God.

In asking for forgiveness, offenders are typically seeking relational forgiveness (reconciliation), but the abuser's mere request for this is often reabusive. For instance, one expert notes that for incest victims, the request by their fathers to be forgiven is often "covert incest," for in asking for forgiveness, the fathers are treating the daughters as someone special, as the only ones who can help them with their problem, as their saviors.[27] This puts the child in a horribly difficult, unfair, and destructive position. I still affirm the propriety and desirability of relational forgiveness under the

---

25. See Ralph H. Earle, Marcus R. Earle, and Kevin Osborn, *Sex Addiction: Case Studies and Management* (New York: Brunner/Mazel, 1995), 63–64. Lenore E. Walker similarly notes the powerful role of apology and contrition in helping physical abusers convince themselves and their partners that they don't have a problem (*The Battered Woman* [New York: HarperCollins, 1979], 65–70).

26. Hilary Eldridge and Jenny Still, "Apology and Forgiveness in the Context of the Cycles of Adult Male Sex Offenders Who Abuse Children," in *Transforming Trauma: A Guide to Understanding and Treating Adult Survivors of Child Sexual Abuse*, ed. Anna C. Salter (Thousand Oaks, CA: Sage, 1995), 153–54.

27. See Sharon Lamb, *The Trouble with Blame: Victims, Perpetrators, and Responsibility* (Cambridge, MA: Harvard University Press, 1996).

right circumstances, but given the dynamics of abuse, it is generally inappropriate for the offender to make an unsolicited request for forgiveness of their victim.

To determine the propriety of relational forgiveness, indicators of genuine repentance must be identified.[28] To do this we need to distinguish characteristics of true repentance versus pseudorepentance. The clearest contrasting examples we can think of are found in 1 and 2 Samuel, in the characters David and Saul. Both were guilty of horrific acts of abuse, including multiple murders (2 Samuel 11:24; 1 Samuel 22:6–19). David was guilty of what many scholars have termed the "power rape" of Bathsheba (recorded in 2 Samuel 11).[29] Saul was guilty of multiple attempted murders, including of those in his own household (1 Samuel 19:10; 20:33). Both ostensibly repented and made virtually identical confessions, asserting that they had sinned against the Lord (1 Samuel 15:24; 2 Samuel 12:13). But only David was pronounced forgiven by God (2 Samuel 12:13). Even after Saul acknowledged his sin and asked for divine forgiveness, Samuel doesn't offer it but instead proclaimed that God was done with Saul. Clearly, Saul's sins, including abuse, had not been forgiven by God. His repentance was not genuine. So let's contrast the characteristics of genuine versus false repentance by abusers.[30]

Characteristics of Pseudorepentant Abusers

They Proclaim Innocence While Boldly Disobeying God

Abusers—particularly ones who are religious leaders—often act self-righteously. Their bold cries of innocence can easily fool people. King Saul directly disobeyed God's command to completely destroy the Amalekites and to take no spoil. Yet when Samuel the priest came, Saul greeted him

---

28. See Lewis Smedes, "Forgiving People Who Do Not Care," *Reformed Journal* 33 (1983): 13–18.

29. Richard Davidson gives eighteen different arguments to support his assertion that this was a "power rape" by a sovereign Jewish monarch to whom citizens were expected to come when he told them to come (*Flame of Yahweh: Sexuality in the Old Testament* [Peabody, MA: Hendrickson, 2007], 523–32); see also Sarah Bowler "Bathsheba: Vixen or Victim?" in *Vindicating the Vixens: Revisiting Sexualized, Vilified, and Marginalized Women of the Bible*, ed. Sandra Glahn (Grand Rapids: Kregel Academic, 2017), 81–100; Larry Spielman, "David's Abuse of Power," *Word & World* 19, no. 3 (1999): 251–59, https://wordandworld.luthersem.edu/content/pdfs/19-3_Politics/19-3_Spielman.pdf. Note, for instance, that neither the prophet Nathan nor any writer of Scripture hold Bathsheba culpable for their sexual activity. Nathan comes to David and solely condemns him (2 Samuel 12:7).

30. The following section is taken by permission from Steven and Celestia Tracy, *By His Wounds: Trauma Healing for Africa* (Phoenix, AZ: Mending the Soul Ministries, 2014), 162–66.

in a religious manner: "The LORD bless you! I have carried out the LORD's instructions" (1 Samuel 15:13). This was a bald-faced lie—he tried to cover up his disobedience with false righteousness.

In the New Testament, the Pharisees did the same thing, and Jesus called them spiritual hypocrites and murderous abusers (Matthew 23:29–35). Sometimes abusers are so bold in their spiritual-sounding statements that it's uncertain what they really mean, such as when murderous Joseph Kony called his Ugandan rebel group "The Lord's Resistance Army." Most of the time, abusers' proclamations of innocence are so strong that they are convincing. Sexual abusers often proclaim their goodness and innocence to anyone who will listen to them, in spite of a mountain of evidence against them. And most often, even when the proof of their abuse is uncovered, they *still* proclaim their innocence.

They Offer Clever Excuses for Their Sin

Samuel wasn't fooled by Saul's lies and confronted him with the clear evidence of his disobedience (animal cries from livestock that should have been destroyed). Saul offered a spiritual-sounding excuse to justify his sin. He said they had "spared the best of the sheep and cattle to sacrifice to the LORD your God, but we totally destroyed the rest" (1 Samuel 15:15). It is astonishing how clever abusers can be when their sin is discovered. For instance, I (Steven) knew a missionary who had molested numerous boys on the mission field. Because of his cleverness, it took a long time for the mission agency to expel him. As witnesses came forward with firsthand reports of his abuse, he would boldly deny their allegations. He claimed, for example, that he was just innocently helping the young boys bathe themselves. He was so bold in his assertions that for several years many believed him and the sexual abuse continued.

They Shift Blame onto Others

When Samuel kept pressing Saul regarding his direct disobedience, Saul resorted to blaming the soldiers. In spite of the fact that he was the sovereign king, Saul said it wasn't his fault that spoil was taken: "The soldiers took sheep and cattle from the plunder" (1 Samuel 15:21). *Blame shifting is one of the most notable characteristics of abusers.* Sexual abusers will often blame their victims for "seducing" them or for wearing immodest clothes. Physical abusers often blame the victims for "making them mad." When soldiers are caught raping and murdering civilians, they often shift the blame on leaders and proclaim that it wasn't really their fault because they were just "following orders." But God doesn't accept abusers' excuses—and neither should we.

They Deceptively Confess and Apologize When Caught

Sometimes abusers will continue to repeatedly proclaim their innocence. But other times—especially when they are caught and fear consequences—they will say all the right things, giving the appearance they have repented. Notice that Saul—after Samuel refused to be fooled by Saul's excuses—finally said, "I have sinned. I violated the LORD's command and your instructions. I was afraid of the men and so I gave in to them. Now I beg you, forgive my sin and come back with me, so that I may worship the LORD" (1 Samuel 15:24–25). However, wise Samuel, being a godly prophet, recognized that these were mere words that didn't reflect a changed heart. He refused to go and instead pronounced God's judgment on Saul.

Years later, Saul repeated this deceptive pattern. On two separate occasions, as he was chasing David, trying to kill him, David spared Saul's life (1 Samuel 24:1–22; 26:1–25). Again, Saul attempted to deceive by spiritual language accompanied by weeping, confessing, pronouncing David as more righteous than himself, calling David his dear son, and promising never to harm David again (24:16–17; 26:21). However, these were deceptive, cheap words. Saul soon went back to his old abusive behavior.

They Harshly Judge Others

Unrepentant abusers can be harsh and judgmental toward others who are committing the same or even a less serious sin than they are. For instance, King Saul slaughtered eighty-five innocent priests and their families, accusing them of disloyalty to the king, while he was acting in blatantly disloyal ways toward God (1 Samuel 22:18–19). We must not be fooled by these deceptive and confusing patterns.

There are many biblical examples of abusers harshly judging others, such as Judah wanting to have Tamar burned to death for sexual sin when in fact he was the one who had gotten her pregnant (Genesis 38:24). If Judah had applied the same standard of justice to himself that he applied to Tamar, he would have also been put to death. Similarly, King David, before he truly repented, burned with anger toward a rich man who stole a lamb, declaring that the man deserved to die. In reality, David had stolen a man's wife and was guilty of two sins that deserved the death sentence—rape and murder (2 Samuel 12:5–6).

Characteristics of True Repentance

Below are some ways to recognize genuine repentance. Keep in mind that the New Testament speaks of the "fruit" of repentance and that it takes time to confidently recognize these characteristics because fruit takes time to grow.

They Confess and Take Full Responsibility for the Abuse (with No Excuses or Blame Shifting)

After Nathan the prophet cleverly confronted David for his sin, Scripture describes David as simply saying, "I have sinned against the LORD" (2 Samuel 12:13). Notice that he did not in any way qualify this confession. Most importantly, he didn't blame his abuse on Bathsheba for bathing on the roof (which, in fact, was an accepted cultural practice); he didn't place any blame on the servants who brought Bathsheba to him; he didn't blame his other wives for not meeting his sexual needs; and he didn't blame Uriah for not being a good husband. David made no excuses for his sin. He took full responsibility.

We also see this in Psalm 51, which David wrote after Nathan confronted him. David's focus is solely on his sin and his need for God's forgiveness. David doesn't minimize his behavior but instead describes it as "evil" (Psalm 51:4).

So when you hear an abuser "confess" their sin but after the confession explain why others also are responsible, you know you're not hearing true repentance.

They Accept the Consequences for Their Abuse without Complaining

If an abuser truly owns their sin and sees it as God does—an evil, destructive act—they will accept the consequences they receive from God, the church, or the civil authorities. In David's case, one of the consequences for his abuse was that the child conceived during the sexually abusive act would die. David pleaded to God for the child's life, since sometimes prayer can stop God's judgment (Exodus 32:11–14; Jonah 3:7–10.) However, once the child died, David accepted God's sentence without complaint (2 Samuel 12:19–23). Furthermore, David described his sin as being "always before him"—he took it seriously—and confessed that God's judgment for sin was justified (Psalm 51:3–4). It's helpful to contrast David's acceptance of God's harsh consequences for his sin of rape and murder with Cain's response to God's consequences for his sin of murder. Cain complained that his punishment was too difficult to bear (Genesis 4:13). *The way an abuser responds to painful consequences for their abuse is profoundly helpful in determining whether they are truly repentant.*

They Acknowledge the Extensive Damage Done to the Victim and Demonstrate Remorse

Cain wouldn't have complained of God's punishment if he truly recognized the impact of his sin on his brother (Genesis 4:8–13). Cain's punishment was that his farming would be more difficult, but Abel wouldn't farm at all. Cain was sentenced to be a "wanderer on the earth," but his brother no longer lived on the earth. On the other hand, David, in true repentance, had "a broken and contrite heart" over his sin (Psalm 51:17). Repentant abusers feel deep and sincere "godly sorrow" for the harm they've done to God's name and to their victims.

As a pastoral counselor, Steve ministers to many abusers. After they confess, one of the things he has them do is compile a list of all the ways their abuse has damaged their victims physically, sexually, emotionally, relationally, and spiritually. They need to take time to prayerfully reflect on their behavior as they compile the list. Then, when they have finished, they're to give their list to the victim(s) so any consequences they have missed can be added to the original list. This is an incredibly humbling exercise for an abuser and can greatly help him or her experience a deeper level of understanding, repentance, and commitment to change.

They Make Restitution for the Harm Done

When abusers truly "own" their sin and recognize the extent of the damage they've caused, they're willing to make appropriate restitution. Restitution is an attempt to compensate a victim for the damage created by the abuse. It's important to note here that abuse generally causes so much damage that no amount of restitution could fully repay the loss. But making restitution is a biblical concept and helps both the abuser and the victim experience a future that holds promise of being different from the harmful past. With restitution the perpetrator accepts ownership and consequences for the abuse, and the victim receives encouragement and hope.

Restitution is built into Mosaic Law. In ancient Israel, there are many examples: when one stole livestock, it was to be repaid double for what was stolen (Exodus 22:4); if a Jew accidentally burned his neighbors' crops, he was to give restitution (payment) for the lost income (Exodus 22:6); when a Jew harmed someone, he was to confess it and make full restitution to the one harmed (Numbers 5:7–8). Biblically, the restitution should relate as directly as possible to the nature of the loss, should be substantial, and should be truly meaningful to the victim. Thus, there are countless types of appropriate restitution. *When abuser's resist making costly restitution, they're most likely* not *repentant.*

They Change the Sinful Pattern of Behavior That Led to the Abuse

Confession is an important starting place for repentance, but it's just that—just the beginning. Remember, repentance involves a *thorough* change of behavior. This means that the abuser must be helped to recognize the faulty thinking, unhealthy habits, and sinful actions that set them up to perpetrate harm. Then, the abuser must make a private and public commitment to change. This will require much reflection, prayer, and effort, but it's essential for long-term transformation. All humans are sinners, but not all humans abuse. Abuse is a more severe type of sin (see Psalm 5:6; Proverbs 6:16–17) and requires more significant consequences and a significant plan for change. In order to change, an abuser must understand the factors that influenced the abuse so that he or she can prevent it from happening again in the future.

Steps in the Practice of Forgiveness

It is one thing to argue for the biblical propriety of forgiving abusers and quite another matter to practice it. The following is a brief practical sketch to guide victims in forgiving their abusers. The steps are in logical order, but after the first two are taken, the sequencing of the remaining ones may vary.

Clarify the Offense(s) and Resultant Negative Emotions

This essential preliminary step precedes actual forgiveness. One cannot truly forgive such a destructive offense as abuse until the specific offense(s) and emotional impact have been assessed and clarified. This is necessary, first of all, by virtue of the nature of forgiveness. Lewis Smedes correctly observes that human forgiveness is appropriate only for real offenses.[31] Thus, the victim must clarify the nature of the offense(s) he or she is considering forgiving. True forgiveness can only happen in the light of a careful moral judgment.

On the one hand, it's common for abuse victims to minimize or deny sin

---

31. Lewis B. Smedes, *Forgive and Forget: Healing the Hurts We Don't Deserve* (San Francisco: HarperSanFrancisco, 1984), 5–9.

against them. On the other hand, bitterness can cause abuse victims to take offense at behavior that in reality was *not* harmful or abusive. In either case, one must prayerfully clarify the nature of the offense before forgiveness can be offered. To do otherwise is to offer trivial forgiveness that is superficial, inappropriate, and unhealthy—unhealthy both for the abuse victim and the perpetrator, for it inevitably involves excusing or minimizing sin.

In judicial forgiveness, God knows precisely what he is forgiving, which includes the heinousness of our behavior and its destructive results (see Psalms 32:1–5; 51:4; Isaiah 1:18; 40:27–28; Revelation 20:12). This is, in fact, what makes his forgiving grace so beautiful. One cannot begin the real process of forgiving an abuser without painstakingly clarifying the nature and emotional consequences of the abuse.

This first step is necessary in light of the nature and impact of abuse. Abuse victims often protect themselves through denial, distortion (such as self-contempt), and dissociation. They commonly blame themselves, not the perpetrators, for the abuse and often minimize the full extent of the abuse and its effects on them. Clarifying the offense and negative impact stimulates the victim to break the pattern of denial and misplaced blame.

One can now see how dangerous it is for counselors or church leaders to urge prompt (and hence premature) forgiveness of abusers. This is incredibly insensitive and destructive to the victims. It can also have the unintended consequence of hindering their healing by strengthening unforgiveness.[32] It amplifies further abuse in the Christian community by promoting individual and corporate minimization and denial of evil. One theologian who works with abuse victims summarizes the allure and danger of immediate, premature forgiveness:

> Premature forgiveness may seem to smooth things over temporarily, and it appeals to most of us who were brought up to believe that being nice was a primary Christian virtue. But it has the effect of driving anger and pain underground where they then fester like a poisonous stream, under our houses and our churches and our communities. And it has the effect of relieving the abuser of any true responsibility to examine his behavior and to change. Because premature forgiveness bypasses consequences and rehabilitation for the offender, it is, in fact, tacit permission—perhaps even an invitation—to continue the violence.[33]

---

32. See Paul C. Vitz, "Kernbergian Psychodynamics and Religious Aspects of the Forgiveness Process," *Journal of Psychology and Theology* 25, no. 1 (1997): 72–80.

33. Cooper-White, *Cry of Tamar*, 255.

Set Appropriate Boundaries to Check
Evil and Stimulate Repentance

Since abuse is inherently about the perpetrator's abuse of power to violate personal boundaries, the victim must determine appropriate boundaries for self-protection. This element of boundary setting is preliminary to actual forgiveness, for we cannot truly forgive unless we can freely forgive—which likely can't happen, particularly for a minor, until the cycle of victimization and powerlessness has been broken. When churches or families press abuse victims to forgive their abusers before protective boundaries are in place, they in essence mock the victim. Church leaders, counselors, and families must instead take seriously the biblical mandate to protect the vulnerable (Proverbs 24:11–12; Isaiah 1:16–17; 58:6; James 1:27). Then, and only then, should forgiveness be considered.

A second element of boundary setting will in many cases be the first aspect of actual forgiving. Here the boundaries are set not only to protect the victim but also to check the offender's evil and, in so doing, to stimulate repentance. Dan Allender and Tremper Longman note that many evil people such as abusers are manipulative and cunning and are accustomed to winning for their sordid purposes; therefore, erecting boundaries to prevent abuse also serves to thwart, or check, their evil, giving them the "gift of defeat" that can be used by God to stimulate their repentance.[34]

If after the boundaries are put in place abusers are unrepentant and persist in their abusive behavior, then they must be given the "gift of excommunication." As with corporate church discipline, the abuse victim does this to open the door to loneliness and shame for the abuser, so that they may be led to repent and find God's healing (1 Corinthians 5:5; 2 Thessalonians 3:14–15).

Let Go of the Right to Hurt an Abuser for Hurting You

We've already given considerable attention to this aspect of forgiveness. We only want to add here that this is an act of faith in which the victim prayerfully turns over the need for justice and redress to God, who is the just Judge.

Reevaluate the Abuser and Discover Their Humanity

Forgiveness is in large measure a mental "reframing process" in which one reinterprets experiences and conclusions by means of biblical truth.[35]

---

34. See Allender and Longman, *Bold Love*, 243–49.
35. See Bobby B. Cunningham, "The Will to Forgive: A Pastoral Theological View of Forgiving," *Journal of Pastoral Care* 34, no. 2 (1985): 143.

As one begins the work of forgiveness, the abusive events, the abuser, God, and many other entities and factors are reframed and given a fuller, more biblically accurate understanding.

Victims have an understandable tendency to reduce those who wounded them to the sum total of their hurtful act or acts. While the abusive act is the most significant thing for a victim—and must in no way, shape, or form be minimized—it's helpful for victims to begin seeing the offender as a fellow human being that includes other aspects of their life as a whole. It may help victims both understand the factors that led to the abuse (thus reducing the tendency to somehow blame themselves for the abuse) and gain a measure of compassion for those who hurt them.

Michael McCullough, Steven Sandage, and Everett Worthington Jr. have developed a helpful empathy-humility model of forgiveness that relates this fourth forgiveness step to the transformation of a victim's memory.[36] Victims need to acknowledge the harmful actions committed against them, but they also must reflect on the neediness of their offenders—and on their own moral fallibility too. In Colossians 3:12–13, we see that putting on a heart of compassion immediately precedes forgiving, implying that the former leads to the latter. It is well-known that a high percentage of abusers were themselves abused or neglected. Every abuser was once a vulnerable, needy child. Every abuser is a human being made in God's image. Every abuser has been manipulated by Satan into seeking to meet legitimate needs and cope with real pain in inappropriate, sinful ways.

Reflecting on an abuser's humanness, including their own trauma experiences, does not soften blame or lessen the reprehensibility of the behavior. But it may give the victim, who is learning to forgive, a renewed ability to see the offender as a whole person—a mixture of hurts, fears, and evil responses. This in turn can help a victim loosen the grip of hatred in their own heart so they can extend psychological forgiveness.

Extend Appropriate Grace

Lewis Smedes describes the last stage of forgiveness as "revising our feelings" toward the one who sinned against us.[37] In this step, the victim moves from inner hatred toward the abuser to an inner desire that good things will come their way. This may well describe the first portion of the last phase, because

---

36. See Michael E. McCullough, Steven J. Sandage, and Everett L. Worthington Jr., *To Forgive Is Human: How to Put Your Past in the Past* (Downers Grove, IL: InterVarsity, 1997), 110–26.
37. See Smedes, *Forgive and Forget*, 10–11.

full Christian forgiveness culminates in an active commitment for one's abuser to experience God's healing and blessing.

Christians are called to extend grace even to evil, destructive people, desiring that this grace will transform them by God's power. Extending grace takes countless forms and can't be formularized, for the needs of each abuser and the personality and abilities of each abuse victim are different. Since the boundary steps determined in step 2 will seriously limit and in some cases preclude personal interaction with unrepentant abusers, this final step will for many abuse survivors primarily involve prayer for their abusers to be stripped of distorted beliefs, to repent, and to find God's forgiveness and healing. This is, in fact, a far more significant action than most realize. In many cases, it may be all the grace a survivor can extend, particularly when the victim has no contact with the abuser.

As noted earlier, Dan Allender and Tremper Longman also emphasize "bold love" as an act of grace toward evildoers.[38] This involves a willingness to do what it takes to bring about the abuser's health and salvation, including articulation of one's sorrow over the abuser's sin, confrontation (Proverbs 27:5–6), exhortation (2 Thessalonians 3:14–15), and excommunication (1 Corinthians 5:1–13). In other circumstances, God has led abuse survivors to extend grace by visiting abusers in prison, by writing letters to abusers that explain the gospel, and by providing financial assistance for abusers to obtain professional counseling.

To Forgive or Not to Forgive?

In conclusion, does God want us to forgive abusers? Yes. Is this always possible? No. It is God's desire to forgive evildoers. It is also his desire to create a community of forgiven sinners who are reconciled to each other. However, we aren't always able to implement fully the three aspects of biblical forgiveness.

Only God can provide judicial forgiveness for the horrific sin of abuse. We can merely avoid hindering the process by pressing abusers to own their behavior and by never endorsing premature relational forgiveness. Relational forgiveness should only be offered when the abuser has shown a clear willingness to take responsibility for their abuse, is taking clear steps toward changed behavior, and is willing to enact firm and appropriate behavioral boundaries—and when the victim is not in danger of being revictimized.

---

38. See Allender and Longman, *Bold Love*, 243–54.

We should, however, offer psychological forgiveness to abusers—even to unrepentant abusers.

In time, we can learn to let go of our attempts to exact personal revenge on abusers and can, where possible, extend not hatred but grace and kindness toward them. We do this with a view toward their healing, recognizing that their unrepentant evil abuse will be judged righteously and decisively by God. A forgiveness that follows these principles breathes hope into malevolent human evil. It offers the transformation of healing for survivors and a call to repentance for those who have perpetrated abuse.

A Word from Mary

Mary, the missionary daughter whose childhood story of abuse was told at the beginning of the book, wrote this epilogue to update readers on God's healing work.

Healing from abuse has been a long process for me. When I look back on my journey, it's hard to believe I'm the same person I was a few years ago. Last year I finished graduate school and now serve as a social worker for homeless and impoverished families. I recently celebrated five years of marriage to an amazing Christian man, and all of my anger and bitterness toward God has been replaced by a trusting, honest relationship with him. I can now view God as my redeemer and rescuer.

Hearing songs such as "Amazing Grace" never fails to bring tears to my eyes. I now support children and families who come from difficult places. I believe that I can help them on a level that someone who has not been abused can't, because I can literally step into their shoes. I will never cease to be amazed at the way God uses evil for good if we let him.

In the beginning of my healing journey, I thought that I would get to a place where I would say, "I'm healed. It's all behind me now." I now realize that healing is a lifelong journey and that every trauma trigger provides an opportunity to face something unexpected—to integrate another layer of my story. The first few years after my disclosure were the hardest years of my life. I want to remind readers that healing from abuse takes time, patience, and a lot of support from others. You can't heal as a lone survivor. We need each other, which is actually a very good thing. Don't beat yourself up if the process is taking much longer than you expected.

My healing came slowly. It started with my parents, who loved me tenaciously. They loved me when I was acting unlovable, and they stuck by my side when I was angry. If possible, abuse victims should find someone who will love them like this. It could be a parent, a sibling, a friend, a pastor, or a counselor. Before victims can accept and love themselves, they must experience unconditional love from someone else.

After I accepted that my parents would love me no matter what, I began to trust other people. I started by telling a close friend about the abuse. I gradually began to trust people in seemingly little ways, such as going on dates with guys or letting more of my true self show through to friends. I encourage abuse victims to open up to people when they feel ready, so they can experience trust again. In my journey, I found the more I trusted other people, the more I could trust God.

As an abuse victim, healing my relationship with God has been the hardest thing I've ever done. It took the most time and was the most painful, but eventually it happened. For a long time, I was furious at God. Although I continued to attend church, I didn't feel a lot of love for God, and that was okay. We are not responsible for our feelings; we're just responsible to keep obeying and pursuing God. During my healing I learned that it's okay to feel angry at God! He even wants us to *tell* him about this anger. I found it helpful to write letters to God about how confused and angry I was toward him and to ask him to show himself to me.

My last step of healing from abuse was forgiving my abuser and those who had enabled him. I believe forgiving one's abuser can only be accomplished after your relationship with God has been healed. Forgiving one's abuser is a supernatural event, and it can only be accomplished with God's help.

I'd like to reiterate to anyone reading this book who has been abused that deep healing takes time. Please don't rush the process. Pray for God to show you the good he wants to bring out of your abuse. Claim his promise in Jeremiah 29:11: "'For I know the plans I have for you,' declares the LORD, 'plans to prosper you and not to harm you, plans to give you hope and a future.'" Look at the story of Joseph and read Genesis 50:20. What people intended for evil, God used for good. Claim these biblical promises and pray that God will reveal their truth to you.

I'd like to conclude with some tips for pastors and others who want to help victims of abuse. First, *be very careful to support and believe the victim.* Abuse victims, as well as their abusers, deny and minimize abuse, so the story of abuse a victim discloses to you will most likely represent just a fraction of the actual abuse they experienced. It's extremely difficult and painful for victims to disclose abuse to anyone, let alone an authority figure. So the last thing they need is for someone they trust—someone who's trying to help them—to question or deny the abuse. They desperately need your support.

Second, *remember that healing from abuse takes time.* It often takes years. This doesn't mean abuse is too damaging for healing to occur quickly or that God is too weak to heal abuse damage instantly—but it's not the way God typically works. Accepting the fact that healing from abuse is generally a long and arduous process doesn't impugn God's power; it's simply a recognition of the way God has made us. Abuse is a powerful tool in Satan's hands because it creates such deep soul damage.

Third, *allow the victim to be angry*—angry at God, angry at the abuser, even angry at you. Just love them and validate that it's okay they're angry— they have a lot to be angry about! Validating feelings is very important for any victim of abuse. Abuse has stripped them of worth, of feelings, and of life. Thus they need all the validation they can get.

The final and perhaps most important tip is to *love, love, love.* If the victim is being mean and harsh, love them. If they are being self-destructive, love them. If they are being hurtful, love them. Victims must *experience* love before they can *embrace* love and begin to trust others. Your role in this healing is vital. You have great potential for help, as well as great potential for harm—never forget that. Most of all, remember that if you are open and available, you get to be a vessel through whom God will work to bring tremendous healing to someone you love. I am only where I am today because God has been working in people like you! I truly believe that if I can experience healing, anyone can!

Bible Passages That Address Abuse

Jesus' View of Children and Those Who Harm Children

Jeremiah 32:31–32, 35—"From the day it was built until now, this city has so aroused my anger and wrath that I must remove it from my sight. The people of Israel and Judah have provoked me by all the evil they have done . . . They built high places for Baal in the Valley of Ben Hinnom to sacrifice their sons and daughters to Molek, though I never commanded—nor did it enter my mind—that they should do such a detestable sin and so make Judah sin."

Matthew 18:5–6—"And whoever welcomes one such child in my name welcomes me. If anyone causes one of these little ones—those who believe in me—to stumble, it would be better for them to have a large millstone hung around their neck and to be drowned in the depths of the sea."

Matthew 19:13–14—"Then people brought little children to Jesus for him to place his hands on them and pray for them. But the disciples rebuked them. Jesus said, 'Let the little children come to me, and do not hinder them, for the kingdom of heaven belongs to such as these.'"

Condemnation of Physical Abuse

Psalm 11:5—"The LORD examines the righteous, but the wicked, those who love violence, he hates with a passion."

Proverbs 1:15–19—"My son, do not go along with them, do not set foot on their paths; for their feet rush into evil, they are swift to shed blood. How useless to spread a net where every bird can see it! These men [abusers] lie in wait for their own blood; they ambush only themselves! Such are the paths of all who go after ill-gotten gain; it takes away the life of those who get it."

Proverbs 6:16–19—"There are six things the LORD hates, seven that are detestable to him: haughty eyes, a lying tongue, hands that shed innocent blood, a heart that devises wicked schemes, feet that are quick to run into evil, a false witness who pours out lies, and a person who stirs up conflict in the community."

Ezekiel 9:9–10—"The sin of the people of Israel and Judah is exceedingly great; the land is full of bloodshed and the city is full of injustice. They say, 'The LORD has forsaken the land; the LORD does not see!' So I [God] will not look on them [abusers] with pity or spare them, but I will bring down on their own heads what they have done."

Ezekiel 18:10–13—"Suppose he has a violent son who sheds blood or does any of these other things . . . He defiles his neighbor's wife. He oppresses the poor and needy. He commits robbery . . . Will such a man live? He will not! Because he has done all these detestable things, he is to be put to death."

Romans 3:15–18—"Their feet are swift to shed blood; ruin and misery mark their ways, and the way of peace they do not know. There is no fear of God before their eyes."

Condemnation of Sexual Abuse

Deuteronomy 22:25–26—"But if out in the country a man happens to meet a young woman pledged to be married and rapes her, only the man who has done this shall die. Do nothing to the woman; she has committed no sin deserving death."

Judges 19:25—"But the men would not listen to him. So the man took his concubine and sent her outside to them, and they raped her and abused her throughout the night, and at dawn they let her go."

Lamentations 5:11—"Women have been violated in Zion, and virgins in the towns of Judah."

Ezekiel 22:11, 21—"One man commits a detestable offense with his neighbor's wife, another shamefully defiles his daughter-in-law, and another violates his sister, his own father's daughter . . . I will gather you and blow on you with my fiery wrath, and you will be melted inside her."

Effects of Sexual Abuse

2 Samuel 13:19–20—"Tamar put ashes on her head and tore the ornate robe she was wearing. She put her hands on her head and went away, weeping aloud as she went . . . And Tamar lived in her brother Absalom's house, a desolate woman."

Condemnation of Neglect

1 Timothy 5:8—"Anyone who does not provide for their relatives, and especially for their own household, has denied the faith and is worse than an unbeliever."

Condemnation and Effect of Verbal Abuse

Proverbs 12:18—"The words of the reckless pierce like swords, but the tongue of the wise brings healing."

Proverbs 15:4—"The soothing tongue is a tree of life, but a perverse tongue crushes the spirit."

Proverbs 18:21—"The tongue has the power of life and death."

Romans 3:13–14—"Their throats are open graves; their tongues practice deceit. The poison of vipers is on their lips. Their mouths are full of cursing and bitterness."

James 3:5–6, 8–9—"Likewise, the tongue is a small part of the body, but it makes great boasts. Consider what a great forest is set on fire by a small spark. The tongue also is a fire, a world of evil among the parts of the body. It corrupts the whole body, sets the whole course of one's life on fire, and is itself set on fire by hell . . . But no human being can tame the tongue. It is a restless evil, full of deadly poison. With the tongue we praise our Lord and Father, and with it we curse human beings, who have been made in God's likeness."

Condemnation of Spiritual Abuse

Ezekiel 22:25–26, 28—"There is a conspiracy of her princes within her like a roaring lion tearing its prey; they devour people, take treasures and precious things and make many widows within her. Her priests do violence to my law . . . Her prophets whitewash these deeds for them by false visions and lying divinations. They say, 'This is what the Sovereign LORD says'—when the LORD has not spoken."

Matthew 23:1–5, 11–13—"Then Jesus said to the crowds and to his disciples: 'The teachers of the law and the Pharisees sit in Moses' seat. So you must be careful to do everything they tell you. But do not do what they do, for they do not practice what they preach. They tie up heavy, cumbersome loads and put them on other people's shoulders, but they themselves are not willing to lift a finger to move them. Everything they do is done for people to see . . . The greatest among you will be your servant. For those who exalt themselves will be humbled, and those who humble themselves will be exalted. Woe to you, teachers of the law and Pharisees, you hypocrites! You shut the door of the kingdom of heaven in people's faces.'"

Mark 7:5–8—"So the Pharisees and teachers of the law asked Jesus, 'Why don't your disciples live according to the tradition of the elders instead of eating their food with defiled hands?' He replied, 'Isaiah was right when he prophesied about you hypocrites; as it is written: "These people honor me with their lips, but their hearts are far from me. They worship me in vain; their teachings are merely human rules." You have let go of the commands of God and are holding on to human traditions.'"

Responsibility of Leaders to Aid and Protect the Vulnerable

Proverbs 24:11–12—"Rescue those being led away to death; hold back those staggering toward slaughter. If you say, 'But we knew nothing about this,' does not he who weighs the heart perceive it? Does not he who guards your life know it?"

Isaiah 1:17—"Learn to do right; seek justice. Defend the oppressed. Take up the cause of the fatherless; plead the case of the widow."

Jeremiah 22:3—"This is what the LORD says: 'Do what is just and right. Rescue from the hand of the oppressor the one who has been robbed. Do no wrong or violence to the foreigner, the fatherless or the widow; and do not shed innocent blood in this place.'"

Jeremiah 22:15–17—"'Did not your father have food and drink? He did what was right and just, so all went well. He defended the cause of the poor and needy, and so all went well. Is not that what it means to know me?' declares the LORD. But your eyes and your heart are set only on dishonest gain, on shedding innocent blood and on oppression and extortion."

Responsibility of Leaders to Confront Abuse and Other Types of Evil

1 Samuel 3:13—"For I told him that I would judge his family forever because of the sin he knew about; his sons blasphemed God, and he failed to restrain them." (Eli was judged for failing to confront and stop his sons from physical and sexual abuse—see 1 Samuel 2:16, 22.)

1 Timothy 5:20—"Those elders who are sinning you are to reprove before everyone, so that the others may take warning."

Titus 3:10–11—"Warn a divisive person once, and then warn them a second time. After that, have nothing to do with them. You may be sure that such people are warped and sinful; they are self-condemned."

God's Righteous Judgment on Abusers

2 Kings 17:17–18—"They sacrificed their sons and daughters in the fire [burned them alive]. They practiced divination and sought omens and sold themselves to do evil in the eyes of the LORD, arousing his anger. So the LORD was very angry with Israel and removed them from his presence. Only the tribe of Judah was left."

Joel 3:19—"Egypt will be desolate, Edom a desert waste, because of violence done to the people of Judah, in whose land they shed innocent blood."

Nahum 3:1, 3, 5, 7—"Woe to the city of blood [Nineveh, the capital of the abusive, ruthless Assyrians], full of lies, full of plunder, never without victims! . . . Charging cavalry, flashing swords and glittering spears! Many casualties, piles of dead, bodies without number [of her murder victims] . . . 'I am against you,' declares the LORD Almighty . . . All who see you will flee from you and say, 'Nineveh is in ruins—who will mourn for her?'"

Philippians 1:27–28—"I will know that you stand firm in the one Spirit . . . without being frightened in any way by those who oppose you. This is a sign to them that they will be destroyed, but that you will be saved—and that by God."

Revelation 21:8—"The vile, the murderers, the sexually immoral, those who practice magic arts, the idolaters and all liars—they will be consigned to the fiery lake of burning sulfur. This is the second death."

Condemnation of Abusive Leaders

Ezekiel 22:6–7, 13, 15—"See how each of the princes of Israel who are in you uses his power to shed blood . . . In you they have oppressed the foreigner and mistreated the fatherless and the widow . . . I will surely strike my hands together at the unjust gain you have made and at the blood you have shed in your midst . . . I will disperse you among the nations and scatter you through the countries, and I will put an end to your uncleanness."

Micah 3:1–4, 9–10, 12—"Listen, you leaders of Jacob, you rulers of Israel. Should you not embrace justice, you who hate good and love evil; who tear the skin from my people and the flesh from their bones; who eat my people's flesh, strip off their skin and break their bones in pieces; who chop them up like meat for the pan, like flesh for the pot? Then they [the abusive leaders] will cry out to the LORD, but he will not answer them. At that time he will hide his face from them because of the evil they have done . . . Hear this, you leaders of Jacob, you rulers of Israel, who despise justice and distort all that is right; who build Zion with bloodshed, and Jerusalem with wickedness . . . Therefore because of you, Zion will be plowed like a field, Jerusalem will become a heap of rubble."

True Nature of Godly Leadership

Deuteronomy 24:5—"If a man has recently married, he must not be sent out to war or have any other duty laid on him. For one year he is to be free to stay at home and bring happiness to the wife he has married."

Luke 22:25–26—"Jesus said to them, 'The kings of the Gentiles lord it over them; and those who exercise authority over them call themselves Benefactors. But you are not to be like that. Instead, the greatest among you should be like the youngest, and the one who rules like the one who serves.'"

Ephesians 5:25, 28—"Husbands, love your wives, just as Christ loved the church and gave himself up for her . . . In this same way, husbands ought to love their wives as [they love] their own bodies."

Colossians 3:19, 21—"Husbands, love your wives and do not be harsh with them . . . Fathers, do not embitter your children, or they will become discouraged."

1 Peter 3:7—"Husbands, in the same way, be considerate as you live with your wives, and treat them with respect as the weaker partner and as heirs with you of the gracious gift of life, so that nothing will hinder your prayers."

1 Peter 5:2–3—"Be shepherds of God's flock that is under your care . . . not lording it over those entrusted to you, but being examples to the flock."

God's Redemption of Abuse

Genesis 50:20—"You intended to harm me, but God intended it for good to accomplish what is now being done, the saving of many lives."

Isaiah 53:5—"But he was pierced for our transgressions, he was crushed for our iniquities; the punishment that brought us peace was on him, and by his wounds we are healed."

1 Corinthians 1:18—"For the message of the cross is foolishness to those who are perishing, but to us who are being saved it is the power of God."

2 Corinthians 4:8–10—"We are hard pressed on every side, but not crushed; perplexed, but not in despair; persecuted, but not abandoned; struck down, but not destroyed. We always carry around in our body the death of Jesus, so that the life of Jesus may also be revealed in our body."

APPENDIX 2

Warning Signs of Potential Abusers

Symptom: Are extremely possessive, jealous

Description: Insecure people may interpret this behavior as love (and an abuser will defend it this way), but healthy people do not endlessly scrutinize who their girlfriends, boyfriends, or spouses spend time with, call multiple times a day to check up on what they are doing and with whom, and so forth.

Symptom: Display smothering, controlling behavior

Description: Abusive people often seek to control virtually every aspect of another's life. They don't allow their loved ones to have their own views, their own lives, their own schedules, or their own possessions. Abusive husbands may not even allow their wives to buy the groceries on their own. Some don't even allow their wives to drive. Often every single purchase is scrutinized and controlled.

Symptom: Have unpredictable, extreme mood changes

Description: Some have described this as a "Dr. Jekyll and Mr. Hyde" pattern that is very confusing and often makes victims doubt their own judgment. The abuser can be very sweet one minute but explode in anger the next. Abusers' bad moods are unpredictable, causing family members to "walk on eggshells" so that they don't set them off.

Symptom: Are unable or unwilling to acknowledge personal fault or responsibility

Description: This is a nearly universal characteristic of abusers. They simply will not take full responsibility for their behavior; it's always someone else's fault. Abusers have an uncanny knack for find-ing unhealthy partners who struggle with low self-esteem and can be easily bullied and shamed into believing they (the non-abusers) are always the problem.

Symptom: Are hypercritical

Description: One of the ways abusers avoid taking responsibility for their unhealthy and sinful behavior is to be hypercritical of others, which is largely the result of their own deep-seated shame. Furthermore, abusers tend to be hypersensitive, so that any little thing upsets them. Family members of abusers can never "get it right" and constantly find themselves being scolded and shamed for their mistakes.

Symptom: Abuse alcohol

Description: Roughly 50 percent of domestic physical abusers have a serious drinking problem. They may blame their abusive behavior on the alcohol, but it's nothing but blame shifting. Alcohol and/or drug abuse is often their sinful way of numbing past trauma.

Symptom: Have unresolved family of origin trauma

Description: The most predictable trait of physical abusers (particularly men) is that they experienced physical abuse in their own childhood homes. They learned early in life that violence is an acceptable way to solve frustrations. Childhood trauma, especially physical or sexual abuse and neglect, can create deep-seated soul damage that may lead to abusive behavior in adulthood unless the wounds are dealt with. One warning sign for potential abuse is seen in an adult who, in spite of having grown up in a dysfunctional or abusive family, denies or minimizes the abuse and its impact.

Symptom: Isolate the victims from family and friends

Description: Abusers cut off their victims from all other social resources. They accuse others of causing trouble. They may try to pull the victim away from family members by saying the victim is too dependent on their family or that the family is not sup-portive. They'll accuse the victim of having an affair if they have any opposite-sex friendships or even casual relationships.

Sometimes abusers will even make victims quit their jobs to cut them off from other relationships (and to make them more dependent on the abusers).

Symptom: Insult and ridicule victims' family and friends
Description: Abusers justify isolating their partners from family and friends and promote their own superiority by insulting and ridiculing these individuals.

Symptom: Prevent victims from leaving
Description: Because an abuser likes to control all behavior and has no sense of appropriate boundaries, he will often refuse to allow a wife or girlfriend to leave, especially during an argument. He may do this by physically stopping her, by verbally harassing her, or by verbally manipulating her.

Symptom: Employ a rigid model of gender roles
Description: Abusers typically have a rigid, extremely conservative understanding of male-female roles. They often place great emphasis on male headship and on the need for women and children to be submissive. They typically ignore the fact that the Bible never teaches that the husband is to be "the boss" who demands obedience from his wife; rather, the Bible calls men to be loving servant-leaders. Females are often viewed and treated as inferior to men. Thus, female opinions and feelings can be readily discounted. Abusers often believe they must make their wives and children submit completely to them, even if they have to use physical force to do so. Ironically, while abusers demand unqualified submission from others, they tenaciously resist submitting to civic or ecclesiastical authorities (child protective services workers, the police, court-appointed counselors, their pastors, and so forth).

Symptom: Threaten to harm themselves
Description: Abusers often successfully manipulate their partners into remaining in an abusive relationship by threatening to harm themselves if the partner breaks off the relationship.

Symptom: Threaten to hurt victims or their families

Description: This is another common way abusers manipulate their partners to stay in the relationship and to passively accept abusive behaviors.

Symptom: Insult and degrade victims in private

Description: Often abusers are charming to their partners (and others) in public but are demeaning and degrading in private.

Symptom: Ignore or ridicule victims' feelings and wishes

Description: Abusers' inappropriate domination, control, and sense of superiority is evidenced by the way they constantly ignore, reject, and even ridicule their partners' feelings and wishes.

Symptom: Have a volatile history of broken romantic relationships and friendships

Description: Abusers often have extensive histories of broken relationships, and in these cases, it was always the other person's fault. Often abusers were physically and/or verbally abusive in these previous relationships.

Symptom: Always posture themselves as victims

Description: Everyone is out to get them; everyone mistreats them; their boss is unfair; they are never given a fair shake; and so forth.

Symptom: Cause victims to fear confronting or even disagreeing with them

Description: Abusers systematically and chronically erode their partners' self-confidence, sense of safety, and emotional well-being through manipulation, violent outbursts, and verbal intimidation. This makes partners of abusers fearful of ever disagreeing with or confronting them, even over trivial issues.

Symptom: Blame the victims for their feelings

Description: Abusers blame others for "making them mad," for "making them feel bad about themselves," and so forth.

Symptom: Have intense, quick development of romantic relationships

Description: Abusers are often very intense in the early stages of dating relationships. They smother and overwhelm the other person with attention and demonstrations of affection. They often press for quick commitment and even marriage before the other person has a chance to really get to know them. Victims of abusers often report they had many nagging doubts when dating them, but they felt so pressured that they ignored their feelings and proceeded to get married and found themselves being abused.

Symptom:	Place impossible demands on family members
Description:	Abusers are very insecure and have quite distorted views of what others can and should do for them. Family members, girlfriends, or boyfriends are made out to be 100 percent responsible for their happiness. In a very strange and sick way, abusers need to physically, emotionally, and verbally control family members because they have transferred responsibility for their emotional well-being to their spouses or children. Abusive mothers also tend to do this with their children.

Recommendations to Parents for Reducing the Risk and Responding to Child Sexual Abuse[1]

Reducing the Risk[2]

1. Above all, make your relationship with your children a top priority. Children who have a close relationship with their parents, know they are loved unconditionally, and are able to talk freely with their parents are much less likely to be sexually abused. Abusers prey on children's vulnerabilities. For instance, I know of one child molester who would take baseball equipment to the park to identify boys whose fathers did not play catch with them.

2. Address your own wounds, especially those that have resulted from abuse. Unhealed abuse wounds create toxic shame, cognitive distortions, emotional numbing, unhealthy coping strategies, and relational disconnection. This helps explain why children of mothers who experienced childhood sexual abuse are much more likely than their peers whose mothers didn't experience CSA to experience sexual abuse themselves (not abuse from their mother but from someone else, often a boyfriend or a husband). Mending the Soul created a workbook (*Mending the Soul Workbook for Men and Women*) that many have found helpful for addressing their own wounds. It is designed as a twelve-week curriculum

---

1. A similar document for church leaders can be found on the Mending the Soul website (www.mendingthesoul.org). It is titled "Recommendations to Churches for Reducing the Risk and Responding to Child Sexual Abuse."

2. An excellent supplemental resource created by Darkness to Light is "5 Steps to Protecting Our Children: A Guide for Responsible Adults," www.d2l.org/wp-content/uploads/2016/10/FINAL _D2L_5-STEPS-BOOKLET.pdf.

for small groups directed by two trained facilitators (MTS has online facilitator trainings).

3. Empower your children. Teach in word and deed that your child's opinions and feelings matter, that just because they are a child doesn't mean they aren't a human being who should be treated with respect and dignity. Teach in word and deed that your child has a right to (respectfully) say no to things done to them they don't feel good about. For instance, a child should be able to say "please, no" to tickling, teasing, or rough-housing that they don't like. Appropriate empowerment is a concept many Christian parents in their (appropriate) zeal to teach children to respect and obey adults minimize or deny. Child abusers look for passive, compliant children whose emotional and physical boundaries can be easily violated. An excellent Christian resource is Rachael Denhollander's book *How Much Is a Little Girl Worth?*[3] It is intended to empower girls to recognize and experience their own worth before God, thus making them less vulnerable to the manipulations and lies of abusers.

4. Be vigilant about protecting your children from others. Historically, parents have focused on "stranger danger" with their children. While some perpetrators do molest children they don't know, this is actually quite rare. Research shows that 90 percent of child sexual abuse victims know their abuser.[4] Be very careful about allowing children to go on sleepovers; be very cautious about leaving children with coaches; be very careful about using male babysitters; don't ignore nagging suspicions or concerns; don't put anyone on a pedestal and assume they could never hurt a child—including relatives and pastors. Darkness to Light (www.d2l.org) has some excellent tip sheets, such as "Checklist for Safer Sleepovers," "Safety at Summer Camp," and "Tips for Youth Serving Organizations."[5]

5. Carefully monitor your child's computer, cell phones, and social media accounts. Even though many parents strongly criticize other parents

---

3. Rachel Denhollander, *How Much Is a Little Girl Worth?* (Carol Stream, IL: Tyndale Kids, 2019).

4. David Finkelhor, "Characteristics of Crimes against Juveniles" (Durham, NH: Crimes against Children Research Center, 2012); see also "10 Common Myths of Child Abuse," National Children's Advocacy Center, https://nationalcac.org/wp-content/uploads/2018/02/FINAL-10-Common-Myths-with-References.pdf.

5. See Darkness to Light's resource page, www.d2l.org/resources. "Checklist for Safer Sleepovers" (www.d2l.org/wp-content/uploads/2019/06/One-Sheet_Safer-Sleepovers_-JTM.pdf); "Safety at Summer Camp" (www.d2l.org/camp); "Tips for Youth Serving Organizations" (www.d2l.org/wp-content/uploads/2017/05/SAMPLE-CODE-OF-CONDUCT.pdf; www.d2l.org/wp-content/uploads/2020/02/D2L-Training-One-Pager-2020-Partner-in-Prevention.pdf).

who monitor their child's technology use, it's important to realize that God has given parents a primary responsibility to protect their children. Modern technology has as much power for evil as for good. Satan knows that far better than we do. Darkness to Light has an excellent tip sheet titled "Talking to Children about Digital Safety."[6] The FBI has also produced a great resource called "A Parent's Guide to Internet Safety."[7]

6. Stay involved in your children's world and get to know the adults who have significant access to them, particularly schoolteachers, church workers, youth pastors, music teachers, and coaches. If you have concerns about any of these people, don't ignore it. Be cautious about leaving your child alone with these individuals. If any of these people don't respect your child's boundaries or don't treat them appropriately, step in and advocate for your child as vigorously as is needed.

7. Have ongoing age-appropriate discussions of sexuality, healthy relationships, and abuse. Specifically discuss possible dangerous situations and advise them on how they should respond. While educating our children on "good touch / bad touch" and abuse dangers, be careful, particularly with younger children, not to provide information they may not be emotionally prepared for and that may cause undue emotional distress and distrust of others.[8] This step (abuse education) is deliberately listed as the last of the seven risk reduction steps. Historically, parents and society have placed the burden on minors to protect themselves and report concerns, which has proven to be a highly ineffective primary strategy for sexual abuse risk reduction, in large part because this strategy is based on several faulty assumptions related to the ability of minors.[9] These flawed assumptions are that:

   i. Minors are able to recognize and properly interpret the nuances of an exploitive encounter, touch, relationship, or situation.

   ii. Minors are able to successfully counter the manipulations or threats of an abuser.

   iii. Minors are able to successfully challenge an adult's authority.

   iv. Minors are able to forgo affection, attention, and/or material incentives given by the abuser.

6. "Talking to Children about Digital Safety," Darkness to Life, www.d2l.org/wp-content/uploads/2020/03/Talking-to-Kids-About-Digital-Safety-2020.pdf.
7. "A Parent's Guide to Internet Safety," U.S. Department of Justice, Federal Bureau of Investigation, www2.fbi.gov/publications/pguide/pguidee.htm.
8. See Julia Rudolph et al., "Child Sexual Abuse Prevention Opportunities: Parenting, Programs, and the Reduction of Risk," *Child Maltreatment* 23, no. 1 (2018): 97–98.
9. Adapted from Rudolph, "Child Sexual Abuse Prevention," 97.

     v. Minors are able and willing to report abuse perpetrated by someone they like.

    vi. Minors are able and willing to report abuse that has caused them to feel conflicted, confused, foolish, guilty, or shameful.

While recognizing we must not put the primary responsibility on children to protect themselves, it is essential that we properly educate them on sexuality, relationships, and abuse. Darkness to Light has compiled an extensive list of helpful educational resources.[10] RAAIN has a useful tip sheet on talking to your children about sexual abuse.[11] Searching "Sexual Abuse Prevention" on Amazon will yield a plethora of resources.[12]

Responding to Abuse Disclosures[13]

1. Prayerfully gather your thoughts. Sexual abuse is one of the most disturbing disclosures a parent can receive, but panic will inevitably precipitate harmful responses. Keep reminding yourself that God's presence, power, and love does not change in the midst of suffering and evil (Psalm 46:1–2). Ask him to give you wisdom and courage as you face this stressful trial (Psalms 23:4; 34:4–8).

2. Calmly and gently talk to the child. Sexually abused children have experienced great trauma. They feel great shame that is often coupled with fear. So the parents' calm, loving response is vitally important and helpful.

3. Calmly yet honestly share your own sorrow over the abuse. Let the child know how sorry you are that this was done to them. Let them know that God grieves over what was done to them; it hurts God when his children suffer (Hosea 11:8; John 11:35). He hates abuse and is grieved and angry when his children are hurt by abusers (Psalm 5:6).

4. Assure the child that it wasn't their fault. Shame causes abused children to instinctively feel they are responsible for the abuse. Additionally, sexual abuse perpetrators often tell the child it is their fault. It may take a very long time for the child to truly believe the abuse wasn't their fault, so repeated verbal assurances from parents are very important.

---

10. See Darkness to Light's resource page (www.d2l.org/resources).

11. "Talking to Your Kids about Sexual Assault," RAINN, www.rainn.org/articles/talking-your-kids-about-sexual-assault.

12. See "Sexual Abuse Prevention" search results, www.amazon.com/s?k=sexual+abuse+prevention&i=stripbooks&ref=nb_sb_noss_2.

13. A helpful, concise resource for parents or children's workers is "Reporting Child Sexual Abuse," Darkness to Light, January 2017, www.d2l.org/wp-content/uploads/2017/01/Reporting_Child_Sexual_Abuse-Small-File.pdf.

5. Assure the child that you will get them help. Abused children don't expect parents to have all the answers or to fix every problem. They just need to know that parents will boldly pursue getting the necessary help.

6. Contact law enforcement and report the abuse immediately. If the perpetrator is a family member, Child Protective Services should also be contacted.

7. Do not immediately confront the perpetrator. While this is often the first thing parents attempt to do, it can easily backfire. First of all, for the sake of the legal investigation, it is important for law enforcement to be the first ones to interview the perpetrator. Second, parents need time to work through the complex issues and intense feelings. Otherwise, they might act and speak rashly in ways that are counterproductive and even destructive.

8. Protect the child from the perpetrator and, if necessary, the extended family and the community. It is the parents' responsibility to protect the child from the perpetrator. Abusers should have no contact with or access to the child. Parents must establish all necessary boundaries with the extended family or community to protect the child. Furthermore, if family, church, or community doesn't accept these boundaries or seeks to minimize or deny the abuse, then parents need to protect the child from those individuals as well. Their denial can be highly damaging to the child. Denial and victim blame are some of the most common responses to sexual abuse—responses that are strongly condemned by God (Proverbs 17:15).

9. Seek professional help. Sexual abuse is confusing, complex, and deeply damaging. Hence, it is advisable to find a licensed Christian counselor experienced in dealing with sexual abuse to work with the child and your family.

10. Consider utilizing Mending the Soul's *Caring for the Vulnerable Child* four-book curricula designed for preadolescent children who have experienced any type of trauma. It was also created for the parents or caregivers of traumatized children. It has a book for parents and caregivers explaining from Scripture and social science the world of a traumatized child and how parents can best respond to these children's unique needs. It also has a workbook for parents and a workbook for children. Finally, it has a teacher's guide so this material can be taught in a church or other setting as a class for parents of traumatized children.[14]

---

14. See "Caring for the Vulnerable Child," Mending the Soul, accessed May 20, 2022, https://mendingthesoul.org/vulnerable-child.

11. Be careful who you tell about the abuse. Scripture tells us there is a time to speak and also a time to be silent (Ecclesiastes 3:7). Sexual abuse is one of the most shameful things that can happen to someone. Furthermore, people often don't how to respond to an abuse report. Therefore, be careful and selective in speaking about the abuse to other people, especially if the child is present. It is important that you respect your child's privacy.

12. Be patient. Sexual abuse creates soul damage that takes considerable time to heal. Remember that God is infinitely committed to the well-being and healing of his children (Romans 8:28, 31–37; Philippians 1:6). Prayerfully commit to God the pain caused by the abuse and entrust healing to him (Psalm 18:1–6; 1 Peter 5:7). Trust that he is working in his wise way on his timetable.

Scripture Index

Subject Index

Abel, 48, 282
Abraham, 18, 99
Absalom, 94–95, 105, 107
abuse
    abuse cycle, 210–11
    effects of, 1–3, 27–28, 33, 113–21
    faith undermined by, 186–89
    family relationships, 193–94
    healing from, 7, 195–98, 203–212, 289–91
    in Christian families, 14–15
    in church, 7–9, 19–20, 37, 54–57, 87–88, 108–10
    in marriage, 190–92
    in Mosaic law, 118
    in peer relationships, 194–95
    rates of, xiv, 7–16, 28–34, 37–40, 49, 55, 76
    redeemable, 23–26
    responses to, xiii, 5–6, 40–41
    sexual harassment and, xiii–xiv
    sexual intimacy and, 190–92
abusers
    adolescent molesters, 82–83
    adult child molesters, 76–81
    children who violate other children, 83–84
    domestically abusive men, 84–88
    female molesters, 81
    pedophiles, 78–79
    profile of, 63–75
    pseudorepentant, 278–80
    warning signs of, 300–304
abusive families, profile of, 89–108, 110–11
Adam and Eve, 17, 29, 31, 180, 240
addictions, 135
Ahab, King, 18, 73–74
Ahaz, King, 230–31
amnesia, 166–67
Amnon, 18, 91–108, 139, 230
anchoring in trauma therapy, 225–26

Asa, King, 231
attachment, 34
Auschwitz concentration camp, 186

Bathsheba, 41, 66, 68, 94, 269, 278, 281
betrayal, 236
blame shifting, 275–76
boundaries, 281
brain, the, 149–54
breathing in trauma therapy, 219–21
    belly breathing, 219–20
    breath prayers, 220–21
    square breathing, 220
brokenness, 201–8
Brothers Karamazov, The, 233–34
Buckenwald concentration camp, 182

Cain, 21, 48, 281–82
Center for the Protection of the Destitute and Mentally Ill (CEPIMA), 115–16
change of behavior, 283
character of God, 255–59
child abuse, 33
child maltreatment, 13–14
child neglect, xiii–xiv
Chowchilla school bus kidnapping, 157, 165–66
code of silence, 106–7
community, authentic, 141–42
compassion of God, 259–62
confession of sin, 281
connection, 179–180, 195–98, 228–29, 231
consequences of and for abusers, 269, 281–82
constriction, 158, 162–64, 171–73, 183–85, 214, 231, 240
Congo, Democratic Republic of the, xiv–xv, 24–25, 115, 174–75, 216–17
criminal violence, 38–39

Dig Deeper into
Mending the Soul

The *Mending the Soul Workbook for Men and Women* is an interactive guide to be used as a companion resource to this book. It provides a path to recovery and wholeness for those isolated by the effects of abuse in all its forms, promoting healing within safe and nurturing relationships. Expressive art, contemplative meditations, and interactive exercises deepen one's intimate connections with God and others, providing individual healing that facilitates mentors and friends in trauma-informed and holistic care of one another. Men and women alike will find their own redemptive stories to tell.

Additional abuse education and healing resources for children, teens, families, and adults—including facilitator and other trainings—can be found on our website:

www.mendingthesoul.org.

We want to know your story!